www.wadsworth.com

wadsworth.com is the World Wide Web site for Wadsworth and is your direct source to dozens of online resources.

At *wadsworth.com* you can find out about supplements, demonstration software, and student resources. You can also send email to many of our authors and preview new publications and exciting new technologies.

wadsworth.com
Changing the way the world learns®

Psychopathology

A Competency-Based Assessment Model for Social Workers

Marilyn R. Zide
Barry University
Ellen Whiteside McDonnell School of Social Work

Susan W. Gray
Barry University
Ellen Whiteside McDonnell School of Social Work

BROOKS/COLE

THOMSON LEARNING Australia • Canada • Mexico • Singapore • Spain • United Kingdom • United States

BROOKS/COLE

THOMSON LEARNING™

Social Work Executive Editor: Lisa Gebo
Assistant Editor: JoAnne von Zastrow
Editorial Assistant: Sheila Walsh
Marketing Manager: Caroline Concilla
Marketing Assistant: Jessica McFadden
Signing Representative: Miguel Ortiz
Project Editor: Teri Hyde
Print Buyer: Tandra Jorgensen
Permissions Editor: Stephanie Keough

Production Service: Scott Hitchcock, Electronic Publishing
  Services Inc., N.Y.C.
Photographer: Mark Safra Photography
Cover Designer: Cuttriss and Hambleton
Cover Image: Courtesy of PhotoDisk
Cover Printer: R.R. Donnelley & Sons
Compositor: Electronic Publishing Services Inc., N.Y.C.
Printing and Binding: R.R. Donnelly & Sons Company

For permission to use material from this text, contact us
Web: http://www.thomsonrights.com
Fax: 1-800-730-2215
Phone: 1-800-730-2214

Library of Congress Cataloging-in-Publication Data
Zide, Marilyn R.
        Psychopathology : A competency-based assessment model for social workers /
        Marilyn R. Zide, Susan W. Gray.
                p. cm.
        Includes bibliographical references and index.
        ISBN 0-534-36766-6
        1. Mental illness--Diagnosis. 2. Psychology,
Pathological. 3. Psychiatric social work.
        I. Gray, Susan Walker–   II. Title.

RC469 .Z53 2001
616.89'075--dc21
00-060853

Wadsworth/Thomson Learning
10 Davis Drive
Belmont, CA 94002-3098
USA

For more information about our products, contact us:
Thomson Learning Academic Resource Center
1-800-423-0563
http://www.wadsworth.com

International Headquarters
Thomson Learning
International Division
290 Harbor Drive, 2nd Floor
Stamford, CT 06902-7477
USA

UK/Europe/Middle East/South Africa
Thomson Learning
Berkshire House
168-173 High Holborn
London WC1V 7AA
United Kingdom

Asia
Thomson Learning
60 Albert Street, #15-01
Albert Complex
Singapore 189969

Canada
Nelson Thomson Learning
1120 Birchmount Road
Toronto, Ontario M1K 5G4
Canada

To our husbands, Nelson R. Zide, MD, and Kenneth E. Gray, JD,

... they know.

About the Authors

Photograph by Mark Safra

Marilyn R. Zide earned her baccalaureate from Barry College, and her master's and doctorate in social work degrees from Barry University, Ellen Whiteside McDonnell School of Social Work. She has worked for many years in the mental health field, both as a supervisor and as a unit director. Currently, Marilyn is a full-time faculty member at Barry University, School of Social Work. She is an associate professor teaching in the Human Behavior in the Social Environment and the Methods of Direct Practice sequences. She has presented more than 85 scholarly papers on the local, state, national, and international levels. She has also authored numerous articles reflecting her wide area of interests, including runaway adolescents and family bonding, bereavement groups, intergenerational family assessment, the brief solution-focused model of practice, methods of classroom teaching, and aspects of cultural diversity. In addition, Marilyn provides agency-based consultation, conducts training workshops for the preparation of practitioners for social work licensure examination, and maintains a private clinical practice in Davie, Florida.

Photograph by Mark Safra

Susan W. Gray earned her baccalaureate from Caldwell College for Women, her master's degree from Rutgers–the State University, a doctorate in education from Nova Southeastern University, and her doctorate in social work from Barry University, Ellen Whiteside McDonnell School of Social Work. Prior to joining the full-time faculty at Barry University's School of Social Work, she worked for many years in the fields of health and mental health. She is a full professor, teaching graduate courses in the Human Behavior in the Social Environment and the Methods of Direct Practice sequences. She also teaches an elective, Crisis Intervention, and a course in social work education in the university's doctoral program. Susan is active in the professional community having served as secretary for the Florida Chapter of the National Association of Social Workers (NASW). She was appointed three years ago by then

Florida Governor Lawton Chiles to the state licensure board where she continues to serve. In addition, Susan maintains an appointment to the Association of Social Work Boards (ASWB) where she serves on the continuing education committee. She is recognized as an informative, engaging presenter and has given papers and workshops on the local, state, national, and international levels. Her publications reflect her wide interests including supervision, professional regulation and licensure, rural practice, bereavement groups, family assessment tools, brief solution–focused therapy, classroom teaching, and aspects of cultural diversity. She maintains a private clinical practice in the Florida Keys.

Professors Zide and Gray have collaborated on numerous projects, and their current work includes a companion book, *Psychopathology: A competency-based treatment model for social workers*, forthcoming from Brooks/Cole (2003).

Contents

Chapter Four

Mood Disorders   80

Chapter Five

Anxiety Disorders   110

Chapter Six

Somatoform, Factitious, and Malingering Disorders   151

Chapter Seven

Dissociative Disorders   200

Chapter Eight

Eating Disorders   225

Preface

Social workers are the largest group of mental health care providers in the United States (O'Neill, 1999). In fact, social workers perform a wider array of professional functions with a more diverse population of clients than has been previously documented (Egan & Kadushin, 1999; Iversen, 1998; Vourlekis et al., 1998). More than ever before, social workers are providing services to clients instead of other professionals, such as psychiatrists or psychologists. The national policy emphasizing de-institutionalization suggests that caring for those with mental illness in the community is expected to continue. Social work has always been stressful and even more so considering today's practice climate that emphasizes consumer advocacy, service linkages, monitoring, and self-help. Professional social work includes casework, case management, group work, group therapy, individual and family counseling, and community organization. The challenge is to avoid adopting shortcuts and to make every effort to keep up to date (Fellin, 1996; Siporin, 1992; Walsh, 2000).

The clients that we work with have a right to expect that we will provide services in a manner consistent with prevailing practice and ethical standards (Reamer, 1998; Rubin, 1992). Those professionals working with mental health issues and clients need to know how to make an assessment. It is the fundamental premise of this book that competent social work practice understands and evaluates clients within the person-in-situation perspective. In particular, the competency-based model provides a framework for an individualized assessment of human behavior within an ecosystems perspectives; one that considers the client's biological, psychological, interpersonal, environmental, and cultural factors. The competency-based assessment focuses on client strengths, coping capacities, and those environmental stressors that influence debilitated patterns of relating and behaving. This approach underscores helping clients find ways to resolve real-life problems (Gambrill, 1994).

Integral to the social work profession's core values and traditions, each person is considered unique in the way he or she deals with problems in living.

Sometimes, however, the client's ability to describe and evaluate his or her situation may be hampered by their current state of mind. Being able to recognize these factors underscores the importance of understanding the multiple circumstances that might often influence a client's "life story." Locke (1992) cautions that generalizing about a particular group is dangerous. The competency-based assessment emphasizes the uniqueness of each person's reactions and the situations in which these occur. The client's context is important for understanding how the person's phenomenological presentation of self has developed not only over time but through interpersonal influences. Additionally, the practitioner considers the multiple influences of family, community, and cultural values. This approach to clinical assessment lays the foundation for systematic observation and exploration rather than unsupported inference and guessing. This text is meant to support social work practice within the traditional confines of our profession. Our book breaks new ground as the first of a new generation of psychopathology textbooks that offers an integrative and multidimensional social work frame of reference.

Now a bit about how our book is organized. Our first chapter describes the basic principles supporting the competency-based assessment—that is, the process of reviewing and understanding an individual's past in order to distinguish and interpret their presenting concerns. It is our intention to weave together empirical findings with biological, psychological (including cognitive), and social systems variables thus creating a competency-based tapestry that provides the organizing framework for assessing psychopathology. It is beyond the scope of this book to include an in-depth discussion of theories of etiology, causation, or interviewing skills. (Our forthcoming book, *Psychopathology: A competency-based treatment model for social workers,* will address these issues as they relate to advanced clinical practice.)

Subsequent chapters will begin with an overview of each of the major disorders found in the *Diagnostic and statistical manual of mental disorders (DSM),* Fourth Edition-TR (APA, 2000). The text is arranged to provide a full discussion of the significant major adult psychiatric disorders. The DSM was first published in the early 1950s by the American Psychiatric Association and now is in its fourth edition. The DSM-IV-TR is considered the standard for clinical evaluation. You will notice an absence of the disorders of childhood. This decision allowed for a more extensive and cogent discussion of each major adult disorder. Our book includes relevant statistical data, for example, prevalence, gender, age of onset, and the general course or pattern for each of the disorders.

We have included case vignettes that will help you, the reader, appreciate the humanization of information that might otherwise be boring and dull. By using the client's voice, we hope to emphasize the many ways that real people respond to life's challenges. These client stories were chosen for their intrinsic value of representing those who are seen in clinical practice and to underscore the resilience of the human spirit. In putting this case material together, we tried to convey how culture, gender, sexual orientation, or social and economic status impacts on making a diagnosis of mental illness. Several vignettes address the multicultural issues social workers may encounter in their practice. For example, the case of Jada Wu illustrates someone who is struggling to overcome specific phobias and how culture influences coping with a mental health condition. Margarethe Jean-Baptiste, an illegal immigrant, illustrates the experiences found in a person who encountered a traumatic life event. Aleta Austin, diagnosed with pain disorder, reveals many other interpersonal variables going on in her life. She is going through a divorce from her husband of five years and is beginning to acknowledge her homosexuality. Matilda Suarez, in addition to having agoraphobia, is dealing with being evicted from her home.

The clinical vignettes are intended to help you remember salient points about symptomatic features and begin to formulate a differential assessment. The case illustrations are derived from the authors' combined practice of over 50 years. They were developed from our own direct practice, clinical supervision, and teaching experiences. Our text is peppered with the stories of real-life clients and often are composites of several individuals. We have included more than 50 cases in order to more fully convey the complexities of the real-life situations of clients.

Following the case vignettes are assessment summaries that focus on differentiating among similar symptom pictures. The DSM, in conjunction with the competency-based assessment model, provides a fuller multidimensional view of clients with major mental illness. The cases are intended to be much more than just cases. We anticipate that they will be used by the practitioner as a tool to integrate the competency-based assessment with the DSM format. The book illustrates the multiaxial diagnosis that complements the assessment of each client's unique competencies.

The vignettes present some of the subtle nuances of case material that illustrate the complexity of psychopathology, and they provide a believable context for the disorders found in this textbook. Our intention is to help convey the "flavor" of information that social workers need to know about understanding a client's story. We want to stretch your thinking and at the same time hold your interest.

We have provided vignettes for nearly all of the major mental health categories but there were some omissions, and no one book can adequately cover all the specific categories. Our aim is to provide an overview of the essential aspects of mental health problems that social workers typically encounter in their clinical practice. Following "best practice," every attempt was made to avoid stigmatizing or labeling. For example, terms such as "people with schizophrenia" were used rather than "schizophrenics." We tried to simplify the diagnostic criteria and make them more understandable. At the same time, the material essential for social work practice was emphasized. We purposely chose a writing style that is less formal than typically seen in most other texts. Our intent is to provide meaningful descriptions of mental disorders that are written in plain language. We hope this book will provide you with a strong sense of direction in taking the first step toward making a competency-based assessment. It will also help to serve as an easily accessible reference for those who work in the many other practice settings found in the social work arena.

At the end of each chapter we have included a section entitled Practitioner Reflections. These are exercises designed to help the reader consider the full range of the client's life experiences. While knowing the signs and symptoms of mental disorders is necessary, it is also essential for the practitioner to tune in to the client's concerns. The exercises are intended to help the reader appreciate the many experiences the person and their family encounter living with mental illness.

For each case we have provided a pictorial representation, featuring biological, psychological, and social factors in the client's life. (Refer to the case of Zelda "Jean" Pfohl in Chapter 2, for an example of this pedagogical tool.) This visual summary is intended to help the reader to integrate the competency-based assessment when diagnosing mental illness. To assist readers further, we have included two appendices as well as a glossary. The first contains the DSM-IV classification system. The second provides a series of questions designed to measure your clinical competencies in psychopathology. These questions can be reviewed either before or after reading each chapter to gauge your level of knowledge.

Each chapter is free-standing and autonomous. We have also listed the references at the end of each chapter in order to simplify where to find more information for further reading. We made every effort to use the most current and relevant professional literature. Much of the work cited is not social work driven, and we say this with some caution because social workers have not had a commanding presence in writing about adult psychopathology and related mental health issues. Our effort is to add to the social work knowledge base concerning mental illness from a social work perspective. It is our hope that this book will fill that gap.

This book is written by social workers for social workers who are in different "seasons" of their professional development. This includes graduate students taking a psychopathology or human behavior course, practitioners (both neophyte and experienced), supervisors needing a current reference, and practitioners who just want to review the basics or prepare for their state licensure examination. The challenges for us were to cover all the material without overwhelming the reader, dispelling the myth that understanding the *Diagnostic and statistical manual* is synonymous with labeling or stereotyping people in a negative way, and covering a broad range of psychopathological conditions in reasonable detail at the level of description and differential assessment. By helping readers understand psychopathology and become familiar with the language of the DSM, the authors hope to balance the tensions found between the medical model and the ecological approach.

This book is intended to be a major text for courses in psychopathology, human behavior in the social environment, or mental health electives. We also intend it to be a useful adjutant for workers in other disciplines such as mental health counselors and family therapists. Major objectives in writing this book have been to convey that psychopathology is an interesting and challenging subject; to help the clinical practitioner better understand their clients; and to appreciate the influence the client's life situations has on mental health. The intent is to encourage working with other interdisciplinary cohorts in a collaborative manner. In our view, social workers are fortunate in that we have a unique opportunity to spend quality time with clients and we get to know them on a deeper, more personal level. Because of our unique practice perspective, we view all aspects of the client versus other disciplines who may only hospitalize, prescribe medications, or conduct psychological testing. We wear many different hats in our social work role and in our need to understand human behavior and its strong ties to psychopathology. It is our ultimate hope that this text will help you gain a working knowledge of psychopathology concepts and the related vocabulary in order to focus on the real work ahead.

ACKNOWLEDGMENTS

A book of this magnitude cannot be brought to fruition solely through the vision of the authors. Many people assisted us from behind the scenes throughout this process. We want to take the opportunity to thank them for their faith in us, and for their encouragement throughout the past two years. The idea for this book began with our classroom experiences teaching content about psychopathology, a topic so often associated with a deficit perspective in social work. We saw our students struggle with trying to maintain the profession's values, applying social work ethics and ideals, while at the same time balancing the tensions associated with learning about psychopathology. So many of the textbooks we used were written by psychologists or psychiatrists, and the social work orientation was further obscured. Our idea to write a book by social workers and for social workers took shape with the assistance of our sponsoring editor, Lisa Gebo. We thank Lisa for her support and encouragement, as well as her delightful exuberance and wonderful sense of humor. The support staff was equally outstanding. They were always available to answer our questions and paid attention to even our smallest concerns. Our thanks and appreciation goes to JoAnne von Zastrow, Assistant Editor; Teri Hyde, Senior Project Editor; and our marketing team, Caroline Concilla and Jessica McFadden, for all their hard work. We want to thank the art department at Electronic Publishing Services N.Y.C. and especially to Cuttriss and Hambleton for the unique design of our cover. A special note of appreciation goes to Scott Hitchcock, our Production Editor, who made the end process a delightful experience. We enjoyed our long conversations learning about the editorial process, exchanging Key lime pie recipes, and queries about how to make this manuscript even better. He was joined by Andrew Schwartz, our manuscript copyeditor, who added many useful suggestions. We are looking forward to working with you all again.

We wish to acknowledge our Dean, Stephen M. Holloway. He was instrumental in creating the organizational climate where an endeavor like ours could become a reality. We appreciate the efforts of our former colleague Richard Caputo, for his remarks and comments on an earlier draft of this manuscript. We are grateful for the support and enthusiasm of one of our doctoral students and colleague, Terry Blakley. She was especially helpful to us in writing the book's glossary. We thank all of our students who shared the classroom with us. They brought their difficult cases, asked the hard questions, and continually reminded us of what the profession of social work is all about.

We are grateful for the thoughtful comments and suggestions made by our reviewers, who took time out of their own busy schedules to read our manuscript. We are indebted to Jose Ashford of Arizona State University, Mary Jo Blazek of the University of Maine, Augusta, Kia Bentley of Virginia Commonwealth University, William Bradshaw of the University of Minnesota, Renee Daniel of Daemen College, Marian Dumaine of Florida International University, Denise Gammonley of the University of North Carolina, Chapel Hill, Alex Gitterman of the University of Connecticut, Eda Goldstein of New York University, Nina Heller of the University of Connecticut, David E. Pollio of Washington University, Michael Rothery of the University of Calgary, and Vikki Vandiver of Portland State University.

Last, but certainly not least, we are grateful to our husbands, families, and friends for their continuing patience and loving support throughout the writing of this book.

REFERENCES

American Psychiatric Association [APA]. (2000) *Diagnostic and statistical manual of mental disorders* (4th ed.-TR). Washington, DC: APA.

Egan, M., & Kadushin, G. (1999). The social worker in the emerging field of home care: Professional activities and ethical concerns. *Health and Social Work*, 24(1): 43–55.

Fellin, P. (1996). *Mental health and mental illness: Policies, programs, and services.* Itasca, IL: F. E. Peacock Publishers, Inc.

Gambrill, E. (1994). Social work research: Priorities and obstacles. *Research on Social Work Practice,* 4(3): 359–388.

Iversen, R. R. (1998). Occupational social work for the 21st century. *Social Work,* 43(6): 551–566.

Locke, D. C. (1992). *Increasing multicultural understanding.* Newbury Park, CA: Sage.

O'Neill, J. V. (1999, June). Profession dominates in mental health. *NASW News,* 44(6): 1.

Reamer, R. G. (1998). Client's right to competent and ethical treatment. *Research on Social Work Practice,* 8(5): 597–603.

Rubin, A. (1992). Case Management. In S. M. Rose (Ed.), Case management and social work practice (pp. 5–24). New York: Longman.

Siporin, M. (1992). Tough economic times require innovation and flexibility in social work education and practice. *Journal of Continuing Social Work Education,* 5(3): 2.

Vourlekis, B. S., Edinburg, G., & Knee, R. (1998). The rise of social work in public mental health through aftercare of people with serious mental illness. *Social Work,* 43(6): 567–575.

Walsh, J. (2000). *Clinical case management with persons having mental illness: A relationship-based perspective.* Pacific Grove, CA: Brooks/Cole.

AN INTRODUCTION TO THE COMPETENCY-BASED ASSESSMENT MODEL

INTRODUCTION

The now century-old tradition of psychiatric social work was one of several specializations, including medical social work and child welfare, that emerged during the early part of the twentieth century. While the field of psychiatric social work grew during the 1900s, workers struggled against seeking employment because of negative professional attitudes directed toward them. French (1940) noted problems associated with early psychiatric social work positions were large caseloads, low pay, and in some cases, requirements to live on the institution's premises and perform nonprofessional duties within the institution.

During the past five decades, social workers have had considerable flexibility in assessing clients, with the choice of using diagnostic categories found in various editions of the *Diagnostic and Statistical Manual of Mental Disorders* (DSM), or other psychosocial or behavioral criteria. During the last part of the twentieth century, the presence of social workers serving all areas of the public and private mental health sectors is well documented (Abramson & Mizrahi, 1996, 1997; Berkman, 1996; Ell, 1996; Lee, 1994; Netting & Williams, 1996, 1997; Simon, 1994). As the profession enters the new millennium, some of the ways social workers have historically looked at clients is in jeopardy, especially regarding specific diagnostic descriptions and interventions based on presenting symptoms. Accountability is considered one of the central themes for contemporary social work practice (Franklin, 1999). While the DSM classification system is often used to meet requirements for "accountability" and third-party payments, social workers, we hope, will continue to balance their objectivity when using the focus found in the DSM. The aim of this book is to help encourage social workers to practice within the philosophical underpinnings of the profession when working with individuals with mental illness. The competency-based model presented in this book seeks to keep sight of the uniqueness of our clients and of their environments.

Mailick (1991) suggests "re-assessing" the assessment in clinical social work practice based on the advent of managed care, changes in the service delivery structure of agencies, and significant cost containment efforts. The implications of the movement toward managed care, as suggested by Paulson (1996), are the merging of public and private services; shifting of financial risk to service providers; the development of community-based service alternatives; and an increased emphasis on client strengths and social supports. This underscores the importance of the practitioner's expertise and competence in assessment. Managed care is revolutionizing the way social workers provide services, and issues around job security and funding have been linked to achieving results and demonstrating effectiveness. Some concern exists that managed care coerces the worker to weigh services for the client's good against the organization's best interests (Strom-Gottfried, 1997). Regretfully, Keigher (1997) concludes that unfortunately social workers have a peripheral influence in effecting service delivery.

About 20 percent of Americans have experienced psychiatric disorders (Johnson, 1995). Despite one's career direction within the field of social work, practitioners are likely to encounter clients with mental illness. Those who work with individuals considered mentally ill realize the need to learn how to decipher the DSM format. Part of the problem in using the manual is that one might come away from it questioning how the diagnostic criteria presented translate to real life clients seen in practice. Social workers must know not only how to effectively assess individuals but also how to develop an intervention plan that addresses client needs.

The DSM format is not for amateurs and should not be considered a substitute for professional training in assessment or the other skills needed to work with clients. For example, tasks such as performing mental status exams and monitoring of medication, historically the sole domain of psychiatrists, are now routinely handled by social workers. It is important to recognize that using a classification system can never replace assessment obtained through the "fluid, personal process of exchange between people" (Meyer, 1993, p. 130). The DSM is not without flaws (Dumont, 1987; Kirk & Kutchins, 1988, 1994). Being social workers ourselves, one of our primary reasons for writing this book is to help make the DSM format more understandable and accessible to other social workers. This book does not take a linear or "traditional" psychiatric approach; rather, it incorporates the competency-based assessment as a vehicle to support social work norms and values.

Developing a working knowledge of psychopathology is similar to mastering a foreign language; at first everything seems confusing, but gradually the language becomes understandable. Similarly, beginning social work students are often anxious when asked to formulate an initial diagnosis (Andreasen & Black, 1995), feeling they are somehow perpetuating "pigeonholing, stereotyping or labeling" people. The process is complicated because most textbooks about mental disorders are written by psychiatrists or psychologists, and tend to be biased toward their own professional alliances (Austrian, 1995). The authors recognize using the DSM format has been a long-standing and controversial topic within social work practice (see, for example, Kirk & Kutchins, 1992; Kirk et al., 1989; Kutchins & Kirk, 1987). Since its first introduction in the early 1950s, the manual has been used to describe and classify mental disorders. The DSM admittedly is an imperfect system, and it has the potential to stigmatize through labeling. Despite its drawbacks, the manual continues to serve as the standard for evaluation and diagnosis. Our aim in writing this book is not to reinvent the proverbial wheel by creating a "wannabe" mini-DSM. A concern for social work practitioners is the emphasis placed on "disease" and "illness" obscuring the profession's orientation that centers on client strengths. While this book is organized around the *Diagnostic and Statistical Manual of Mental Disorders*, the authors hope to simplify the language of psychopathology in a way that will help decide the kind of information to gather, how to organize it, and interpret data collected.

THE MULTIAXIAL SYSTEM

A DSM evaluation involves making an assessment on five distinct dimensions or axes each referring to a different domain of information that can be organized around the competency-based assessment. An individual's behavior is divided into two distinct axes. Axis I, Clinical Disorders and Other Conditions that May Be a Focus of Clinical Attention (including V codes), is used to denote all mental disorders except the personality disorders and mental retardation, which are only reported on Axis II. If there is more than one Axis I disorder, the practitioner lists each individually in order of primary severity. Table 1-1 summarizes the major groups of disorders found on Axis I.

TABLE **1-1**   **AXIS I—CLINICAL DISORDERS AND OTHER CONDITIONS THAT MAY BE A FOCUS OF CLINICAL ATTENTION**

Disorders usually first diagnosed in infancy, childhood, or adolescence (excluding mental retardation, which is diagnosed on Axis II)

Delirium, dementia, and amnestic and other cognitive disorders

Mental disorders due to a general medical condition

Substance-related disorders

Schizophrenia and other psychotic disorders

Mood disorders

Anxiety disorders

Somatoform disorders

Factitious disorders

Dissociative disorders

Sexual and gender identity disorders

Eating disorders

Sleeping disorders

Impulse-control disorders not elsewhere classified

Adjustment disorders

Other conditions that may be a focus of clinical attention

TABLE **1-2**   AXIS II—PERSONALITY DISORDERS AND MENTAL RETARDATION

Paranoid personality disorder

Schizoid personality disorder

Schizotypal personality disorder

Antisocial personality disorder

Borderline personality disorder

Histrionic personality disorder

Narcissistic personality disorder

Avoidant personality disorder

Dependent personality disorder

Obsessive-compulsive personality disorder

Personality disorder not otherwise specified

Mental retardation

Source: Reprinted with permission from the *Diagnostic and statistical manual of mental disorders,* Fourth Edition-TR. © 2000 American Psychiatric Association.

Axis II, Personality Disorders and Mental Retardation, is used to note various aspects of personality functioning and the presence of maladaptive personality features. It can also be used to note an individual's characteristic coping style, for example, the defense mechanisms of splitting, projection, or denial. A diagnosis of mental retardation needs to be noted prior to age 18. A diagnosis of personality disorder is *never* assigned to anyone under the age of 18. Table 1-2 summarizes Axis II.

The rationale behind having both an Axis I and an Axis II diagnosis is the concern that practitioners might give most of their attention to the more florid and dramatic Axis I disorders. By considering an Axis II diagnosis, the practitioner also pays attention to the less striking, longer lasting symptoms of mental retardation and especially the personality disorders (Wilson et al., 1996). Axis III, General Medical Conditions, includes all general medical diseases or conditions that may be clinically relevant to the mental disorders reported on Axis I and Axis II. In this way, Axis III encourages the practitioner to conduct a thorough evaluation of their client. Additionally, collaboration among the various treatment providers increases. The assessment process in social work is ongoing, taking note of, for example, changing medical circumstances or medications. Refer to Table 1-3 for a listing of the general medical conditions found on Axis III.

Axis IV, Psychosocial and Environmental Problems, calls attention to clinically relevant psychosocial and environmental issues found in many of the DSM disorders. This category includes problems or difficulties associated with the client's primary support group, their social environment, or other interpersonal factors. Table 1-4 summarizes Axis IV.

TABLE 1-3   AXIS III—GENERAL MEDICAL CONDITIONS

Infectious and parasitic diseases

Neoplasms

Endocrine, nutritional, and metabolic diseases and immunity disorders

Diseases of the blood and blood-forming organs

Diseases of the nervous system and sense organs

Diseases of the circulatory system

Diseases of the respiratory system

Diseases of the digestive system

Diseases of the genitourinary system

Complications of pregnancy, childbirth, and the puerperium

Diseases of the skin and subcutaneous tissue

Diseases of the musculoskeletal system and connective tissue

Congenital anomalies

Certain conditions originating in the perinatal period

Symptoms, signs, and ill-defined conditions

Injury and poisoning

Source: Reprinted with permission from the *Diagnostic and statistical manual of mental disorders,* Fourth Edition-TR. © 2000 American Psychiatric Association.

Axis V, or the Global Assessment of Functioning (GAF) Scale, is used to assess the individual's overall psychological, occupational, and social functioning (Frances et al., 1995). It is particularly useful in tracking the individual's clinical progress. Scores may be assigned at the time of admission and/or at the time the client ends treatment. It can also be used during other time periods, for example, in the course of the client's highest level of functioning during the past six months.

The scale scores range from 100, "superior"; 80, "transient symptoms"; 70, "mild symptoms"; 60, "moderate symptoms"; 50, "serious symptoms"; 40, "some impairment in reality testing"; 30, "behavior is considerably influenced by delusions or hallucinations," "serious impairment in communication/judgment," or "inability to function in almost all areas"; 20, "danger of hurting self," "occasionally fails to maintain minimal personal hygiene," or "gross impairment in communication"; 10, "persistent danger of severely hurting self or others," "inability to maintain minimal personal hygiene," or "serious suicidal act with clear expectation of death; to 0, indicating "insufficient information." In practice, the GAF score tends to vary. This is due to each social worker's subjective assessment of the client's situation. Despite this drawback, it is seen as the accepted language of clinicians. In sum, a score of 100 indicates optimal functioning and the lowest score of 10 denotes extreme danger that the client will hurt himself/herself or others. The rating measures are summarized in Table 1-5.

TABLE **1-4**   AXIS IV—PSYCHOSOCIAL AND ENVIRONMENTAL PROBLEMS
Problems with primary support group (for example, divorce or physical abuse)
Problems related to the social environment (for example, death of a friend)
Educational problems (for example, academic difficulties)
Occupational problems (for example, unemployment or stressful work conditions)
Housing problems (for example, homelessness or inadequate housing)
Economic problems (for example, living on a fixed income)
Problems with access to health care services (for example, inadequate health insurance)
Problems related to interaction with the legal system and crime (for example, serving time in jail)
Other psychosocial and environmental problems (for example, discord with nonfamily caregivers such as social worker or physician)

Source: Reprinted with permission from the *Diagnostic and statistical manual of mental disorders,* Fourth Edition-TR. © 2000 American Psychiatric Association.

The multi-axial system becomes a tool to gather information that supports the competency-based assessment. That is, the practitioner considers factors above and beyond diagnostic signs and symptoms. Clients do not exist in a vacuum. There is more to a person and their life story than a description of symptoms. The partnership between the DSM classification format and the competency-based assessment individualizes the client, looks at the full range of factors affecting their life, examines the lack of "fit" between the person and their environment, and extends the practitioner's understanding of psychopathology. Social workers who assess a client's condition solely in terms of whether they meet the DSM criteria fail to appreciate the ways that clients cope with life's challenges, influencing factors, and available supports. Competency-based practice emphasizes the importance of identifying client competencies, and it focuses on assets instead of deficits. More precisely, it focuses on building and enhancing the client's own skills as they attempt to deal with life conditions.

The mental disorders found in the DSM will be presented from a social work perspective. Sometimes interesting historical information will be included, and at other times editorial asides about exploration and assessment will be offered. In most cases, the authors present a clinical case vignette to help the reader keep in mind the major features of assessment. Above all, we try to provide what the worker will need in a format that is clinically relevant, understandable, and practitioner friendly.

This book is not intended to address all of the specific DSM classifications, nor does it include all specific disorders. We hope to advance assessment criteria from a social work perspective while balancing the tensions inherent in the medical model. We emphasize a competency-based assessment that encompasses both an ecological approach and systems theory to determine what biopsychosocial factors have contributed to the client's problems, as well as factors that may be useful in intervention planning (Maxmen & Ward, 1995). The struggle is shifting the lens away from defining pathology to one of looking beyond internal processes where multiple social and environmental factors that influence functioning are considered.

TABLE 1-5   AXIS V—GLOBAL ASSESSMENT OF FUNCTIONING (GAF) SCALE

Code *(Note: Use intermediate codes when appropriate, for example, 75, 45)*

100 Superior functioning in a wide range of activities, life's problems never seem to get out of hand, is sought out by others because of his or her many positive qualities. No symptoms.

90 Absent or minimal symptoms (for example, mild anxiety before a job interview), good functioning in all areas, interested and involved in a wide range of activities, socially effective, generally satisfied with life, no more than everyday problems or concerns (for example, a disagreement with a friend).

80 If symptoms are present, they are transient and expectable reactions to psychosocial stressors (for example, changing jobs or moving); no more than slight impairment in social, occupational, or school functioning (for example, receiving a poor job evaluation).

70 Some mild symptoms (for example, not able to sleep well occasionally) OR some difficulty in social, occupational, or school functioning (for example, staying out after curfew), but generally functioning pretty well, has some meaningful interpersonal relationships.

60 Moderate symptoms (for example, occasional panic attacks) OR moderate difficulty in social, occupational, or school functioning (for example, lack of friends and unable to maintain employment).

50 Serious symptoms (for example, suicidal ideation) OR any serious impairment in social, occupational, or school functioning.

40 Some impairment in reality testing or communication (for example, irrelevant speech) OR major impairment in several areas, such as work or school, family relationships, judgment, thinking, or mood (for example, avoids friends).

30 Behavior is considered influenced by delusions or hallucinations OR serious impairment in communication or judgment (for example, acting inappropriately) OR inability to function in almost all areas (for example, has no friends, has no job, and is reclusive).

20 Some danger of hurting self or others (for example, violent outbursts) OR occasionally fails to maintain minimal hygiene (for example, does not shower, cut hair) OR gross impairment in communication (for example, does not talk).

10 Persistent danger of severely hurting self or others (for example, repeatedly violent) OR persistent inability to maintain minimal personal hygiene OR serious suicidal act with clear expectation of death.

0 Inadequate information.

Source: Reprinted with permission from the *Diagnostic and statistical manual of mental disorders,* Fourth Edition-TR. © 2000 American Psychiatric Association.

Many current textbooks (see, for instance, Maxmen & Ward, 1995; Wilson et al., 1996) use terminology describing those considered mentally ill as "patients." While the DSM format has begun to move away from these descriptions, it remains to be seen how quickly the rest of the literature follows suit. The ultimate challenge is to know when to utilize the DSM effectively and when to keep its classification system in perspective.

THE COMPETENCY-BASED ASSESSMENT MODEL

A competency-based assessment is the process of reviewing and understanding an individual's past in order to distinguish and interpret presenting concerns. By looking at the person and their history, the worker gains a greater insight into current functioning. Attention is focused on examining biological, psychological (including cognitive), and social systems variables. In his classic article, Bronfenbrenner (1979) suggests practitioners who do not consider all the various environmental influences lose the breadth and depth of the client's life experiences. The biopsychosocial framework, together with an ecological perspective and systems theory, explicates this competency-based assessment model. The ***ecological perspective*** draws attention to the client's multiple interactions with their environment; the ***biopsychosocial framework*** validates the potential importance of biogenetic, psychological, social, and environmental factors in understanding human behavior; and ***systems theory*** integrates these principles. Individualizing how each person is affected by the "illness" is at the heart of this conceptualization.

A brief overview of the components comprising the competency-based assessment model follows. The first element is the biopsychosocial framework.

The Biopsychosocial Framework

George Engel (1977, 1980, 1997) is considered the leading proponent of the biopsychosocial framework. According to Engel, the biological component addresses relationships among factors that include normal biology, disease processes, genetic influences, and their relationship to the person's biological functioning. The psychological component addresses those factors that include thoughts, feelings, perceptions, motivation, and reaction to "illness." The social component examines cultural, environmental, and familial influences. According to Bandura (1969, 1977), reciprocal interactions are assumed between a person's behavior and their environment. Understanding the client's functioning at all levels helps provide a more complete clinical picture and one that identifies competencies that may be built upon. Based on this, it is essential to discern the client's medical status, individual psychology, and sociocultural factors affecting behavior.

Historically, there have been two major models explaining behavior; one is the biomedical model and the other is the psychodynamic model. The ***biomedical model*** delineates diagnostic criteria, whereas the ***psychodynamic model*** focuses on symptoms, behaviors, and underlying psychological processes. According to Stoudemire (1994), these two models, when integrated, form a biopsychosocial framework. This framework for assessment considers (a) genetic and biological factors in the pathogenesis of certain disorders (such as schizophrenia and mood disorders); (b) developmental experiences or/and conflicted family and social relationships (some individuals may be more vulnerable to certain types of illness); (c) current life stresses (that may precipitate the onset of certain psychiatric disorders and symptoms, or contribute to the relapse of preexisting conditions).

The biopsychosocial framework supports the competency-based assessment model in several ways. First, the significance of understanding the client's present functioning and its relationship to past events underscores the need for fully understanding each client's unique history. Second, this model relies on a thorough assessment and prioritizing of problems. Third, it pays attention to the multiple systems that affect the client, such as the biological, psychological, social, and cultural aspects of the client's life. A fourth characteristic is the focus on positive behaviors and events in the client's life rather than emphasizing deficits. Finally, a competency-based assessment focuses on the relationship between behavior and surrounding events—that is, those events that can either elicit or maintain problematic behaviors. According to McDaniel (1995), this helps the client and family maintain an identity apart from the "illness." Applying a competency-based assessment model underscores the importance of evaluating all aspects of the client's difficulties while looking for strengths.

The second element important to discussion of the competency-based assessment model incorporates an ecological perspective.

The Ecological Perspective

More than 25 years ago, Germain (1973) introduced the "ecological metaphor" as a way to expand the focus of social work practice by emphasizing the interaction between persons and their environment. The ecological perspective primarily focuses on human ecology, or the way human beings and their environment accommodate to each other (Germain, 1991; Germain & Gitterman, 1995). This interaction is considered dynamic; that is, the goodness of "fit" between individuals and their surroundings is achieved through mutual interaction, negotiation, and compromise. Zastrow (1995) highlights the importance of understanding clients through an ecological point of view:

> Human beings are viewed as developing and adapting through transactions with all elements of their environments. An ecological model gives attention to both internal and external factors. It does not view people as passive reactors to their environments, but rather as being involved in dynamic and reciprocal interactions with them. (p. 24)

The mental disorders described in the DSM describe a disease process, not people; individuals with the same diagnosis often look very different from one another in terms of behaviors, personality, life experiences, or problems in living. Depending on the diagnostic criteria offered, clients may have remarkably different life experiences. While the DSM may be recognized as a useful diagnostic tool, it tells the practitioner little or nothing about the "whys" of mental illness, nor does it address client individuality.

One of the strengths of the ecological perspective is that it draws attention to each person's unique history and considers the complexity of the human experience. Some of the more salient concepts of the ecological perspective take into consideration:

Person:environment fit—This is viewed as the actual "fit" between an individual's or a group's needs and their surroundings. Considered a defining characteristic of social work practice, the person:environment fit requires an assessment that encompasses the person, their environment, and the interactions between them.

Adaptations—Adaptations are regarded as the continuous, change-oriented, cognitive, sensory-perceptual, and behavioral processes people use to sustain or raise the level of "fit" between themselves and their environment.

Life stressors—Life stressors include difficult social or developmental transitions, traumatic life events, or other issues disturbing the existing "fit."

Stress—Considered the response to life stressors, stress is characterized by troubled emotional or physiological states (or both). It may be characterized by anxiety, guilt, anger, fear, depression, helplessness, or despair.

Coping measures—Coping includes efforts to regulate negative feelings. According to Antonovsky (1980), the most basic category of coping resources consists of beliefs and attitudes toward life. Other coping mechanisms include the person's knowledge, successful experiences with life tasks, and cognitive capacities and the ability to reason; the ability to control and use emotional affective responses to stress; and skills to carry out planned action, which usually come from past successful experiences.

The ecological perspective views individuals as moving through a series of life transitions that require environmental supports and coping skills. Stress may result if there is not a good "fit" between internal and external demands and resources (Germain and Gitterman, 1996). The practitioner looks at those transactions that either promote or inhibit growth and development. In addition, this perspective helps the practitioner to work collaboratively with clients to mobilize strengths and coping, locate resources, and explore opportunities within the client's environment that may pave the way for the client to achieve success rather than being powerless or disenfranchised.

The third and last element composing the competency-based assessment model is systems theory.

Systems Theory

Systems theory was developed during the 1940s and 1950s by Ludwig von Bertalanffy (1968), as an approach to understanding the interconnectedness of the various relationships within a person's life. From the beginning, systems theory postulated that the behavior of any living system was not fixed by its initial conditions. Bertalanffy suggested all social sciences could be integrated by using systems as a unit of analysis—that is, the biological system and the personality system as well as the social system. Systems theory organizes the practitioner's understanding of human development. The theory does not attempt to explain human behavior, but asserts that human behavior is viewed through three distinct frames of reference: the biological, psychological, and social. Systems theory clarifies the person-situation gestalt by conceptualizing the client's world. It moves away from a linear explanation of cause and effect to appreciate the complex interactions between the individual and all aspects of their biopsychosocial system. In other words, the true role of systems theory is to help the social worker pay attention to those complex interactions between clients and their environment. The competency-based assessment complements using the DSM for assessing mental illness. This approach to assessment includes exploring how the client's current thoughts, feelings, *and* factors within the environment relate to functioning versus focusing solely on behavior as a sign of underlying intrapersonal concerns. Using the biopsychosocial framework fosters an evaluation based on "behaviors-in-situations" rather than behaviors or situations alone. The competency-based assessment also considers capacities, motivation, and environmental qualities as components of ecological competence for the multiple transactions between people and their social environments. This leads to a change in the type of assessment questions asked, where the worker is more interested in finding out what is right about the client than what is wrong. This summary of the central ideas supporting the competency-based assessment model sets the stage for the constructs discussed in the following chapters.

Assessment is an ongoing process with a focus toward valuing client strengths. According to Gambrill (1983), assessment differs from diagnosis in a number of ways:

> Observable behaviors are not used as signs of something more significant but as important in their own right as samples of relevant behaviors. Behavior is considered to be a response to identifiable environmental or personal events such as specific thoughts or feelings. Rather than using behavior as a sign of underlying intrapersonal causes, assessment includes an exploration of how current thoughts, feelings, and environmental events relate to these samples of behaviors. (p. 34)

This changes the emphasis in the type of assessment questions asked. For example, when working with a client who is socially isolated and may be depressed, asking questions about how they manage to get through the day shifts the inquiry away from pathology and toward the client's own competency. The competency-based assessment provides the foundation for examining effective problem solving, self-change, viable alternatives, and solutions. From this example, using a wide-angle lens in formulating the assessment provides the opportunity to gather data that focuses on the client's experiences in coping with depression. The biological, psychological, and social elements found in the competency-based assessment, when merged with the DSM multi-axial classification system, provide an individualized way of looking at the client and their social context.

In subsequent chapters, the connections among the biological, psychological, and social factors are presented. Figure 1-1 is a graphic representation that depicts this approach. This pedagogical feature is repeated throughout the book, each time focusing on a specific disorder. The case illustrations are not to be considered as the final word, but as representations of assessment data. By envisioning the convergence of these perspectives, it is hoped that the practitioner will get a fuller picture of assessing for competence or those skills that enable the client to function effectively and the client's unique experience with mental disorders. The competency-based assessment is the process of clarifying competence within the client system, the unique features of their environment, the goodness of "fit" between clients and their environment, and the impact of mental illness. Notes Compton and Galaway (1999):

> In this perspective, clients are regarded as active, striving human beings who are capable of organizing their lives and realizing their potentialities, as long as they have appropriate family, community, societal, and environmental resources. (pp. 354–355)

The competency-based assessment is directed toward finding ways to support the client's resilience and coping strategies.

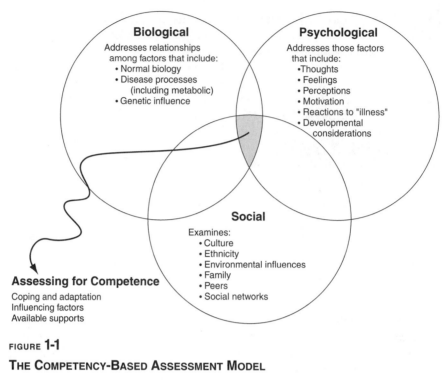

FIGURE **1-1**

THE COMPETENCY-BASED ASSESSMENT MODEL

The interactions of the biological, psychological, and social variables in the client's life.

UNDERSTANDING THE CLIENT

According to Shulman (1999), professional practice should be guided by "obtaining relevant information (study), using models to guide our understanding of our client's circumstances (assessment), developing intervention strategies (treatment), and assessing our impact on the process and outcome (evaluation).... All play important roles" (p. 117–118). Assessment should ask, "What's the matter?" (Meyer, 1993, p. 2). Unlike the model borrowed from medicine where the focus is on examining how past events have affected individuals, it is important to understand the context of current issues. Important assessment categories adapted from Compton and Galaway (1999), de Jong and Berg (1998), Franklin and Jordan (1992), Germain and Gitterman (1996), Jordan and Franklin (1995), Shulman (1999), and Woods and Hollis (2000) include the nature of the presenting problem; the client's current life situation including intrapersonal issues and interpersonal concerns such as family, work or school, and peers; context and social support networks; relevant historical data, and sociocultural factors. The specific information elicited about the nature of the presenting problem is summarized on Table 1-6. It is not our intent to provide a comprehensive list, but to outline a beginning guide to exploring presenting concerns with the client in a systematic way.

Formulating a competency-based assessment is more than relying on "gut feelings" or worker intuition. This is not to say that clinical judgment is unimportant, only

---

TABLE 1-6   THE NATURE OF THE PRESENTING PROBLEM

Identify the reason for referral:

What made the client seek help now and not before?

How has the client sought to solve the problem previously including other therapy (and with what results)?

What is the client's ability to identify and define problems; or to discuss probable causative factors?

Describe the events leading up to the referral or other factors precipitating the referral.

Identify the contributing conditions and components of the problem:

History

   When did the problem first occur?

   Is this a long-standing unresolved problem, or a recent one?

Duration

   How long has the problem been going on?

Frequency

   How often does the problem occur?

Magnitude

   What is the intensity of the problem?

Antecedents

   What happens immediately before the problem occurs?

Consequences

   What happens immediately after the problem occurs?

Clarify the client's competence:

What are the unique capacities, skills, attitudes, motivations, strengths, and potentialities of the client?

What are the particular areas of coping strengths?

What are indicators of resilience in the person?

Which areas of competence need to be reinforced or supported?

Which life experiences can be mobilized to stimulate or support the process of change?

What client resources are available for solving the problem?

How does the client relate to the worker and demonstrate the ability to use help?

What is the social worker's perception of the problem? How much agreement is there between the worker and the client concerning these problems?

Are there other difficulties associated with (or in addition to) the problem?

---

that effective judgments concerning clients must instead be grounded in empirical observations and documentation of client characteristics. In the authors' experience, there is a temptation for workers to prematurely diagnose first and then to ask questions to support this clinical picture. Typically, the worker should look at the multiple influences in the client's life, for example, *intrapersonal issues, patterns of interpersonal relationships, social context,* and *support* networks (Table 1-7). Table 1-7

TABLE **1-7**   THE CLIENT'S CURRENT LIFE SITUATION

I. Intrapersonal issues:
Cognitive functioning
What is the client's perception of the problem?
Is there evidence of the client's capacity to solve problems?
Is there evidence of rational versus irrational thoughts?
Emotional functioning
Describe the client's affect.
Is there evidence of appropriate versus inappropriate affect?
Has the client been under stress or recently experience pressure that has been difficult to manage?
Behavioral functioning
What is the client's physical appearance?
Mannerisms?
Disabilities?
Physiologic functioning
Has the client been seen medically during the past year?
If so, what are the results?
Has the client had any recent illness, or surgery?
Is there evidence of drug or/and alcohol usage?
Any medications taken?
Describe diet, caffeine use, and so forth.
Mental status
Note:
Disturbances in appearance, dress, or posture.
Disturbance in thoughts, such as hallucinations or delusions.
Disturbances in level of awareness, such as memory, attention.
Disturbances in emotional tone, such as either deviations in affect or is there a discrepancy in the client's verbal report of mood/affect and what the practitioner observes.
Degree which client seems aware of the nature of the problem and the need for treatment.
Client roles and role performance
What roles does the client perform, such as wife, mother?
Are the client's issues related to role performance?
Are the client's issues related to role satisfaction or dissatisfaction?
Has the client had any serious problems with their children, their marriage or other close relationships?
Developmental considerations
Trace the birth, developmental history (including the mother's pregnancy), developmental milestones, or illness.

Sexual, marital and family history (such as domestic violence, abuse).
Is there a legal history?
What has family life been like when the client was growing up?
Does the client recall any specific events while growing up, such as a parent dying or divorcing when the client was young?

II. Interpersonal family issues:
What is each family member's perspective of the problem(s)?
Marital status
What is the client's sexual, dating, or marital history?
What is the quality of the client's intimate relationships?
What year (or years) did the client marry?
If married more than once, how many times?
Family structure
What is the quality of the client's family interactions?
Describe the family system: composition; structure; boundaries; cohesion; flexibility; rules; family alliances; family power; negotiation; family decision making; problem solving; and communcation patterns.
Has there been any recent serious illness or death in the client's family?
How does the client describe his or her parents?

III. Interpersonal work or school:
Occupation or grade in school
Satisfaction with work/school
Are there indicators of successful achievement in this setting?
Are there issues related to grades, pay, or promotions?
Describe the client's relationships with colleagues/peers.
Does the presenting problem(s) occur in this setting also?
If so, how does the client get along with peers, teachers, boss or other authority figures?
What is the academic/work history?
Is the client having any problems with money or with their job?
Is the client seriously in debt?

IV. Interpersonal peers:
Who are the client's friends, and what is the quality of these relationships?
Is the client satisfied with their friends/peers?

TABLE **1-8**   THE CLIENT'S CONTEXT AND SOCIAL SUPPORT NETWORKS

Clarify the environmental characteristics that influence coping and adaptive patterns of the client:

What environmental resources does the client have?

   How adequate are the client's material circumstances—housing, transportation, food?

   What does the client know about community resources and how to use them?

What actual or potential supports are available in the environment?

   Does the client have access to family or peer supports or support from agencies in the neighborhood that are not being used?

What are the risks and vulnerabilities in the client system?

What blocks, obstacles, or/and deficits interfere with the client's life processes and adaptive strivings?

What is the goodness of "fit" between the client system and their environment?

Ethnic/cultural considerations:

What is the client's ethnic or cultural group?

What is the degree of acculturation?

Is there evidence of prejudice or discrimination by others toward the client?

To what extent is there isolation from (or participation in) extra-familial groups and associations, such as ethnic or cultural groups?

What is the client's perception of how ethnic/cultural group identification has helped or not helped?

How do sociocultural factors interfere with the client's functioning (such as racism, sexism, cultural values) and social and economic injustice?

Can the client draw from the resources of his or her culture or ethnic group?

---

provides suggestions for examining biopsychosocial functioning and areas that may begin to delineate the "fit" between the person and his or her social network.

Other areas to explore include the client's *context* and *social support* networks (Table 1-8). This includes culture and ethnicity, which are an integral part of one's identity. It is important to explore the extent to which these factors can affect persons with a mental illness (Voss et al., 1999). Along with respect for these considerations, the practitioner takes into account his or her own attitudes and biases (Weaver, 1998; Weaver, 2000).

SUMMARY

The competency-based assessment framework operationalizes the process of summarizing, prioritizing, and classifying the information found in the DSM. However, the practitioner looks for strengths and resources in the individual and their related social systems that can be developed and supported. Additionally, individual, family, and socio-environmental systems in the client's life are reviewed. A thorough understanding of the client's problems often demystifies using a diagnostic label and provides clinical insight into what seems to be a complicated symptom picture (Gray & Zide, 1999). The worker must be knowledgeable about many factors related to presenting issues. Therefore, familiarity with the diagnostic conditions and the ability to apply them correctly is important to the competency-based assessment for social workers.

An important social work value relates to appreciating human worth and respecting dignity. We often see people who are not at their best. The profession is committed to helping people who are oppressed and disempowered (DuBois & Miley, 1996). The social worker focuses on the strengths of the person, thereby promoting both personal and societal competence despite the obstacles associated with mental illness. Siporin (1975) noted 25 years ago, "a chief mandate of the social work profession is to work with people who are disenfranchised and oppressed" (p. 4). Social work values both the strengths and vulnerabilities of people. These values are integral to the competency-based assessment model, which incorporates both biopsychosocial factors and the relationship between behavior and the client's context. This perspective provides a more complete picture describing the individual's functioning at all levels.

The competency-based assessment focuses on relationships between behavior and surrounding events—those events that elicit or maintain problematic behaviors. The individual's present functioning is examined in relationship to past events, while considering biopsychosocial factors as well as environmental systems. The focus is on client strengths rather than deficits. In sum, a competency-based assessment assumes that clients have the capability to reorganize their lives as long as they have appropriate family, community, societal, and environmental resources and supports.

REFERENCES

Abramson, J., & Mizrahi T. (1996). When social workers and physicians collaborate: Positive and negative interdisciplinary experiences. *Social Work*, 41: 270–281.

Abramson, J., & Mizrahi, T. (1997). Models of effective collaboration between social workers and physicians: A typology. Paper presented at the Annual Program Meeting of the Council of Social Work Education, Chicago, Illinois.

American Psychiatric Association. (2000). Diagnostic and Statistical Manual of Mental Disorders (4th ed.-TR) Washington, DC: APA.Chicago.

Andreasen, N. C., & Black, D. W. (1995). *Introductory textbook of Psychiatry* (2nd ed.). Washington, DC: American Psychiatric Press.

Antonovsky, A. (1980). *Health, stress, and coping.* San Francisco: Jossey-Bass.

Austrian, S. G. (1995). *Mental disorders, medications, and clinical social work.* New York: Columbia University Press.

Bandura, A. (1969). *Principles of behavior modification.* New York: Holt, Rinehart & Winston.

Bandura, A. (1977). *Social learning theory.* Englewood Cliffs, NJ: Prentice-Hall.

Berkman, B. (1996). The emerging health care world: Implications for social work practice and education. *Social Work*, 41: 541–551.

Bronfenbrenner, U. (1979*). The etiology of human development: Experiments by nature and design.* Cambridge, MA: Harvard University Press.

Compton, B. R., & Galaway, B. (1999). *Social work processes* (6th ed.). Pacific Grove, CA: Brooks/Cole.

de Jong, P., & Berg, I. K. (1998). *Interviewing for solutions.* Pacific Grove, CA: Brooks/Cole.

DuBois, B., & Miley, K. K. (1996). *Social work: An empowering profession* (2nd ed.). Boston: Allyn and Bacon.

Dumont, M. P. (1987). A diagnosis parable. *Readings*, 2(4): 9–12.

Ell, K. (1996). Social work and health care practice and policy: A psychosocial research agenda. *Social Work*, 41: 583–592.

Engel, G. L. (1977). The need for a new medical model: A challenge for biomedicine. *Science*, 196: 120–136.

Engel, G. L. (1980). The clinical application of the biopsychosocial model. *American Journal of Psychiatry*, 137: 535.

Engel, G. L. (1997). From biomedical to biopsychosocial: Being scientific in the human domain, *Psychosomatics*, 38(6): 521–528.

Franklin, C. G. (1999). Research on practice: Better than you think? *Social Work in Education*, 21(1): 3–9.

Franklin, C., & Jordan, C. (1992). Teaching students to perform assessment. *Journal of Social Work Education*, 28(2): 222–241.

Frances, A., First, M. B., & Pincus, H. A. (1995). *DSM-IV guidebook.* Washington, DC: American Psychiatric Press.

French, L. M. (1940). *Psychiatric social work.* New York: The Commonwealth Fund.

Gambrill, E. (1983). *Casework: A competency-based approach.* Englewood Cliffs, NJ: Prentice-Hall.

Germain, C. B. (1973). An ecological perspective in case work practice. *Social Casework*, 54: 323–330.

Germain, C. B. (1991). *Human behavior in the social environment: An ecological view.* New York: Columbia University Press.

Germain, C. B., & Gitterman, A. (1995). Ecological perspective. In J. G. Hopps and G. Lloyd (Eds.), *Encyclopedia of social work* (19th ed.), pp. 816–824. Washington, DC: NASW Press.

Germain, C. B., & Gitterman, A. (1996). *The life model of social work practice.* New York: Columbia University Press.

Gray, S. W., & Zide, M. R. (1999, June). Working with individuals who have personality disorders: Demystifying and depathologizing the process. Paper presented at the National Association of Social Workers, Inc., Florida Chapter, Annual State Conference, Ft. Lauderdale, Florida.

Johnson, H. W. (Ed.). (1995). *The social services: An introduction* (4th ed.). Itasca, IL: F. E. Peacock Publishers.

Jordan, C., & Franklin, C. (1995). *Clinical assessment for social workers.* Chicago: Lyceum Books.

Keigher, M. (1997). What role for social work in the new health care practice paradigm? *Health and Social Work*, 22(2): 149–155.

Kirk, S. A., & Kutchins, H. (1988). Deliberate misdiagnosis in mental health practice. *Social Service Review*, 62: 225–237.

Kirk, S. A., & Kutchins, H. (1992). *The selling of DSM: The rhetoric of science in psychiatry.* New York: Aldine de Gruyer.

Kirk, S. A., & Kutchins, H. (1994). Is bad writing a mental disorder? *New York Times*, June 20, A17.

Kirk, S. A., Siporin, M., & Kutchins, H. (1989). The prognosis for social work diagnosis. *Social Casework*, 70: 295–304.

Kutchins, H., & Kirk, S. A. (1987). DSM-III and social work malpractice. *Social Work*, 32: 205–211.

Lee, J. A. B. (1994). *The empowerment approach to social work practice.* New York: Columbia University Press.

Mailick, M. D. (1991). Re-assessing assessment in clinical social work practice. *Smith College Studies in Social Work*, 62(1): 3–9.

Maxmen, J. S., & Ward, N. G. (1995). *Essential psychopathology and its treatment.* New York: W. W. Norton and Company.

Mc Daniel, S. H. (1995). *Counseling families with chronic illness: Family psychology and counseling services.* Alexandria,VA: American Counseling Association.

Meyer, C. H. (1993). *Assessment in social work practice.* New York: Columbia University Press.

Netting, F. E., & Williams, F. G. (1996). Case management-physician collaboration: Implications for professional identification, roles, and relationships. *Health & Social Work*, 21: 216–224.

Netting, F. E., & Williams, F. G. (1997, March). Preparing the next generation of geriatric social workers to collaborate with primary care physicians. Paper presented at the Annual Program Meeting of the Council on Social Work Education, Chicago.

Paulson, R. I. (1996). Swimming with the sharks or walking in the garden of Eden? In P. R. Raffoul & C. A. McNeece (Eds.), *Future issues for social work practice*, pp. 85–96. Needham Heights, MA: Allyn and Bacon.

Shulman, L. (1999). *The skills of helping individuals, families, groups, and communities* (4th ed.). Itasca, IL: F. E. Peacock Publishers.

Simon, B. L. (1994). *The empowerment tradition in American social work: A history.* New York: Columbia University Press.

Siporin, M. (1975). *Introduction to social work practice.* New York: Macmillan.

Stoudemire, A. (1994). *Clinical psychiatry for medical students* (2nd ed.). Philadelphia: J. B. Lippincott Company.

Strom-Gottfried, K. (1997). Implications of managed care for social work education. *Journal of Social Work Education*, 33(1): 7–18.

Weaver, H. N. (1998). Teaching cultural competence: Application of experiential learning techniques. *Journal of Teaching in Social Work*, 17(1/2): 65–79.

Weaver, H. N. (2000). Balancing culture and professional education: American Indians/Alaskan natives and the helping professions. Paper presented at the 46th Annual Program Meeting of the Council on Social Work Education, New York, New York, February.

Wilson, G. T., Nathan, P. E., O'Leary, K. D., & Clark, L. A. (1996). *Abnormal psychology: Integrating perspectives.* Boston: Allyn and Bacon.

Woods, M. E., & Hollis, F. (2000). *Casework: A psychosocial therapy* (5th ed.). New York: McGraw-Hill.

von Bertalanffy, L. (1968). General system theory: A critical review. In W. Buckley (Ed.), *Modern systems research for the behavioral scientist*, pp. 11–30. Chicago: Aldine.

Voss, R. W., Douville, V., Little Soldier, A., & Twiss, G. (1999). Tribal and shamanic-based social work practice: A Lakota perspective. *Social Work*, 44(3): 228–241.

Zastrow, C. (1995). *The practice of social work* (3rd ed.). Pacific Grove, CA: Brooks/Cole.

COGNITIVE DISORDERS: DELIRIUM AND DEMENTIA

INTRODUCTION

It is well known that people today are living longer (Park, 1994), and it is not uncommon to find 80-, 90-, and 100-year-olds living active and productive lives. How old is old? What does the concept of chronological age really mean? When are people no longer deemed productive or valuable? "Beliefs about aging are maintained by language. Expressions like the 'decline' of old age; metaphors such as the 'autumn years' or the 'twilight of one's life'; and characterizations such as 'old codger,' 'curmudgeon,' 'doddering,' and 'senile' are words reserved for older people" (Witkin, 1999, p. 510). People seem more impressed with being young, staying healthy, and maintaining their productivity. This is often characterized as searching for the proverbial Fountain of Youth. Moody (1995) suggests that "instead of 'normal' or 'successful aging,' we begin on the contrary to think of aging as a 'disease' to be conquered and cured" (p. 172). In contrast to the normal, healthy aging process, this chapter will describe three classes of cognitive disorders; they include delirium, dementia, and amnestic disorders (amnesia).

Delirium is characterized as a temporary condition that often accompanies a short and fluctuating course. Persons affected with delirium cannot think or reason clearly, and subsequently they lose contact with the world around them. Delirium can occur at any age, and under many different circumstances. It includes prominent disturbances in alertness, and the individual is confused and disoriented. Individuals who have delirium generally do not know what day it is or where they are. They might be able to focus on one thing, but this focus only lasts a few moments. Additionally, individuals with delirium cannot relate their present situation to anything they experienced in the past; in other words, their thinking should be considered disconnected. One of the ways to recognize the presence of delirium is the person's tendency for restlessness, agitated behavior, and constantly moving around without purpose. This behavior is considered unusual for the person. Delirium can occur at any age, but its effects are almost always time-limited. The various types of delirium included in the DSM-IV-TR are due to a general medical condition;

substance-induced (including medication complications); and due to multiple eti-ologies. This chapter focuses on substance-induced delirium as it is commonly seen by the practitioner in hospital or medically related settings.

Dementia is an advancing, progressive, and degenerative condition, which is marked by a gradual deterioration of a broad range of cognitive abilities. It is impor-tant to recognize that as people age they continue to develop and experience many changes both individually and in their relationships, thus taking their rich personal history and life experiences along with them (Antonucci & Akiyama, 1995). During the latter part of the aging process, the adult faces the loss of support for their role identity, loss of family relationships, and the erosion of functioning (Antonucci, 1994; Siebert et al., 1999). Some cultures view the aged as productive members throughout their entire lives, and treat them as treasured jewels. Others regard the aged as inconvenient burdens or nuisances.

The population is graying rapidly, and the very old are the fastest growing group in the United States, although it is not nearly as fast as the general population growth in other industrialized countries, for example, Germany and Japan (Ozawa & Kono, 1997). It is expected that by the year 2050, the elderly population will make up 66.9 percent of the total U.S. population (U.S. Bureau of the Census, 1993). This means that the average 20-year-old today should expect to live beyond their 75th birthday (National Center for Health Statistics, 1997). Currently, it is estimated that there are somewhere from 2.3 to 5.8 million older adults living with Alzheimer's disease and other dementias living in the United States (Khachaturian & Rade-baugh, 1996; Toseland et al., 1999). Those with Alzheimer's disease alone are expected to quadruple in number over the next 50 years, at which time it will affect 1 in 45 Americans (Brookmeyer et al., 1998).

Dementias are characterized by prominent memory disturbances and central nervous system (CNS) damage, and a dementia is likely to have a protracted course (Shaner, 1997; Wilson, et al., 1996). Individuals with dementia experience a global deterioration in their intellectual, emotional, and cognitive abilities. They experience a great deal of difficulty performing tasks that require them to remember or learn things or to use information they once knew. It becomes difficult for the person with dementia to maintain attention, and even harder for them to sustain this attention. A gradual decline in the normal richness of their thought process takes place.

The various types of dementia included in the DSM-IV-TR are dementia of the Alzheimer's type; vascular dementia; dementia due to HIV, head trauma, Parkinson's disease, Huntington's disease, Pick's disease, Creutzfeldt-Jakob dis-ease, or other general medical disorder; and substance-induced persisting demen-tia due to multiple etiologies. The competency-based assessment is especially suited to working with people with dementia and their families because of the inte-gration of biological, psychological, socio-environmental, and economic concerns; this integration emphasizes persons and their multiple interactions with their envi-ronment (O'Neill, 1999). Dementia is the most expensive disorder in terms of use of formal services and its financial cost. This chapter will focus on dementia of Alzheimer's type to underscore the importance of looking at the medical under-pinnings associated with this disorder.

Amnestic disorders are characterized by prominent memory disturbances, levels of alertness or other cognitive complications that are also found in delirium or dementia. However, the primary characteristic in this disorder is the individual's inability to remember and perceive things. Typically, the person has difficulty using both short-term and long-term memory. For example, the individual might have an easier time remembering something that happened to them 50 years ago than remembering what they ate for breakfast yesterday. It should be noted that the competency-based assessment of amnestic disorder rules out other symptoms such as the difficulty making decisions (executive functioning) or the failure to recognize family or friends (agnosia). Associated features include disorientation, **confabulation**, emotional blandness, and apathy. The amnestic disorder is meant to describe a specific defect involving the loss of memory rather than a pattern featuring multiple cognitive impairments. There are three types of amnestic disorders noted in the DSM-IV-TR: amnestic disorder due to a general medical condition; substance-induced persisting amnestic disorder; and amnestic disorder due to multiple etiologies.

Cognitive disorders are characterized by syndromes of delirium, dementia, and amnesia; all of these are caused by either a general medical condition, "substance" use (both prescribed and illicit, and including alcohol), or a combination of these factors. These disturbances in cognition involve mental confusion, memory impairment, problems maintaining attention, difficulty thinking, and the inability to plan or engage in self-actualized daily living. We begin with a discussion describing delirium and how it affects individuals.

DELIRIUM

Delirium is one of the first mental disorders to be described in history. Descriptions of individuals with these symptoms appeared in writings more than 2,500 years ago (Lipowski, 1990). Over time, delirium has been known by many different names including acute confusional state, toxic psychosis, acute brain syndrome, and metabolic encephalopathy (Morrison, 1995). Although the brain can be directly involved, as in the case of a seizure disorder, the actual cause of delirium is usually a process initiated outside of the person's central nervous system. Delirium is known to have many causative factors, including fevers, drug allergies, chemotherapy, anesthesia, and/or the effects of drug use or an overdose. The delirium process can include effects from hypo- or hyperactive endocrine dysfunction (thyroid disease); infections (meningitis); liver disease (hepatic encephalopathy); renal disease (uremic encephalopathy); vitamin deficiency diseases (thiamine, folic acid, nicotine acid); drug withdrawal or toxicity (anticholinergic agents, antipsychotic drugs, and others); poisons (carbon monoxide); and the effects of postoperative states (anesthesia).

These multiple factors underscore the importance of making the competency-based assessment due to the interplay between their cognitive functioning and biological influences. Of particular importance to the practitioner is a thorough exploration of biological factors. For example, the practitioner considers those who have high fevers, are taking certain medications, or are undergoing a surgical procedure. Because most of the medical conditions are potentially treatable, delirium can often be reversed in a relatively short period of time. Delirium should be thought of as a *syndrome and not a disease*.

Prevailing Pattern

Perhaps because of its transient nature, in that it can occur and then resolve itself quickly (often within hours or days), delirium has been a difficult entity to study. Estimates of the actual number of people affected are lacking. However, Kaplan and Sadock (1998) suggest that delirium is a common disorder, occurring in approximately 15 percent of those who undergo general surgical procedures. Interestingly, it has been estimated that 30 percent of those admitted to surgical intensive care units have been found to experience delirium sometime during their hospital stay. Delirium often signals the presence of a medical situation or a medical emergency that is causing brain dysfunction. It behooves the practitioner to provide help as soon as possible. Many medical conditions have been linked to the onset of delirium, including intoxication from drugs, toxins, and poisons; withdrawal from drugs; infections; head injuries; and various other types of trauma to the brain (Lipowski, 1990). The pattern of delirium is typically short term, and it is this pattern that helps to distinguish it from the other cognitive disorders, especially dementia. Delirium tends to develop quickly, and its course can vary over the day. Symptoms of delirium tend to worsen during early evening hours, known as **sundowning** and when the person is in unfamiliar and unstructured environments (Exum et al., 1993).

The competency-based assessment pays particular attention to the person's mental status including *clouding of consciousness* (the inability to focus, sustain, or shift attention). Individuals appear confused, bewildered, or alarmed. In addition, they may have difficulty in responding to reassurance or in following directions. *Impaired* cognition often includes a marked disturbance of recent memory, and the individual may be unable to provide meaningful psychosocial history. They may be disoriented to time and place; their speech may have a rambling or incoherent quality; they may have trouble finding words, or identifying commonly recognized objects or people. Perceptual disturbances may also be present and may include illusions and visual hallucinations. Often actual perceptions are misinterpreted, and ordinary noises or objects can be perceived as dangerous, threatening, and disturbing. Persecutory delusions based on sensory misperceptions are fairly common. However, once the "causative factor" is eliminated, the individual gradually returns to their prior (or premorbid) level of functioning. Delirium has a short and fluctuating course that is not better explained by dementia (Scully, 1996). Associated features include the following:

- *Disturbance in the sleep-wake cycle*—The individual sleeps during the day and remains awake and agitated at night.
- *Disturbance in psychomotor behavior*—The person may appear disorganized, with purposeless movements, or have increased or decreased psychomotor activity.

Periods of irritability (the individual striking out), belligerence (attempting to flee), or euphoria (resulting in being injured, for example, falling out of a bed) can also occur. The following case vignette is an example of delirium.

The Case of Salvador Cullotto

Adeline Cullotto brought her husband Salvador to Memorial General Hospital's emergency room. She entered the reception area pleading, "Please, please can someone help my husband? He's talking out of his head and I don't know where else to go!" The social worker on duty attempted to calm Mrs. Cullotto down, and asked, "Can you tell me what's been happening to your husband?"

Mrs. Cullotto responded, "Well, Sal doesn't know his name, he doesn't know who I am, and he's talking out of his head. He seems very confused. On top of all that, he has not slept a wink all night. I'm really so worried about him. He's terribly frail right now. Do you think he's becoming senile?" The social worker said he needed more information and asked Mrs. Cullotto, "What has been happening recently or differently that might explain your husband's current behavior?"

She replied, "Well, Sal does have some anemia, you know low blood counts." After a moment of thought, she replied, "Oh you mean like Sal undergoing chemotherapy treatments for chronic lymphocytic leukemia? Now that you mention it, Sal's oncologist changed his protocol regimen several days ago, but Sal never had any problems before with medication changes. You know, come to think of it Sal is really out of it. While we were driving over here he whispered to me, 'The doctor is taking blood out of one arm and putting it right back into my other arm.' Sal made me promise to tell the proper authorities, whoever that is, and 'not to let them charge us double.'" When the social worker asked Mrs. Cullotto to explain further, she said, "Sal insists that the doctor is selling his blood back. He takes blood from one arm and then puts it right back into the other arm. He doesn't want to let him get away with that." She stated, "I've never seen Sal like this before. That's really a screwy idea, and I don't know what's gotten into him. He absolutely loves Dr. Canner. He's been taking care of Sal for years." Mrs. Cullotto added that they had been married for 55 years, both were retired (she a hairdresser and he a factory worker), and they had one son who lived nearby.

The emergency room social worker asked Mr. Cullotto a series of questions about his memory and orientation that included: "What is your name? Do you know where you are right now? Do you know what today's date is? How old are you? What is your wife's name? Do you know what you ate for breakfast this morning? How are you feeling?" The social worker observed in his progress notes, "Mr. Cullotto appears unable to focus, sustain, or shift his attention enough to answer the questions posed to him. His attention wanders, and he is distracted by room sounds around him. He is unable to follow instructions, complete a thought, or reply fully to questions posed to him. His speech has a rambling quality, and is difficult to follow."

The emergency room social worker first reassured Mrs. Cullotto, and then he promised to speak with Mr. Cullotto's doctor. Mr. Cullotto was subsequently hospitalized. When the social worker followed up with the Cullottos after admission, he learned that Mr. Cullotto's chemotherapy protocol had indeed been changed. Two days after admission, Mr. Cullotto's symptoms began to lessen, and he was subsequently discharged three days later. Upon discharge Mrs. Cullotto was overheard commenting to her husband, "Sal, it's just so wonderful to see you back to your usual self. You really weren't you, and I was really scared that your were starting to get Alzheimer's disease. Let's go home, order pizza, and rent a Bruce Willis movie."

Assessment Summary

The interactions of the biological, psychological, and social elements in Sal Cullotto's life are not illustrated here, because they play a small role in the vignette. The key issue in making an assessment of delirium is the recognition of causative factors. A case in point is when the social worker asked Mr. Cullotto to talk about the strength of his belief that his blood was being sold back to him. "It is often only in the specific details that errors of inference become apparent" (First et al., 1995, p. 41). The features of Mr. Cullotto's delirium, in contrast to dementia, were that they had an acute beginning, a relatively brief duration, and the minute-to-minute shifting of his mental status. Unfortunately, the diagnosis of delirium is all too often missed in medical settings, especially in those individuals who tend to be quiet and subdued as opposed to those who are agitated (Frances et al., 1995).

Dementia can be distinguished from delirium by the absence of confusion (Moore & Jefferson, 1996), but both may occur concurrently. Assessing delirium should be distinguished from other mental disorders that present with features of confusion, disorientation, and perceptual disturbances. Intoxication or withdrawal from many drugs of abuse can also cause these symptoms, but the assessment of substance-induced delirium should not be made unless the symptoms exceed those that would be expected during typical intoxication or withdrawal. When schizophrenia is present, the individual's hallucinations and apparent confusion can resemble a delirium, but the individual does not have the disorientation, memory loss, and (daily) sleep disturbance seen in delirium. Those with generalized anxiety disorder may present with agitation, but it is without disorientation, confusion, and memory loss.

The specific coding noted in the DSM determines the differentiation:

- Due to a General Medical Condition (293.0) (List/indicate the general medical condition.).
- Substance Intoxication Delirium (291.0) (Code based on the substance used; for example, 291.0 includes alcohol, amphetamine or amphetamine-like substance, cannabis, hallucinogen, inhalant, opioid, phencyclidine or phencyclidine-like substance, sedative, hypnotic, or anxiolytic, other, or unknown substance.)
- Substance Withdrawal Delirium (Code based on specific substance.)
- Delirium Due to Multiple Etiologies (Code based on specific etiology.)
- Delirium Not Otherwise Specified (NOS) (780.09)

If the delirium is caused by a general medical condition, the practitioner should note both the delirium (Axis I) and the identified general medical condition (Axis III) that is judged to be causing the disturbance. For example, if a client has delirium due to congestive heart failure, it would first be noted on Axis I as Delirium Due to Congestive Heart Failure (293.0), and then on Axis III as Congestive Heart Failure (428.9). The practitioner should be certain to record all causative agents on Axis III, as in the case vignette of Mr. Cullotto's chemotherapy.

Mr. Cullotto's DSM multi-axial designation would be specified as:

Axis I	292.81 Delirium (Chemotherapy)
Axis II	V71.09 (No diagnosis)
Axis III	208.10 Chronic Lymphocytic Leukemia
	280.9 Anemia
Axis IV	Retired
Axis V	GAF = 35 (on admission)
	65 (on discharge)

The competency-based assessment model focuses on underlying causative factors and the client's environment in order to determine the necessary steps to reverse and correct the person's condition. The challenge for the practitioner is to assess for delirium because, if left unrecognized, delirium can often result in serious medical complications or irreversible cognitive impairments. The vignette illustrates questions about Mr. Cullotto's memory and orientation as a part of the assessment process. It is also helpful for the practitioner to gather data from collateral sources such as family members or friends. For example, Adeline Cullotto was the first one who observed sudden and observable changes in her husband; that is, she noticed Sal was confused, disoriented, and illogical. Ultimately, Mr. Cullotto experienced a substance-induced delirium brought on by a reaction to changes in his new chemotherapy treatment. Once his treatment was adjusted, Sal returned to his prior level of functioning.

DEMENTIA

When Alois Alzheimer, a German psychiatrist, first described this disease in 1906, it was considered to be relatively rare. Perhaps this was because life expectancy at the turn of the century was 47 years old as opposed to the current figure of 77 years. It is believed that one in five Americans between the ages of 75 and 84, and almost 50 percent of those 85 years and older are now affected. Why some people are stricken in their 50s while others stay unaffected well into their 90s remains a question.

While there is no foolproof way to diagnosis Alzheimer's disease, other than perhaps after death at autopsy (Shope et al., 1993; Whitehouse, 1993), medical science has made several critical discoveries about how Alzheimer's affects and destroys the brain. This mystery has been slowly unfolding over the past 15 years. Sometime during the late 1980s, scientists isolated and identified a molecule called APP, or amyloid precursor protein. APP is a normal protein that is produced by healthy neurons, and the human body produces at least three enzymes, dubbed alpha, beta, and gamma secretase, that eventually cleave APP into shorter forms. It is not known what the exact purpose of these enzymes serves, but what is clear is that they can build up in the fluid surrounding neurons to form plaques. The medical community used to believe that individuals with Alzheimer's disease produced too many of these enzymes known as A-beta, but that is not currently found to be the case. Persons with Alzheimer's disease produce A-beta at the same rate as a healthy person.

Researchers reexamined the issue and found it was not so much the process of buildup in the fluid surrounding the neurons, but one of how these fluids are disposed. In persons without Alzheimer's, A-beta usually dissolves after it drifts away from the cell. It was found that sometimes A-beta folded into insoluble forms called fibrils, which stick together and form plaques. We all produce some plaques as we go through the aging process. However, the real problem begins when these fibrils trigger an inflammatory response in the brain. What occurs next is that the brain then generates toxic agents called free radicals, which fight off infections. The formation of fibrils causes the same reaction; that is, the free radicals kill off both the healthy neurons and fibrils indiscriminately. Much of the current work in Alzheimer's research involves how enzymes, vitamins, heredity, environmental factors, the use of anti-inflammatory drugs, and hormones play a role in the onset of this disease. Treatment is aimed toward preventing the destruction of healthy neurons while stalling the production of A-beta.

Dementia has often been confused with organic mental syndrome, chronic organic brain disorder, rapid-onset brain syndrome, slow-onset brain syndrome, amnestic disorder (amnesia), and delirium (Weiner, 1991). Perhaps no other mental disorder has had more confusion surrounding it in terms of inaccurate terminology or interchangeable names.

According to Weiner (1991), the term *dementia* was derived from using a combination of fragmented Latin words—*de*, meaning "out of," plus *mens*, meaning "mind," plus *ia*, meaning "state of"—and suggests that the person was deprived of their mind. Recent research regarding brain functioning suggests that several important mental functions are localized in specific areas and that injury to these areas can result in certain types of cognitive impairment. Our understanding of the brain has greatly improved. We know the brain is divided into many different components, but in order to do its job it must function as a well-integrated system (Nietzel et al., 1998). The essential feature of dementia is a deterioration of a person's memory, their awareness, thought, and perception. How a person remembers and understands language and how they learn can greatly affect their lives.

The practitioner should consider dementia when the cognitive decline has been present for at least several months and is not a manifestation of a fluctuating course of delirium (discussed earlier). Conditions such as Alzheimer's disease oftentimes produce degeneration across many areas of the brain, producing a mosaic of cognitive problems. "Although cognitive disorders are found in people of all ages, some of them occur more often in older people, in part because many diseases that cause brain deterioration are more likely to affect the elderly" (Nietzel et al., 1998, p. 378). A 1996 Consensus Conference, cosponsored by the National Institute on Aging and the Reagan Institute of the Alzheimer's Association, focusing on Alzheimer's disease, recommended uniform evaluation procedures and diagnostic assessment (Wisniewski & Silverman, 1997).

Age-related cognitive decline is important to consider when making a competency-based assessment (Caine, 1994). In addition to memory loss, at least *one* of the following must be present for a diagnosis of Alzheimer's:

- *Agnosia*—The failure to recognize familiar friends, family members, or commonly used objects (such as eating utensils).

- *Aphasia*—The individual loses their ability to understand written language, yet he or she is still able to comprehend speech.

- *Apraxia*—Difficulty coordinating motor behaviors even though the necessary motor functions are intact and the person is physically capable of performing these motor behaviors.

- *Loss of* **executive functioning**—Judgment and impulse control are affected, and the ability to analyze, understand, and adapt to new situations is impaired.

- Other cognitive impairments—Includes the inability to remember events (even those happening minutes earlier), the loss of appropriate judgment about behavior, confusion and disorientation, and/or difficulties in accurately perceiving spatial arrangements.

As discussed above, the three A's—agnosia, aphasia, and apraxia—tend to be more commonly seen in dementia. They are also most likely to occur later on in the person's dementia experience. Dementia is the reduction or impairment of intellect, emotion, and behavioral functioning severe enough to cause some detriment in social, occupational, and other important interpersonal areas in the person's life. It is almost as if the person has lost their "road map of life." They experience difficulty with short-term memory and, to a lesser degree, long-term memory. For example, when short term-memory problems occur the person may forget where they left their purse or wallet, not remember to turn off the stove (sometimes with food still cooking), or forget to lock the doors before going to bed. Problems experienced with long-term memory are considered less severe; for example, the person cannot remember where they live or how to get home.

"Personality changes" are often manifested by a lack of appropriate grooming. The individual might begin to wear their clothing inside out (or sometimes no clothing at all), display a major decline in personal hygiene including bowel and urinary incontinence, poor oral care, shaving, and the overall inability to care for oneself. It is generally this loss of "good judgment" and lapse of previously "normal" behavior that often prompts family members to seek help. In one of the authors' clinical practice experience, a family member described her loved one in the following manner: "My mother once could vie for the regalness of being the Queen of England.

She always had such impeccable table manners and social graces. Now mother eats butter with her fingers, and throws the bread on the floor or tries to stuff peas up her nose." It is often this heartbreak of seeing family members unable to sustain their former standard of behavior that is so tragic for the family to endure. Along with the progressive decay of appropriate judgment, the family often describes the heartbreak of losing their family member. In some cases, a person described as easygoing and friendly may become extremely rigid, anxious, hostile, or aggressive (Ragneskog & Kihlgren, 1997; Sadavoy & LeClair, 1997).

Social workers often encounter families struggling with caring for their loved one at home. Having to make the difficult decision to institutionalize a beloved family member with dementia usually occurs when there is an excessive amount of night-time activity, a history of falls and injuries, immobility or difficulty in walking, incontinence, and a situation of being cared for by a female, usually a relative (Hope et al., 1998; van Dijk et al., 1993). Other factors include caretaker burden and depression, emotional distress, financial worries, loss of work, and family conflict (Brodaty & Luscombe, 1998; Donaldson et al., 1998; Kosberg & Cairl, 1991; Luscombe et al., 1998; Magai & Cohen, 1998; Ponder & Pomeroy, 1996; Walker & Pomeroy, 1996).

The second most common type of dementia the social worker may find in practice is vascular dementia, sometimes referred to as multi-infarct dementia. Vascular dementia is caused by at least one stroke. Risk factors include diabetes, hypertension (high blood pressure), heart disease, and medical disorders leading to cerebral emboli. The precise relationship between a cerebral infarct and manifesting dementia requires further research, but an association has been found to exist (Rubin, 1997).

By far the most common type of dementia is *Alzheimer's type*, which accounts for approximately two-thirds of all dementia seen in the older population (Rubin, 1997; Small, 1998). Making a competency-based assessment is vitally important to both the client and to their family in helping to understand the "personality changes" that will occur (Robinson et al., 1998). Even though only one person in a marital relationship is likely to have dementia, it really has two or more victims— the affected spouse, the caretaker spouse, and the family.

It is important that the practitioner recognize the various warning signs of Alzheimer's:

THE EARLY STAGE

- Memory loss (recent) begins to affect the individual's performance
- Loss of initiative
- Mood or personality changes, for example, avoiding family or friends
- Confusion about where they are, for example, being at home
- Takes longer to perform usual chores

THE MIDDLE STAGE

- Increasing problems recognizing family and/or friends
- Escalating memory loss and confusion

- Making repetitive statements
- Occasional muscle jerking or twitching
- Difficulty in reading, writing, or understanding numbers
- Problems thinking logically
- Struggles to find "the right words" to express themselves
- Needs close supervision, for example, they may wander away from home
- May exhibit suspiciousness, irritability, or restlessness
- May have trouble bathing or with self-care

THE LATE STAGE

- Difficulty swallowing/feeding self, and loses weight
- Does not recognize their family members or lifelong friends
- Does not distinguish familiar everyday objects, for example, how to use a fork or spoon
- Becomes incontinent, and unable to control bladder and/or bowels
- Unable to care for self
- Unable to communicate with others, for example, cannot speak or respond to others

The following vignette will illustrate an example of dementia, Alzheimer's type.

The Case of Zelda "Jean" Pfohl

"Mr. Pfohl, why don't you follow me and I'll show you our nursing home facility," said the social worker. "You know, I'm still not so sure about putting Jean in here. Actually, I'm really sick about it. This June we'll be married 55 years. You know a lot of people can't say that these days," said Mr. Pfohl. "Jean and I promised each other that if ever the other one should ever 'get so bad' as to need a nursing home, well, we just wouldn't do it. We'd do everything in our power to maintain our home life together, but things are just so terrible right now [starting to cry]. I hired a very nice woman who took wonderful care of my wife six days a week. She'd cook meals, bathe Jean, and provided 24-hour care, but then one of her own relatives got sick and she had to leave us. I found myself just unable to care for Jean by myself. I couldn't lift or bathe her, but the most depressing part was changing her diapers. I mean, how much can someone have to deal with? It became impossible to see the one person I love most in this world reduced to being a baby. It's just too much … just too much. She's not the Jean I knew. She doesn't recognize me, our children, grandchildren, or great-grandchild."

The social worker found a quiet corner in the home's formal parlor away from the activity of the residents and staff. She invited Mr. Pfohl to sit down and asked him to talk about what precipitated his decision to visit the nursing home.

Mr. Pfohl related, "We had it pretty good for many years. Sure we had rough times, but mostly times were good for us. We were two young kids when we married in 1929. Neither one of us finished high school, but not many people did in those days. I left school, got a job and a model-T Ford in that order. Although Jean was the only girl in her family, and the third of four children, she was a 'mother' to her brothers. Their parents died during the swine flu epidemic in 1918, and Jean was still a baby herself. But she was determined that she and her brothers wouldn't be separated, and they weren't. Once she made up her mind, everybody better watch out.

"We've been married almost 56 years, and for the most part it has been a good marriage. We have two wonderful children, and they both live nearby. Our daughter is divorced, but she's doing very well. She has three grown children of her own, and recently earned a master's degree in teaching. On top of that, she's a world-class musician. We have always been proud of her accomplishments. Our son is a physician who married his high school sweetheart. At first, we didn't approve of their relationship, but as time went on we could see they really were meant for each other. They have three children and are also doing very well. Our daughter-in-law has been very helpful bringing food and meals over, but how much can we expect her to take care of us? Our grandchildren are wonderful, but they have their own lives to live.

"I forgot to mention to you that Jean earned a broker's real estate license after our children were grown and out of the house. I wasn't too thrilled with her working outside of the home, you know, in those days women usually were homemakers, but she was stubborn about this. She told me that she was tired of cleaning the house and she only wanted to sell real estate for 'pin money.' She did a pretty good job, too. In a few years, Jean had a thriving business and several people working for her. She'd buy 'fixer upper' houses, and after the necessary repairs she'd sell them for a nice tidy profit. She put whatever commissions she earned back into buying other houses. I tell you Jean really had a nose for business, and she made a good deal of money. We're lucky that we don't have any financial worries, but that's because of Jean's business sense. It sure wasn't because of what I earned in my seat cover business. She was the brains in our family, and that's why her being this way is so hard for me.

"These are supposed to be the 'golden years' in our lives. We used to have lots of friends, but now no one wants to go out with us. I guess I really don't blame them. Around our condo development I now watch other couples holding hands, playing golf or cards, and going out to dinner. Whereas Jean is reduced to wearing diapers, not recognizing me, and blabbing nonsense. How do you go from all we had to all of this?"

The social worker asked what kinds of things he began to recognize in Jean that told him "something was happening to her that was different from her usual behavior." Mr. Pfohl responded, "I guess I knew things weren't going right when Jean forgot where she left her purse, or when she left the stove on. Five or six years ago, I didn't think too much of it, but then as time went on it got worse. Several times she almost burned the house down when she left food cooking on the stove and then walked away. After that, I wouldn't let her cook anymore, but the problems didn't end there. She'd forget who she was talking to on the telephone, or else didn't remember how to get home when she went out on errands. Two times the police picked her up for driving erratically, and I had to promise them I wouldn't let her drive anymore. Sometimes I think I've been at fault for trying to let her continue to 'be normal.' I'd give her the car keys and hope for the best. I just didn't want to face the truth that she was changing. She wasn't the Jean I knew, but a shell of the person I loved. You can't imagine how painful this has been for me. I've lost my best friend."

When asked to describe Jean's behavior, he related, "Sometimes she's as placid as a lamb, and other times she gets so agitated that she physically lashes out at others trying to help bathe or care for her. Several times she accused me of stealing her money. A few times she got so riled up that I gave her a small change purse filled with dollar bills. It seems that being able to touch or feel the money calmed her down. If she happens to tell me I took her money, I show her the change purse and she becomes quiet again." Mr. Pfohl's eyes again filled with tears. He took his glasses off and began to clean them with a well-worn handkerchief before continuing.

"We used to go to the all the spring training baseball games; we knew all the players, especially the rookies. We'd do all the typical things, you know, eat hot dogs, drink soda pop, and sing all those terrific old songs like 'Take Me Out to the Ball Game.' Jean sure loved going to those games. Sometimes we'd take a glove with us, you know, to try to catch pop flies. One time we actually caught a ball, and we gave it to our youngest grandson, Kenny." Mr. Pfohl paused, and said to the social worker, "I seem to be talking your ear off. I guess I've needed someone to talk to. Am I taking up too much of your time? Do you have someone else you need to see?" The social worker reassured Mr. Pfohl that she really wanted to hear about what had been happening to him and Jean and added, "I have all the time in the world."

He continued, "Jean keeps me up at night. Several times she started to open the front door and wander away. I used to let her dress herself, but she would put her clothes on backwards or sometimes she just sat naked until I dressed her. Until recently, she was able to walk around our condo, but now she has fallen several times. Three months ago she fractured her left arm, and let me tell you it was no picnic taking care of her with a full arm cast. More times than not I use a wheelchair to get her around because she's so unsteady on her feet. It just seems easier than letting her walk. I got one of those gizmos that fits on the back of my car so it makes using a wheelchair easier, but nothing is really easy."

Mr. Pfohl sat quietly, struggling to hold back his tears. He appeared visibly upset, and the social worker reassured him that what he was experiencing was very normal. He replied, "Yeah, that's what everyone says. What I'm feeling is very normal, but it doesn't help when I have to break my promise and put Jean in a nursing home because I'm too weak to take care of her. I used to think of myself as a very capable and strong man, but not anymore. [He looked defeated.] I guess that's the real problem of getting old. You begin to become vulnerable to health problems, financial fluctuations, and limits in what you once handled with complete ease.

"I haven't had a good night's sleep in months. Jean is really restless, especially at night, and she keeps me up half the night. That's when I knew I had to hire someone to help me take care of her. Now I'm in a real bind because I don't want to put

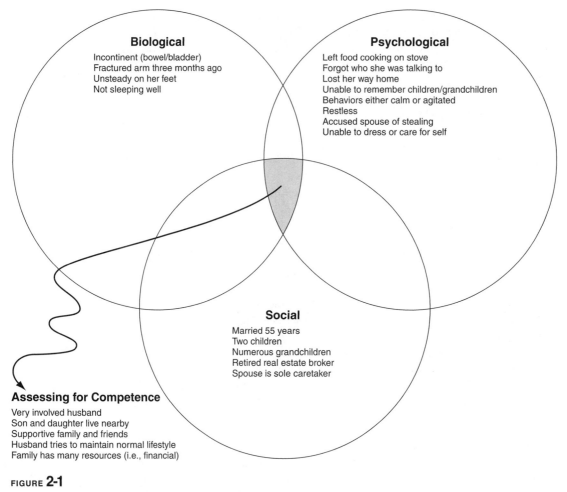

Biological
Incontinent (bowel/bladder)
Fractured arm three months ago
Unsteady on her feet
Not sleeping well

Psychological
Left food cooking on stove
Forgot who she was talking to
Lost her way home
Unable to remember children/grandchildren
Behaviors either calm or agitated
Restless
Accused spouse of stealing
Unable to dress or care for self

Social
Married 55 years
Two children
Numerous grandchildren
Retired real estate broker
Spouse is sole caretaker

Assessing for Competence
Very involved husband
Son and daughter live nearby
Supportive family and friends
Husband tries to maintain normal lifestyle
Family has many resources (i.e., financial)

FIGURE **2-1**

DEMENTIA, ALZHEIMER'S TYPE

The interaction of the biological, psychological, and social variables in Zelda Jean Pfohl's life.

Jean in a nursing home, but I don't seem to have much choice these days. Thankfully, money is not an issue for us. I feel like I've betrayed her somehow, but if I don't get some relief this will kill me. I used to think that getting old with the one you love was going to be an exciting and wonderful experience. We always planned to have lots of time to travel, play cards, hold hands, and spend quality time together. Well, it turned out to be just the opposite. Getting old is really just an awful experience, especially if it's spent without your best friend."

Assessment Summary

To accurately assess dementia, Alzheimer's type, the practitioner must first rule out potential medical and neurological explanations (Callaway, 1998; Morrison, 1995).

In the natural course of events, the nursing home social worker is generally among the last professionals to be consulted (Reinardy, 1995; Reinardy & Kane, 1999). Although the vignette refers to Jean's fall and subsequent broken arm, not mentioned were her complete medical and neurological evaluations to rule out other general medical problems.

There are several ways to code dementia of the Alzheimer's type, depending on the age of onset and the various accompanying signs and symptoms, for example, uncomplicated, with delusions, with depressed mood, and with delirium. It is important to differentiate between early onset (or under 65) and late onset (over 65).

Other types of dementia include **vascular dementia**, which has also been termed multi-infarct dementia because it is presumed to be caused a series of strokes. The differential diagnosis for vascular dementia is that persons generally become worse through a series of small debilitating steps (as these strokes occur), whereas those with Alzheimer's dementia experience a more gradual deterioration of function.

Parkinson's disease (with dementia) is a slow and progressive neurological condition characterized by tremors, rigidity, involuntary and rhythmic movements of extremities, motor restlessness, and posturing instability.

Pick's disease usually occurs between age 45 and 50. Impairments are in memory, concentration, abstract thinking, and speech, along with disorientation and apathy. It is considered a degenerative disease, particularly of the frontal and temporal lobes of the brain.

Creutzfeldt-Jakob disease is a rare illness and believed to be caused by a newly discovered agent known as a prion. Individuals lose their mental alertness (which is why it is often confused with Alzheimer's disease), experience memory loss, and are disoriented. A distinctive feature of this disease is myoclonus, a shocklike contraction of muscles. Myoclonus is not unique to Creutzfeldt-Jakob disease, but when it is present (in combination with the signs of mental deterioration), it can serve as an indicator of what is happening to an individual.

Huntington's disease is inherited through a single dominant gene, and it is a progressive and degenerative disease that includes difficulties in cognition, emotion, and movement. Symptoms generally begin between 30 and 50 years of age, and death usually occurs within 10 to 20 years of its onset. The individual exhibits involuntary tremors and twitching of the head, torso, and extremities, lurching gait, and explosive speech. It is usually associated with excessive levels of dopamine, deficient GABA, and atrophy in the caudate nucleus and frontal-temporal lobes of the brain.

Usually it is not difficult to make an assessment of dementia, at least in an overall sense, except in the very early stages (Shader, 1994). Because effects of delirium present with features similar to dementia (disorientation and memory loss), dementia cannot be assessed until after the delirium clears. In addition, agnosia, aphasia, and apraxia are much more common in Alzheimer's dementia than in delirium.

Mrs. Jean Pfohl's DSM multi-axial designation would be:

Axis I	209.0 Alzheimer's Dementia, late onset, uncomplicated
Axis II	V71.09 No diagnosis
Axis III	331.0 Alzheimer's Disease

(continued)

733.10 Fractured left arm

Axis IV   None

Axis V   GAF = Deferred

In looking at Jean's past and present history, the practitioner can gain a greater insight into her current functioning. Specific attention focuses on understanding biological, psychological (including cognitive), and social systems variables. The competency-based assessment notes that Jean has a very strong support system in her husband, Harry, and in both of her children, who live nearby. Mr. Pfohl is currently in a crisis himself. However, he is very resilient in that he is able to talk openly with the social worker about his feelings and seeks outside assistance. While Mrs. Pfohl is the "identified client," in actuality it is Mr. Pfohl who becomes the focus of the assessment. Several key competencies include his role as the sole caretaker, a strong desire to keep his family together, and his intention to maintain a normal lifestyle.

AMNESTIC DISORDER (AMNESIA)

Although this disorder is relatively uncommon, it is important to carefully sort through a symptom picture of amnesia that imitates either delirium or dementia. The individual should be described as having an amnestic syndrome when loss of memory is clearly severe and is the most outstanding defect noted. The competency-based assessment helps the practitioner to discern differences between problems that may be psychological in origin and whatever organic processes might be involved.

While there is more than one amnestic syndrome, the differences among them revolve mainly around what individuals can and cannot remember. The most common example of the amnestic disorder is alcoholic Korsakoff syndrome (also referred to as **Korsakoff psychosis**). This disorder is characterized by the individual's striking inability to form new memories, with subsequent "blank spots," often filled in with confabulation. If amnesia is not detected, the person may suffer residual disabilities and the family may experience unnecessary frustration (Isenberg, 1997).

SUMMARY

Dementia is an insidious and progressively deteriorating process. It has been called "the longest good-bye" because its features can last ten or more years. Delirium can be recognized by its acute onset and its brief duration. Amnestic disorder is fairly well circumscribed and thus easier to diagnose than delirium or dementia. Recent memory is extremely damaged. However, the individual is able to deal with an

TABLE **2-1**   THE DIFFERENTIAL FEATURES BETWEEN DELIRIUM AND DEMENTIA

Characteristics	Delirium	Dementia
Onset	Sudden/acute. Occurs at any age	Insidious. Generally occurs after 55 years of age
Duration	Fluctuates, lasting hours to weeks	Long term; months to years ("the longest good-bye")
Prevailing Pattern	Temporary reversible condition while "causative factors exist." Examples: drug allergies, chemotherapy, anesthesia, substance use	Permanent, irreversible condition
Attention	Lacks direction, distractibility, fluctuates during the day	Relatively unaffected
Speech	Incoherent	Confabulates
Personality Changes	No long-standing change	Person is "shell" of former self
Environment	Difficulties generally do not arise due to short-term nature of syndrome	Interpersonal difficulties. Example: caregiver stress, financial worries
Common Features	Memory loss	Memory loss
	Confusion	Confusion
	Decreased alertness and orientation	Decreased alertness and orientation
	Problem with perception, mood, and behavior	Problem with perception, mood, and behavior

immediate situation or problem. This inability to remember what they cannot underscores the importance of gathering collateral information. Chronic alcohol use (Korsakoff syndrome) with insufficient thiamine (vitamin B1) is the most frequent cause of amnestic disorders (Morrison, 1995). Associated features include confusion and disorientation, confabulation (or imagining events), and subtle emotional changes. Two of the most frequently undetected disorders in the clinical setting are delirium and dementia. While delirium can occur at any age, dementia is generally associated with those over 55. In contrast, the less common disorder, amnesia, is the inability (commonly caused by chronic alcohol use) to learn new information or to recall previously learned material. Table 2-1 summarizes the differential features between delirium and dementia.

PRACTITIONER REFLECTIONS

One of the key challenges the practitioner faces is knowing how to differentiate between delirium and dementia or the related cognitive disorders. The competency-based assessment underscores the importance of exploring biological, psychological, and social influences.

Activities

- List two problems you anticipate you may encounter in trying to interview Mr. Sal Cullotto.

- Identify how other cultures may treat persons with delirium and dementia.

- Imagine for a moment that you are referring one of your clients with dementia-like symptoms to a neurologist. How would you present your case?

- If you were interviewing someone with a delirium-like picture, what kinds of questions would you ask to determine the presence of the disorder?

- List all of the problems, obstacles, and challenges that you anticipate that a family might encounter with a member who is diagnosed with dementia.

REFERENCES

Antonucci, T. C. (1994). A life-span view of women's social relations. In B. F. Turner & L. E. Troll (Eds.), *Women growing older*, pp. 239–269. Thousand Oaks, CA: Sage Publications.

Antonucci, T. C., & Akiyama, H. (1995). Convoys of social relations: Family and friendship within a life span context. In R. Bleiszner & V. H. Bedford (Eds.), *Handbook of aging and the family*, pp. 355–371. Westport, CT: Greenwood Press.

Brodaty, H., & Luscombe, G. (1998). Psychological morbidity in caregivers is associated with depression with patients with dementia. *Alzheimer Disease and Associated Disorders,* 12(2): 62–70.

Brookmeyer, R., Gray, S., & Kawas, C. (1998). Projections of Alzheimer's disease in the United States and the public health impact of delaying disease onset. *American Journal of Public Health*, 88: 1337–1342.

Caine, E. D. (1994). Should aging-associated memory decline be included in DSM-IV? In T. A. Widiger, A. J. Francis, H. A. Pincus, M. B. First, R. Ross, & W. W. Davis (Eds.), *DSM-IV Sourcebook*, Vol. I, pp. 329–337. Washington, DC: American Psychiatry Association.

Callaway, J. T. (1998). Psychopharmacological treatment of dementia. *Research on Social Work Practice*, 8(4): 452–474.

Donaldson, C., Tarrier, N., & Burns, A. (1998). Determinants of carer stress in Alzheimer's disease. *International Journal of Geriatric Psychiatry*, 13(4): 248–256.

First, M. B., Frances, A., & Pincus, H. A. (1995). *DSM-IV handbook of differential diagnosis.* Washington, DC: American Psychiatric Press.

Frances, A., First, M. B., & Pincus, H. A. (1995). *DSM-IV Guidebook*. Washington, DC: American Psychiatric Press.

Hope, T., Keene, J., Gedling, K., Fairburn, C. G., & Jacoby, R. (1998). Predictors of institutionalization for people with dementia living at home with a carer. *International Journal of Geriatric Psychiatry,* 13(10): 682–690.

Isenberg, K. E. (1997). In S. B. Guze (Ed.), *Adult psychiatry*, pp. 169–195. St. Louis, MO: Mosby-Year Book.

Kaplan, H. I., & Sadock, B. J. (1998). *Synopsis of psychiatry* (8th ed.). Baltimore, MD: Williams & Wilkins.

Khachaturian, Z., & Radebaugh, T. (Eds.). (1996). *Alzheimer's disease: Cause(s), diagnosis, treatment, and care*. Boca Raton, FL: CRC Press.

Lipowski, Z. J. (1990). *Delirium: Acute confusional states.* New York: Oxford University Press.

Luscombe, G., Brodaty, H., & Freeth, S. (1998). Younger people with dementia: Diagnostic issues, effects on carers and use of services. *International Journal of Geriatric Psychiatry*, 13(5): 323–330.

Magai, C., & Cohen, C. I. (1998). Attachment style and emotion regulation in dementia patients and their relation to caregiver burden. *Journal of Gerontology*, 53(3): 147–154.

Moody, H. R. (1995). Ageing, meaning and the allocation of resources. *Ageing and Society*, 15: 163–184.

Moore, D. P., & Jefferson, J. W. (1996). *Medical psychiatry*. St. Louis, MO: Mosby-Year Book.

Morrison, J. (1995). *DSM-IV made easy*. New York: Guilford Press.

National Center for Health Statistics. (1997). Report of final morality statistics, 1995. *Monthly Vital Statistics Report*, 45: 1–80.

Nietzel, M. T., Speltz, M. L., McCauley, E. A., & Bernstein, D. A. (1998). *Abnormal psychology*. Boston: Allyn and Bacon.

O'Neill, J. (1999, January). Aging Express: Can social work keep up? *NASW News*, 44, p. 3.

Ozawa, M. N., & Kono, S. (1997). Child well-being in Japan: The high cost of economic success. In G. A. Cornia & S. Danziger (Eds.), *Child poverty and deprivation in the industrialized countries, 1945–1995*, pp. 307–334. London: Oxford University Press.

Park, D. C. (1994). Research on aging deserves top priority. *Chronicle of Higher Education*, 41: A40.

Ponder, R. J., & Pomeroy, E. C. (1996). The grief of caregivers: How pervasive is it? *Journal of Gerontological Social Work*, 27(1/2): 3–21.

Ragneskog, H., & Kihlgren, M. (1997). Music and other strategies to improve the care of agitated patients with dementia. *Scandinavian Journal of Caring Sciences*, 11(3): 176–182.

Reinardy, J. (1995). Relocation to a new environment: Decisional control and the move to a nursing home. *Health and Social Work*, 20: 31–38.

Reinardy, J., & Kane, R. A. (1999). Choosing an adult foster home or nursing home: Residents perceptions about decision making and control. *Social Work*, 44(6): 571–585.

Robinson, P., Ekman, S. L., & Wahlund, L. O. (1998). Unsettled, uncertain and striving to understand: Toward an understanding of the situation of persons with suspected dementia. *International Journal of Aging and Human Development*, 47(2): 143–161.

Rubin, E. H. (1997). Cognitive disorder: Dementias. In S. B. Guze (Ed.), *Adult psychiatry*, pp. 197–210. St. Louis, MO: Mosby-Year Book.

Sadavoy, J., & LeClair, J. K. (1997). Treatment of anxiety disorders in late life. *Canadian Journal of Psychiatry*, 42(Suppl. 1): 28S–34S.

Scully, J. H. (1996). *Psychiatry*. Baltimore, MD: Williams & Wilkins.

Shader, R. I. (1994). *Manual of psychiatric therapeutics.* Boston: Little, Brown, & Co.

Shaner, R. (1997). *Psychiatry*. Baltimore, MD: Williams & Wilkins.

Shope, J. T., Holmes, S. B., Hogan, J., Tang, G., Izenson, S., Gilman, S., & Jones, M. Z. (1993). Pathologists' participation in postmortem examinations for patients with dementia. *The Gerontologist*, 33(4): 461–467.

Siebert, D. C., Mutran, E. J., & Reitzes, D. C. (1999). Friendship and social support: The importance of role identity to aging adults. *Social Work*, 44(6): 522–533.

Small, G. W. (1998). Differential diagnosis and early detection of dementia. *American Journal of Geriatric Psychiatry*, 6(2 Suppl. 1): S26–33.

Toseland, R. W., McCallion, P., Gerber, T., Dawson, C., Gieryic, S., & Guilamo-Ramos, V. (1999). Use of health and human services by community-residing people with dementia. *Social Work*, 44(6): 535–548.

U.S. Bureau of the Census, (1993). *Population projection of the United States, by age, sex, race, and Hispanic origins: 1993 to 2050* (Current Population Reports P25-1104). Washington, DC: U.S. Government Printing Office.

van Dijk, P. T. M., Meulenberg, O. G. R. M., van de Sande, H. J., & Habbeman, J. D. F. (1993). Falls in dementia patients. *The Gerontologist*, 33(2): 200–204.

Walker, R. J., & Pomeroy, E. C. (1996). Depression or grief? The experience of caregivers of people with dementias. *Health and Social Work*, 21(4): 247–254.

Weiner, M. F. (Ed.). (1991). *The dementias: Diagnosis and management*. Washington, DC: American Psychiatric Press.

Whitehouse, P. J. (1993). Autopsy. *The Gerontologist*, 33(4): 436–437.

Wilson, G. T., Nathan, P. E., O'Leary, K. D., & Clark, L. A. (1996). *Abnormal psychology*. Boston: Allyn and Bacon.

Wisniewski, H. M., & Silverman, W. (1997). Diagnostic criteria for the neuropathological assessment of Alzheimer's disease: Current status and major issues. *Neurobiology of Aging*, 18(4 Suppl.): S43–50.

Witkin, S. L. (1999). How "ripened" are you? *Social Work*, 44(6): 509–511.

SCHIZOPHRENIA AND OTHER PSYCHOTIC DISORDERS

INTRODUCTION

Dr. John Haslam, an early pioneer in the field of mental illness, published *Observations on Madness and Melancholy*, in 1809. He conceptualized schizophrenia as "a form of insanity," stating:

> The sensibility appears to be considerably blunted; they do not bear the same affection towards their parents and relations; they become unfeeling to kindness, and careless of reproof.... I have painfully witnessed this hopeless and degrading change, which in a short time has transformed the most promising and vigorous intellect into a slavering and bloated idiot. (p. 65)

Forty years later, Benedict Morel (1809–1873), a Belgian psychiatrist, standardized and formally described symptoms of schizophrenia using the terms *demence* ("loss of mind"), and *precoce* ("premature"); the term in Latin is dementia praecox.

The story of schizophrenia begins in 1896, with Emil Kraepelin, a German professor of psychiatry. He brought together under one heading several types of mental abnormalities previously viewed as separate and distinct disorders even though they shared similar underlying features. Kraepelin distinguished three subtypes. The first was "catatonia" (alternating immobility and excited agitation); the second was "hebephrenia" (silly and immature emotionality); and the third was known as "paranoia" (delusions of grandeur or persecution) (Kraepelin, 1919/1971). He postulated that although clinical manifestations might differ, the central feature of the disorder was its early onset that ultimately developed into a "mental weakness." He went on to identify several features occurring in dementia praecox, such as hallucinations, delusions, and negativism. Further, Kraepelin believed that changes in the brain were of some importance in its cause. He was the first to suggest that dementia started in early adolescence and evolved into a long-term chronic course due to brain deterioration.

In 1911, Eugene Bleuler, a Swiss psychiatrist, extended Kraepelin's conceptualizations and described a group of "different" schizophrenias characterized by disturbances of feelings, thinking, and relationships to the outside world. He coined the term *schizophrenia* from the Greek word *schizo*, meaning "split," and *phrene*, meaning "mind." This new term replaced terms such as "madness," "lunacy," and "dementia praecox." Bleuler believed that underneath the person's unusual behaviors was an "associative splitting" of the basic functions of personality. He felt the most prominent feature of schizophrenia was the tearing apart of the individual's psychic functions. This, he believed, was especially evident in the loosening of associations between ideas, inappropriate behavior, and disorganization of thought, affect, and actions. Bleuler did not intend to suggest the "split mindedness" represented two distinct personalities found in the person with dissociative identity disorder, rather that it denoted a shattered personality. Bleuler believed the split referred to the widening gap between internal and external realities. This schism between thought, emotion, and behavior established what continues to remain as the most enduring description of schizophrenia. Bleuler isolated four fundamental diagnostic features, sometimes called "the four A's" to identify the "splitting" of external reality. They are:

- *Associations* are logical thought processes. When altered, speech loses its coherence (or a loosening of associations), and connections among ideas are absent or obscure. Communication may become highly idiosyncratic and individualized; that is, the person may create his or her own words (neologism) according to some form of special symbolism. An example of a neologism would be, *"Every time I hear the clinks, snaps, and bangs on the grass. I guess, I think, I know that's where Jesus clicks and clocks."*

- *Affect* is the observable manifestation of a person's mood or emotion, in schizophrenia characterized by diminished emotions (flat or blunted), feeling disconnected from surrounding events (impersonating or performing within a role), and/or emotional indifference to the surrounding world (reduction in pleasurable experiences).

- *Autism* is characterized by significant impairment in social interactions, communication, and restricted patterns evidenced by behavior, interest, or activity.

- *Ambivalence* is described as positive and negative values that often exist simultaneously; they include uncertainty about taking a particular direction or frequently vacillation between two different perspectives and courses of action.

In the 1930s, Kurt Schneider introduced "first- and second-rank symptoms," now known as positive and negative symptoms. They have become a significant factor in assessing schizophrenia. Schneider's first-rank symptoms are summarized in Table 3-1, his second-rank symptoms in Table 3-2.

Understanding Schizophrenia

Psychosis is traditionally defined as the loss of reality testing and the impairment of mental functioning manifested by delusions, hallucinations, confusion, impaired memory, and the inability to function within the interpersonal domain (Thomas, 1997). The

TABLE **3-1**   SCHNEIDER'S CRITERIA: FIRST-RANK SYMPTOMS
(POSITIVE SYMPTOMS)

Disturbances of audible thoughts

Voices arguing

Voices commenting to each other

Somatic passivity experiences or inertia

Thought withdrawal

Thought broadcasting

Delusional perceptions

All other experiences involving "avolition" or the inability to initiate or participate in important
activities

exact cause of schizophrenia is unknown, but there is growing support for genetic and biological factors associated with its origin (Mueser, 1997). Schizophrenia is characterized by a broad range of behaviors marked by a loss of the person's sense of self, significant impairment in reality testing, and disturbances in feeling, thinking, and behavior. The individual is unable to distinguish the accuracy of their own perceptions and thoughts from external reality. More narrowly defined, psychosis describes characteristics and behaviors involving delusions, prominent hallucinations, grossly disorganized or catatonic behavior, incoherent speech, aimless agitation to total immobility, and an affect that ranges from apathy and withdrawal to incoherent thinking (Barlow & Durand, 1995; Farmer & Pandurangi, 1997). To complicate the practitioner's understanding of this syndrome, many of the above-mentioned features are not found in everyone with schizophrenia and can be found as a part of other mental disorders. To understand each person and their distinctive course of schizophrenia better, the competency-based assessment encourages the practitioner to look at the individual's capacity for interpersonal relationships, cultural influences, environmental and social factors, and coping resources.

Despite the reality that some persons with schizophrenia can function productively, it remains a misunderstood picture of symptoms. Attitudes about those with mental disorders have varied throughout history, but no matter what the era,

TABLE **3-2**   SCHNEIDER'S CRITERIA: SECOND-RANK SYMPTOMS
(NEGATIVE SYMPTOMS)

Disturbances of perception

Sudden delusional ideas

Perplexity

Depressive and euphoric mood changes

Feelings of emotional impoverishment

persons with schizophrenia have been maligned (Fink & Tasman, 1992). Popular books, movies, and television have exploited and contribute to this misinformation. Sometimes newspaper headlines report, "Ex-Mental Patient Goes on Wild Shooting Spree." While this may have occurred on some occasions, it contributes to fostering a false picture that persons with schizophrenia should be considered dangerous. These accounts help perpetuate a detrimental and negative picture.

Schizophrenia interferes with almost every aspect of a person's intrapersonal functioning and interpersonal world. It disrupts how they see their social environment, the manner in which they think, speak, and even move (Marley, 1998). While the emotional aspect takes a tremendous toll, the long-term financial expenses can also be quite devastating (National Foundation for Brain Research, 1992). A complex symptom picture characterizes schizophrenia—specific patterns or features that tend to appear together (Palfai & Jankiewicz, 1991).

Schizophrenia has a chronic course, which generally includes a prodromal phase, an active phase (characterized by delusions, hallucinations, or both), and a residual phase in which the prevailing features are in remission. In assessing for schizophrenia, the specific psychotic features and behaviors must be present for at least one month (or less, if successfully treated) during the active phase, and the disturbance must persist for at least six months (APA, 2000; Scully, 1996). Persons with schizophrenia do not always fit into these specific subcategories, thus causing confusion among practitioners about the usefulness of their assessment guidelines.

Cultural Considerations

Schizophrenia is known around the world (Shaner, 1997), and in most cultures and socioeconomic groups (Whaley, 1998). When psychosis occurs, it is not viewed as a normal phenomenon and is always seen as an indication of some profound mental process. In some industrialized countries, researchers contend that schizophrenia is a culturally created label for those people who behave in ways that are outside accepted cultural norms (Sarbin & Mancuso, 1980; Barlow & Durand, 1995). As part of the competency-based assessment, the practitioner should take into consideration how mental illness is perceived within the person's culture. Also helpful is to examine the composition, structure of social and family support, and level of social communication (Bland, 1998; Stromwall & Robinson, 1998). As discussed in the following case of Rudy Rosen, a person with schizophrenia can challenge the resources of family members.

Prevailing Pattern

One of the first tasks confronting the practitioner is to determine the extent of psychotic symptoms. According to Zimmerman (1994), the assessment includes inquiries into manic and/or depressive features (if they have ever been present).

For most people with schizophrenia, their symptoms come and go. The following three phases are indicative of the schizophrenic cycle:

- The *prodromal phase*, or before the features of schizophrenia become very apparent, during which the person's level of functioning deteriorates prior to the onset of the active psychotic phase.

- The duration of the *active phase*, wherein the individual exhibits psychotic features including hallucinations, delusions, and grossly disorganized behavior and speech, or negative features such as flat affect must be present at least six months, including one month of active or acute phase. (Kaplan & Sadock, 1998)

- The *residual phase* follows the active phase. This is sometimes considered a "filler" category, because the individual has either been helped successfully or they have improved to the point where they no longer have enough features for the practitioner to ascertain the presence of schizophrenia. (Barlow & Durand, 1999)

The following metaphor may be helpful in visualizing the residual phase. Imagine for a moment that you have a full glass of milk in front of you. Everyone can easily identify it as a glass of milk because of its color, texture, smell, and taste. This could be considered analogous to the active phase of schizophrenia; that is, the individual has all the attributes characteristic of schizophrenia. Further imagine this glass of milk has now been emptied. Enough of a residue remains so one can still identify that its contents were once milk. This residual phase suggests that the person has some remaining features but not to the extent to be fully assessed for schizophrenia.

While at least 50 percent of individuals with schizophrenia improve significantly, there are those who experience the disorder as a chronic illness characterized by frequent hospitalizations, incarceration, and social and legal consequences. The overall course tends to be a progressive deterioration of functions, at least during the first few years. This includes both the exacerbations of symptoms and the partial remissions. It is this small group that often comes to the practitioner's attention. The general outlook tends to be guarded, as the disorder can be quite devastating in terms of impaired interpersonal and social functioning. Suicide, depression, substance abuse, and social withdrawal often coexist (Taubes et al., 1998; Wassink et al., 1999).

A better outlook includes an acute emergence of symptoms, later life onset, previously good functioning at work or with personal relationships, the ability to comply with a treatment regimen (Smith et al., 1999), and the presence of adequate informal social contact (Cohen, 1990; Harding et al., 1987). Features that suggest a chronic course with schizophrenia include an insidious onset, previous personal or family history of schizophrenia, evidence of social withdrawal, inappropriate or shallow affect, the prior assessment for schizoid, schizoaffective, schizophreniform, or schizotypal personality disorders, and difficulties conforming to treatment regimens.

Understanding Positive and Negative Symptoms

Some practitioners may find positive and negative categorizations of psychotic behaviors confusing. Another way to conceptualize *positive symptoms* is to envision those outward psychotic signs *present* in the person with schizophrenia (such as delusions or hallucinations) but *absent* in a person without psychosis (Fowles, 1992; Rossi-Monti, 1998). There are several different types of delusions including grandeur, guilt, jealousy, persecution, and ideas of reference. Positive symptoms vary widely, and no one single feature is common to those with schizophrenia. Individuals with a psychotic disorder must have at least one (or more) positive symptoms.

Negative symptoms are those characteristics that are notably absent though they are normally present in people's experience. For example, the person with schizophrenia has a blunted affect instead of the full range of emotions; is emotionally withdrawn instead of socially connected; has poor rapport with others instead of being able to relate easily; shows difficulty in abstract thinking or stereotypical thinking instead of being oriented and "connected"; lacks spontaneity instead of relating freely; or shows poor self-care instead of maintaining proper diet and hygiene (Carpenter, 1993, 1994). Speech and motivation (Debowska et al., 1998) are also features that are absent but should be present. For example, negative symptoms of motivation are seen as a loss of goal-directed behavior. As well, the individual may be ambivalent about approaching social situations. Overall, negative symptoms severely reduce the singular characteristics of an individual's personality. To assess for the presence of schizophrenia, at least two negative features must occur in the sensory areas of the body, such as sight, hearing, taste, smell, and touch.

A summary of both positive and negative symptoms follows:

- *Delusions* are false and fixed beliefs based on incorrect deductions or misrepresentation of the person's reality. These beliefs are not considered as normative within the individual's cultural or religious group. The two most common are delusions of grandeur or the belief that one is special, famous, or important, and delusions of persecution where the person believes others intend harm. The practitioner can explore delusions by suggesting an alternative scenario to the individual, saying, for example, "Suppose those people who followed you were not going to harm you, but rather they were just going to the same place you were." If the individual cannot acknowledge the possibility of this alternative explanation, then chances are that the practitioner is seeing a delusion at work.

Delusions are of major importance in understanding schizophrenia. These delusional beliefs are firmly maintained despite evidence to the contrary (Andreasen et al., 1995; Maher & Spitzer, 1993). The following is a representative sample of the types of delusions that the practitioner might encounter. Included are a series of questions aimed at exploring them further.

DELUSIONS OF GRANDIOSITY

"Do you think you have exceptional talents, unique powers, or mysterious abilities that no one else has?"

If YES, "Could you describe them?" "Could you tell me more about this?" "Do they happen during special times?"

DELUSIONS OF PERSECUTION

"Do you think people are against you, following you, or are trying to hurt you?"

If YES, "Could you tell me more about that?" "Why do you think that people are out to get you?" "Are people plotting against you?" "Do they want to hurt you?"

If YES, "Why do you think someone would want to hurt you?" "When you notice this happening to you, what do you think this means?"

DELUSIONS OF REFERENCE

"When you are watching television, reading a newspaper, or listening to the radio, do you believe that 'they' are referring specifically to you? Or that there are special messages intended just for you to see or hear?"

If YES, "What kinds of things have you noticed?" "What does this mean to you?"
"Do you think that strangers in stores, the mall, or in a movie theater take special notice of you, or talk about you behind your back?"
If YES, "How do you know this?" "What does this mean to you?"

THOUGHT BROADCASTING
"Have you ever thought about something so strong or hard that other people could hear your thoughts?"
If YES, "Do you think that people can hear what you are thinking even if you don't say anything out loud?" "How do you know this?"

THOUGHT INSERTION
"Are there thoughts inside of your head that have been placed there by somebody from the outside?" (Be sure to clarify that you are referring to thoughts inserted by others.)
If YES, "Could you tell me more?" "Have you noticed there is a special time or place when this happens?"

- *Hallucinations* are experiences of sensory events without environmental stimulation. To count as a symptom when assessing for the presence of schizophrenia, the hallucination must be considered prominent. Auditory hallucinations or "hearing voices" is considered the most common feature of schizophrenia (Holroyd et al., 1994). These auditory hallucinations can be present in other mental disorders, but in schizophrenia they typically talk about, as well as to, the individual. Often these "voices" sound so real that the person is convinced that they are coming from outside, such as from hidden microphones. The voices are often described as abusive and critical in nature, or else command the performance of certain unpleasant or harmful tasks. Tactile or somatic hallucinations are considered the least common, and include sensations similar to electrical tingling or burning sensations (Nietzel et al., 1998). A former client of one of the authors related feeling as if "a boa constrictor was slithering down inside my body. It went around my chest, and when it split in half one part went down my arms and the other part went down my legs." It is important to take into account hallucinations, as they occur in relatively few other psychiatric disorders.

- *Disorganized speech* is not governed by logic and sometimes can be exhibited by rhymes or puns. Sometimes disorganized speech may take the form of mimicking speech patterns of those around the person by articulating the tone and repeating overheard words or fragments of conversations (**echolalia**). Other examples include condensing or inventing new words (**neologism**). Some may continuously repeat the same words or sentence (**perseveration**) or use rhyme or puns (**clanging**). Two other manifestations of disorganized speech include failure to answer specific questions, or going off on a tangent), and the random or arbitrary leaping from topic to topic (**derailment).** These patterns of speech complicate the person's ability to communicate with others (Manschreck, 1993). **Alogia** involves a speech disturbance in which there is either relative scarcity in the amount of speech or poverty in its content. It is important to note that only speech that is seriously disorganized and extremely difficult to understand and/or interpret should be considered a symptom of schizophrenia. Disorganized speech can be seen in other disorders, such as delirium or dementia, which must be ruled out.

- **Disorganized behavior** involves physical actions that do not appear to be goal-directed—for example, taking off one's clothes in public, assuming or maintaining unusual postures, pacing excitedly, or moving fingers or extremities in idiosyncratic and repetitive ways. This form of behavior is seen as severe and causing a great deal of impairment to the individual, unlike something seen as "odd" or "eccentric" as in a tic or compulsion. Similar to disorganized speech, disorganized behavior is seen in other disorders, such as substance intoxication, and must be ruled out.

- *Flat affect* is exhibited by gazing with "vacant eyes." The individual is seemingly unaffected by what is going on around them or displays little change in facial expressions (Berenbaum & Oltmanns, 1992). Often, inappropriate affect is displayed by laughing or crying at incongruous times.

- *Bizarre behavior* refers to a pattern of conduct or demeanor far removed from normal and expected experiences. Determining what is bizarre and what is not becomes especially important.

- *Avolition* involves the inability to make goal-directed choices and the expression of little or no interest in activities. The individual is generally disorganized, behaves inappropriately, and may be excessively controlled and rigid. Avolition is the indifference and unresponsiveness to even the most basic everyday activities, such as maintaining personal hygiene, and the inability to independently sustain other important self-care activities. The term *avolition* was derived from the prefix *a*, meaning "without," and *volition*, meaning "an act of choosing, or deciding."

Perhaps an easier way to conceptualize schizophrenia is in terms of comprising three factors: one is the presence of a psychotic factor, another is a disorganized factor, and the third is a negative factor. For a significant portion of time since the onset of the disorder, one or more major areas of social functioning will have deteriorated, such as occupational, social, or self-care. Duration includes continuous signs and symptoms that must persist for at least six months. During this period, at least one month must include features of psychosis (or the active phase). Periods of either prodomal or residual traces are not enough to represent a full-blown episode of schizophrenia. Additionally, the person must display negative symptoms, and at least two other features, such as poor personal hygiene, plus an increased belief that people are talking about them behind their back.

Differential Assessment

The lifetime prevalence of schizophrenia in the United States (including the closely related schizophreniform disorder and schizoaffective disorder) is approximately 1 percent; worldwide prevalence ranges between 0.01 and 3 percent (Gottesman, 1991; Keith et al., 1991; Wilson et al., 1996). In general, this wide variation is a result of how various diagnostic criteria are defined among different demographics, environmental conditions, and levels of industrialization (Jablensky, 1989). For example, in Third World countries men are reported to have higher rates of schizophrenia.

It has been suggested schizophrenia affects men and women equally, but evidence suggests it occurs slightly more in men (Iacono & Beiser, 1992). Additionally, important gender differences are noted around the age of onset (Gorwood et al., 1995; Jeste & Heaton, 1994; Remschmidt et al., 1994; Stober et al., 1998), especially because the initial schizophrenic episode occurs 10 to 15 years earlier in men. Schizophrenia can happen to persons as early as 8 years of age (although this is not a common pattern), or as late as 60 years old (Castle & Murray, 1993). It is not known why men experience an earlier onset of schizophrenia; however, this age-related pattern has been reported in virtually all countries where schizophrenia has been studied (Hafner et al., 1994).

Familial and Biological/Genetic Considerations

There is considerable debate among various professional disciplines concerning the validity of a schizophrenia-specific onset occurring in childhood (Caplan et al., 1990; Gordon et al., 1994). Several studies indicate that of approximately 50 percent of individuals who experience schizophrenia in childhood show significant symptoms throughout their adulthood. Having a family history of schizophrenia worsens the overall prognosis. Genetic factors, as discussed earlier, appear to imply a relationship to the development of schizophrenia through "increased genetic loading or a complicated interaction between biologic vulnerability and the environment" (Lewis & Volkmar, 1990, p. 352). Evidence of genetic transmission of the risk for schizophrenia has been widely accepted and some twin, adoption, and family studies support the genetic component in schizophrenia (Dworkin, 1992; Kallmann, 1938; Kendler & Diehl, 1993; Kety et al., 1994; Tierari, 1991). What remains unclear is exactly how that factor is expressed. For instance, schizophrenia could be caused by a genetic predisposition toward a particular biochemical imbalance, the deficiency of a specific enzyme, or attributed to other biological causes (McGuffin et al., 1995). Gottesman (1991) summarizes schizophrenia as follows: "While the genes are necessary for causing schizophrenia, they are not sufficient or adequate by themselves, and one or more environmental contributors are also necessary for schizophrenia but they are not specific to it" (p. 164). Nevertheless, there is still sufficient evidence to support the fact that those with schizophrenia have a different biochemical makeup.

Classical studies comparing monozygotic (or identical) to dizygotic (or fraternal) twins confirm the hypothesis that genetics plays a large role in the predisposition and vulnerability to schizophrenia (Levinson & Mowry, 1991; Walker et al., 1991). In monozygotic twins, if one is diagnosed with schizophrenia, there appears to be a 50 to 60 percent probability that both will eventually have the disorder. Such prevalence is between 10 and 15 percent for dizygotic twins, the same rate existing for all siblings (Grinspoon & Bakalar, 1990).

Magnetic resonance imaging (MRI) provides a way to view the structure of the brain without the use of unnecessary radiation. In principal, an MRI operates on the premise that human body cells contain certain elements sensitive to magnetic fields (Altman, 1999). Current research suggests there are significant differences occurring between the brain ventricles of discordant identical twins; that is, the twin with schizophrenia has been found to have larger brain ventricles than their nonschizophrenic twin counterpart (Pahl et al., 1990; Suddath et al., 1990). Decreased brain volume in the temporal region suggests the relationship between the severity of auditory hallucinations and disorganized language (Gur & Pearlson, 1993), and blunted affect and motivation (Klausner et al., 1992). Other variations occur in areas pertaining to cognitive competency skills, levels of concentration, memory, and perception. While many practitioners continue to believe schizophrenia is a disorder of the brain, no evidence of brain abnormality (structure or function) has been found common to those persons who have schizophrenia.

Biochemical theories suggest that the presence of neurotransmitters in the brain is clearly involved in the pathophysiology of schizophrenia. However, their specific role remains undetermined. Some maintain schizophrenia may be caused by alterations in these neurochemical systems resulting from some other more fundamental pathophysiologic process occurring in four areas of the brain: limbic system, frontal lobes, temporal lobes, and basal ganglia. However, there is probably no single area of the brain associated with the cause of this disorder. These four areas are so interconnected that dysfunction in one area often causes primary pathology in another.

The Role of Dopamine

The role of the neurotransmitter dopamine remains the basis for one of the foremost and enduring biochemical theories regarding the etiology of schizophrenia. Because certain antipsychotic medications block the effect of the neurotransmitter dopamine, there has been much interest in the dopamine hypothesis. The following discussion is a brief overview and is intended to familiarize the practitioner with the major concepts of the role of dopamine in schizophrenia.

The simplest formulation of the dopamine hypothesis points to the possibility that somehow the dopamine system is too active. Excessive dopamine may mediate the positive symptoms of auditory hallucinations or delusions, while deficient dopamine in cortical regions of the brain may mediate the negative symptoms of schizophrenia: the emotional blunting, social withdrawal, apathy, and so forth. These observations when combined led some researchers to theorize that schizophrenia in certain people was attributable to excessive dopamine activity (especially involving the D2 receptors). Others dispute the theory that schizophrenia is related to excess dopamine (Carson & Sanislow, 1993; Su et al., 1993). What seems clear is that the answer of whether dopamine is involved in the development of schizophrenia is more complicated than once thought (Potter & Manji, 1993).

Briefly, the human brain is made up of billions of neurons, which all send and "fire" messages back and forth between each other. These messages are received from presynaptic neurons; they continue to cross over gaps and progress toward the synapse, moving onto a receptor, and finally being delivered to a postsynaptic neuron. The basic dopamine hypothesis does not really elaborate on whether dopaminergic hyperactivity is due to too much release of dopamine, too many dopamine receptors, hypersensitivity of the dopamine receptors to dopamine, or some combination of those mechanisms. It is important to note that dopamine continues to be seen as an important neurotransmitter that is involved in the regulation of cognitive, sensory processes, and mood.

There are two major limitations associated with the dopamine hypothesis. First, dopamine antagonists are effective in treating virtually all psychotic and severely agitated individuals, not just those with schizophrenia. Other clinical investigations have been looking into several other neurotransmitters suspected of being involved in the pathophysiology of schizophrenia, for example, serotonin, acetylcholine, glutamate, and gamma aminobutyric acid (GABA). There is continued debate among some practitioners whether the impact or presence of specific neurotransmitters can endorse making the assessment of schizophrenia alone. There seems to be some evidence that dopaminergic hyperactivity is not seen uniquely in individuals with schizophrenia. Second, some electrophysiological data suggest that dopaminergic neurons may increase their firing rate in response to long-term exposure to antipsychotic drugs.

Increasing attention has been paid to other neurotransmitters, specifically, serotonin, norepinephrine, and amino acids (GABA). There is a great deal of evidence suggesting that norepinephrine may somehow be involved in the pathophysiologic process of schizophrenia. However, there is little statistical evidence regarding its precise role. Consensus suggests that norepinephrine is not thought to act alone in the pathogenesis of schizophrenia; interestingly, *serotonin* has engendered a great deal of interest in the pathogenesis of schizophrenia because it is seen as the modulator of other systems, such as dopamine (Andreason & Carpenter, 1993).

Suicide and Substance Use

Suicide is a profoundly serious complication associated with schizophrenia. Approximately 50 percent attempt suicide at least once, and 2 percent complete suicide (Waldinger, 1990). Men and women are equally likely to commit suicide due to the risk factors of depression and young age at onset (Addington & Addington, 1992). Often individuals see suicide as the only reasonable alternative to living with this devastating and chronic disorder. Persons with schizophrenia often lead lonely, isolated lives and tend to be highly suspicious and/or ambivalent in their relationships with others. Their behavior appears erratic and inconsistent. They have major problems relating to others and have little insight into their problems. They frequently demonstrate either a strong dependency on familiar people, or become bothersome, annoying, or intrusive to strangers. Real friendships rarely exist. The content of their delusions and hallucinations may frighten, estrange, or alienate others.

In addition to the features noted and cognitive disturbances commonly present in schizophrenia, individuals have approximately a 50 percent lifetime history of substance use (Mueser et al., 1995). The presence of comorbid substance use disorders suggest a poorer course of schizophrenia, including increased hospitalizations, homelessness, violence, family emotional and financial strain, and noncompliance with treatment modalities (Bartles et al., 1993; Bentley & Walsh, 1996; Clark, 1994). "Schizophrenia is a disorder that sometimes defies our desire for simplicity" (Barlow & Durand, 1995, p. 566). The prevailing consensus suggests that schizophrenia is more complicated than other disorders due to the combination of factors that play a large role in determining its outcome.

SCHIZOPHRENIA: THE FIVE SUBTYPES

The types of schizophrenia are not based on any understanding of the mechanisms of the disorder; they simply organize sets of symptoms that tend to appear together. In our earlier historical discussion, we discussed Kraepelin's initial concept of schizophrenia including his formulations regarding some differences noted between various categories of schizophrenia which he later identified as subtypes. Subsequent classification models identified specific divisions between these subtypes of schizophrenia. Although symptoms can cut across several subtypes, only one subtype can be assessed at any time. The five subtypes are **catatonic type, paranoid type, disorganized type, undifferentiated type,** and **residual type**. In practice, people do not "fit" precisely into specific subcategories, because they generally do not remain "true" to just one subtype classification; what is known, though, is that people display a defined pattern of features. Schizophrenic features are also divided into two specific types, positive and negative symptoms (discussed earlier in this chapter).

The competency-based assessment involves a careful evaluation of the client and what others in their social world have observed. The assessment carefully explores thoughts, speech, perception, affect, psychomotor activity, and interpersonal functioning. Other noteworthy areas to explore include:

- *Absence of insight*—The person is noncompliant taking their medications because they do not believe they have a problem.
- *Disturbance of sleep*—The person may experience trouble sleeping, especially when the onset of auditory hallucinations and delusions keep him or her awake.
- *Dysphoria*—The individual exhibits anxiety, hypersensitivity, anger, and depression.

For much of the time, the disorder has substantially impaired the individual's ability to socialize, work, or maintain some level of self-care. When this disorder develops during late childhood or adolescence, the person tends to fall short of realizing and achieving normative expected scholastic, social, or occupational status. Mood disorders (see Chapter 4) associated with psychotic features and schizoaffective disorder have been ruled out, because no major depressive, manic, or mixed episodes have occurred during active phase symptoms. (If for some reason they have already occurred, then their total duration has been very brief.) The disturbance is not due to the effects or use of a substance (e.g., drug of abuse, prescription medication). The disturbance is not directly caused by a general medical condition, such as cerebrovascular disease, herpes encephalitis, **Wernicke encephalopathy** (vitamin deficiency of thiamine, which metabolizes poorly in heavy drinkers resulting in confusion, loss of muscle coordination, and unintelligible speech), or **Korsakoff psychosis** (amnesic disorder caused by damage to the thalamus from chronic, heavy alcohol use). If the individual has had a past history of an autistic disorder, *or* another type of pervasive developmental disorder, then schizophrenia is considered only if prominent and pronounced hallucinations, or delusions are also present and last for a month or more (less, if the individual has been treated successfully).

PARANOID-TYPE SCHIZOPHRENIA

In schizophrenia of paranoid type, persecutory delusions are present, for example, delusions of grandeur, auditory hallucinations, or an unsubstantiated fear that they will be harmed or persecuted by others. The person does not display negative symptoms, such as disorganized speech or catatonic behavior and, on the surface, they often seem to be the most "normal-appearing" despite psychotic ideation. The delusions are dominated by themes of persecution or grandiosity. This is frequently accompanied by auditory hallucinations related to these themes.

Individuals are generally older when they experience their first episode, and they are usually better able to take care of daily needs, even when most symptomatic. These individuals are characterized as tense, suspicious, guarded, reserved, hostile, or aggressive. It is helpful for the practitioner to explore the content of the individual's delusions, particularly if the theme is one of violence or aggression. This is even more important if the person has incorporated the practitioner into their delusional, violent thoughts. Keeping in mind the safety of both client and practitioner, one should proceed slowly and respectfully during the interview while also providing detailed explanations for what is occurring.

To help better differentiate among the various subtypes, the following vignette provides an opportunity to become familiar with the specific features of schizophrenia, in particular, the paranoid type. The case illustrates the influence of biopsychosocial factors that help individualize Rudy Rosen's experience with schizophrenia. This vignette addresses how this disorder has affected the client and his family, life span development, and the effects of frequent hospitalizations, medication, and chronic relapse.

The Case of Rudy Rosen

Rudy is a 76-year-old white male who is currently hospitalized because of a recent suicide attempt. Persecutory hallucinations are reflected in his statement to the social worker on admission, "My medication is poisoned by my wife." He was escorted to a large, metropolitan psychiatric hospital by a mobile crisis unit because he refused to voluntarily admit himself for observation.

During the intake process, Rudy's wife, Ruth, revealed a history that began approximately 25 years ago when her husband was first diagnosed as "schizophrenia, paranoid type." Adds Mrs. Rosen, "That statement changed my life." At that time, Rudy had been employed as an auto mechanic. According to Ruth, one day he suddenly and without warning began to recount bizarre symptoms. Ruth remembered her husband saying, "Our home telephone is bugged and the people at work tampered with it." Rudy accused some of the other mechanics of stealing his tools, and claimed several people were following him home while plotting to harm him. His wife noted that soon after, Rudy began accusing her and their two children of plotting against him. However, his rationale for this blaming attitude remained vague. She went on, "Rudy ran around the house, screaming that I thought he was crazy, and I was working with the police and his employer to put him in the 'crazy' hospital."

During Rudy's initial hospitalization 25 years ago, he had a difficult time understanding his illness or why he had been put in the "hospital for crazy people." Rudy did not believe what the psychiatrists, social workers, or his family were trying to tell him about his illness. He remained steadfastly convinced that people were plotting against him, his phone was bugged, and his medicine could not help him because "it's poisoned." Rudy began a six-week trial course of Thorazine, his symptoms abated, and he was discharged from the hospital. Rudy did relatively well for a long period of time, although he did have several episodes of first-rank symptoms after he refused to take his medications. Whenever Rudy's symptoms became worse his wife brought him to the hospital, where he was usually readmitted, especially if he was actively suicidal.

The social worker reviewed Rudy's chart and found a family history noting that he was the youngest of five children. Three of his siblings are still living and include a brother, Harry, aged 90, and two sisters, Natalie, 85, and Miriam, 87. The details about Rudy's oldest sister are vague; one sentence notes she died while hospitalized in a mental institution more than 50 years ago. Apparently she had been hospitalized for what was termed "depression" following the birth of her only child. Further exploration of family history reveals that Rudy's mother was described as being "very strange" (by almost everyone in the family). His mother accused people of being against her, out to hurt her, and (reported by others) that she "heard voices that were not heard by anyone else." Rudy's father and older siblings raised him, as the mother was considered "unfit and crazy." Of noteworthy physical importance, both of Rudy's eardrums were punctured from a serious infection when he was five years old. The etiology remains unknown; however, he was treated for many years, including several surgeries for chronic ear infections. This condition left Rudy with a very significant hearing deficit throughout his life. Rudy also had a history of rheumatoid heart disease as a youngster. Rudy's wife reports that one of his sisters, Miriam, exhibits "bizarre-like" behavior. However, no diagnosis has been determined, and the 87-year-old sister remains under the care of a full-time paid nursing companion.

Rudy has been married a little over 55 years, and he has two children; his daughter is age 54, and his son is 50. Both children are professionals, and they live in the same community with their parents. Rudy has six grandchildren and one great-grandchild. He is retired, with no outside hobbies, interests, or friends. He is in poor cardiac health, having had a quadruple heart bypass five years ago. In addition, he has a pacemaker, suffers from congestive heart disease (ASHD), cataracts, and chronic ear infections. Rudy experiences severe tardive dyskinesia (TD) from his many years of taking high doses of antipsychotic drugs. His symptoms include hand tremors, tongue thrusting, and unsteady gait. In addition, Rudy takes a cadre of daily medications including Coumadin (a blood thinner); Resperdal (for his psychosis); Valium (for sleep); Cogentin (for TD); Wellbutrin, Paxil, and Buspar (for his positive symptoms); and Synthryoid (to treat his slow metabolism).

Rudy's wife is a retired office manager. She looked quite tired and sad during the intake interview, and commented that she had retired to become "Rudy's full-time nurse, appointment keeper, and jailer." Although she and Rudy had a "good marriage" despite his illness, she had maintained the hope that their "golden years" would be filled with quality time spent together going on vacations, family activities, and fun. She always thought that if he took good care of himself and took his medication that his schizophrenia would abate. Instead, her days are spent driving Rudy from doctor to doctor, to the dentist, or to hearing aid technicians. Rudy's behavior makes it difficult for him to keep any one doctor for an extended period of time. With a sigh, Ruth explains that this is because he accuses them of "cheating, giving him the wrong medicine, or trying to kill him." Rudy changes doctors and dentists very often.

Rudy's wife no longer allows him to take his medications without close supervision. She recently found evidence (pills on the bathroom floor) that he flushes his medications down the toilet. She is not sure how long this had been going on, but suspects this may have led to this current hospitalization when he again began to have active signs and symptoms of delusions and hallucinations.

Assessment Summary

Rudy's life, as depicted in this vignette, illustrates the signs and symptoms of paranoid-type schizophrenia. Although his initial onset occurred late in life, the course illustrated in this case example is chronic. Rudy's interpersonal and social functioning have exacerbated over his lifetime, especially when he neglects taking his medication. It is important to note the impact this disorder has had on his family. Rudy's wife has borne the emotional and financial brunt of his illness over the past 25 years. While his children were growing up, they had to constantly cope with the loss of a meaningful parental relationship, with their father's bizarre behavior, and with his frequent hospitalizations.

The multi-axial designation would be specified for Mr. Rosen as:

Axis I	295.30 Schizophrenia, Paranoid Type
Axis II	V71.09 (No diagnosis)
Axis III	366.9 Cataracts

(continued)

389.9 Hearing Loss

333.82 Neuroleptic-Induced Tardive Dyskinesia

428.0 Congestive Heart Failure (pacemaker)

Axis IV   Deferred

Axis V   GAF = 25 (on admission)

50 (on discharge)

The competency-based assessment examines effective problem solving and viable alternatives. What has helped Rudy to cope with such a devastating mental disorder has been the devotion shown by his wife, Ruth. They have been married

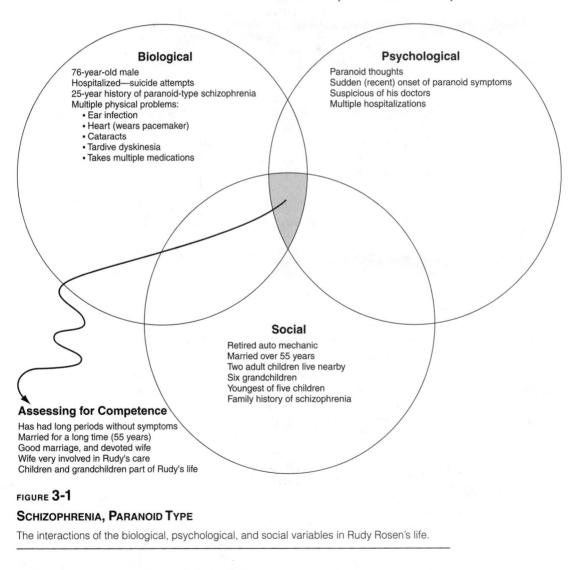

Biological

76-year-old male
Hospitalized—suicide attempts
25-year history of paranoid-type schizophrenia
Multiple physical problems:
• Ear infection
• Heart (wears pacemaker)
• Cataracts
• Tardive dyskinesia
• Takes multiple medications

Psychological

Paranoid thoughts
Sudden (recent) onset of paranoid symptoms
Suspicious of his doctors
Multiple hospitalizations

Social

Retired auto mechanic
Married over 55 years
Two adult children live nearby
Six grandchildren
Youngest of five children
Family history of schizophrenia

Assessing for Competence

Has had long periods without symptoms
Married for a long time (55 years)
Good marriage, and devoted wife
Wife very involved in Rudy's care
Children and grandchildren part of Rudy's life

FIGURE **3-1**

SCHIZOPHRENIA, PARANOID TYPE

The interactions of the biological, psychological, and social variables in Rudy Rosen's life.

for 55 years and according to his wife, "It was a very good and satisfying marriage." In addition, Rudy was emotionally supported by his children and his grandchildren. There were long periods of time when Rudy took his medication and experienced periods of remission. During this time, the family had a sense of cohesiveness. This set the foundation for a shared memory of "normalcy" that seemed helpful for the family during the times when Rudy relapsed.

CATATONIC-TYPE SCHIZOPHRENIA

Persons with catatonic-type schizophrenia exhibit many of the basic features mentioned previously. However, it is the abnormal and striking physical movements, or lack of physical movements, that distinctly sets this category apart from the other four subtypes of schizophrenia. More than likely, the practitioner will easily recognize psychomotor disturbances; they alternate between the extremes of excitement and stupor. Because of this, the person with the catatonic subtype may require medical supervision in order to prevent hurting themselves or others. They may be unable to eat or drink on their own, and even the process of normal body elimination may require monitoring. In addition, these individuals may experience complications from untreated malnutrition, dehydration, electrolyte disturbances, or exhaustion.

At times, the person's physical motor activity may appear to look "speeded up," but the more typical catatonic behavior is described as being a slow, retarded, or a stuporlike state. The amount of activity and its seemingly driven quality generally ranges between extremes of agitation, as in an excited catatonic state, to a withdrawn and inactive state usually associated with catatonic stupor. Several characteristics usually dominate an individual's behavior. They may, for example, adopt and maintain rigid postures for hours at a time, assume bizarre positions, exhibit stuporlike states, and/or become mute (the most common occurrence). The person is seemingly oblivious to the external world, and he or she may resist being moved by others. Another pattern is to rapidly alternate between excitement and immobility (Morrison, 1995).

The bearing and manner of the person with catatonic-type schizophrenia is often described as artificial and stilted. They will spontaneously pose or display bizarre, inappropriate silliness and "odd" mannerisms, for example, using their face to create facial grimacing or "silly faces." These strange postures can be held for very long periods of time, akin to a wax statue frozen in a fixed position. This is referred to as *catatonic posturing*. Someone else may try to manipulate or move the individual's semistiff or waxlike limbs, but once moved the limbs can then remain "fixed" for hours or days. This is referred to as *waxy flexibility*. Disturbances of volition include *negativism*, which is characterized by an almost mulish refusal to follow any course of action suggested or expected. In some cases this negativism is passive, for example, if food is served to the person and they do not eat it. Another example may be if someone asks a question, the person does not answer.

At other times, the person's negativism becomes "active"; for example, they maintain rigid posturing despite attempts to move them. Sometimes the person exhibits a tendency to repeat or mimic spoken words of others; this is known as *echolalia*. For example, if the person is asked a question, they will repeat it over and over, sometimes for an hour or more. *Echopraxia* occurs when the person with catatonic-type schizophrenia mimics the physical gestures and movements of others, for example, in a mirrorlike pantomime. This behavior may continue long after the other person has left the room. Echolalia and echopraxia are seen as involuntary and meaningless repetitions of others words and/or actions.

Certain mannerisms often have a special meaning to the individual that is connected to delusions or hallucinations. Seemingly purposeless repetitive movements or verbalizations are seen in a variety of conditions. For example, a person folds a piece of paper along the same creases until it disintegrates; their movements are referred to as *stereotyped behaviors* or *stereotypy*. They commonly involve the entire body, and the person may, for example, rock or sway. These movements generally represent some special significance, but it is generally not discernible to others and seems purposeless in nature. When asked, "Why are you folding this piece of paper over and over again?" they offer no reason. Involuntary repetition of tasks, such as repeating an answer to a question until the individual is asked to stop, is referred to as *perseveration*. The use of perseveration does not include using standard filler words such as, "you know," "like," or "I mean."

Catatonic-type schizophrenia should include *at least two* of the following features:

- Stupor or motor immobility (cataplexy) or a sudden and transient episode of paralysis, with no loss of consciousness, and affecting nearly all voluntary muscles; or waxy flexibility

- Hyperactivity that is not influenced by external stimuli

- Mutism (deficit of communication through speech or interaction with others, or marked negativism)

- Peculiar or odd behaviors evidenced by posturing, stereotypes, or mannerisms

The following case vignette describes the important features of catatonic-type schizophrenia. The case discussion includes other conditions that may complicate making an accurate assessment. As you read about Joey Esterson, it is helpful to differentiate among features of catatonic-type schizophrenia from a general medical condition, substance and/or alcohol abuse, or other types of psychosis.

The Case of Joey Esterson

Joey is a 20-year-old single man who was admitted to a large metropolitan hospital's mental health service. He was not verbal and offered no chief complaint on admission. Joey's older cousin, Lenny Pasternak, brought him to the hospital. He expressed the concern, "Joey is going crazy again." He added, "Joey probably needs to go back to the state hospital." Lenny Pasternak was a poor historian and provided very little coherent information about his cousin's background, except, "Joey is the middle child of three children. His older sister and younger brother both live in New York, but they don't have any contact with Joey. Joey's father died from a heart attack five years ago." The only other information provided was that Joey's father had been diagnosed as schizophrenic many years earlier. There was even less information regarding Joey's mother, who apparently had abandoned him and his siblings when they were young children.

Lenny described his cousin, saying, "Joey always talked funny, even when he was 10 or 12 years old. Joey heard and saw things that no one else in the family did." Eventually, at the age of 17, Joey was diagnosed with catatonic-type schizophrenia.

During the current episode, Joey almost had to be carried into the hospital because he walked in a greatly hobbled fashion on the outside arches of his feet, and refused to be moved. The social worker noted Joey's appearance as that of a slightly built, disheveled young man who paid no attention to his current surroundings. During the initial meeting, he sat with his eyes closed, shut tight, did not look up when spoken to, and did not answer questions directed to him. Joey refused to participate in a conversation with the social worker and did not answer any questions.

While it appeared Joey understood things happening around him, he did not interact with anyone. He sporadically introduced phrases he had apparently heard before into his speech, and he accomplished this without opening his eyes or looking up. His speech was affected in such a manner that he babbled babylike, often with a lisp or stammer, and occasionally broke out in a fragmentary remnant of a tune unexpectedly in the middle of what he was "saying." Joey made many facial grimaces and various other kinds of seemingly senseless physical movements. For example, Joey crossed his legs in a rigid manner; that is, his legs were assembled in odd positions while his hands were in constant motion on top of his head.

The social worker attempted a mental status examination that revealed the following information: Joey was admitted in a semimute state; and very little could be explored regarding his thought content, cognitive processes, insight, or judgment. Joey was retained at the hospital involuntarily for a 72-hour period. During that time, he remained essentially motionless and sat in a chair for many hours at a time. This practitioner noted Joey showed evidence of a noticeable tremor in his extremities, a common sign of agitation. In addition, when Joey's arms or legs were placed in any position, for example, extended straight out, he maintained this position for a long period of time, even when he was told he could resume his former position. If others attempted to bend Joey's extremities, their movement was met with resistance. If Joey was approached from one side of his body, he gradually would turn his head away in order to look in the opposite direction. In addition, Joey wrinkled his nose, made twitching movements with his mouth, and pursed his lips with no apparent purposeful reason. These purposeless movements often lasted over several seconds, and were not accompanied by any other motions of the tongue, which might implicate the effects of tardive dyskinesia.

Assessment Summary

Joey exhibits classic features of catatonic-type schizophrenia. Once considered rare, it is often inadequately diagnosed (Fink et al., 1995). From this case discussion, it is clear that these features have persisted far longer than the required six months duration.

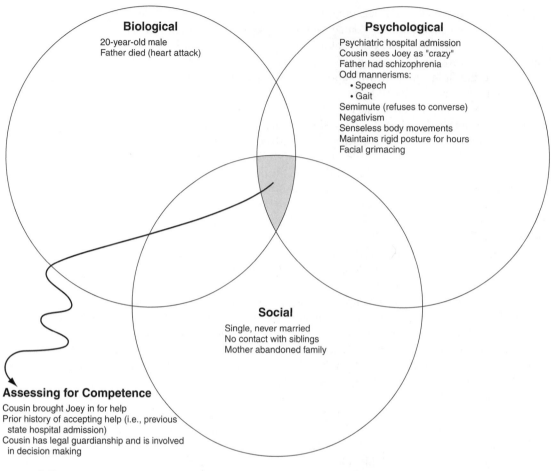

Biological
20-year-old male
Father died (heart attack)

Psychological
Psychiatric hospital admission
Cousin sees Joey as "crazy"
Father had schizophrenia
Odd mannerisms:
  • Speech
  • Gait
Semimute (refuses to converse)
Negativism
Senseless body movements
Maintains rigid posture for hours
Facial grimacing

Social
Single, never married
No contact with siblings
Mother abandoned family

Assessing for Competence
Cousin brought Joey in for help
Prior history of accepting help (i.e., previous
  state hospital admission)
Cousin has legal guardianship and is involved
  in decision making

FIGURE **3-2**

SCHIZOPHRENIA, CATATONIC TYPE

The interactions of the biological, psychological, and social variables in Joey Esterson's life.

Joey demonstrates other important characteristics such as muteness, negativism, catatonic excitement, posturing, waxy flexibility, and facial grimacing. An important distinction should be noted in that Joey was not considered stuporous because he was alert enough to turn away from an approaching stimulus (negativism).

The DSM multi-axial designation for Joey Esterson would be as follows:

Axis I	295.20 Schizophrenia, Catatonic Type
Axis II	V71.09 (No diagnosis)
Axis III	None
Axis IV	Problems related to the social environment
	Occupational problems

(continued)

        Economic problems

        Problems with primary support group

   Axis V   GAF =   20 (on admission)

                   50 (on discharge)

In this case vignette, the competency-based assessment model pays particular attention to ruling out general medical conditions. In Joey's situation, there was no evidence of medical disorders that could have produced or mimicked catatonic behavior, such as epilepsy and/or certain strokes. The practitioner, in this case, referred Joey for a complete general medical and neurological evaluation to rule out other disorders. It is expected that a laboratory inquiry, including urine and blood analysis for toxic substances and drug(s) of abuse, will be conducted. There is one major source of support in Joey's social environment, his cousin Lenny. This relative not only brought Joey to the hospital but has also cared for him for most of his life. Despite being abandoned at an early age by his mother, Lenny continues to express concern and apparently cares for Joey.

DISORGANIZED-TYPE SCHIZOPHRENIA

In contrast to the paranoid type of schizophrenia, individuals with the disorganized type exhibit marked disruption in their speech patterns (disorganized speech) and behavior (disorganized behavior). They may display flat or inappropriate affect, such as silliness at inappropriate times, or laugh without apparent reason. Incongruous facial grinning and grimacing are quite common. If hallucinations or delusions are present, they are not organized around a central theme, as in the paranoid type, and are seen as more fragmented and disjointed. This subtype was previously known as "hebephrenia." These individuals show early signs of difficulty with life problems, and the course tends to be chronic.

    The disorganized subtype of schizophrenia is characterized by marked regression toward primitive, disinhibited, and unorganized behavior, and the absence of symptoms that meet the criteria for the catatonic type. The early symptoms can start as deterioration in personal grooming and inappropriate social behavior. Personal hygiene is often described as shabby or unkempt. Family and friends often are the first to observe these personality changes and often describe the person as "just not the same as they used to be."

    These individuals are usually active, but in an aimless and unproductive manner. Their thought disorder is seen as very pronounced, and their connection with reality is seen as limited. Their prognosis is generally poor, and few have significant remissions.

    The criteria for disorganized-type schizophrenia is disorganized behavior, disorganized speech, and flat or inappropriate affect. The following case vignette illustrates the signs and symptoms of disorganized-type schizophrenia. Pay particular attention to the onset and duration of symptoms.

The Case of Sarah MacDonald

Sarah is a 30-year-old African-American woman who looks a lot younger than her stated age. She was brought to the hospital emergency room by her brother, Jack, who was not sure how many times his sister had previously been admitted to the psychiatric unit, "but it's been a lot of times." Sarah has lived with her brother, his wife, and their two children during the past ten years. Jack stated, "Most times things around the house were all right, but when Sarah started her crazy stuff, things got pretty chaotic."

Jack added that recently he has become more fearful for the safety of his two children. He was unable to be specific, but claimed that "Sarah stays in her room banging her closets and dresser drawers open and closed all day." She throws things around, and "it sounds as if she is talking to someone in her room except she doesn't have a telephone and no one ever visits her. My sister has never been very sociable, and we always thought of her as a loner even when she was a young child." He was asked to elaborate more regarding her relationships with others. He continued, "My sister rarely laughs, she always seems distant, you know almost unfeeling, and she never appears to enjoy anything very much."

When Jack was asked about Sarah's moods, he stated, "My sister's mood ranges between anger and senseless giggling. Sometimes she makes up 'silly words' and sometimes her mood doesn't match what she's saying." He continued, "Sarah's speech and manner can only be described as 'childlike.' She often walks with a bouncing step, you know, she exaggerates her hip movements. I'm not sure what she's doing. She really acts silly and often breaks out in a fit of giggling for no apparent reason."

Additional history provided by Jack confirms that Sarah abruptly stopped taking her medications six weeks ago; her prescriptions included clozapine (Clorazil), clonazepam (Klonopin), and alprazolam (Xanax). Soon after discontinuing her medication, she began to hear voices again and act bizarre, and her physical appearance deteriorated. She sometimes disappeared from the house for weeks at a time, but eventually the police picked her up "wandering the street." There is no known history of drug or alcohol abuse, or other general medical condition that might account for Sarah's appearance and behavior.

Sarah was first hospitalized when she was 18 years old. At that time she had been exhibiting a variety of psychotic symptoms that included disorganized speech and behavior. According to Jack, his sister never really attended school on a regular basis, nor was she able to maintain any real employment or live independently. During her initial hospitalization, Sarah had been successfully treated with antipsychotic drugs, and within several weeks her psychotic symptoms abated. She was discharged to the care of her brother. For the next few years, Sarah seemed to be getting along okay. That is, she attended a day care program and through that activity she made a few friends and enrolled in a restaurant worker program. She took her medication consistently and appeared to be coping well.

During the past ten years, Sarah has had numerous hospitalizations, medication trials, and subsequent releases into her brother Jack's care. Once Sarah was home, she would sporadically take her medication, and ultimately became symptomatic and disorganized again. During this current admission, Sarah's speech made little sense and was interspersed with frequent rhyming. Sometimes she would make sounds, rather than articulate specific or meaningful words. She was involuntarily admitted for three days and discharged with medications and a scheduled follow-up visit in the hospital's outpatient department.

Assessment Summary

Nothing in Sarah's history suggests a general medical condition. Although her affect had been described as "flat," she does not exhibit anything remotely similar to the severely depressed mood of a major depressive disorder with psychotic features. Sarah has never expressed suicidal ideation, nor has she had any symptoms suggestive of manic-type features. The fact that these features have persisted longer than six months rules out schizophreniform disorder or brief psychotic disorder. Sarah's personal appearance, social behavior, pronounced thought disorder, negative symptoms, poor hygiene, social withdrawal, poor rapport, and emotional responses are seen as inappropriate, contributing to the assessment of disorganized-type schizophrenia. The vignette describes behaviors that include incoherent speech, inappropriate affect, auditory hallucinations, grossly disorganized behavior, and an onset that occurred at an early age; she was 18 when first hospitalized.

Sarah MacDonald's DSM multi-axial designation would be:

Axis I	295.10 Schizophrenia, Disorganized Type	
Axis II	V71.09 (No diagnosis)	
Axis III	None	
Axis IV	Occupational problems with unemployment	
	Occasionally homeless	
	Problems with access to health care services	
Axis IV	GAF =	20 (on admission)
		30 (on discharge)

Despite Sarah's struggle with a serious diagnosis, the competency-based assessment explores potential strengths and resources. The most important resource she has is her brother, who is involved actively in her life. Even though Jack is concerned for his own family's safety, he continues to take care of her. He provides her with housing, attempts to make sure she takes her medication on a regular basis, brings her to therapy appointments, and watches for possible signs of relapse.

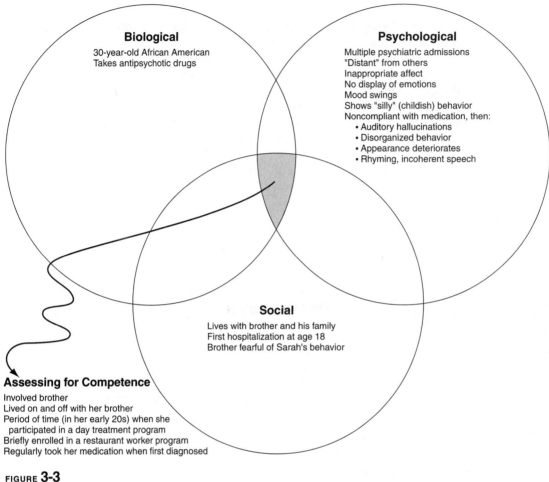

Biological
30-year-old African American
Takes antipsychotic drugs

Psychological
Multiple psychiatric admissions
"Distant" from others
Inappropriate affect
No display of emotions
Mood swings
Shows "silly" (childish) behavior
Noncompliant with medication, then:
• Auditory hallucinations
• Disorganized behavior
• Appearance deteriorates
• Rhyming, incoherent speech

Social
Lives with brother and his family
First hospitalization at age 18
Brother fearful of Sarah's behavior

Assessing for Competence
Involved brother
Lived on and off with her brother
Period of time (in her early 20s) when she
  participated in a day treatment program
Briefly enrolled in a restaurant worker program
Regularly took her medication when first diagnosed

FIGURE **3-3**

SCHIZOPHRENIA, DISORGANIZED TYPE

The interactions of the biological, psychological, and social variables in Sarah MacDonald's life.

UNDIFFERENTIATED-TYPE SCHIZOPHRENIA

Those who exhibit the major features of schizophrenia but have not met the full assessment distinctions for paranoid, disorganized, or catatonic types are considered of undifferentiated type. The characteristics are virtually indistinguishable from the three other schizophrenia categories; essentially this determination is made of exclusion rather than that based entirely on symptomatology. The process of making an assessment of undifferentiated-type schizophrenia is basically using "what's left over." Some individuals do not quite "fit" into the previously reviewed subtypes. In other words, the person has met all the basic criteria for schizophrenia, but has *not* met specific criteria for paranoid, disorganized, and catatonic types of schizophrenia. The following case vignette provides an opportunity for the reader to become acquainted with undifferentiated-type schizophrenia and what it might look like.

The Case of Shayla Patterson

Shayla is a 20-year-old female who was born to a single teenage mother. Her father came from Trinidad; Shayla has never had contact with him. She was referred to the XYZ Community Mental Health Agency by her next-door neighbor who once attended a parenting group there. The neighbor told Shayla, "It's a real good place to go and get help, and besides the 'shrinks' are real nice."

Shayla and her mother, Mrs. Beth Shafer, both attended the intake interview. Shayla is a petite young woman who exhibited poverty in the amount and content of her speech (alogia), and she appeared unkempt and disheveled (avolition). Shayla's mother appeared quite anxious, distraught, and urgently wanted "someone to help my daughter." Mrs. Shafer described her daughter's childhood as one exemplified by a cadre of difficulties including poor school performance, aggressive behavior at home, speaking in "funny voices," hearing people talk back to her (not validated by others), and being in contact with "beings from outer space." Mrs. Shafer stated, "You know, Shayla's father used to talk to himself, too," and, "He had to be placed in a mental institution a time or two when he got too crazy." Mrs. Shafer was unable to provide reliable information regarding Shayla's father other than, "He was just a crazy old coot a lot of the time." She added, "I just love my baby and I don't want anything to happen to her."

During the time of intake, the social worker carefully explored intrapersonal and interpersonal functioning. Shayla exhibited a variety of psychotic symptoms that included delusions. Shayla stated that she was in contact with "George Washington, Abraham Lincoln, and Cleopatra," and they talked back to her (auditory hallucinations). However, there were no clear systemized themes or patterns involved (which would have been suggestive of paranoid-type schizophrenia). There was no evidence of a mood disorder, specific organic factors, or drug and/or alcohol abuse. Shayla has been unable to keep any type of job, and her social functioning is described as very limited at best. As a next step, Shayla was referred for a psychiatric evaluation.

Assessment Summary

Several features described in this vignette support making the assessment for undifferentiated-type schizophrenia. Contributing to this diagnosis was Shayla's extreme decline in functioning over a period of several years, occasional delusions, and her many oddities of behavior and speech. There is no evidence of a mood disorder, a general medical condition, or substance of abuse that could better account for these

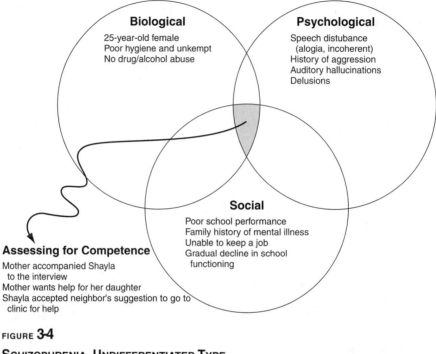

FIGURE 3-4

SCHIZOPHRENIA, UNDIFFERENTIATED TYPE

The interactions of the biological, psychological, and social variables in Shalya Patterson's life.

symptoms. It is important to note the emergence of features occurring during Shayla's middle adolescent years. Her delusions frequently had different themes versus a specified pattern, in that they were not systematized, thereby ruling out the paranoid subtype. The absence of any notable or prominent catatonic features rules out the catatonic subtype. Although Shayla's speech was at times viewed as incoherent, her affect was unremarkable and not seen as particularly flat or grossly inappropriate, thereby ruling out the disorganized type. Thus undifferentiated-type schizophrenia was left.

According to the DSM multi-axial system, Shayla's diagnosis would be:

Axis I   295.90 Schizophrenia, Undifferentiated Type

Axis II   V71.09 (No diagnosis)

Axis III   None

Axis IV   None

Axis IV   GAF = 35 (current)

To formulate a correct diagnosis for Shayla, the practitioner needs to know the information found in the DSM. This requires the ability to differentiate among the various subtypes of schizophrenia. However, the worker also looks for strengths and resources. In this case, Shayla's mother talked with others about getting help for her daughter and followed through with appropriate recommendations, for example, going to the clinic. Additionally, the mother came to the intake appointment and appeared very supportive and nurturing.

RESIDUAL-TYPE SCHIZOPHRENIA

Residual-type schizophrenia classification has changed very little over time. It describes circumstances and conditions of individuals who continue to exhibit a schizophrenic-like picture but with *no current active phase* in evidence. To consider the residual subtype, an individual must have had at least one episode of schizophrenia, while not currently manifesting active symptoms. Even though there is no evidence of bizarre delusions or hallucinations, the person still exhibits remnants, or "leftovers," of previous active disease. Emotional blunting, social withdrawal, eccentric behavior, illogical thinking, and some loosening of associations are present. However, the symptoms are not as pronounced. Some fragmentary symptoms still exist, and the individual is seen by others as somewhat unusual, odd, or peculiar, but the person is able to maintain some level of social functioning.

This subtype is essentially a "filler" component and tends to be infrequently utilized in clinical practice. The residual category is addressed in this chapter, as it underscores the importance of formulating an accurate clinical assessment. Unfortunately, there is little additional information regarding the prevalence or other important demographic data concerning this subtype. Other important features to consider:

- The person has at one time met the specific criteria for one of the other four subtypes of schizophrenia—that is, catatonic, paranoid, disorganized, or undifferentiated.

- There are no longer features of catatonic behavior, hallucinations, delusions, or disorganized behavior or speech.

- The person is still beset with specific features, as indicated by *either* of the following:

  Flat affect, minimized speech, or lack of volition (negative symptoms)

  A diminished pattern of at least two basic features of schizophrenia, for example, odd beliefs, distorted perceptions, odd speech, or peculiar behavior

Positive symptoms are often reported, such as hearing one's thoughts spoken aloud or auditory hallucinations that comment on the individual's behavior. Individuals self-report that their thoughts are being controlled, the ability to extend their thoughts onto others, delusions, or experience that includes others controlling or influencing the individual from the outside.

In summary, a number of causative factors have been implicated in the cause of schizophrenia, including genetic influences, role of brain structure, neurotransmitter imbalances, and psychological stressors. Regardless of the various assumptions about the etiology of schizophrenia, it is clear that this disorder affects each individual differently. Each person may have the same set of symptoms, but their level of functioning may appear very different. This underscores the importance of the competency-based assessment, which examines the interplay of interpersonal, social, environmental, and cultural influences in a person's life.

UNDERSTANDING OTHER PSYCHOTIC DISORDERS

Schizophreniform Disorder

Sometimes people display something akin to a schizophrenic-like picture, but not at the same level as those found in schizophrenia. Schizophreniform disorder presents, but differentiates from, the symptoms suggestive of schizophrenia. To complicate the clinical picture, these symptoms can disappear just as quickly as they appear. This could be attributed to a successful treatment regimen, or there is no clear explanation. When the presence of schizophreniform disorder is assessed, there is no detected organic cause of psychotic symptoms, the psychotic features must last *less than six months*, and include a prodromal, active, and residual phase.

In schizophreniform disorder, it appears as if the person has schizophrenia, but he or she subsequently recovers completely with no residual aftereffects. This provisional category can be a valuable tool, as it avoids coming to premature conclusions about a person's behavior. It may also serve as a warning that the underlying cause of a specific psychosis may not yet be determined.

It is often quite confusing that the symptoms and criteria for schizophreniform disorder are identical to those of schizophrenia. The important distinction is in duration and intensity. An easy way to distinguish between the two disorders is remembering that the duration of schizophrenia must be longer than six months, and schizophreniform symptoms must exist for at least a substantial part of one month (less, if successfully treated), but less than six months. If an assessment is made without waiting for the "duration interval" or possible recovery (which is sometimes the case), "schizophrenia, provisional" should be noted; if the person's recovery is complete within six months, this notation should be eliminated.

The following sample of a social work student's process recording illustrates the conversation between the intern and a client, Claudia Benjamin, who was involuntarily placed in a general medical hospital's psychiatric unit. The process recording includes both the word-for-word conversation and the student's reactions to the contents of the interaction. It is presented to illustrate the schizophrenic-like picture a person with schizophreniform disorder may have and the subtle distinctions between the two. The biopsychosocial features are not illustrated in this case. The intent, instead, is to illustrate through the vignette how the symptom picture may emerge from the scope of the therapeutic conversation.

The Case of Claudia Benjamin

Ms. Benjamin is a 23-year-old Jamaican female who was brought to the hospital by the police who found her wandering naked around 14th Street and Ocean Drive on South Beach. According to the police report, the woman appeared to be distraught and claimed, "My mother is coming from the moon to pick me up." The police officers felt the young woman was delusional and hallucinating at the time and decided to transport her to the hospital's emergency room. During transit the police called their dispatcher reporting their status, and they were informed of a missing person's bulletin describing the young woman they had just picked up. A social work intern was assigned to the emergency room as a part of her hospital rotation. The transcript begins:

CONTENT	REACTIONS TO PROCESS
W: "Hi, Ms. Benjamin? I'd like to introduce myself. I'm a social work intern here at General. How are you feeling now?"	I'm really nervous about working with someone who might be psychotic.
CB: [The client shrugs her shoulders and begins to play with her hair and hum some kind of tune. There is no eye contact.]	I heard that no eye contact is bad.
W: "Are you comfortable?"	I'm trying to make her like me, but I don't think I'm getting anywhere with her.
CB: "Get them away! Get them away!"	
W: "I'm not sure what you want me to get away from you. Could you be clearer?"	Oh, boy. This isn't going the way I want it to. What should I do now?
CB: "Those things, things, that are after me."	That sounds like paranoia, but is it enough paranoia? I'm confused whether she is having delusions or hallucinations. Oh, boy.
W: "Ms. Benjamin, what 'things' are you referring to? I'm not quite sure I understood what you wanted me to know. Could you be a bit clearer?"	
CB: [The client cocked her head to one side and closed her eyes very tightly. It appeared to me that she wasn't listening to me, but to another conversation…inside her head.]	I haven't a clue as what to do next.

At this point, I thought it was time to have a talk with my supervisor. I need help in finding out what was going on for my client. Mary Jo Cringle, my field supervisor, suggested I talk with Claudia's family, who was sitting in the waiting room. As I spoke with the Benjamin family, the information they supplied helped to clear up some of my confusion.

According to Ms. Benjamin's mother, Claudia has been "acting this way" for only a few months. Her family told me that before this incident they cared for Claudia at home. After she wandered away from home today, they realized she needed more care than they could provide. Mrs. Benjamin said, "My daughter was a really good kid growing up. You know, it's very difficult to watch your own child talk to someone she thinks is there, but who really isn't. She thinks we are going to poison her food or harm her in some way." Mrs. Benjamin denied that Claudia ever experienced depressive or manic episodes, and she denied any medical problems or the use of substances ("Claudia doesn't even take aspirin").

"I just don't understand what happened to my wonderful daughter. She was all right up until just a few months ago and now this. Do you think you can help her?"

Assessment Summary

The purpose of this vignette was to look at the worker's process rather than to illustrate the client's life story. The process transcript describes the social work intern's uncomfortable feelings about the interview and illustrates how unsettling it can be for the neophyte practitioner to attempt to relate to someone who is not responding "rationally." The client's odd mannerisms and delusions leave the social worker frightened and confused. While the student intern valiantly attempts to understand the client's "reality," Claudia Benjamin's response leaves the student feeling bewildered and inept. The differential diagnosis of brief psychotic disorder was not considered in the above vignette because the duration of symptoms was more than 30 days. Schizophreniform disorder is regarded to have a more hopeful outlook than does schizophrenia (Shaner, 1997). However, most of what we know about the clinical course suggests that approximately one-third to one-half of those with schizophreniform disorder advance toward developing schizophrenia, and these two disorders probably share a common pathogenesis.

The DSM multi-axial designation is:

Axis I	295.40 Schizophreniform
Axis II	V71.09 (No diagnosis)
Axis III	None
Axis IV	Unknown
Axis V	GAF = 30 (on admission)

Schizoaffective Disorder

Historically, individuals who showed symptoms of schizophrenia and also a mood disorder, such as depression, have been grouped together under the umbrella of schizophrenia. This was often viewed as a "mixed bag of problems" for the practitioner who attempted to understand these complex behaviors. Some suggest that schizoaffective disorder is either a mixture of a mood disorder and schizophrenia (*affect* always refers to, or is affiliated with, "mood"), or a form of bipolar disorder (because individuals often respond well to medication, specifically lithium treatment). Others hold that this is an entirely separate type of psychosis. Still others believe this is simply a collection of confusing and contradictory symptoms (Barlow & Durand, 1995; Berenbaum & Oltmanns, 1992; Carson & Sanislow, 1993; Grinspoon & Bakalar, 1990; Wassink et al., 1999).

Complicating the symptom picture further, depression frequently accompanies schizophrenia. Because of this, it becomes more difficult to distinguish schizophrenia from schizoaffective disorder and other forms of mood disorders. Schizoaffective disorder presents with features of both psychosis and a mood disturbance. If the periods of depression or mania are brief in relation to schizophrenia, the presence of schizophrenia is taken into account; however, if they are lengthy, a mood disorder or schizoaffective disorder should be considered. Chapter 4 contains a more detailed discussion of mood disorders.

The competency-based assessment is helpful to distinguish among a person with schizophrenia, someone with a mood disorder, or someone who has both conditions. In particular, practitioners should obtain pertinent intrapersonal information, including history of medical, neurological, or psychiatric problems as well as pertinent family history. The prognosis is better for someone with schizoaffective disorder than for an individual with schizophrenia, but it is worse than someone having a mood disorder.

Differential Assessment

While there is little data available, schizoaffective disorder appears less common than schizophrenia. To consider the presence of schizoaffective disorder, both a mood episode and the psychotic features of schizophrenia (such as social impairment and poor self-hygiene) must be present *concurrently* for a substantial and uninterrupted period of time. During this same time, there must be *at least two weeks* of delusions or hallucinations in the absence of a mood episode. The person's mood is manifested as either a major depressive episode, manic episode, or mixed episode. For example, the person may be depressed for two weeks, or they may be depressed for one week and show manic symptoms for another week. The mood should be seen as a very significant part of the total clinical picture.

As a part of the competency-based assessment, the practitioner should carefully explore the client's history, looking for alternative explanations of their behavior such as the presence of a general medical condition, for example, AIDS. This careful exploration of the client's life story helps the practitioner avoid coming to premature conclusions about what is already a confusing picture.

To establish a diagnosis the person must have all of the following during a single and unremitting period:

- They meet the basic requirements noted for schizophrenia including delusions or hallucinations without a major mood disorder in evidence for two weeks or more.

- They meet the requirements for either major depressive disorder, manic disorder, or a mixed episode for at least two weeks.

The following case discussion of Sydney Sutherland attempts to show the importance of thoroughly understanding the client's presenting concerns. Clients often come to the attention of the social worker when they are disoriented and unable to provide accurate information. This underscores the importance of talking with others close to the client, such as family or friends, who may be able to provide more reliable factual data.

The Case of Sydney Sutherland

Sydney Sutherland was rushed to the hospital after being found unconscious by her brother, Jerry Sutherland, in his home. Within her reach were an empty liquor bottle and an assortment of medicine bottles, including barbiturates, benzodiazepine-based tranquilizers, stimulants, painkillers, and a collection of several unknown drugs. Sydney's condition was stabilized in the emergency room, and she was transferred up to the psychiatric ward for observation.

The record room called to inform the social worker that Sydney had several prior admissions both to the psychiatric unit and to the acute medical hospital over the course of ten years. The medical records also indicated Sydney had been treated for unspecified bacterial pneumonia three months ago. The psychiatric records indicated she was diagnosed as "schizophrenia, paranoid type." She is being followed by Dr. Irene Morrell, and attends the day treatment program at Bethune Shores Mental Health Agency. Mr. Sutherland thinks the name of his sister's social worker "is something like Lee or Leslie Wagner." This worker will contact Bethune Shores to find out Ms. Sutherland's current status. I asked her brother, Mr. Sutherland, to sign a release of information form that will enable me to contact Dr. Morrell and the day treatment program.

"Hello, this is Martina Lopez, I'm a social worker at Regional Hospital, psych unit. Is it possible to speak with a Lee or a Leslie Wagner?"

"Lee Wagner speaking, can I help you?"

"I certainly hope so," I replied. I introduced myself and assured Ms. Wagner that I had the necessary signed permission forms allowing us to inquire about Ms. Sutherland. I provided some of the current information and asked if she could fill in the gaps and tell me anything more relevant regarding Ms. Sutherland's treatment.

Ms. Wagner responded, "I've seen Sydney on and off for the past three years. She's been pretty unreliable throughout the time that I've known her. Most of the time she doesn't show up for her appointments, and she doesn't like to take her meds. She was diagnosed with paranoid-type schizophrenia, and pretty much stays in the 'active phase.' You know, she'd have a fair chance to go into some type of remission, but as I said before, she's noncompliant with her medications. Whenever I ask her about why she doesn't take the medicine, she tells me that we put poison in the pills because we want to kill her."

I asked, "Has Sydney had ever shown evidence of having a depressed, manic, or mixed episode?" Ms. Wagner replied, "I can't remember her ever having a mood component to her psychosis, but that sounds like what's going on for her right now.

Is that what you are thinking?" I said, "Yes, it seems that way to me, but I also need to talk with her brother to see if he's noticed any changes in her behavior recently." Ms. Wagner ended our conversation asking if I would let her know how Sydney was doing. I promised I would be in touch.

I spoke with Mr. Sutherland soon after my telephone conversation with Ms. Wagner. We found a quiet corner in the day room to talk. He appeared to be in shock and stated, "Geez! I knew my sister was having mental problems, but I didn't think she'd try to kill herself. Man!" I asked him to tell me what his impressions were of his sister's behavior the past month or two. In particular, I inquired about anything that may have been different, worse, or better. He replied, "Well, you know she was always seeing things and talking to things that were never there, or at least no one else could see. Sydney could never keep a job more than a day. Mostly she panhandled or hustled, you know to earn money, but she didn't have to do that. Our parents are people of means and could easily take care of her. Mostly she lived at our parents' place, but once in awhile she'd come and stay a day or two at my condo. I tried to feed her a hot meal, give her a place to take a hot shower, but most of the time she just wandered by to 'borrow money.'

"The only thing I noticed different about her was that the last month or so, Sydney seemed really depressed. You know, like if she slept over my house, she couldn't drag herself out of bed until after 4 P.M., and for her that was really unusual. I also remember that she cried more than I've ever seen her. Now that you mention it, she told me a few times that things were 'hopeless' and she wanted to die. Hey, do you think this suicide attempt was my fault? You know I didn't recognize that she'd actually do it."

I offered reassurance to Mr. Sutherland and told him sister was pretty troubled, and that he couldn't possibly follow her around 24 hours a day to make sure she was okay. I told him we could help his sister and that we would stay in touch. After saying good-bye to Mr. Sutherland, I then made my way back to the psychiatric unit.

Assessment Summary

Certain organic mental disorders often have signs and symptoms resembling schizophrenia, such as hallucinations, delusions, and incoherence. Sydney was found unconscious with a number of medications and alcohol nearby. Therefore during the competency-based assessment, it is essential to rule out other factors that might otherwise explain her behavior. The assessment of schizoaffective disorder should be made if periods of depression or mania are brief in relation to the ongoing symptoms of schizophrenia. In the case vignette, Sydney has a long history of schizophrenia as reported by her brother and the social worker at the day care center; that is, Sydney experiences (auditory and visual) hallucinations. However, within the last month she also began to show signs of major depression. She slept all day and cried more than usual. On some occasions, Sydney confided to her brother that things were "hopeless" and that she wanted to die. Since Sydney's depression is prolonged (lasting at least the past "month or so"), a schizoaffective disorder is considered.

Sydney's complete diagnosis would be as follows:

Axis I	295.70 Schizoaffective Disorder
Axis II	V71.09 (No diagnosis)
Axis III	482.9 Pneumonia, Unspecified Bacterial Infection
	970.9 Stimulants
	967.0 Barbiturates
	969.4 Benzodiazepine-Based Tranquilizers
Axis IV	Occupational problems
	Economic problems
Axis V	GAF = 20 (on admission)

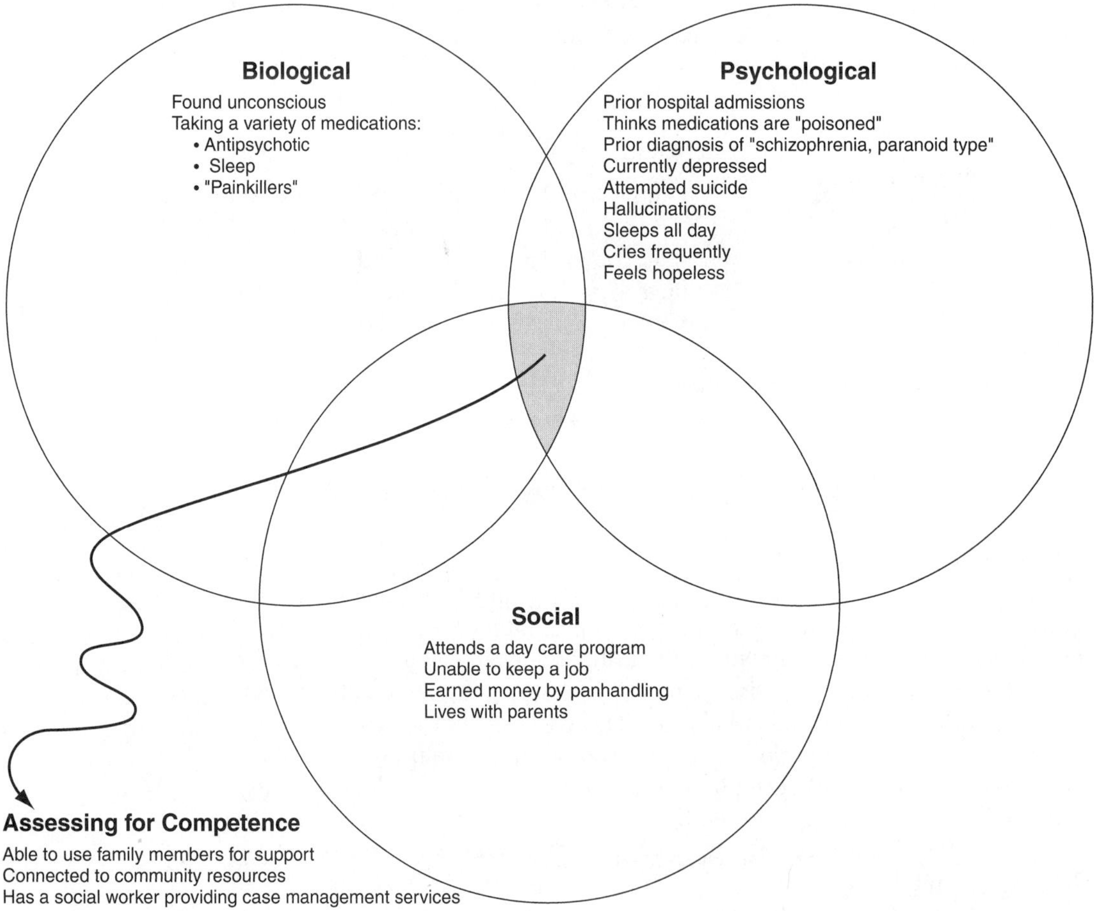

Biological
Found unconscious
Taking a variety of medications:
 • Antipsychotic
 • Sleep
 • "Painkillers"

Psychological
Prior hospital admissions
Thinks medications are "poisoned"
Prior diagnosis of "schizophrenia, paranoid type"
Currently depressed
Attempted suicide
Hallucinations
Sleeps all day
Cries frequently
Feels hopeless

Social
Attends a day care program
Unable to keep a job
Earned money by panhandling
Lives with parents

Assessing for Competence
Able to use family members for support
Connected to community resources
Has a social worker providing case management services

FIGURE **3-5**

SCHIZOAFFECTIVE DISORDER

The interactions of the biological, psychological, and social variables in Sydney Sutherland's life.

Brief Psychotic Disorder

Brief psychotic disorder is seldom assessed in clinical practice, and unfortunately it has received minimal attention. It is included in this chapter to help the practitioner carefully explore all aspects of the client's life as a part of making the competency-based assessment. There is not a great deal of reliable information regarding the incidence, prevalence, sex ratio, average age of onset, or subsequent course of this disorder.

Typically, brief psychotic disorder *lasts more than one day, but less than 30 days*, with an eventual return to the individual's prior level of functioning. If these psychotic features persist beyond 30 days, the assessment would then suggest one of the other psychotic categories, such as schizophreniform disorder. If these features occur within four weeks of childbirth and the mother, for example, threatens to harm or kill her infant, has bizarre delusions or hallucinations, disorganized speech, or catatonic behavior, than the postpartum onset should be specified. However, if these features are culturally sanctioned (or perceived as a normative coping response), then the practitioner would not consider using the diagnosis.

Features *always* include at least one major symptom of psychosis. This usually occurs with an abrupt onset, but does not always include the characteristic patterns seen in schizophrenia. For example, a person may experience some extreme or overwhelming situation(s) and show erratic emotions, screaming or muteness, impaired memory of recent events, and eccentric "odd" behavior. These situations generally include the kind of major life events that would cause any one significant emotional upheaval, for example, the loss of a parent, a life-threatening accident, or even the birth of a child. Practitioners should consider "the event" within the context of the stress it may cause or if any type of secondary gain is involved.

Overall the outcome is generally good, and the person does not experience long-term major psychiatric problems. It is useful to include information gathered from friends and family as a part of the competency-based assessment. It is especially important to inquire about the individual's prior level of intrapersonal functioning, past history regarding similar reactions to stress, and the chronological relationship between the current life stressor and the onset of symptoms. Other differential assessment distinctions should include the consideration of factitious disorder (refer to Chapter 6), malingering (Chapter 6), psychotic disorder due to a general medical condition (as in epilepsy or delirium), substance-induced psychotic disorder, dissociative identity disorder (Chapter 7), and psychotic episodes associated with borderline and schizotypal personality disorders (Chapter 9).

Delusional Disorder

As the name implies, the central characteristic of *delusional disorder* is the person's persistent belief about something that is contrary to reality. The individual may also imagine events that could be happening but, in fact, are not. At face value, these thoughts seem completely plausible in that they are nonbizarre. Individuals with this disorder tend not to have some of the other features commonly associated with schizophrenia, such as flat affect or other negative symptoms. Compared with some of the other disorders, the onset is relatively late in life, the disorder beginning when the individual is between 40 and 50 years old. It is not known why this disorder has such a late onset, but there is some speculation that perhaps these individuals lead relatively normal lives and do not feel the need to seek help. The person comes to the social worker's attention at the point when their symptoms become problematic and ego-dystonic.

When considering a delusional disorder, the individual must exhibit one or more positive symptoms of schizophrenia lasting less than one month (often precipitated by stressful situations), *but lasting at least for one day* (APA, 2000). Unfortunately, relatively little is known about the biopsychosocial influences, for example, the prevalence or course of the illness. However, the disorder is rare, is seen more in women than men, and has a genetic component (Carson & Sanislow, 1993; Keith et al., 1991).

The practitioner should keep in mind that several other disorders cause delusions, and these should be ruled out before making an assessment of delusional disorder. Generally, a good rule of thumb is to consider the use of substances such as alcohol or/and illicit drugs, which can also cause the features associated with delusional disorder. Additionally, brain tumors, vascular dementia, and cognitive-type dementia can manifest similar features and should be discounted.

Shared Psychotic Disorder (formerly known as Folie à Deux)

The last of the psychotic disorders addressed in this chapter is known as **shared psychotic disorder**. When the practitioner evaluates the client's interpersonal relationships as a part of the competency-based assessment, there are times when a significant other person is identified who exerts undue influence on the client's life. The following discussion is intended to help the practitioner carefully explore aspects of the client's social world.

Relatively little is known about this exotic and rare disorder. The syndrome has been known by many different names, including communicated insanity, infectious insanity, and double insanity as well as folie à deux. The main features include a slow development of delusions resulting from being in a symbiotic-like relationship with an "other." Usually one person is under the influence of another person who is having delusions, for example, a long-standing submissive relationship between a parent and their child, a husband and wife, or members of a cult group. Usually these persons live together in social isolation, and they move frequently to escape the difficulties associated with their delusional behaviors. There are usually no other associated features other than the shared delusion(s). The age of onset is variable, and it is considered more common in women (APA, 2000; Barlow & Durand, 1995). The development of these delusions is gradual, and the disorder usually remits spontaneously.

SUMMARY

While many persons with schizophrenia have some symptoms in common, each individual's course and outlook may be vastly different. This underscores the importance of the competency-based assessment, which examines the extent of the individual's coping, resources, capacity for interpersonal relationships, life stressors, and cultural influences, and the impact of his or her social environment. Each variable plays an important part in the assessment process. To summarize the major features:

- Schizophrenia is characterized by a wide spectrum of cognitive and emotional features including symptoms of delusions, hallucinations, disorganized speech and behavior, and inappropriate emotions.

- Symptoms of schizophrenia are divided into "positive" and "negative" symptoms.

    Positive symptoms refer to the more outward signs and symptoms, or those characteristics that are present and should be absent. These include abnormal behavior, or an excess or distortion of normal behavior, including delusions, hallucinations, and disorganized speech.

    Negative symptoms refer to the more inward signs and symptoms, or those symptoms that are absent and should be present. These involve deficits in normative behavior in the dimensions of affect, speech, and motivation.

- Schizophrenia is subdivided into five categories:

    Those with the *paranoid type* have prominent delusions or hallucinations. At the same time, their cognitive skills and affect remain relatively intact.

    Those with the *catatonic type* have unusual and striking motor responses such as remaining in a "fixed position" (referred to as waxy flexibility), excessive activity, and being oppositional in remaining rigid. In addition, they display odd mannerisms with their bodies and faces, which often include grimacing.

    Those with the *disorganized type* exhibit marked disruption in their speech (disorganized) and behavior (disorganized). They also display flat or inappropriate affect.

    Some individuals do not fit neatly into these subtypes and are classified as *undifferentiated type*.

    Individuals who have had at least one episode of schizophrenia but who no longer have the major symptoms of the disorder should be considered *residual type*.

- There are several other disorders that are characterized by a "psychotic-like" picture, and include symptoms such as hallucinations and delusions. These include:

    Schizophreniform disorder—Symptoms of schizophrenia experienced for less than 6 months.

    Schizoaffective disorder—Individuals have symptoms of schizophrenia and also exhibit the characteristics of mood disorders as in major depressive disorder and bipolar affective disorder.

    Delusional disorder—A persistent delusion or belief that is contrary to reality, in the absence of the other characteristics of schizophrenia.

    Brief psychotic disorder—Includes one or more "positive" symptoms such as delusions, hallucinations, disorganized speech, or disorganized behavior occurring over the course of less than a month.

    Shared psychotic disorder—Individuals develop delusions simply as a result of an intensively close relationship with a delusional individual.

Practitioner Reflections

While knowing the various signs and symptoms of schizophrenia is necessary, it is also essential for the practitioner to tune in to the client's "story." In many ways, persons with schizophrenia and other psychotic disorders can function productively. At other times, they may struggle with the broad range of their symptoms. The reflections provided here are designed to help you consider the full range of the person's experience.

Activities

- List all of the myths and reactions to people diagnosed with schizophrenia that you or others that you know have heard about, seen in the media, or read in books.

- Write down all of the words you can think of associated with the word *psychotic*. Going back over this list, how many of them are positive and how many are negative? What does this tell you about how persons with psychotic disorders are perceived?

- Review the case of Joey Esterson. What are some of the problems related to interviewing someone who is so reticent and responds the way that Joey does?

- Looking back over the cases discussed in this chapter, identify some of the obstacles each person may pose in developing a therapeutic relationship.

- An appointment was made with you and the receptionist has just told you that Rudy Rosen is in the waiting room. You greet him, help him to get settled in your office, and exchange some general pleasantries. You are now ready to start. Write the first four to five minutes of your session as you imagine it to have happened. This might, typically, involve eight to ten exchanges. (Refer to the case of Claudia Benjamin for an example of what this process recording might look like.) Looking back over your work, what prompted you to say what you did, ask the questions you asked, and how you were feeling at the time?

References

Addington, D. E., & Addington, J. M. (1992). Attempted suicide and depression in schizophrenia. *Acta Psychiatrica Scandinavica*, 85: 288.

Altman, N. R. (1999). Personal conversation (April 1).

American Psychiatric Association [APA]. (2000). *Diagnostic and statistical manual of mental disorders* (4th ed.-TR). Washington, DC: APA.

Andreasen, N. C., & Carpenter, N. T. (1993). Diagnosis and classification of schizophrenia. *Schizophrenia Bulletin*, 19: 199–214.

Andreasen, N. C., Arndt, S., Alliger, R., Miller, D., & Flaum, M. (1995). Symptoms of schizophrenia: Method, meaning and mechanisms. *Archives of General Psychiatry*, 53: 341–351.

Barlow, D. H., & Durand, V. M. (1995). *Abnormal psychology*. Pacific Grove, CA: Brooks/Cole.

Bartles, S. J., Teague, G. B., Brake, R. E., Clark, R. E., Bush, P., & Noordsy, D. L. (1993). Substance abuse in schizophrenia: Service utilization and costs. *Journal of Nervous and Mental Disorders*, 181: 227–232.

Bentley, K. J., & Walsh, J. (1996). *The social worker and psychotropic medication*. Pacific Grove, CA: Brooks/Cole.

Berenbaum, H., & Oltmanns, T. F. (1992). Emotional experience and expression in schizophrenia and depression. *Journal of Abnormal Psychology*, 101: 37–44.

Bland, R. (1998). Understanding grief and guilt as common themes in family response to mental illness: Implications for social work practice. *Australian Social Work*, 51(4): 27–34.

Caplan, R., Perdue, S., Tanquay, P. E., & Fish, B. (1990). Formal thought disorder in childhood-onset schizophrenia and schizotypal personality disorder. *Journal Child Psychological Psychiatry*, 31: 1103–1114.

Carpenter, W. T. (1993). The negative symptom challenge. *Archives of General Psychiatry*, 49: 236–237.

Carpenter, W. T. (1994). The deficit syndrome. *American Journal of Psychiatry*, 151: 327–329.

Carson, R. C., & Sanislow, C. A. (1993). The schizophrenia's. In P. B. Sutker & H. E. Adams (Eds.), *Comprehensive handbook of psychopathology*, pp. 295–333. New York: Plenum Press.

Castle, D. J., & Murray, R. M. (1993). The epidemiology of late-onset schizophrenia. *Schizophrenia Bulletin*, 19: 691–700.

Clark, R. E. (1994). Family costs associated with severe mental illness and substance use: A comparison of families with and without dual disorders. *Hospital and Community Psychiatry*, 45: 808–813.

Cohen, C. I. (1990). Outcome of schizophrenia into later life: An overview. *Gerontologist*, 30: 790–797.

Debowska, G., Grzyuwa, A., Kucharska-Pietura, K. (1998). Schizophrenia. *Comprehensive Psychiatry*, 39(5): 255–260.

Farmer, R. L., & Pandurangi, A. K. (1997). *Diversity in schizophrenia: Toward a richer biosocial understanding for social work practice. Health and Social Work*, 22(2): 109–116.

Fink, M., Bush, G., & Petrides, G. (1995). What is catatonia? *Harvard Mental Health Letter*, 11(8): 8.

Fink, P. J., & Tasman, A. (Eds.). (1992). *Stigma and mental illness*. Washington, DC: American Psychiatric Press.

Fowles, D. C. (1992). Schizophrenia: Diathesis stress revisited. *Annual Review of Psychology*, 43: 303–336.

Gordon, C. T., Frailer, J. A., McKenna, K., Giedd, J., Zametkin, A., Hommer, D., Hong, W., Kaysen, D., Albus, K. E., & Rapoport, J. L. (1994). Child onset schizophrenia: An NIMH study in progress. *Schizophrenia Bulletin*, 20: 697–712.

Gorwood, P., Leboyer, M., & Jay, M. (1995). Gender and age of onset of schizophrenia: Impact of family history. *American Journal of Psychiatry*, 152: 208.

Gottesman, I. I. (1991). *Schizophrenia genesis: The origins of madness*. New York: Freeman.

Grinspoon, I., & J. B. Bakalar. (1990). *Schizophrenia*. Cambridge, MA: Howard College.

Gur, R. E., & Pearlson, G. D. (1993). Neuroimaging in schizophrenia research. *Schizophrenia 1993: Special report*, pp. 163–179. Washington, DC: National Institute of Mental Health, Schizophrenia Research Branch.

Hafner, H., Maurer, K., Fatkenheuer, B., An Der Heiden, W., Riecher-Rossler, A., Behrens, D., & Gattz, W. (1994). The epidemiology of early schizophrenia: Influence of age and gender an onset and early course. *British Journal of Psychiatry*, 164(Suppl.): 29–38.

Harding, C. M., Brooks, G. W., Ashikakga, T., Strauss, J., & Brier, A. (1987). The Vermont longitudinal study of persons with severe mental illness, II; Long-term outcome of subjects who retrospectively met DSM-III criteria for schizophrenia. *American Journal of Psychiatry*, 144: 727–735.

Haslam, J. (1809/1976). *Observations on madness and melancholy*. New York: Arno Press.

Holroyd, S., Robins, P., Finklestein, D., & Lavrisha, M. (1994). Visual hallucinations in patients from an ophthalmology clinic and medical clinic population. *Journal of Nervous and Mental Disorders*, 182: 273–276.

Iacono, W. G., & Beiser, M. (1992). Are males more likely than females to develop schizophrenia? *American Journal of Psychiatry*, 149: 1070–1074.

Jablensky, A. (1989). Epidemiology and cross-cultural aspects of schizophrenia. *Psychiatric Annals*, 19: 516–524.

Jeste, D., & Heaton, S. (1994). How does late-onset compare with early-onset schizophrenia. *Harvard Mental Health Letter*, 10(8) 8–10.

Kallmann, F. J. (1938). *The genetics of schizophrenia*. New York: Augustin.

Kaplan, H. J., & Sadock, B. J. (1998). *Synopsis of psychiatry* (8th ed.). Baltimore, MD: Williams & Wilkins.

Keith, S. J., Regier, D. A., & Rae, D. S. (1991). Schizophrenic disorders. In L. N. Robins & D. A. Reiger (Eds.), *Psychiatric disorders in America: The epidemiologic catchment area study*, pp. 33–52. New York: Free Press.

Kendler, K. S., & Diehl, S. R. (1993). The genetics of schizophrenia: A current genetic-epidemiologic perspective. *Schizophrenia Bulletin*, 19: 261–285.

Kety, S. S., Wender, P. H., & Jacobsen, B. (1994). Mental illness in the biological and adoptive relatives of schizophrenic adoptees. *Archives of General Psychiatry*, 51: 442.

Klausner, J., Sweeney, J., Deck, M., Hass, G., & Kelly, A. B. (1992). Clinical correlates of cerebral ventricular enlargement on schizophrenia. Further evidence for frontal lobe disease. *Journal of Nervous and Mental Disease*, 180: 407–412.

Kraepelin, E. (1919/1971). *Dementia praecox and paraphrenia*. (R. M. Barclay, Trans.). New York: Krieger.

Levinson, D. F., & Mowry, B. J. (1991). Defining the schizophrenic spectrum: Issues for genetic linkage studies. *Schizophrenia Bulletin*, 17: 491–514.

Lewis, M., & Volkmar, F. (1990). *Clinical aspects of child and adolescent development*. Philadelphia: Lea & Febiger.

Maher, B., & Spitzer, M. (1993). Delusions. In C. G. Costello (Ed.), *Symptoms of schizophrenia*, pp. 92–120. New York: John Wiley & Sons.

Manschreck, T. C. (1993). Psychomotor abnormalities. In C. G. Costello (Ed.), *Symptoms of schizophrenia*, pp. 261–290. New York: John Wiley & Sons.

Marley, J. A. (1998). People matter: Client reported interpersonal interaction and its impact on symptoms of schizophrenia. *Social Work*, 43(5): 437–444.

McGuffin, P., Owen, M. J., & Farmer, A. E. (1995). Genetic basis of schizophrenia. *Lancet*, 346: 678.

Morrison, J. (1995). *DSM-IV made easy*. New York: Guilford Press.

Mueser, K. T. (1997). Schizophrenia. In S. M. Turner & M. Hersen (Eds.), *Adult psychopathology and diagnosis* (3rd ed.). New York: John Wiley & Sons.

Mueser, K. T., Bennett, M., & Kushner, M. G. (1995). Epidemiology of substance use disorder among persons with chronic mental illnesses. In A. Lehman & L. Dixon (Eds.), *Double jeopardy: Chronic mental illnesses and substance abuse*, pp. 9–25. Chur, Switzerland: Harwood Academic.

National Foundation for Brain Research. (1992). *The care of disorder of the brain*. Washington, DC: National Foundation for Brain Research.

Nietzel, M. T., Speltz, M. L., McCauley, E. A., & Bernstein, D. A. (1998). *Abnormal psychology*. Boston: Allyn & Bacon.

Pahl, J. J., Swayze, V. W., & Andreasen, N. C. (1990). Diagnostic advances in anatomical and functional brain imaging in schizophrenia. In A. Kales, C. N. Stefanis, & J.

A. Talbott (Eds.), *Recent advances in schizophrenia*, pp. 163–189. New York: Springer-Verlag.

Palfai, T., & Jankiewicz, H. (1991). *Drugs and human behavior*. Dubuque, IA: Wm. C. Brown Publishers.

Potter, W. Z., & Manji, H. K. (1993). Are monoamine metabolites in cerebral spinal fluid worth measuring? *Archives of General Psychiatry*, 50: 653–656.

Remschimdt, H., Schulz, E., Martin, M., Wornke, A., & Trott, G. E. (1994). Childhood onset schizophrenia: History of the concept and recent studies. *Schizophrenia Bulletin*, 20: 727–745.

Rossi-Monti, M. (1998). Whatever happened to delusional perception? *Psychopathology*, 31(5): 225–233.

Sarbin, T., & Mancuso, J. (1980). *Schizophrenia: Medical diagnosis or moral verdict?* Elmsford, NY: Pergamon Press.

Scully, J. H. (1996). *Psychiatry*. Baltimore, MD: Williams & Wilkins.

Shaner, R. (1997). *Psychiatry*. Baltimore, MD: Williams & Wilkins.

Smith, T. E., Hull, J. W., & Clarkin, J. F. (1999). Dimensions of social adjustment in schizophrenia: A factor analysis. *Journal of Nervous and Mental Disease*, 187(1): 55–57.

Stober, G., Franzek, E., Haubitz, I., Pfuhlmann, B., & Beckmann, H. (1998). Gender differences and age of onset of catatonia subtypes of schizophrenia. *Psychopathology*, 31(6): 307–312.

Stromwall, L. K., & Robinson, E. A. R. (1998). When a family member has a schizophrenic disorder: Practice issues across the family life cycle. *American Journal of Orthopsychiatry*, 68(4): 580–589.

Su, Y., Burke, J., O'Neill, F. A., Murphy, B., Nie, L., Kipps, B., Bray, J., Shinkwin, R., Ni Nuallain, M., Maclean, C. J., Walsh, D., Diehl, S. R., & Kendler, K. S. (1993). Exclusion of linkage between schizophrenia and D2 dopamine receptor gene region of chromosome 11q in 112 Irish multiplex families. *Archives of General Psychiatry*, 50: 205–211.

Suddath, R. L., Christison, G., Torrey, E. F., Casanova, M. F., & Weinberger, D. R. (1990). An anatomical abnormality in the brains of monozygotic twins discordant for schizophrenia. *New England Journal of Medicine*, 322: 789–794.

Taubes, T., Galanter, M., Dermatis, H., & Westruch, L. (1998). Crack cocaine and schizophrenia as risk factors for PPD reactivity in the dually diagnosed. *Journal of Addictive Diseases*, 17(3): 63–74.

Thomas, C. L. (1997). *Taber's cyclopedic medical dictionary* (18th ed.). Philadelphia: F. A. Davis.

Tierari, P. (1991). Interaction between genetic vulnerability and family environment: The Finnish adoptive family study of schizophrenia. *Acta Psychiatrica Scandinavica*, 84: 460–465.

Waldinger, R. J. (1990). *Psychiatry for medical students* (2nd ed.). Washington, DC: American Psychiatric Press.

Walker, E., Downey, G., & Cospi, A. (1991). Twin studies of psychopathology: Why do the concordance rates vary? *Schizophrenia Research*, 5: 211–221.

Wallis, C., & Willwerth, J. (1992). Schizophrenia: A new drug brings patients back to life, *Time*, July 7, 53–60.

Wassink, T. H., Flaum, M., Nopoular, P., & Andreasen, N. C. (1999). Prevalence of depressive symptoms early in the course of schizophrenia. *American Journal of Psychiatry*, 156(2): 315–316.

Whaley, A. L. (1998). Cross-cultural perspective on paranoia: A focus on the black American experience. *Psychiatric Quarterly*, 69(4): 325–343.

Wilson, G. T., Nathan, P. E., O'Leary, K. D., & Clark, L. A. (1996). *Abnormal psychology*. Boston: Allyn & Bacon.

Zimmerman, M. (1994). *Interview guide for evaluating DSM-IV psychiatric disorders and the mental status examination*. Philadelphia: Psych Press Products.

MOOD DISORDERS

INTRODUCTION

Depression has been described throughout the ages, and accounts of what are currently referred to as mood disorders can be found in many ancient documents (Kaplan et al., 1994). The DSM-IV (APA, 1994) expanded in size by approximately 50 percent from its predecessor DSM-III-R (APA, 1987), and the space allocated to mood disorders tripled in size. Mood disorders refer to a group of emotional disturbances with serious and persistent difficulty maintaining an even, productive emotional state. The term *affective disorders*, although currently somewhat dated, continues to be used interchangeably to describe these mood conditions. The DSM attempts to define and differentiate between these two closely related concepts (APA, 1994, 2000). The DSM-IV glossary defines *affect* as:

> A pattern of observable behaviors that is the expression of a subjectively experienced feeling state (emotion). Common examples of affect are sadness, elation, and anger. In contrast to mood, which refers to a more pervasive and sustained emotional "climate," affect refers to more fluctuating changes in emotional "weather." (p. 763)

A mood disorder generally involves varying degrees of depression, elation, or irritability. However, the presence of an altered mood is not sufficient to warrant the assessment of a mood disorder. In practice, the social worker may hear the person with a mood disorder say, "I just can't seem to get myself out of bed," or "When I try to remember anything, it's like trying to fight through a thick fog." The person's reduced interest, energy, and motivation begin to adversely affect their interpersonal life. They may have difficulty making normal everyday decisions, lose interest in pleasurable activities, have difficulty sleeping, and show decreased interest in sexual activities.

Negative ideation and low self-esteem characterize the intrapersonal domain; they view themselves as worthless and valueless. Individuals with a mood disorder are generally pessimistic and possess little or no sense of hope for themselves or their future. Often they tend to "forget" about their accomplishments and fixate on present failures, misdeeds, and flaws (Moore & Jefferson, 1996; Rubin, 1997). The person may experience restless thoughts, and complain of somatic ailments, such as constipation, headaches, and menstruation irregularity. If left on their own, they may not bathe or change their clothing for days at a time. As a result, major depressive episodes often lead to interpersonal difficulties such as unemployment, scholastic failure, divorce, and social isolation.

The practitioner must always look for a mood disorder when a client comes in for help. The competency-based assessment underscores the need for a thorough investigation into the client's life and helps the practitioner look beyond the chief complaint. Morrison (1995) notes that the presence of mood disorders accounts for almost half of a typical mental health practice and can be found in all social classes, races, and cultural backgrounds. While mood disorders have many different levels of severity, they can be reduced to a few main principles.

This chapter will pay particular attention to the two major mood disorders, *major depression* (or those individuals who experience only depressive episodes previously referred to as unipolar depression, which is not a DSM term) and *bipolar disorder*, previously known as manic depression (or those individuals who exhibit manic, extreme euphoric or heightened mood, and depressive episodes at the same time, or manic episodes alone). The chapter will also focus on two "minor" mood disorders, **dysthymia** (more chronic in nature) and **cyclothymia** (more fluctuating in nature). These latter two disorders present symptoms less severe than those found in major depressive disorder and bipolar disorder.

The DSM defines mood as "a pervasive and sustained emotion that colors the perception of the world. Common examples of mood include depression, elation, anger, and anxiety" (p. 768). Four types of mood episode are outlined in DSM. They are:

- *Major depressive episode*—At least two weeks of depressed mood accompanied by a characteristic pattern of depressive symptoms

- *Manic episode*—At least one week of exhilarated, heightened, or irritable mood accompanied by a characteristic symptom pattern

- *Mixed episode*—At least one week of a combination of manic and depressive symptoms

- *Hypomanic episode*—At least four days of exhilarated, heightened, or irritable mood that is less extreme than a manic episode (APA, 1994, 2000).

The competency-based assessment helps the practitioner to decipher among the confusing relationships of the aforementioned types of mood episode and the several other types of mood disorders. These mood episodes are not seen as separate disorders. For example, an individual's symptom presentation cannot be legitimately diagnosed as a manic episode but must be considered within the larger context of the mood disorder (Francis et al., 1995).

Individuals usually experience depression as a "downing down" or the lowering of mood. Many of us experience a "bad day" when, for no apparent reason, we feel glum, irritable, grumpy, or "out-of-sorts." However, what is considered clinical depression lasts for more than a day or two versus occasionally feeling "blue." The person who lives with clinical depression will relate that they do not bounce back, and this down feeling consumes their entire life. Nothing seems interesting or fun any more. In this same vein, many of us go through periods feeling elated or "floating on a cloud." These elevated "moods" usually do not linger over an extended period of time. In other words, people bounce back and move on.

Experiences that might normally raise someone's mood, for example, spending a fun evening with a friend, do not seem to have any impact on the person who is depressed. A client once described their depression to one of the authors as, "I just don't enjoy eating food, making love to my wife, sleeping, or spending time with friends anymore. I always feel either sluggish or restless. I can't concentrate, and making the smallest decision tends to paralyze me into inaction. Sometimes it takes me all day just to get out of bed, and then I go out on the couch watching TV until it's time to go back to bed. That's no life." Gelman (1987) aptly dubbed depression as "the common cold of mental illness" (p. 7); unfortunately, unlike a cold, depression does not resolve itself after a few weeks. In summary, differentiating between the experience of "moods" as a normal occurrence versus the depressive disorder includes:

- The depressed mood is not temporary or easily shaken off, and it typically persists for weeks, months, or years.
- The depressive disorder is significant and severe enough to impair important areas of a person's interpersonal functioning.
- Depressed individuals exhibit both physical and behavioral signs and symptoms, such as sleep disturbance, loss of interest in pleasurable pursuits, and changes in appetite.

Francis et al. (1995) identify some problems related to defining who is depressed and how depression is shown. For example:

- Not all clients can accurately describe how they feel.
- Presenting symptoms of depression can vary greatly—one person might sleep too much, whereas another sleeps too little, or one eats too much and another cannot touch food.
- Practitioners may not recognize the impact culture plays on the assessment of depression.
- Mood disorders commonly occur as presenting features in a wide variety of other disorders.
- The terms *affect* and *mood* continue to be used interchangeably, causing some confusion among practitioners. For instance, "Remnants of this designation still are found in the name *schizoaffective disorders* rather than *schizomood disorder*" (Francis et al., 1995, p. 193).

THE MAJOR DEPRESSIVE DISORDERS

Major depressive disorder, most often referred to as "major depression," is characterized by the presence of one (single episode) or more (recurrent) depressive episodes during an individual's life. There are many features in addition to feeling "sad" or "blue." The language of the client may reflect other expressions of depression such as feelings of worthlessness, loss of energy, and a marked loss of ability to experience pleasure (*anhedonia*). While all are important in assessing for depression, the work of Buchwald and Rudick-Davis (1993) suggest that *vegetative features* (that is, bodily symptoms) are critical to the assessment of mood disorders. These often serve as warning signals in the form of changes in sleep patterns, energy levels, or appetite fluctuations (Rubin, 1997).

The core issue in looking for the presence of major depression is whether the features are the primary problem or if they are related to another disorder. This distinction is complicated by the fact that both situations tend to create problems in living for the individual. Almost everyone at some point in his or her life has experienced feeling "depressed." What makes these feelings different is that a setback, for example, losing one's job, is very different from the experience of having major depression. The competency-based assessment recognizes that getting a new job or moving on in life does not necessarily eliminate these feelings of sadness. The practitioner considers major depression when the following features have been present over a *two-week period* of time and represent a change from earlier ways of coping:

- Despondent mood most of the day, nearly every day
- Markedly diminished interest or pleasure in most activities
- Significant changes in weight (either gain or loss)
- Vegetative features such as insomnia (cannot sleep) or hypersomnia (sleeping too much)
- Psychomotor agitation (hand wringing or restless pacing), or retardation (a slowing down in activities such as walking or talking)
- Fatigue and/or loss of energy
- Feeling worthless or excessive guilt
- Inability to concentrate or think
- Recurring thoughts of death, or suicidal ideation
- Significant distress or impairment in social, occupational, or other important areas of interpersonal functioning.

At least one of the features is *either* a depressed mood *or* a loss of interest or a loss of pleasure. Major depression is *not* caused by street drugs, medication, physical illness, or alcohol. In addition, these features are *not* related to the process of normal bereavement.

Prevailing Pattern

There is growing evidence that genetics plays a role in etiology. Major depression appears, in part, to be inherited, and Kaplan et al. (1994) note the prevalence is two to three times higher among first-degree relatives of those who have suffered a major depressive episode than among the general population. Onset can occur at any age, presents itself in a variety of ways, and includes varying degrees of severity (Reid et al., 1997). The first episode usually occurs gradually and becomes more prominent during the individual's mid-20s. The first episode more commonly occurs during adolescence. In rare instances, it may occur in early childhood or during the later stages of life. Typically, the depressive episode lasts anywhere from months to years, after which the individual generally returns to their previous psychosocial functioning. Although some individuals may have only one episode during their life span, the majority of persons go on to have two or more (Moore & Jefferson, 1996; Hagerty et al., 1997).

One might begin to consider major depression as occurring in specific episodes or in cycles; that is, individuals "cycle" down into and then back up from periods of depression. Exceptions do occur, but for the most part this periodic or cycling depressive process is more typically seen in clinical practice (Mendelberg, 1995; Jefferson & Griest, 1994). Thase (1992) suggests individuals who have experienced a major depressive episode have a higher probability that it will reappear, and each new episode carries renewed risks of psychosocial difficulties and suicide. Moore and Jefferson (1996) suggest that up to 25 percent of individuals with major depression experience at least partial relief from its effects. A greater clinical uncertainty is whether an individual will experience new episodes, as there is no way to reliably predict the influence of the biological, psychological, and social factors in a person's life. Research suggests that the chances of a recurrence are, unfortunately, rather high; perhaps as many as 75 percent of persons who have experienced a major depressive disorder will have this happen again (Nietzel et al., 1998).

Complications Associated with Major Depression

Thoughts about *suicide* are almost always present, and often the risk is greatest when the individual begins to recover from their depression. While coming out of their depressive fatigue they may acquire enough energy to carry out a suicide strategy (Thase, 1992; Zisook & Shuchter, 1993). In addition, some may experience panic attacks or other problems such as obsessions or compulsions (refer to Chapter 5) (Schatzberg, 1992; Taylor et al., 1996; Rubin, 1997).

Complications typically center on interpersonal difficulties related to employment, relationships with others, marital discord, and substance abuse (Brown et al., 1995). The practitioner should consider any drug a client is taking when assessing for a mood disorder (Kaplan et al., 1994). The following two cases illustrate different pictures of depression. The first vignette introduces Anita Richards, who has experienced recurring episodes of major depression in contrast to the subsequent case of Alice Jackson, who has experienced her first episode.

The Case of Anita Richards

Anita Richards was admitted to the hospital psychiatric unit after being brought in by the Mobile Crisis Unit (MCU) who responded to her suicide threat made over the telephone. The intake report noted that she threatened to slash her wrists with a razor blade. Anita Richards is a 38-year-old Hispanic divorced mother of four (ages 15, 12, 11, and 9). Ms. Richards had been hospitalized on three previous occasions. According to her medical records, she was treated for "major depressive disorder, recurrent." The following case vignette is a partial account of the practitioner's interview.

The social worker entered Ms. Richards' hospital room and immediately noted her disheveled and unkempt appearance. Ms. Richards' hair was tousled and "wild," and her eyes were puffy and swollen. Ms. Richards related, "I've got lots and lots of problems that just don't seem to go away. My boss fired me six months ago and I haven't been able to find work since. Every time somebody calls him about me, he tells them not to hire me because I was always late to work. Sure I overslept a few times, but that's not enough to ruin my getting another job, is it? Because of that, I can't support my four kids. The oldest two live with their father in another state, and I never see them. My younger two live with my mother, and I'm going to get them back as soon as I can."

I asked Ms. Richards, "What happened to bring you back to the hospital this time?" She began to sob quietly; "I don't know what gets into me. I get into these crying jags and I just can't seem to stop." I asked if Ms. Richards was still taking the antidepressants prescribed during the last hospitalization. She closed her eyes and became silent. I noticed she twisted a tissue in her fingers into shreds. Ms. Richards responded, "I hated being so constipated all the time. I gained 15 pounds and none of my clothes would fit me. But I know I should take those damn pills! After awhile, I just didn't think they helped." When it appeared she had calmed down somewhat, I asked her to tell me what happens when she gets into those "crying jags."

Ms. Richards continued, "I feel really rotten. I hate myself and don't feel I deserve to live. I hate the way I look, hate the way I feel, I hate…[sobbing harder]… I hate…hate…I hate all of this. I just want it all to end." Once again she became quiet. I leaned over and gently suggested to her, "Perhaps you really don't want to end it all." (I remembered thinking at this point, that this was a tenuous moment in the interview. I knew that I could not talk her out of suicide. This would only ignore her feelings. My intent at this point was to suggest other options for living and getting help.) I pointed out, "Deep down inside you want someone to help you find a way to get better. You did reach out and make that phone call to MCU." I asked what she thought about what I had just said.

She nodded her head affirmatively, "I just don't think anything in my life is ever going to get better. Jeez, you have no idea how tired I am of fighting life." She seemed lost in thought and then continued, "I got busted by the cops two days ago for selling crack cocaine. I spent the whole night in jail because I didn't have the money to post bail. I called my mother, but she wouldn't help. Some mother, huh? I used my one phone call to hear her tell me that I got into trouble one too many times. She told me, 'I hope the judge throws the book at you, and you rot in jail for ten years.' Listen, this whole deal wasn't my fault. How was I supposed to know the kid was an undercover 'narc'? He looked like a 12-year-old kid, you know what I mean? If you ask me, he was leading me on just to set me up. I don't use drugs, but I got to eat, don't I?"

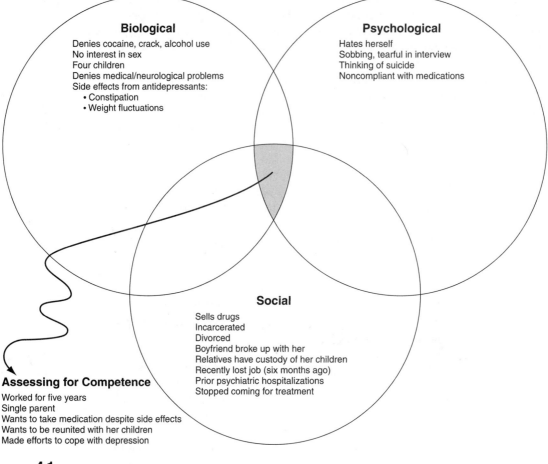

Biological

Denies cocaine, crack, alcohol use
No interest in sex
Four children
Denies medical/neurological problems
Side effects from antidepressants:
  • Constipation
  • Weight fluctuations

Psychological

Hates herself
Sobbing, tearful in interview
Thinking of suicide
Noncompliant with medications

Social

Sells drugs
Incarcerated
Divorced
Boyfriend broke up with her
Relatives have custody of her children
Recently lost job (six months ago)
Prior psychiatric hospitalizations
Stopped coming for treatment

Assessing for Competence

Worked for five years
Single parent
Wants to take medication despite side effects
Wants to be reunited with her children
Made efforts to cope with depression

FIGURE **4-1**

MAJOR DEPRESSION, RECURRENT

The interactions of the biological, psychological, and social variables in Anita Richards' life.

I asked her about her suicidal call to MCU, and she responded, "Well, what do you expect? I don't have a job, I can't ever seem to get caught up, my kids are being raised by my 'ex' and my lousy mother, and, and, I can't eat, can't sleep, can't [sobbing] …"

When she could talk once more, I asked her about what has been happening to her. "Well, it's just like the other times. I can't force myself to eat anything." I asked if she had lost any weight, and she replied, "I think so because my clothes hang on me now, you know sorta baggy." When I asked her about other problems going on, she replied, "I feel down in the dumps all the time. I cry all the time, sleep all the time, and wake up feeling like I never slept at all. I just feel really 'blah.' I'm just tired of life that's all. It's hopeless. I have nothing going for me. I'm a real loser. You know, there's nothing I like about living. I really wanted to wait for the kids to be grown up and independent; then I'd have no more excuse to hold me here." She related this with a wistful half smile and tears streaming down her face.

I asked if she ever had times when she felt different than "down in the dumps." Or more like "up in the clouds" or "really happy and full of energy." She denied experiencing manic or psychotic behavior. Ms. Richards was unable to accurately recount when her last depressive episode occurred. Her hospital chart revealed a history of three previous admissions for major depression, beginning three years ago. Her most recent admission was noted five months earlier.

Our conversation led to a discussion regarding her relationships with others. She related, "I used to have a boyfriend, but he left me stranded. He called me a 'cold, sexless fish.' I just didn't want to have sex, that's all. That's no reason to call me a bunch of nasty names. He's a jerk, that's all."

I asked whether she had any interest in doing things, such as a hobby. She related, "When I was a kid I used to like to read. Now I can't seem to concentrate on what I'm reading, and can't get through two pages before I forget what I read. I guess I don't watch TV for the same reason."

We continued our interview, and I asked her several questions about her past and present medical history. She denied any medical or neurological problems. She denied alcohol or drug use, saying, "I just sell them, I don't use them." (I noted this response and plan to explore this further at a later point in time.) Ms. Richards was subsequently hospitalized for observation.

Assessment Summary

In this case vignette, the social worker needed to decide whether Anita is currently in the midst of experiencing a normal reaction to a series of life events (such as losing her job, being arrested, her boyfriend breaking up with her, her mother refusing to help) or whether they had nothing to do with the onset of her latest depressive episode. The worker may never know causality. A competency-based assessment provides the foundation for the worker to fully explore the client's world as well as to look for Anita's strengths in coping with what she described as a "hopeless situation." It is important to discern normal life events from unfortunate circumstances, especially losses as they are often followed by depressive symptoms (Keller et al., 1992; Scully, 1996). Anita did not provide evidence to the worker that her depression was related to bereavement issues.

Anita Richards' full DSM diagnosis would read as follows:

Axis I	296.33 Major Depressive Episode, Recurrent, Severe, Without Psychotic Features
Axis II	V71.09 (No diagnosis)
	Rule out denial of substance abuse
Axis III	564.0 Constipation
	Weight Loss
Axis IV	Problems related to interaction with the legal system/crime
	Divorced
	Unemployment
	Problems with primary support group
Axis V	GAF = 20 (on admission)

Despite numerous interpersonal difficulties, Anita has shown many strengths in coping with recurring major depression. She has been able to maintain employment for a period of time (five years). Despite the distasteful side effects associated with antidepressant medications, such as constipation and weight fluctuations, Anita realizes the importance of taking them on a regular basis. Finally, she wants to be reunited with her children, who currently reside with her mother and her former husband.

The following vignette recounts the story of Alice Jackson, who experiences her first episode of depression.

The Case of Alice Jackson

Alice Jackson, age 19, gave birth to her second child almost three weeks ago. Since then Alice has been experiencing a "depressed mood" according to her husband, Mark. Mr. Jackson brought his wife into the emergency room because "My wife won't stop crying and I didn't know what else to do."

I was the social worker on duty and introduced myself to Mr. and Mrs. Jackson. It appeared to me that Mr. Jackson was quite upset, and I asked him to have a seat. Mrs. Jackson was having her vital signs taken by a nurse in an examining room nearby. I began the interview by asking him to describe what brought them to the emergency room. Mr. Jackson began to run his hands through his hair and then over his face. He said, "I just don't know what to do with Alice anymore. She's got everything going for her, so I don't know what's the problem. I mean why would she want to hurt herself or not love our new baby?" I asked Mr. Jackson to "go back and tell me something about the incident or circumstances when you felt your wife first began to experience these problems."

"Well, let's see. We were childhood sweethearts and all that, and she never gave any sign of being anything but a 'rock solid' girl. Sure, we married young, I was 19 and she was 17, but most of our friends married young, too. We both got jobs right outta high school. I got a job working at Sweeny's Auto Repair Shop, and Alice got a job as a cashier at K-Mart. Things were going real good for us. We were making good money, rented a nice apartment, and then 'bam,' our first kid's on the way. Hell, we didn't really care, except maybe it was a little too soon, that's all. Well, I'll tell you what, Alice was beside herself with happiness when our baby boy, Ben, was born. She fussed and spoilt him like nobody's business. Of course, she had a little trouble adjusting to staying home with Ben, especially since she had to cut back her hours at K-Mart to part-time, but you never saw a prouder mother."

Mr. Jackson was asked if his wife had ever exhibited any "baby blues" after Ben was born. He stated, "I didn't notice anything unusual, 'cept maybe she was tired more." I asked Mr. Jackson to continue. "Well, let's see here. Everything was going along fine. Ben was growing fat and sassy and was the apple of our eye. We had so much fun showing him off and all. Alice's mother doesn't live too far from us, and she helps out babysitting and stuff every once in awhile, but we try not to trouble her too much 'cause she's got her own problems." When asked to elaborate, Mr. Jackson replied, "Well, I don't like to tell tales outta school you know, but if you think it'll help, I can tell you that Alice's mother had some mental problems in the past. I don't know much about it, but the way I heard it she tried to kill herself a few times using some pills and washing it down with a bottle of liquor. Doesn't that beat all? She stayed in the hospital for some kind of 'depression' or something, but I don't know what it has to do with Alice. You know, come to think of it, Alice's two sisters had something like that, too."

He continued, "Anyhow, back to Alice. When Ben was about six months old we found out that we were gonna have another baby. Alice and I were still glad about another new baby, but we knew it was gonna put a big dent in our lives. We moved into a bigger and more expensive trailer, and I started working more hours at the body shop. Toward the end of her pregnancy, Alice had some problems carrying the baby. She gained a lot of weight and her fingers and toes really got swollen up. She's never been much of a complainer, but she did have lots of aches and pains this time. Then Alice had to quit her job, and let her mom take care of Ben most of the day. Well, just about three weeks ago Alice gives birth to our second son, Josh. We named him after my Dad. Anyhow, once we got home from the hospital, Alice becomes so, I'll call it depressed. She doesn't want to hold the baby or take care of him. She nursed Ben and loved it, but with Josh when she puts him to her breast it's awful. You gotta picture this, here she is nursing the baby and all the while she's crying with great big tears running down her face. It broke my heart to see her like that." He looked sad at this point and continued, "She doesn't want to eat, doesn't take an interest in Ben at all, says she's tired and only wants to go back to bed. I didn't know what to do. She was never like this before. That's the reason I brought her to the hospital. Alice said she didn't deserve to live any more and was gonna do something about it. I think she needs some help, don't you?"

Mr. Jackson related that Alice never used any type of substances, nor did she have any other medical problems. She did not exhibit any psychotic symptoms, nor had she had any manic, mixed, or hypomanic episodes. Alice Jackson was admitted to the psychiatric unit at the hospital for observation.

Assessment Summary

Because Alice had only one major depressive episode and has never exhibited a manic or hypomanic episode, her assessment would be "major depressive disorder, single episode." Alice's single episode in this vignette may have another occurrence either months or years from now. If that were to happen, her assessment would be changed to "major depressive episode, recurrent" as in the case of Anita Richards.

In summary, the practitioner should consider the following differential assessment points to aid in distinguishing between major a single episode of major depression and recurring depression. They are:

• The individual's particular symptoms and whether they are "out of proportion" to the event

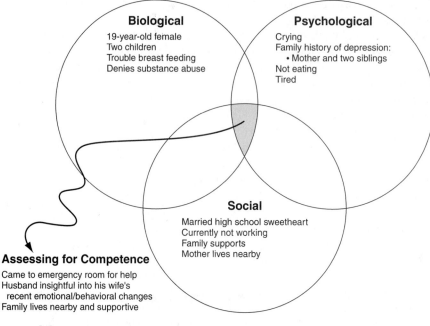

FIGURE 4-2

MAJOR MOOD DISORDER, SINGLE EPISODE, WITH POSTPARTUM ONSET

The interactions of the biological, psychological, and social variables in Alice Jackson's life.

- The duration and intensity of the features of depression
- Whether the individual's mood is "reactive" to changes in life—in other words, whether the individual may "perk up" when something good happens versus those with a depressive episode who are less likely to do so
- The presence of a family history of major depression.

It is important to consider a wide range of other life problems that can be confused with a major depressive disorder (Littrell, 1995). In addition, one determines whether the individual has had episodes of manic-like behaviors, indicating a bipolar disorder or cyclothymia. The competency-based assessment helps the practitioner to carefully examine the multiple influences in a person's life and to distinguish between a depressive episode and a bipolar episode. The competency-based assessment also considers medical conditions that manifest depressive features, such as epilepsy, cerebrovascular diseases, and certain tumors. Other conditions that complicate making an assessment include psychotic disorders commonly associated with depression such as schizophrenia (see Chapter 3), obsessive-compulsive disorder (OCD) (Chapter 5), panic disorder (Chapter 5), and personality disorders (Chapter 9).

Alice Jackson's postpartum depression may confound the practitioner in making this determination because the depressive episode occurs shortly after childbirth and does not occur at any other times (Wisner & Wheeler 1994; Stuart & O'Hara, 1995). The practitioner should pay careful attention to situations of postpartum onset since the likelihood of maternal harm to an infant increases. In Alice's case, her husband Mark reacted quickly to these changes in her behavior. This underscores the importance of collateral contacts.

Schizoaffective disorder can be distinguished from major depression in that it has a defined element of psychosis combined with the presence of a mood disorder lasting more than *two weeks*. The relative absence of fatigue, loss of interest, and insomnia help the practitioner differentiate between depression and generalized anxiety disorder (Taylor et al., 1996). Those individuals with anorexia nervosa (Chapter 5) often exhibit depressive features and the depression occurs around significant weight loss.

The most common emotional change associated with major depression is not the depressed mood per se but rather the *pervasive* loss of interest and pleasure in everyday living (Rubin, 1997). Major depressive episodes are associated with a significant risk of suicide, and individuals suspected of suffering from a mood disorder should routinely be examined for whether they are contemplating suicide.

Alice Jackson's overall diagnosis is as follows:

Axis I	296.23 Major Mood Disorder, Single Episode, with Postpartum Onset
Axis II	V71.09 (No diagnosis)
Axis III	Childbirth
Axis IV	Deferred
Axis V	GAF = 45 (on admission)

BIPOLAR DISORDER

"Individuals suffering from bipolar disorder usually experience periods of depression as well as periods of either extremely elevated mood known as **mania**, or mixed episodes in which mania and depression alternate so rapidly that both are experienced within the same day" (Nietzel et al., 1998, p. 294). The presence of mania or hypomania defines bipolar disorder. Mania is defined as a distinct period during which the predominant mood is either elevated, expansive, or irritable with several associated symptoms such as hyperactivity, pressured speech, racing thoughts, inflated self-esteem, decreased need for sleep, distractibility, and excessive involvement in potentially dangerous activity (Stoudemire, 1994). In addition, the practitioner may observe psychotic symptoms, for example, delusions or perceptual disturbances (hallucinations).

In *mania*, the mood disturbance is severe and causes marked impairment in interpersonal functioning; in a **hypomanic episode**, many of the features found in mania may be present, but the mood disturbance is less severe (APA, 1994, 2000). At times it may difficult to differentiate severe hypomania from mania. Delusions, hallucinations, and disorganization can be seen during manic episodes and are considered *mood congruent*. The important thing to remember is if there are psychotic symptoms or a marked impairment in normal psychosocial functioning. To the extent where hospitalization is needed, the condition has now crossed over an important threshold, that of mania. The term bipolar disorder is a misnomer, since a single manic episode is enough for the practitioner to make the assessment; that is, the individual "swings" to the manic pole (and also to the depressive pole).

How does the practitioner know when the client's "depression" is the result of a major depressive disorder or an aspect of bipolar disorder? For most, this distinction is unclear. In other words, major depressive disorder and bipolar disorder obviously overlap, because the depression shows itself in very similar ways. One might note that while some features are the same, other features are quite different. For example:

- Bipolar disorder occurs almost equally for both men and women (Hamilton, 1989), whereas major depressive disorder is more commonly seen in women (Kessler et al., 1994).
- Bipolar disorder usually starts in adolescence, whereas major depressive disorder appears later in life (Strober et al., 1995).
- Bipolar disorder appears more frequently among higher socioeconomic status groups (Weissman et al., 1991).
- Bipolar disorder is less affected by psychosocial stressors.
- Bipolar disorder has a greater genetic risk component than major depressive disorder (Goodwin & Jamison, 1990).

In bipolar disorder, manic episodes can develop as quickly as within a few hours. However, the more typical pattern is that an episode evolves over a period of a few days. It is not unusual for the individual to go without sleep for several days. Their speech is often rapid, unremitting, and has a "pressured," urgent quality to it. Their judgment tends to be impulsive and poor; for example, they may go on expensive shopping sprees or enter into risky business ventures. Additionally, they experience racing thoughts and become easily distracted. They present with inflated self-esteem (grandiosity), which can take on delusional dimensions including religious, political, financial, or sexual themes. The individual may claim to possess exceptional "powers," for example, believing he or she can change the direction of the wind, or is invincible to harm.

Prevailing Pattern

Despite research, the cause of bipolar disorder remains relatively unclear (Winokur et al., 1993; Strober et al., 1995). What has been studied is the family influence (Goldberg et al., 1995; Werder, 1995), which offers strong evidence of genetic transmission. Although this disorder can be seen in younger children, it is relatively rare for symptoms to emerge after age 40. According to Nietzel et al. (1998), the lifetime risk for bipolar disorder is estimated between 0.4 and 1.6 percent, but there is a higher risk with a family history of major depression or manic symptoms. Children who have one parent affected with bipolar disorder have a 30 percent greater chance of developing a mood disorder sometime in their life. Those with both parents with bipolar disorder have a 50 percent chance of developing a mood disorder (Goldberg et al., 1995).

As noted earlier, bipolar disorder occurs in episodes or cycles. In between, most individuals experience a "normal" (euthymic) interval during which they generally return to their usual state of psychosocial functioning (Soloman et al., 1995; Hirschfeld et al., 1995). A first episode may be either a depressive or a manic one. The majority of persons do not tend to experience a mixed-manic episode initially. There is no way to predict the presenting pattern; subsequent episodes, if they occur, remain variable. It would be highly unlikely for the practitioner to find individuals who alternate between manic and depressive episodes.

Variations of Bipolar Disorder

There are variations in bipolar disorder:

- *Bipolar I*—Refers to severe manic symptoms accompanied by one or more periods of major depression.
- *Bipolar II*—Refers to the same pattern of symptoms, but a major distinction in the degree of severity; typically, the disorder does not lead to psychotic behavior or require hospitalization.

To identify other key variations in this disorder, the practitioner considers two additional aspects. One is rapid cycling, and the other is a seasonal pattern.

- *Rapid cycling* occurs when *four or more* separate bipolar episodes (in any combination) are experienced within a *one-year period* (Altshuler et al., 1995; Calabrese & Wayshville, 1995).
- Those who present a **seasonal affective pattern** tend to experience episodes during a particular time of year, for example, beginning late fall or early winter (Lewy, 1993; Gitlin et al., 1995). The prevalence of seasonal affective disorder is higher in northern than in southern climates due to less sunlight available during the winter months (Allen et al., 1993; Rubin, 1997). The competency-based assessment pays attention to the client's environmental context. Certainly those living and working in the frigid confines of northern climes complain about "winter blues." However, these complaints alone are not severe enough to meet specific guidelines for the bipolar disorder (Barlow & Durand, 1995).

Review of the literature suggests bipolar I has a poorer prognosis than major depressive disorder. Long-term studies suggest that 15 percent of individuals with bipolar I disorder do well, 45 percent experience multiple relapses, 30 percent are in partial remission, and 10 percent are chronically troubled (Hopkins & Gelenberg, 1994; Gitlin et al., 1995).

In distinguishing bipolar disorder from other mood disorders, the single most important differential feature is the sequence of the illness. Up until the 1980s, the term bipolar II was little known (Morrison, 1995). Those individuals assessed as having either bipolar I or bipolar II disorder manifest very similar features. An important distinction between the two is the degree of impairment and discomfort in intrapersonal and interpersonal (and especially occupational) functioning. The following case discussion illustrates the shifts in mood common to those who experience bipolar disorder. Because Carol Bishop's pattern of symptoms does not lead to psychotic behavior nor does she require hospitalization, she can be considered as someone with bipolar II disorder.

The Case of Carol Bishop

I first met 14-year-old Carol when she sometimes stayed in the waiting room while her parents, Frieda and Gerald, came for counseling. I am not sure they really had any hope of saving their 15-year marriage, and I guess, looking back, counseling for them was really just a form of "lip service." It was a way to tell themselves, their child, and their respective families, "we tried." After the Bishops stopped coming, I didn't hear from them for about a year.

I have been affiliated in a private practice group made up of other licensed social workers for more years than I want to acknowledge. Several of us "old timers" wanted to keep our daytime agency jobs, but also branch out into private work. We decided to share office expenses and subsequently put up our respective shingles. Private practice isn't what it used to be; however, it makes a nice departure from working for someone else. While my private practice doesn't generally necessitate checking telephone messages daily, if a client needs to speak with me or has an emergency, the office can always reach me by beeper or cell phone. The other day, coming in for a regularly scheduled office session, I found a message from my former client, Frieda Bishop. Her message asked me to call her, but "nothing urgent."

I called Frieda, and after a few minutes of chitchat and catching up on what had been happening. Frieda shared with me that she and her husband, Gerald, divorced two months ago. He has a girlfriend, and the house is up for sale. Frieda finally got around to telling me the reason for her call. "It's Carol, she has been driving me crazy for the last six or eight months. I mean, I don't want to sound like 'Mommy Dearest' incarnate, but she's really gone off the deep end. Get this, she went to Macy's and charged $3,000 worth of cosmetics and designer purses. Can you imagine how many purses and lipsticks that is? [Silence.]"

"What is she going to do with all that stuff? What could she have been thinking? To top it off, she won't take anything back. How is she going to pay for everything? She earns minimum wage, but nothing is going to help because she just lost her after-school job. I tried to get her boss to rehire her, but he told me Carol hasn't shown up for work in three weeks and he just had to let her go. He also said, 'When Carol did show up for work she was either higher than a kite or deader than a doornail. I don't know what to expect when she comes to work.' He told me he didn't think Carol used drugs, but he couldn't be sure. He said, 'A lot of the customers complained about Carol because sometimes she talked so fast they couldn't understand her or else she looked like she was falling asleep in the middle of a transaction.'"

Frieda continued, "You know, I feel really guilty now, because I've been so wrapped up in my own troubles that I've ignored what's been going on in Carol's life. I always suspected something wasn't quite right, but I guess I just didn't want to deal with it. Is there any chance that I could bring her in and see you sometime soon?"

An appointment was scheduled for the next afternoon. I was left with the impression that Frieda was terribly overwhelmed. I also realized I hadn't gotten in a word edgewise; that in itself was unusual.

When I did see Carol, I was somewhat surprised by the difference I saw in the youngster I had seen only a year ago. Although she looked more mature, she also appeared to be under a great deal of distress. Initially, I saw Frieda and Carol together and gathered relevant family history. Frieda related that her oldest brother, Henry, has been treated for bipolar disorder from the time he was 18. She was uncertain whether one of his daughters had the same kind of problem. Frieda continued, "When Henry was a kid, he'd do all sorts of wacky stuff. You know, in a way it sounds a lot like what Carol has been up to. As I recall, Henry never needed much sleep. He would talk nonstop and did some wild and crazy things. Then, just like somebody turned a switch, all the energy would go out of Henry. You couldn't drag him out of bed because all he wanted to do was sleep. My poor parents had a real hard time with him. They were glad when he joined the Army and moved out."

I spent the remainder of the session with Carol. Currently, she is enrolled in the 11th grade and wants to attend a local community college after she graduates. Carol said her grades could be a lot better and she is only failing a couple of classes. She is an attractive young woman, of average height and slender build. My sense of her was that she was restless. I noticed she tapped her fingers on the arm of the chair, and swung her crossed legs back and forth in a constant motion.

I asked, "Carol, why do you think you are here?" She replied, "I don't know what the problem is because I feel just fine. Maybe the problem is my mother. Now that Daddy is out of the house she has nothing else to occupy her time, so she's putting her nose into my business. She thinks I have a mental problem, but I don't. Just because I don't need as much sleep as she does she gets all bent out of shape. I mean, come on!" I asked her about this, "Carol, were you ever so energetic that instead of sleeping you did household chores or worked throughout the night?" She replied, "Sure. Look, I just feel happy that's all. I don't like wasting my time sleeping, all right? Everybody makes such a big deal out of it. I can sleep when I'm old. Right now I'd rather spend my time on the computer. Did you know they have 24-hour chat lines? I mean you can talk to hundreds of people all night long. It's really cool." I asked her when she stayed up all night on the computer whether she felt tired the next day. "Heck no! Even if I don't sleep a wink I feel really GREAT. Who needs to sleep?"

I asked Carol to describe those times when she felt "really happy." She replied, "It's the best! It's wonderful! It's great! It's terrific! It's like being on top of the world! I love it because I can do anything and everything [laughing]. Did I tell you that someday I'm going to be a famous movie star?" I was very aware of how pressured her speech had become and asked her about this. She related that while she has been told she is a "pretty talkative teenager," she also felt, "I just have a lot to say."

I asked whether there were times in the past months or year when she felt the opposite of being happy. I inquired, "Have you ever felt really sad, tired or cried a lot in a way that is different from the happy feeling you are describing today?" Carol appeared thoughtful for a moment, as if she was thinking about the answer and responded slowly nodding her head, "Yeah, there are some times when I can't lift my head off my pillow or wake up. Sometimes I'm 'on top of the world' and other times, I'm 'down in the dumps.' That's weird huh? For about two months I didn't want to eat and my clothes just hung on me. My mother said I looked 'gaunt.' There were times I couldn't wake up for school or work. I didn't care about anybody or anything. That's all changed now!"

Carol denied using drugs or alcohol. She said she likes to have fun and sometimes "spends too much money." She likes to go out and have a good time with her friends. Carol is currently sexually active with four boys, none of whom know about the others. She admitted she often doesn't use "protection" but "nothing bad has happened, so why bother?"

We set up several appointments for the following week. I referred her to Dr. Beverly Klienaszewski for a medical evaluation to rule out a possible general medical condition such as multiple sclerosis, hyperthyroidism, or AIDS. I also requested a psychiatric consultation with Dr. Dylan Macey to consider medication intervention.

Assessment Summary

It is important to separate a manic episode from schizophrenia. Although difficult, a differential assessment is possible with a few clinical guidelines. Merriment, elation, an infectiousness of mood are more commonly seen in manic episodes than in schizophrenia (Kaplan et al., 1994). The practitioner considers the presenting combination of a manic mood, rapid speech, and hyperactivity to tip the scale in the direction of a manic episode. Individuals who are currently undergoing an acute exacerbation of paranoid schizophrenia are able to sit quietly, whereas individuals who present with acute mania are hyperactive and their conversation takes on a pressured quality (Moore & Jefferson, 1996). Those with catatonic schizophrenia continue to remain self-involved and detached no matter how agitated their behavior, and generally maintain limited interaction with others around them (Marengo et al., 1993; Maher & Spitzer, 1993). By comparison, those individuals experiencing a manic episode (no matter how fragmented their behavior) want to be involved with others.

In Carol's situation, it was her mother who first noticed something unusual. Often, it is a close family member who notices a change in the client's behavior or personality. Carol, on the other hand, had no insight into her behavior and the difficulties that she caused. She explained away her lack of sleep, time spent "chat-

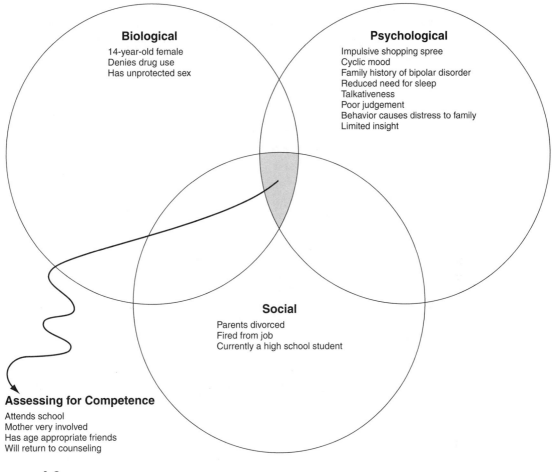

Biological
14-year-old female
Denies drug use
Has unprotected sex

Psychological
Impulsive shopping spree
Cyclic mood
Family history of bipolar disorder
Reduced need for sleep
Talkativeness
Poor judgement
Behavior causes distress to family
Limited insight

Social
Parents divorced
Fired from job
Currently a high school student

Assessing for Competence
Attends school
Mother very involved
Has age appropriate friends
Will return to counseling

FIGURE **4-3**

BIPOLAR II DISORDER, DEPRESSED, MILD

The interactions of the biological, psychological, and social variables in Carol Bishop's life.

ting" 24 hours a day on the computer, incessant talking, and feelings of invincibility as typical teenage behavior. The task before the social worker is to differentiate among a manic episode, a hypomanic episode, mixed episode, major depression, or a cyclothymic disorder.

The practitioner assessed Carol's behavior. At least one manic and one depressive episode characterized her presentation. Carol exhibited bipolar features by cycling "up" into a manic episode, returning to her normal behavior, and then cycling "down" into a depressive episode. As shown in the case vignette, Carol's period of major depression was shown when, for example, she could not get out of bed to go to work. For a short while after, she "bounced back." If nothing else had occurred, the social worker could probably consider only the presence of major depression. However, common to bipolar disorder, especially the first episode, is the unexpected arrival of manic features. At this juncture, the social worker pays particular attention to Carol's shopping spree at Macy's and considers bipolar disorder, the shorthand for all mood disorders that include at least one manic episode. Because of the severity of her behavior, the social worker did not consider the diagnosis of cyclothymia.

Carol Bishop's past history and her typical presentation would make her diagnosis secure:

Axis I	296.89 Bipolar II Disorder, Depressed, Mild
Axis II	V71.09 (No diagnosis)
Axis III	None
Axis IV	None
Axis V	GAF = 70 (highest functioning within the last three months of contact)

The competency-based assessment evaluates Carol's context and social support networks. There are many strengths. Her mother is concerned about her and very involved. Carol has many friends in school and has been able to work, though sporadically. Finally, Carol followed through with the appointment, has a past positive relationship with the social worker (who knows her family history), and is willing to continue treatment.

THE MINOR MOOD DISORDERS

Dysthymia

Dysthymia is characterized by a relatively low-grade, but chronic depression often lasting for years. The term *dysthymia* means "ill humored" and was first introduced in the DSM-III (APA, 1980). It was then known as *depressive personality disorder* or *depressive neurosis*, and the name was subsequently changed to *dysthymic disorder* in the DSM-IV (APA, 1994). The practitioner may encounter individuals with the dysthymic disorder who regard their chronic low mood as "normal." In one of the authors' experiences, their client remarked, "I don't remember a time when I didn't feel depressed."

These individuals usually have chronic symptoms that seem to pervade their entire past and present existence. Dysthymia shares many of the same symptoms of major depressive disorder. However, the symptoms are considered somewhat milder and they remain relatively unchanged over a long period of time (sometimes lasting for 20 or 30 years). Differences between the two disorders appear to be in their levels of *severity* and *chronicity*; dysthymic symptoms are milder but more chronic (Rush, 1993).

Dysthymia is considered when an individual presents with a chronic depressed mood (or irritable mood in children and adolescents) that lasts at least two years or more, is evident more days than not, and during this period does *not* have symptoms severe enough to fit the picture of someone with a major depressive episode. To consider dysthymia, the person must exhibit two of the following:

- Increased or decreased sleep
- Increased or decreased appetite
- Low energy
- Low self-esteem
- Poor concentration or decision-making ability
- Hopelessness.

In addition, the practitioner should rule out a manic, mixed, or hypomanic episode, and cyclothymic disorder.

There has been a great deal of discussion within the professional community about whether dysthymia represents a disorder *sui generis* (unique or singular) or whether it is merely a milder form of major depression. A small percentage of individuals with dysthymia never experience a full depressive episode. However, at some point, a large majority of these individuals do experience a depressive episode. The coexistence of dysthymic disorder and major depression is sometimes referred to as *double depression* (Wells et al., 1992). It may be important for the practitioner to discern this particular patterning of depression, since it is associated with more severe problems in living and a more problematic future outlook (Zisook, 1992).

Prevailing Pattern

Dysthymia typically has an insidious onset beginning in childhood (or adolescent) years. It is less common to find symptoms emerging in adulthood. Those individuals with an onset on or before the age of 21 are characterized as *early onset*, and those after the age of 21 are considered *late onset* (APA, 1994, 2000; APA Taskforce, 1997). The age when a person first begins to experience the symptoms of dysthymia may influence the course and outcome. As an example, Klein et al. (1988, 1995) suggest that individuals with early onset are more likely to develop a major depressive disorder later on in their lives.

A person's mood is characterized as brooding, complaining, sorrowful, gloomy, somber, and nihilistic. Everything seems to be taken very seriously, and life is perceived as a constant struggle bringing little happiness or satisfaction. The biological domain may reflect an assortment of somatic or neuropsychological features, which include fatigue, lack of energy, difficulty thinking, and problems eating and sleeping. The dysthymic disorder is not characterized by episodes but by the perpetual waxing and waning *presence* of symptoms. As a consequence, the individual often feels deficient, unlovable, inferior, and unable to appreciate their value to others. Because of this self-concept, they often experience difficulties in interpersonal domains of their life; for example, marriages and friendships tend to suffer. The combined effects of dysphoria, low sense of self, and poor interpersonal relationships frequently contribute to the individual's vulnerability in using substances and contemplating suicide (Stoudemire, 1994).

There are no universally accepted precipitants for the etiology this disorder, but predisposing factors may include a history of childhood psychiatric illnesses, chronic psychosocial stressors, and a family history of major depressive disorder (Shaner, 1997). The following vignette illustrates dysthymia and how it influences Mario Delucca's life. Note that he did not seek help for the symptoms associated with this disorder but for problems getting along on the job.

The Case of Mario Delucca

Mario Delucca is a 56-year-old married father with three grown daughters. He is a well-respected college professor. Dr. Delucca called my office last week saying he was concerned about how things were going for him at the university. When I saw him, he looked older than his stated age; he carried himself in a stooped and hunched over manner. While he had what I would characterize as the "rumpled, disheveled, absentminded professor look," there was an air about him that made him look depressed and tired. His hair was entirely gray, but it seemed like a haircut was long overdue and his personal appearance could be characterized as sloppy. He could have combed his hair, and he looked like he needed a shave.

He entered my office in a subdued manner and quietly took a seat in the farthest corner possible. I initiated the conversation, "Dr. Delucca, what has been happening that made you decide to come in today?" He replied, "Things are, well, not so good. I know I should have come in to see you before now, but I got caught up in some family stuff. Well, you know, after awhile things just went downhill. I feel embarrassed just having to talk about it." I responded, "Well, you are here now, and that's important."

I commented that he appeared tired. Dr. Delucca stated, "I just don't seem to have very much free time. When I'm not teaching, I'm grading papers, presenting at conferences, or writing. I guess I don't have many opportunities for leisure activities." He smiled sadly and continued, "I know I should have come in sooner but things went alright for awhile, but then about a month or so later everything went back to the way it used to be."

I asked Dr. Delucca to elaborate. "I just feel weary all of the time. I never want to do anything, and I'm having some trouble eating and sleeping, but I can't say I've lost any weight because my clothes still fit me. I saw my doctor last week for a physical, and she wanted to give me a prescription for some sleeping pills, but I told her, 'I'd rather tough it out.' You know, I really can't remember a time when I didn't feel this way. Maybe that's just the way I am or maybe it's my job. I don't know."

We spoke awhile longer, and the following is a summary of our discussion:

- While Dr. Delucca manages to work, he is experiencing problems at the university. According to him, he should have been promoted to full professor status three years ago. However, he admits he does not have the necessary scholarly publications to support his tenure. Dr. Delucca also claims his department chair has been making broad hints that it might be time "to look for another position elsewhere."

- Dr. Delucca's third wife (of five years), Rosemary, recently filed for divorce. He stated, "It's just more evidence that I'm a loser. I cannot seem to do anything right these days."

- Dr. Delucca denies encountering any periods of time when he experienced elated moods or increased energy.

- Dr. Delucca was told by his physician to reduce his stress and salt intake due his hypertension and (mild) congestive heart failure.

- Dr. Delucca denies alcohol or drug use, other than drinking "an occasional beer" on the weekends.

- He experiences recurring depressed moods, which tend to last one to two months at a time; he only experiences a few weeks in between these episodes that he describes as "normal."

- Dr. Delucca denies any psychotic features that include hallucinations, delusions, or bizarre thoughts or ideas.

Assessment Summary

Looking for differences between dysthymia and major depressive disorder can be very complex, because the symptoms are nearly identical. However, while the duration of dysthymia is longer overall, its symptoms are milder. Dr. Delucca's mood symptoms can be described as chronic versus acute or recurring. He has never been without these features for longer than a few weeks at a time, and they are present more days than not. Dr. Delucca describes a poor self-image, fatigue, decreased appetite, and what could be considered a "gloomy outlook" on life.

A normal state of "unhappiness" may, at times, be hard to differentiate from dysthymia. Many times the practitioner will work with individuals who experience reversals in life, life-threatening illness, or other misfortunes in which a state of chronic depression seems understandable. For most, life is not always filled with misfortune, and through careful questioning the practitioner can usually find a period of time where misfortune did not occur. Even if Dr. Delucca experienced a reversal of his own misfortunes, he would still remain "sad and gloomy." Depressive symptoms may occur in individuals with hypochondriasis because they are convinced they have a serious illness, which is considered paramount. However, if depressive symptoms are present, they are almost always transitory. In contrast, individuals with dysthymia will accept the physician's affirmation of well-being, but the depressive symptoms continue (Moore & Jefferson, 1996). In addition, the appearance of any manic episode automatically rules out dysthymia.

Dr. Mario Delucca's overall diagnosis is as follows:

Axis I	300.4 Dysthymic Disorder, Late Onset	
Axis II	V71.09 (No diagnosis)	
Axis III	402.91 Hypertensive Heart Disease with Congestive Heart Failure	
Axis IV	Employment difficulties	
Axis V	GAF = 75 (on initial appointment)	

Learning about Dr. Delucca's intrapersonal and interpersonal functioning provides a more complete clinical picture of what is going on for him as well as identifying competencies within his life that can be later expanded upon in counseling.

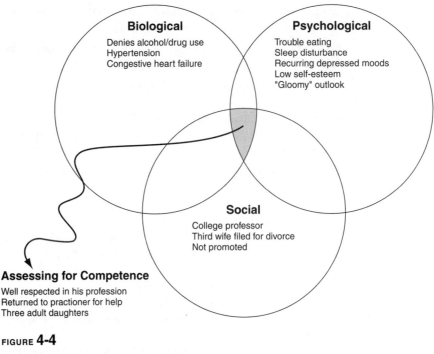

Biological
Denies alcohol/drug use
Hypertension
Congestive heart failure

Psychological
Trouble eating
Sleep disturbance
Recurring depressed moods
Low self-esteem
"Gloomy" outlook

Social
College professor
Third wife filed for divorce
Not promoted

Assessing for Competence
Well respected in his profession
Returned to practioner for help
Three adult daughters

FIGURE **4-4**

DYSTHYMIC DISORDER, LATE ONSET

The interactions of the biological, psychological, and social variables in Mario Delucca's life.

The emphasis shifts to those positive behaviors and events rather than examining "defects." Dr. Delucca's sense of himself is poor, and it would be important to point out the reality of having had a successful career. Additionally, he is well respected in his profession and focuses his concern on ways to achieve tenure and become more productive. Another strength is his willingness to seek professional help.

Cyclothymia

The second minor mood disorder is cyclothymia, which refers to a chronic or cyclic mood disturbance *that lasts at least two years* and has many of the same features found in major depressive episodes. For example, the individual may exhibit low mood, lethargy, despair, problems eating and sleeping, and trouble concentrating (Howland & Thase, 1993). Over a two-year period, individuals are not free of the specific manifestations of cyclothymia for more than two months. Typically, the person regards their chronic low mood as "normal" or the way they have always been. Cyclothymia is considered a milder form of bipolar II disorder; that is, the hypomanic phase alternates with milder depressive phases (Kaplan & Sadock, 1998).

Cyclothymia often begins early in life and represents a risk factor for the eventual development of bipolar I or bipolar II during later stages (APA, 1994, 2000; Scully, 1996; Wilson et al., 1996).

Prevailing Pattern

The symptomatic features of cyclothymia typically alternate in an irregular fashion, lasting for days or weeks. During manic periods an individual may be described as enthusiastic and cheerful, or at times irritable. During the depressive periods these persons may be described as ill humored, peevish, or overly sensitive to slights or criticism. Often fatigue and apathy hamper their efforts, and modest changes in their appetite and sleep are seen with a tendency toward hypersomnia. The following case illustrates the elements of cyclothymia as the client describes her presenting concerns. Carefully look for signs of mood swings found in the bipolar disorder. The interaction of the biological, psychological, and social factors in Ms. Prince's life are not shown since the vignette concentrates on illustrating her prevailing "mood."

The Case of Othello Prince

Ms. Prince made an appointment at a local community family service center and during the intake interview claimed her life has been "just like a roller coaster. Sometimes you go up and sometimes you have to come down." Ms. Prince was assigned to Elaine Pasternak, LCSW, a licensed clinical social worker who described the following at a clinical case staffing:

I had the opportunity to met Ms. Prince, who is a 33-year-old married woman and the mother of a four-year-old son. She is an attractive, African-American woman. Her medical history reveals that she has had diverticulitis of the colon for the past ten years. This condition has responded well to dietary restrictions. Currently, Ms. Prince is employed as a waitress at a local deli. The reason she came to the agency revolves around "mood swings."

Ms. Prince complained that over the past five years these "moods" have become more problematic. Ms. Prince related to me that she generally feels "pretty well," but admitted from time to time she has difficulty eating and sleeping. According to her, "that's because I have so many things to do that I can't stop to eat when I'm involved in one of my projects." She describes herself as "usually upbeat," but goes on to relate, "every few months I experience a few weeks where I really don't enjoy doing much of anything." She continued, "It's just like being on a roller coaster. I don't mean one of those monster things when you go way up and then rush way down. No, it's more like a hill and valley thing." She denies having medical and/or substance-related problems, suicidal ideation, and has never been hospitalized for these "moods."

Assessment Summary

The characteristics of cyclothymia include a hypomanic episode that is similar to a manic episode, except the disturbance is less intense and not severe enough to cause marked impairment in interpersonal functioning. A dysphoric mood described by Ms. Prince was present, but not serious enough to qualify as a bipolar disorder. In contrast to bipolar disorder, cyclothymia is characterized by numerous "up and down" fluctuating periods of hypomanic and depressive features that must exist for at least two years without experiencing a normal range of mood.

Ms. Othello Prince's five axes noted on the DSM would be as follows:

Axis I	301.13 Cyclothymic Disorder
Axis II	V71.09 (No diagnosis)
Axis III	562.10 Diverticulitis of the Colon, Unspecified
Axis IV	Deferred
Axis V	GAF = 75 (on initial appointment)

SUMMARY

A visual summary of the differential course of the mood disorders is presented in Table 4-1.

One complication associated with the mood disorders includes the risk for suicide. No one really knows why people choose to end their lives, or how to predict those who will try. The reasons are complex, and there are many factors to consider (Keck et al., 1996). The competency-based assessment helps to explore those factors that may help identify individuals who have a higher risk for suicide, such as living alone, a recent loss, chronic illness or pain, and a previous history of depression or other suicide attempts (Dantzler & Salzman, 1995). Within the mood disorder cohort, attempted and completed suicide is very common in individuals who experience bipolar I disorder (as well as major depressive disorders) because of the heightened feelings of hopelessness and helplessness (Jamison, 1993; Scully, 1996; Rubin, 1997). Currently, there are 30,000 documented suicides each year in the United States, with the actual number probably much higher (Andreasen & Black, 1995).

Kaplan et al. (1994) suggest the following conditions are important risk factors and warning signs for suicide:

- Previous attempt(s)
- Anxiety, depression, and exhaustion
- Verbalizes suicidal ideation (or more indirectly communicates this by giving possessions away, for example)
- Concern for family being left behind
- Makes plans for death

TABLE **4-1**   A VISUAL SUMMARY OF THE DIFFERENTIAL COURSE
                 OF THE MOOD DISORDERS

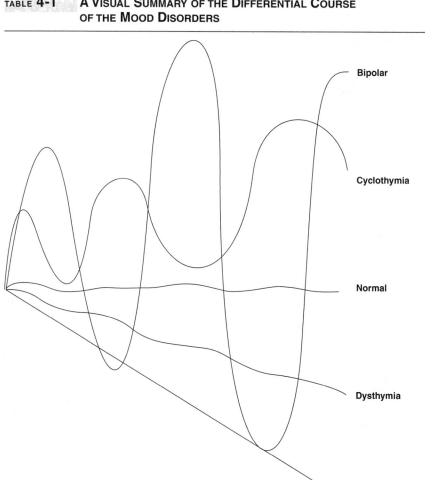

- Has a specific method (and access to the means)
- Family history of suicide.

It is beyond the scope of this book to offer specific guidelines regarding what steps the practitioner should take if a client appears suicidal. However, the following offers key points to consider when the client talks about suicide.

- Take seriously all threats of suicide
- Fully explore reasons for why the person considers suicide
- Minimize opportunities for self-harm
- Involve family and/or friends, when appropriate

- Provide continuing ongoing support
- Revisit the client's issues related to suicide, especially as their depression lifts
- Develop a specific plan between you and the client for continued follow-up care.

PRACTITIONER REFLECTIONS

A variety of biopsychosocial factors are correlated with the onset of depression. The competency-based assessment examines all aspects of the client's life. Competent practice takes into account the varying degrees of depression, euphoria, or irritability found in mood disorders. The following activities are aimed at helping better understand our client's experiences.

Activities

- Persons with a mood disorder present unique challenges for the practitioner. The case of Anita Richards, who struggles with major depression, can evoke many feelings in the practitioner such as incompetence, worry, or anxiety. From the case vignettes presented in this chapter, select a situation reflecting a problem that is a potential struggle for you. Ask a colleague or supervisor to role-play the first minute or two of the interview with you. Take turns assuming the role of the client and the worker, and provide each other with feedback about this experience. Pay attention to the times when your own feelings might potentially get in the way of your therapeutic relationship.

- Can you remember a time in your life when you felt "down" or "depressed"? Write down in as much detail as you can remember what this experience felt like. For example, consider how you felt during this time, what kinds of thoughts you may have had, your level of energy, whether you experienced sleep or any appetite changes, how you related to others who are (or were) important in your life, and what helped you to feel better. Reflect back on the cases presented in this chapter. Consider the interpersonal and/or social obstacles these clients experienced in coping with their mood disorder. Identify the sources of support available to these clients and what you think should be added to be more helpful.

- Think back to the clients you have seen in your own clinical practice who were feeling "sad" or "down in the dumps" but did not qualify for having a mood disorder. What went into making that determination?

- The competency-based assessment determines the influence of contextual events in a person's life and its unique meaning to them. Interview several people who have shared the same kind of stressful life events, for example, divorce, serious illness, or a death of a loved one. During this conversation, inquire how they felt about the *event*. Be aware of how each person assigns different meanings to the same type of event.

REFERENCES

Allen, J. M., Lam, R. W., Remick, R. A., & Sadovnick, A. D. (1993). Depressive symptoms and family history in seasonal and nonseasonal mood disorder. *American Journal of Psychiatry*, 150(3): 443–448.

Altshuler, L. L., Post, R. M., & Leverich, G. S. (1995). Antidepressant induced mania and cycle acceleration: A controversy revisited. *Psychiatry*, 152(8): 1130–1138.

American Psychiatric Association [APA]. (1987). *Diagnostic and statistical manual of mental disorders* (3rd rev. ed.). Washington, DC: APA.

American Psychiatric Association [APA]. (1994). *Diagnostic and statistical manual of mental disorders* (4th ed.). Washington, DC: APA.

American Psychiatric Association [APA]. (2000). *Diagnostic and statistical manual of mental disorders* (4th ed.-TR). Washington, DC: APA.

Andreasen, N. C., & Black, D. W. (1995). *Introductory textbook of psychiatry*. Washington, DC: American Psychiatric Press.

APA Task Force (1997). *The practice of electroconvulsive therapy: Recommendations for treatment, training and privileging* (2nd ed.). Washington, DC: American Psychiatric Press.

Barlow, D. H., & Durand, V. M. (1995). *Abnormal psychology*. Pacific Grove, CA: Brooks/Cole.

Brown, S. A., Inaha, R. K., & Gillin, J. C. (1995). Alcoholism and affective disorder: Clinical course of depressive symptoms. *American Journal of Psychiatry*, 152: 45.

Buchwald, A. M., & Rudick-Davis, D. (1993). The symptoms of major depression. *Journal of Abnormal Psychology*, 102(2): 197–205.

Calabrese, J. R., & Wayshville, M. J. (1995). A medication algorithm for treatment of bipolar rapid cycling? *Journal of Clinical Psychiatry*, 56(Suppl. 3): 11–18.

Dantzler, A., & Salzman, C. (1995). Treatment of bipolar depression, *Psychiatry Services*, 46(3): 229–238.

Francis, A., First, M. B., & Pincus, H. A. (1995). *DSM-IV Guidebook*. Washington, DC: American Psychiatric Press.

Gelman, D. (1987). Depression. *Newsweek*, p. 7, May 4.

Gitlin, M. J., Swendsen, J., Heller, T. L., & Hammen, C. (1995). Relapse and impairment in bipolar disorder, *American Journal of Psychiatry*, 152(11): 1635–1640.

Goldberg, J. F., Harrow, M., & Grossman, L. S. (1995). Course and outcome in bipolar affective disorder: A longitudinal follow-up study, *American Journal of Psychiatry*, 152(3): 379–384.

Hagerty, B. M., Williams, R. A., & Liken, M. (1997). Prodromal symptoms of recurrent major depressive episodes: A qualitative analysis. *American Journal of Orthopsychiatry*, 67(2): 308–314.

Hamilton, M. (1989). Mood disorders: Clinical features. In H. I. Kaplan & B. J. Sadock (Eds.), *Comprehensive textbook of psychiatry (Vol. I)*. Baltimore, MD.: Williams & Wilkins.

Hardy, G. E., Barkham, M., & Shapiro, D. A. (1995). Impact of cluster C personality on outcomes of contrasting brief psychotherapies for depression. *Journal of Consulting Clinical Psychology*, 63(6): 997–1004.

Hirschfeld, R. M. A., Clayton, P., & Cohen, I. (1995). *American psychiatric association practice guideline for treatment of patients with bipolar disorder*. Washington, DC: American Psychiatric Press.

Hopkins, H. S., & Gelenberg, A. J. (1994). Treatment of bipolar disorder: How far have we come? *Psychopharmacology Bulletin*, 30(1): 27–38.

Howland, R. H., & Thase, M. E. (1993). A comprehensive review of cyclothymic disorder. *Journal of Nervous and Mental Disease*, 181: 485.

Jamison, K. R. (1993). *Touched with fire: Manic depressive illness and temperament.* New York: Free Press.

Jefferson, J. W., & Greist, J. H. (1994). Mood disorder. In R. E. Hales, S. C. Yudofsky, & J. A. Talbott (Eds.), *American Psychiatric Press Textbook of Psychiatry* (2nd ed.). Washington, DC: American Psychiatric Press.

Kaplan, H. I., & Sadock, B. J. (1996). *Pocket handbook of clinical psychiatry* (2nd ed.). Baltimore, MD: Williams & Wilkins.

Kaplan, H. I., & Sadock, B. J. (1998). *Synopsis of psychiatry* (8th ed.). Baltimore, MD: Williams & Wilkins.

Kaplan, H. I., Sadock, B. J., & Grebb, J. A. (1994). *Synopsis of psychiatry.* Baltimore, MD: Williams & Wilkins.

Keck, P. E., McElroy, S. L., & Strakowski, S. M. (1996). Factors associated with maintenance antipsychotic treatment of patients with bipolar disorder. *Journal of Clinical Psychiatry*, 57(4): 147–151.

Keller, M. B., Lavori, P. W., Mueller, T. I., Endicott, J., Coryell, W., Hirschfeld, S., & Shea, T. (1992). Time to recovery, chronicity and levels of psychopathology in major depression. A 5-year prospective follow-up of 431 subjects. *Archives of General Psychiatry*, 49: 809–816.

Kessler, R. C., McGongle, K. A., Zhao, S., Nelson, C. B., Hughes, M., Eshelman, S., Wittchen, H., & Kendler, K. S. (1994). Lifetime and 12 month prevalence of DSM-III-R psychiatric disorder in the United States: Results from a national comorbidity survey, *Archives of General Psychiatry*, 51: 442–455.

Klein, D. N., Taylor, E. B., Dickstein, S., & Harding, K. (1988). The early-late onset distinction in DSM-III-dysthymia. *Journal of Affective Disorders*, 14: 25–33.

Klein, D. N., Riso, L. P., & Donaldson, S. K. (1995). Family study of early-onset dysthymia. *Archives of General Psychiatry*, 52: 487.

Lewy, A. J. (1993). Seasonal mood disorder. In D. D. Dunner (Ed.), *Current psychiatric therapy*, pp. 220–225. Philadelphia: W. B. Saunders.

Littrell, J. (1995). Clinical practice guidelines for depression in primary care: What social workers need to know. *Research on Social Work Practice*, 5(2): 131–151.

Maher, B., & Spitzer, M. (1993). Delusions. In C. G. Costello (Ed.), *Symptoms of schizophrenia.* New York: John Wiley & Sons.

Marengo, J., Harrow, M., & Edell, W. S. (1993). Thought disorder. In C. G. Costello (Ed.), *Symptoms of schizophrenia*, pp. 56–91. New York: John Wiley & Sons.

Mendelberg, H. E. (1995). Inpatient treatment of mood disorders. *Psychological reports*, 76(3, pt. 1): 819–824.

Moore, D. P., & Jefferson, J. W. (1996). *Handbook of medical psychiatry.* St. Louis, MO: Mosby-Year Book.

Morrison, J. (1995). *The DSM-IV made easy.* New York: Guilford Press.

Nietzel, M. T., Speltz, M. L., McCauley, E. A., & Bernstein, D. A. (1998). *Abnormal psychology.* Boston: Allyn & Bacon.

Reid, W. H., Balis, G. V., & Sutton, B. J. (1997). *The treatment of psychiatric disorders.* Bristol, PA: Brunner/Mazel.

Rubin, E. H. (1997). Psychopathology. In S. B. Guze (Ed.), (1997) *Adult Psychiatry.* St Louis, MO: Mosby-Year Book.

Rush, J. A. (1993). Mood disorder in DSM-IV. In D. L. Dunner (Ed.), *Current psychiatric therapy*, pp. 189–195. Philadelphia: W. B. Saunders.

Schatzberg, A. F. (1992). Recent developments in the acute somatic treatment of major depression. *Journal of Clinical Psychiatry*, 53(3): 20–25.

Scully, J. H. (1996). *Psychiatry* (3rd ed.). Baltimore, MD: Williams & Wilkins.

Shaner, R. (1997). *Psychiatry*. Baltimore, MD: Williams & Wilkins.

Soloman, D. A., Keitner, G. I., & Miller, I. W. (1995). Course of illness and maintenance treatment for patients with bipolar disorder. *Journal of Clinical Psychiatry*, 56(1): 5–13.

Stoudemire, A. (1994). *Clinical Psychiatry for Medical Students* (2nd ed.). Philadelphia: J. B. Lippincott.

Strober, M., Schmidt-Lackner, S., & Freeman, R. (1995). Recovery and relapse in adolescents with bipolar affective illness: A five-year naturalistic, prospective follow-up. *Journal of American Academy of Child and Adolescent Psychiatry*, 34(6): 724–731.

Stuart, S., & O'Hara, M. W. (1995). Interpersonal psychotherapy for postpartum depression. *Psychotherapy Practice and Research*, 4(1): 18–29.

Taylor, S., Koch, W. J., Woody, S., & McLean, P. (1996). Anxiety sensitivity and depression: How are they related? *Journal of Abnormal Psychology*, 105(3): 474–709.

Thase, M. E. (1992). Long-term treatment of recurrent depressive disorders, *Journal of Clinical Psychiatry*, 53(Suppl. 9): 32–44.

Weissman, M. M., Bruce, M. L., Leaf, P. J., Florio, L., & Holzer, C. (1991). Affective disorders. In L. N. Robins and D. A. Rigier (Eds.), *Psychiatric disorders in America*, pp. 53–80. New York: The Free Press.

Wells, K. B., Burnam, M. A., Rogers, W., Hays, R., & Camp, P. (1992). The course of depression in adult outpatients. *Archives of General Psychiatry*, (9): 788–794.

Werder, S. F. (1995). An update on the diagnosis and treatment of mania in bipolar disorder. *American Family Physician*, 51(5): 1126–1136.

Wilson, G. T., Nathan, P. E., O'Leary, K. D., & Clark, L. A. (1996). *Abnormal psychology*. Boston: Allyn & Bacon.

Winokur, G., Coryell, W., Endicott, J., & Akiskol, H. (1993). Further distinction between manic-depressive illness (bipolar disorder) and primary depressive disorder (unipolar depression). *American Journal of Psychiatry*, 150: 1176–1181.

Wisner, R. L., & Wheeler, S. B. (1994). Prevention of recurrent postpartum major depression. *Hospital and Community Psychiatry*, 45(12): 1191–1196.

Zisook, S. (1992). Treatment of dysthemia and atypical depression. *Journal Clinical Psychiatric Monograph*, 10: 15.

Zisook, S., & Shuchter, S. R. (1993). Uncomplicated bereavement. *Journal of Clinical Psychiatry*, 54: 365.

ANXIETY DISORDERS

INTRODUCTION

Anxiety disorders are considered the most common mental disorders, affecting one in four people in the United States (Kessler et al., 1994; Narrow et al., 1993). Anxiety is regarded as a warning signal that helps alert a person to impending or imminent danger and enables them to deal with the threat of harm. Conversely, fear is a similar warning signal but is markedly different from anxiety. Fear is seen as a response to a definite and/or known hazard, whereas anxiety is a response to an unknown or unspecified threat. The predominant difference between the two is that fear is considered an acute reaction, while anxiety is considered more chronic.

The practitioner considers whether anxiety is a normal response to something going on in a person's life or whether anxiety is excessive. In particular, the competency-based assessment investigates (1) the person's physical resources (physical arousal); (2) cognitive responses and distortions; and (3) coping strategies (Coryell & Winokur, 1991). An anxiety disorder should be considered if the person's response is exaggerated in at least one of the above.

Anxiety is a mood state wherein the person anticipates future danger or misfortune with apprehension. This response causes a markedly negative affect primarily consisting of tension and somatic features (Barlow, 1988). Clients often experience anxiety as a vague feeling of apprehension manifested as worry, unease, or dread. Everyone experiences anxiety from time to time. One might feel a sense of discomfort, "butterflies in the stomach," a rapid heart rate, or "nervous" fidgeting (Barlow & Durand, 1997). Experiencing some anxiety is considered normal, even adaptive. A certain amount of anxiety can motivate a person toward taking appropriate actions that would prevent a "threat." Some anxiety is good, but having too much is not.

Anxiety is a normal reaction to anything that might be threatening to a person's lifestyle, values, self, or loved ones. Some degree of anxiety can appear when things go wrong, and also when things go right or changes in life. To illustrate, When you study and prepare yourself for an exam, that is a good way to reduce anxiety. When you make adequate preparations to be well prepared, you also take steps to avoid the anxiety you would experience if you did not study and failed the psychopathology exam. The anxiety about taking an exam becomes the "early warning system"; that is, it serves as an alert to take anticipatory action, studying hard, and hopefully to pass the course.

For those adversely affected by anxiety, their feelings are characterized by a sense of having no control and being unable to predict challenging life situations. Anxiety becomes problematic when it begins to significantly interfere with the demands of daily living, particularly in social and occupational functioning. A major problem in understanding anxiety is its subjective nature—anxiety can mean many different things to different people. The competency-based assessment begins by distinguishing between what is considered a normal or adaptive response to life stressors. Anxiety rarely occurs in isolation, and other accompanying features such as depression, suicidal ideation, or somatic complaints are commonly noted (Ballenger, 1998; Dunner, 1998; Lecrubier & Ustun, 1998; Overbeek et al., 1998).

The conditions reviewed in this chapter are characterized by anxiety and by behavior calculated to ward it off. Included are those anxiety disorders the social worker commonly encounters in practice: **agoraphobia**, panic disorder with and without agoraphobia, specific and social phobias, obsessive-compulsive disorder, posttraumatic stress disorder (PTSD), generalized anxiety disorder (GAD), and acute stress disorder.

UNDERSTANDING AGORAPHOBIA

Taken from the Greek language, the term *agoraphobia* literally means "fear of the marketplace." When the practitioner begins to explore the presence of anxiety, what will become quite apparent is not the fear of being in a particular place or situation but rather the likelihood of suddenly becoming ill, not being able to escape, or not being able to receive immediate help. The person is afraid of being incapacitated or embarrassed.

There is some research supporting the existence of more than one kind of agoraphobia, but the most common type occurs secondary to panic disorder (Goisman et al., 1995; Harworth et al., 1993). The research notes a small minority of cases where people deny ever having a panic attack, other than the features of dreading "something might happen." In these instances, they are believed to have agoraphobia without the resulting panic component. The majority of what is known comes from studies about agoraphobia with panic disorder (Morrison, 1995). There are not many relevant statistics about agoraphobia without a history of panic, because it is not often seen in clinical practice nor has it garnered the support of empirical research (Turner & Hersen, 1997; Wittchen et al., 1998). In a recent study, Yonkers et al. (1998) identified women as more likely to have panic with agoraphobia than men. In our case presentation of Matilda Suarez, the reader's attention will focus on *agoraphobia without panic*. In the second case, that of Jada Wu, *agoraphobia with panic* will be addressed.

Prevailing Pattern

The age of onset typically occurs during the 20s or 30s, with no difference in age of onset or duration between men and women (Starcevic et al., 1998). Panic attacks are easily identified in adults, but there is some controversy over how often they occur in young children and adolescents (Kearney & Allan, 1995). Although quite rare in young children, panic attacks are more commonly noted in the adolescent years (Ollendick et al., 1994). If left untreated, panic attacks can endure for years with a chronic relapsing course, and remission cannot occur as long as the panic attacks remain. Due to the somatizing that often occurs for those suffering panic attacks, the practitioner may find clients more frequently using the health care system (Rees et al., 1998; Sheikh et al., 1998).

Most of what is known suggests that the avoidance behavior characteristic of persons with agoraphobia is simply one associated feature of severe, unexpected panic attacks. In other words, if someone experiences an unexpected panic attack, they are usually afraid they will experience another one. What the individual wants to do is stay in a place considered safe, in case another episode occurs. There are a number of situations or places the person with agoraphobia generally avoids, such as being in a movie theater, shopping centers, grocery stores, elevators, subways, airplanes, riding in the backseat of a two-door car, driving in tunnels or over bridges, or simply just waiting in line.

In extreme situations of agoraphobia without a history of panic disorder, the individual fears being anywhere except in the safety of their own home; for example, the prospect of walking outside to pick up the morning paper may fill them with debilitating fear. Some people become so incapacitated they refuse to venture out of their home. As illustrated in the following example, this may last for years.

The Case of Matilda Suarez

Matilda Suarez, age 58, has not walked outside of her home for the past 15 years. Her parish priest, Father Michael Krane, referred Ms. Suarez to the Homebuilders' Social Service Agency. He had been quite concerned because of her recent failing health and dwindling financial resources. "Father Michael" recently learned that Ms. Suarez's apartment complex was going to be demolished to make room for a "neighborhood improvement project." A home visit was scheduled by the social worker, and Ms. Suarez was seen the following week.

Ms. Suarez was born in Havana, Cuba, and immigrated to South Florida during the Mariel boatlift during the early 1980s. She has two daughters, aged 22 and 25, both of whom live in the South Florida area. Ms. Suarez divorced her husband almost 20 years ago and has had no further contact with him. It is believed he returned to Cuba.

During our first visit, Ms. Suarez related that she is quite lonely, and, "My daughters have their own lives, but I wish they'd visit me more often. Sometimes I don't see anybody for two or three weeks at a time." The worker asked, "Could you tell me more about this?" Ms. Suarez continued, "Well, did Father Michael tell you I haven't been able to leave my house in 15 years?" (The worker nodded yes.) "I mean I don't even go outside to pick up my morning newspaper. The paperboy knows he has to lean the newspaper right up against my front door or else I don't read the paper that day. I hate to even open up my front door because I'm afraid I'll get an 'attack.' It's no way to live, but what other choice do I have?"

The worker asked Ms. Suarez several other questions. The following is a composite of her responses. Ms. Suarez has no other contact with anyone other than Father Michael, her daughters, and a visiting nurse. She has not left her home in 15 years and completely depends on her girls to "do all my shopping and basic household maintenance." She used to do her own errands, but could not go out alone, at least not without one of the girls accompanying her. Ms. Suarez claimed, "I'm afraid to go out alone." She would get especially nervous if she had to be around a lot of people, because she does not like "closed-in spaces." The last time she went to her doctor's office, she walked out because "the waiting room became too crowded and cramped."

Currently she sees a visiting nurse once or twice a year to follow her medical needs. Ms. Suarez suffers from varicose veins in her lower extremities, which cause her difficulty in walking. She is also monitored for "hot flashes" associated with being postmenopausal. She denied using alcohol or drugs, and denied depression, hallucinations, delusions, or suicidal ideation. Ms. Suarez earns a living as a medical transcriber, and this enables her to do a little work from her home. Ms. Suarez states, "I have no friends in this world that care about me. I'm a prisoner in my own world. My constant companions are these four walls [her arm moving expansively around the room] and my television. Year after year, month after month, day after day nothing ever changes. [She sighs.] I can't leave my house because I don't feel safe, and now the County Reclamation Agency is going to tear my world down. Where can I go from here? Don't they understand I can't walk out of my house? What am I going to do?"

Assessment Summary

Because of her anxiety and fears, Ms. Suarez completely avoids going to different places and being in situations where she does not feel safe. Even with a companion, she still felt unable to leave her home. She was not able to explain to the social worker her exact concerns for what might happen if she left her home. However, Ms. Suarez was able to recognize that she would feel very afraid.

Ms. Suarez's features were too varied for social or specific phobia (Hofmann et al., 1997; Magee et al., 1996). The overriding distinction for assessing agoraphobia is the danger Ms. Suarez perceived from her environment versus social phobia, where the danger would be perceived coming from her relationship with others. She does not have separation anxiety disorder because she does not have a problem being left alone. Her diagnosis would not be posttraumatic stress disorder as she did not claim to experience any traumatic situations, such as being raped. There were no features suggesting obsessive-compulsive disorder, nor did she show evidence of having a panic disorder.

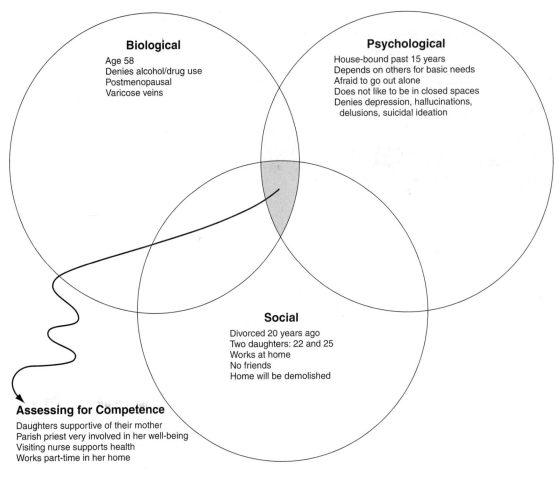

Biological

Age 58
Denies alcohol/drug use
Postmenopausal
Varicose veins

Psychological

House-bound past 15 years
Depends on others for basic needs
Afraid to go out alone
Does not like to be in closed spaces
Denies depression, hallucinations,
   delusions, suicidal ideation

Social

Divorced 20 years ago
Two daughters: 22 and 25
Works at home
No friends
Home will be demolished

Assessing for Competence

Daughters supportive of their mother
Parish priest very involved in her well-being
Visiting nurse supports health
Works part-time in her home

FIGURE **5-1**

AGORAPHOBIA WITHOUT HISTORY OF PANIC DISORDER

The interactions of the biological, psychological, and social variables in Matilda Suarez's life.

Ms. Suarez's diagnosis at this point is as follows:

Axis I	300.22 Agoraphobia Without History of Panic Disorder
Axis II	V71.09 (No diagnosis)
Axis III	454.9 Varicose Veins, Lower Extremities
	627.9 Postmenopausal Disorder
Axis IV	Financial difficulties
	Housing problems
	Lack of friends
Axis V	GAF = 65 (on initial appointment)

Competency-based practice focuses on two specific areas in Ms. Suarez's life. One is her environment, and the other is related to those intrapersonal issues that support her ability to cope with anxiety. There are four key supports in her life: her two daughters, the parish priest, and her visiting nurse. In addition, Ms. Suarez has been able to support herself, though in a limited fashion, working from home as a medical transcriber.

The following is a case example of agoraphobia with panic disorder.

The Case of Jada Wu

Jada Wu, a 27-year-old airline stewardess, was referred to the social worker at the Employee Assistance Program (EAP) two weeks ago. The only information known was what Ms. Wu noted in her pre-intake form, "I suffer from feelings of nervousness." Our first session took place in my office, near the airport concourse where Ms. Wu was employed.

Jada Wu is a very attractive woman of Chinese descent, who appears her stated age of 27. She is of medium height, is slim figured, and wears her long hair in a braid hanging down her back. She had a ready smile and appeared comfortable meeting me for the first time.

To summarize her relevant background history, her parents were originally from Beijing and immigrated to South Florida 25 years ago when Jada was two years old. She remembered growing up in cramped living quarters with several other family members who had also immigrated to the United States around the same time. She related that while there was not a great deal of money for material things, her family always celebrated traditional festivals and holidays, for example, the Chinese New Year, "sweeping of the grave," and mid-autumn festivals. In addition, her family started one of the first Chinese restaurants in their neighborhood. She has fond memories of helping the family business thrive. She described herself as being "social" and gregarious in that she would wait on tables, take orders, and joke with the customers.

Jada was the first woman in her family to complete college. This caused a great deal of controversy among family members, because it seemed like this caused a pull away from family unity. In her family, if a child attempted to act independently, they were labeled as "inconsiderate, ungrateful, and self-indulgent." The family valued "sticking together." In addition, when Jada started her job with the airline, she was the first to work outside of the family business. While she sensed that her parents were tolerant of her accomplishments, Jada offered that there was now a certain degree of tension at family gatherings.

When she settled in her chair, I asked, "Ms. Wu, why do you think you are here?" After a moment's hesitation, she stated, "Please call me Jada." (I nodded yes.) "I guess it's about what's been happening to me lately." She was quiet a few moments and seemed to need a bit of direction. I suggested she talk about what's been happening to her. She continued, "Well, everything was going along just fine until one day I was on a routine flight inbound from Dallas to San Antonio. All of a sudden, I mean really out of the blue [with a nervous laugh] … that sounds like a joke, but it wasn't meant to be. Anyway, I began to feel dizzy. One of other stewardesses sat me down in an empty first-class seat so I wouldn't topple over. I felt nauseous; I was freezing cold; my heart was beating so fast it felt like it was going to pop out of my chest. I felt short of breath, and I thought I was going to die right there on the plane.

"The captain made an overhead announcement asking if there was a physician on board. We didn't have a doctor, but the nicest social worker came forward and offered to help. She took one look at me, and asked lots of medical kinds of questions. For example, was I taking any medication, has this ever happened before, did I have a history of heart disease? I told her I had just passed my annual physical examination, and as a rule was always a very healthy person. I keep my weight down, I'm a vegetarian,…that sort of stuff. The social worker was really nice. She held my hand, and reassured me that what she thought might be happening was something called a 'panic attack.' She said I'd be all right. She suggested I try to breathe into an airsickness bag for about ten minutes. That helped calm me down. Before the social worker left the plane she suggested I seek some counseling and go see my doctor again."

I asked what precipitated this incident. Jada responded, "I can't actually tell you." I began asking a series of questions aimed at exploring whether Jada experienced agoraphobia, "Do any of the following make you feel very fearful, nervous, or anxious? Being away from your home; being in a closed or small room (like an elevator); being on a bridge; in a crowd of people like at a concert hall?" She responded, "Well, yes, I have had problems leaving my house. You know, for the last several months my sister has started to take me grocery shopping, but I didn't make a connection between that and any problems I've been having. Oh, wait a minute! I just remembered, there were a few times when I felt as if I was trapped. I was shopping at the mall. It was really weird, you know. Like I needed to escape and get out of there but I couldn't get anyone to help me. Eventually those feelings went away somehow and I managed to get home myself. Since then, I do most of my shopping on the Internet. Do you know you can even get groceries this way?"

I then asked how long Jada had experienced these panic episodes. Jada replied, "You know, since that first time it happened when I was inbound from Dallas, I've had a lot more. Sometimes they happen every day. They aren't always the same, but they are very terrifying nonetheless. They start suddenly, develop rapidly, and then they are over in 30 or 40 minutes. When you are responsible for several hundred people you have to always be ready to help them, not for it to be the other way around. Several times I had a panic attack when I was walking out of my house to leave for the airport. And twice they happened during a layover stop when the crew went out to dinner together. Of course, I didn't tell them anything was wrong with me. I made up a story that I might be getting a fever, and tried to hide it from them. I'm not sure they bought my story or whether they recognized that I was shaking, breathing hard, and was sweating, but no one said anything. You know, it's not a good thing to have a flight attendant who looks like she's falling apart."

When asked how she was currently doing, she replied, "Well, I'm always worried about when one of these panic attacks are going to occur again. It's like I'm constantly worrying. I have problems leaving my house for work too. It helps if my mother drives me to the airport, but she can't hold my hand forever, can she? I'm thinking about changing my job. The airline offered me a job as a reservation clerk, and I'm seriously thinking about it. I'm too afraid to go through one of these panic attacks while flying. I can hardly think about my life as doing anything differently. Flying is my life, and I will really miss traveling." I asked where she had traveled. With downcast eyes she replied, "Mexico, Japan, China, Thailand, Hong Kong, Bali, Australia, Papua New Guinea, Egypt, Israel, Russia, all throughout Europe and Scandinavia. I guess that's going to be a thing of the past, huh?" I replied, "Not necessarily, but I think we have some work ahead of us."

Assessment Summary

Jada's panic attack was quite typical; it began suddenly, escalated rapidly, and included heart palpitations, shortness of breath and lightheadedness, and nausea. Jada, fearing she was going to die, shows the characteristic fears most people experience during an attack. While a number of general medical conditions can mimic panic attacks, it should be pointed out that Jada recently passed her annual physical examination and was found to be in good health. Making an assessment of specific or social phobia is not likely, because the focus of Jada's anxiety was not directed toward a single situation or to a social situation. Major depressive disorder can accompany panic disorder with or without agoraphobia. However, Jada did not describe a past history of depression.

Understanding Jada's functioning on all levels helps provide a more complete clinical picture as well as identifying her competencies that can be built upon. Based on the competency-based assessment, the practitioner must discern Jada's medical status, intrapersonal factors, and the influence that culture plays in her life. The vignette reveals Jada's insight into her problems interfering with her work, and supportive fellow employees. Her family, while only "tolerant" of Jada moving outside of the family system, were supportive of her independence. When she had fears about going outside, her sister helped with shopping chores. Finally, Jada followed through on the counseling referral and was motivated to work on her problems.

Jada's diagnosis, at this point, would be as follows:

Axis I	300.21 Panic Disorder with Agoraphobia
Axis II	V71.09 (No diagnosis)
Axis III	None
Axis IV	None
Axis V	GAF = 75 (current functioning)

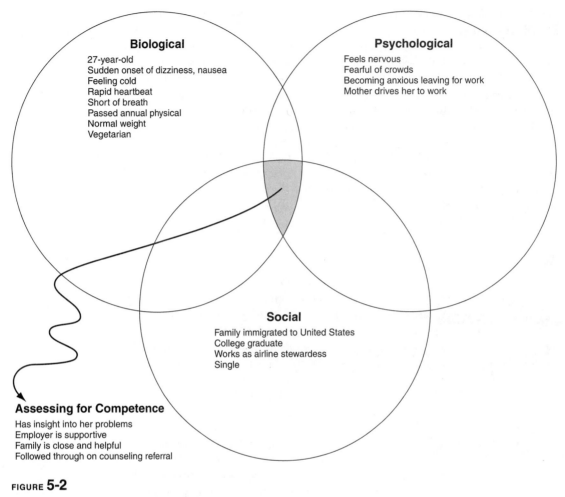

Biological
27-year-old
Sudden onset of dizziness, nausea
Feeling cold
Rapid heartbeat
Short of breath
Passed annual physical
Normal weight
Vegetarian

Psychological
Feels nervous
Fearful of crowds
Becoming anxious leaving for work
Mother drives her to work

Social
Family immigrated to United States
College graduate
Works as airline stewardess
Single

Assessing for Competence
Has insight into her problems
Employer is supportive
Family is close and helpful
Followed through on counseling referral

FIGURE **5-2**

AGORAPHOBIA WITH PANIC DISORDER

The interactions of the biological, psychological, and social variables in Jada Wu's life.

UNDERSTANDING SPECIFIC PHOBIA

The term *phobia* emerged from Phobos, the much-feared Greek deity whose father, Ares, was the god of war. Most of us have the usual kinds of fears that may include ordinary events like going to the doctor or dentist for a checkup. However, these fears do not generally rule our lives to the point where we completely avoid such activities. These fears tend to be considered inconvenient nuisances that we somehow adapt into our lives and try to work around. When a person becomes engulfed in a phobic episode, they usually feel inundated by overwhelming terror that literally obscures almost all other experiences. In its severest form, a phobia becomes extremely incapacitating. Examples of phobic features include profuse sweating, racing heart, a feeling described as choking or smothering, dizziness (or lightheadedness), and trembling, to name a few. Phobias are one of the most commonly seen mental disorders in the United States (Kaplan & Sadock, 1998).

A *specific phobia* is defined as any persistent, unreasonable, and irrational fear of a specific object (dogs or cats, for example), activity (driving), or being in a situation that causes intense distress. Specific phobias markedly interfere with a person's capability to function well, and they result in a compelling desire to avoid the feared object. More than 100 specific phobias have been identified. However, enumerating them seems to add little to understanding this disorder (Moore & Jefferson, 1996).

Specific phobias can occur at any age but seem to peak between the ages of 10 to 13 years (Albino et al., 1996; Strauss & Last, 1993). The best recognized specific phobias include four major types (animal, natural environment, blood-injection/injury, and situational), plus one categorized as "other" type (Antony et al., 1997; Hofmann et al., 1997). Unless the person is truly impaired by these fears and there is marked distress or interference with their usual routines, employment, or other areas of interpersonal functioning, a specific phobia should not be considered. The "other" subtype does not receive very much attention (Antony et al., 1997), but parents of toddlers can recognize the viability of its existence. It originates when the child is startled by a loud noise (fireworks or marching band) or costumed cartoon-type character (familiar or not). The usual scenario includes the child's eagerness to get away from the cause. Even if it is the child's favorite character, for example, "Barney" or "Mickey Mouse," the child becomes quite distressed and fearful. They might cry or even scream in their desire to "get away." Obviously children outgrow their reaction, but until they do parents generally avoid those situations that may be potentially upsetting.

The following vignettes provide a brief picture of each of the four phobias. In general, phobias cause a great deal of intrapersonal and interpersonal distress for people. The competency-based assessment is helpful for understanding each client's unique source of anxiety and stress.

Animal Type

Excessive or unreasonable fear of animals and insects defines *animal phobia* and is considered to be the most common type (Fredrikson et al., 1996). Young children are especially susceptible to animal phobias (Merckelbach et al., 1996). For example:

> Kyle Spector, age eight, was playing in his grandmother's backyard when the dog from next door broke away from his chain restraint and bit Kyle on the arm. The bite did not cause a great deal of damage; in fact, two small Band-Aids adequately covered the small puncture wounds. However, in the ten years since the incident, Kyle will not approach another dog, nor visit his grandmother's home.

Natural Environment Type

Sometimes, children at a very early age develop fears of situations or events occurring in nature. These fears are known as *natural environment phobias* (Unnewehr et al., 1998). For example:

> When Miles Hailey was six years old, he accidentally fell out of his family's fishing boat during a camping trip and almost drowned. Miles states, "My dad put his mouth on top of mine and performed CPR. After I was revived, everybody told me I had stopped breathing and had turned 'blue.' I guess you could say I was dead." Since that incident, Miles refuses to go anywhere near any large body of water. Recently, his parents announced their plans to celebrate their 35th wedding anniversary by taking the family on a cruise to the Caribbean Islands. Miles absolutely refuses to go.

Fear of water, as described in Miles story, is only one of a number of examples that could describe a natural environment type of specific phobia. Other examples include fear of heights, thunderstorms, hurricanes, floods, and tornadoes.

Blood-Injection/Injury Type

Ost (1992) found that those with blood-injection/injury phobias almost always differed in their physiological reaction from individuals with other types of phobias. While it is not known why this difference occurs, this subtype tends to run in families. Interestingly, its prevalence is lower in the elderly, and higher in females and persons with less education (Bienvenu & Eaton, 1998). The following case was recounted to one of the authors.

> Ralph Tyler, a 29-year-old, Hollywood, Florida, policeman came in for a complete medical examination. Mr. Tyler claimed, "I have been in excellent health throughout my entire life, so I don't need any in-depth tests." Mr. Tyler recently moved to the South Florida area and was told he could not get medical insurance with the police department unless he had a medical examination. Under great duress, Mr. Tyler agreed to the exam. However, he canceled six previous appointments.
>
> His physical health was noted as "unremarkable." When he was escorted into the laboratory area he asked, "Can I get you to donate some of your blood? I can't stand the sight of needles. I mean I really freak out. You don't understand, but I can't stand to even think about blood. My mom is the same way. I can't even watch television shows having to do with medicine. Do you know the doctor program *ER*? I can't watch it! Yuk."
>
> After a great deal of reassurance and trying to convince Mr. Tyler that I was "the best drawer of blood" he was ever going to meet, I jokingly told him that I had won many awards for being South Florida's "most painless lab tech." He finally settled his 6'3", 240-pound frame into one of the lab chairs. I laid out a row of tubes, needles, cotton, and alcohol swabs. I tightened the tourniquet on his arm, and began feeling around for a juicy vein. As I made preparations to draw his blood Mr. Tyler weakly said, "I don't feel so good," and then fainted dead away. After he was revived, Mr. Tyler revealed that he always fainted whenever he saw a needle or blood, especially his own. When questioned why he didn't say something to me in

the first place, he admitted, "Look at me. I'm supposed to be this big tough cop and what do I do when I see a little tiny needle. Hey would you tell anybody?"

Situational Type

Persons characterized with situational-type phobia would have difficulty using public transportation, for example, buses, trains, and airplanes, or be in enclosed places, such as elevators. The features sound very similar to panic disorder with agoraphobia, but the key difference is individuals with situational phobia never experience a panic attack outside the context of their phobic object or situation (Barlow & Durand, 1995). The following vignette is an example of a person with a situational-type phobia.

> While called for jury duty several years ago, one of the authors was sitting in the jury box being asked the typical prospective "juror type" questions. I remember I had just finished answering a series of questions when I happened to glance sideways. I noticed a middle-aged women in obvious distress. I leaned over and whispered to her, "Are you alright?" She whispered back, "I have to get out of here. I mean, I really have to get out of here. Can you see an exit door from here?" I told her, "No." "Oh, I knew this was a bad mistake, this always happens to me," she said. I raised my hand, and a very surprised judge asked, "What seems to be the problem?" I suggested that the woman sitting next to me was in need of some immediate attention. The judge quickly took in the situation, and ordered a 15-minute recess. After several minutes of discussion between the woman, the attorneys, and the judge, she was excused from jury duty. As she left the courtroom, she leaned over and said to me, "Thank you so much for helping me out. I always have problems whenever I'm in a place where I can't get out. [Laughing] You should consider yourself lucky that we weren't in an elevator together."

SOCIAL PHOBIA

Social phobia is commonly referred to as "performance anxiety"; that is, the person fears performing publicly because they will be seen as inept, foolish, or inadequate thereby suffering disgrace, humiliation, or embarrassment. While feeling this way, and admitting that their fears are baseless and illogical, they nevertheless become severely anxious and often go to great lengths to avoid being in these situations (Greist, 1995; Jefferson, 1996; Judd, 1994). Several famous stage, screen, and recording artists have stopped performing publicly because they feared they would forget lyrics to a song, their voice would crack, or they would suffer embarrassment in some way. Apparently, it is not the "act" itself that is feared; rather, it is the "doing of the act" and making a mistake in public that exacerbates their fear (Antony et al., 1998). However, if the person performs in private, this may cause little or no anxiety.

Fear of speaking in public is considered the most common (Stein et al., 1995), followed by fear of trembling when writing in public, for example, signing one's name on a charge receipt in front of a salesperson. Other forms of social phobia behavior include worrying about choking on food when eating in a public place or being unable to urinate when others are present (known as bashful bladder). People with this problem often must wait until a stall in a public bathroom becomes available, which can be quite inconvenient depending on the circumstances (Moore & Jefferson, 1996). Many persons with a social phobia avoid being in most social situations. Sometimes they are able to endure their discomfort and go through with the performance situation. Other times they may refuse to perform. In extreme cases, a panic attack may take place. The fear that others will detect their nervousness and see signs of their somatic distress such as trembling hands, blushing (erythrophobia), or nervousness adds to the symptom picture.

Prevailing Pattern

There is some suggestion that lifetime occurrence of social phobias is 10 percent of the general population (Shaner, 1997). However, when only those persons truly incapacitated are considered, the prevalence is probably much lower. Social phobia generally begins during early adolescent years, making its appearance later than specific phobias but earlier than the onset of panic disorder. The rates of phobic disorders in families are less well studied than for many other mental health disorders (Bierut, 1997). However, Fyer and associates (1993) suggest that social phobia can run in families, and first-degree relatives have a significant increased risk of developing this disorder compared with relatives of individuals without social phobia.

When making the competency-based assessment, other common features of social phobia are noted in the interpersonal areas of the person's life; for example, problems can include the inability to sustain employment, suspended educational pursuits, lack of career promotion, and severe social restrictions (Katerndahl & Realini, 1998; Kessler et al., 1998; Schenier et al., 1992).

The Case of Herbert Wilks

I received a referral from a social work colleague who was concerned that a personal friend, Herbert Wilks, was beginning to experience problems whenever he had to speak publicly. The following is a brief description of my first session with Mr. Wilks.

I walked into the waiting room and identified myself to Mr. Wilks. We shook hands and introduced ourselves. I told him, "I like to be called Marilyn," and he said, "I like to be called Herb. My mother is the only one that still calls me Herbert." We made our way down to my office. After a few moments, Herb began to explain the difficulties that brought him in.

"Well, to tell you the truth, this is sort of embarrassing, but I've been having problems for the past four years doing my job," he said. I asked Herb, "What do you do for a living?" He replied, "Well, actually I do several things. To make financial ends meet I drive an 18-wheel tractor-trailer truck on the weekends. In addition, every semester I teach a language arts course at a small community college. But I consider my 'regular job' being a motivational speaker for a large national corporation. I like what I do, don't get me wrong. It's just that during the last year or so I just can't get up and talk in front of a bunch of people. It's the 'kiss of death' for someone like me who teaches, and is a motivational speaker. It's gotten so bad that I may lose both my jobs."

I asked whether he had fears of being watched or embarrassed by others. Herb replied, "Exactly, that's exactly right! I am just so afraid of being humiliated if I give the wrong answer, or if I can't finish my lecture." I asked Herb what happens when this occurs. He continued, "I become sweaty, my hands tremble, sometimes my voice cracks, and a few times I blushed bright red. It's terrible. I worry I'll get tongue-tied, and it's gotten to the point where I broke six speaking engagements that were for really prestigious companies. I just couldn't perform. A few times, I would hide in the men's restroom before I had to present I just didn't want to come out. Several times I literally forced myself to do the presentations. I have to tell you it's just awful. I feel so anxious about it. I know my clients don't get their money's worth. I'm sure they thought I was stupid, and wonder why I'm supposed to be such an expert motivational speaker. I can't stand the humiliation. I have canceled a number of my language arts classes because I just can't teach feeling this way. I'm sure the students love when the class is canceled, but if news of this should ever get back to the dean of the school, my job is 'cooked.' You know, I'll be finished."

I asked him why he thought he had these problems. Herb continued, "You know, I'm a clean and decent fella. I don't use drugs. I don't smoke. I don't drink alcohol. I'm a dedicated family man. My wife is a 'stay-at-home mom.' I might not have mentioned it, but we were childhood sweethearts. I have three great kids, and go to church on Sundays. I have no history of any medical problems. I just don't know how to explain what's going on."

Asked if he experienced other kinds of distress connected to his public speaking, Herb replied, "Yes. I think about this all the time. My wife, Dora, has been giving me a hard time. She tells me to 'snap out of it,' but don't you think I would if I could? I mean, I realize I'm blowing this out of proportion, but what can I do? Do you think you can help me?"

Assessment Summary

Herb had some insight about his fears of public speaking and teaching. He did not provide any indication of experiencing panic attacks, nor did he show evidence of anxiety due to a general medical disorder or substance-induced anxiety disorder. Ultimately, Herb's assessment boils down to the differences among the phobias. Herb manifested none of the features of a specific phobia, agoraphobia, or a personality disorder. Specific and social phobias could be difficult to ascertain from persons who are naturally shy and retiring. Many people worry about or feel uncomfortable when involved in social situations. Unless the person is significantly affected occupationally, socially, or in other interpersonal areas of their lives, they should not be considered as having social phobia. Herb's excessive fears of speaking and teaching certainly "fit" with a diagnosis of social phobia.

Using the competency-based assessment model, the practitioner is more interested in finding out about what is right about Herb than what is wrong. Asking

Herb questions about how he manages to get through the day shifts away from a focus on deficits and toward Herb's own competency. Herb presents himself as a very hardworking, well-educated man. He is married to his childhood sweetheart, and he works very hard at three jobs to keep his family together. He is active in his church community. Another identified strength is his insight and willingness to change and to seek help.

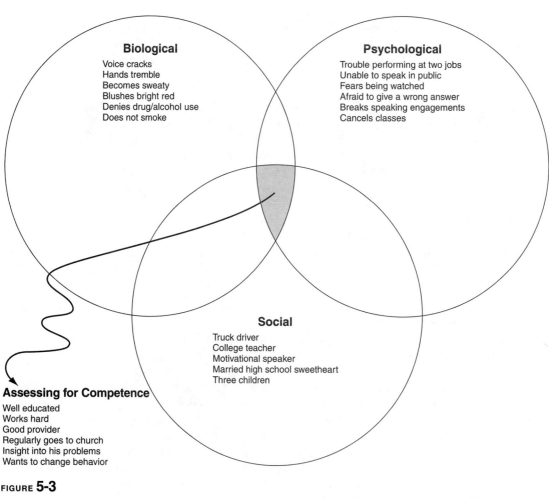

Biological
Voice cracks
Hands tremble
Becomes sweaty
Blushes bright red
Denies drug/alcohol use
Does not smoke

Psychological
Trouble performing at two jobs
Unable to speak in public
Fears being watched
Afraid to give a wrong answer
Breaks speaking engagements
Cancels classes

Social
Truck driver
College teacher
Motivational speaker
Married high school sweetheart
Three children

Assessing for Competence
Well educated
Works hard
Good provider
Regularly goes to church
Insight into his problems
Wants to change behavior

FIGURE **5-3**

SOCIAL PHOBIA

The interactions of the biological, psychological, and social variables in Herb Wilk's life.

Based on the above, Herb Wilk's diagnosis is:

Axis I	300.23 Social Phobia
Axis II	V71.09 (No diagnosis)
Axis III	None
Axis IV	Occupational problems
Axis IV	GAF = 75 (during intake)

OBSESSIVE-COMPULSIVE DISORDER

As children, most of us carefully tip-toed down sidewalks in an effort not to "step on the cracks." If unsuccessful in this game, friends joyously chanted, "Step on a crack, break your mother's back." It is this same process of rituals and superstitions that drives persons with *obsessive-compulsive disorder (OCD)*. While not sure why we avoided "the cracks," we in some way were acting to protect someone against "harm" by performing the ritual. We realize this is a somewhat simplistic example, but most of us can identify with it.

Now imagine you knew people who spent their entire lives trying to avoid stepping on cracks or were driven to counting rituals and so totally afraid that their every impulse would bring disaster to them or their family. It would no longer be considered a game or fun. People who are considered "obsessive" or "compulsive" are the not the same as those who have *obsessions* or perform *compulsions*. The difference between the two is that obsessive or the "ive" and obsession or the "ion" is more than just a word ending. **Obsession** is a personality *style* (with some adaptive features), and "obsessive" represents a mental *disorder* often considered debilitating (Maxmen & Ward, 1995).

Persons with obsessive-compulsive disorder are plagued with unwanted recurrent *obsessions* or *compulsions* (or both). Most have experienced, at some time or another, a temporary obsession; for example, when one cannot seem to get a song lyric or advertising sales pitch out of their mind. It just spins round and round. Have you ever gone out for the evening and worried whether you locked your front door, or turned off the oven? Sound familiar? Often we do not initiate these thoughts. Has anyone ever asked you something so simple as the name of an actress in a movie? You know the answer, but you just cannot immediately give the correct response. The answer is on the "tip of your tongue." It starts to bother you. In fact, it bothers you a lot. You might even stop thinking about everything else while you struggle to remember the name of "that" actress. While you might not recognize it, you are experiencing a mild form of an obsession. The "not knowing" is certainly irritating and bothersome. However, after awhile you either remember the name of the actress or your need to know diminishes. This is considered perfectly normal, because it stops and does not take over your entire life. Not everyone exhibits these features to the extent that someone with obsessive-compulsive disorder does.

Consider the person who has OCD and fights this battle every minute of every hour of every day, day after day for most of their lives. Those with clinical obsessions are different because they suffer recurrent obsessions or compulsions that take over their lives; they are severe enough to be time consuming, cause marked distress, or result in significant impairment in life functioning.

The most common obsession or "the thinking aspect" includes *recurrent thoughts* such as becoming contaminated when shaking hands with others. Other obsessions include *repeated doubts*, for example, when a person thinks they failed to lock the front door. Obsessions can also include *ideas* in which the person "injures" someone while driving an automobile; for example, a bump in the road translates into running over a body even though it never really occurred. Obsessions can also include *impulses* in which the person must have "things" aligned in a particular order, for example, pictures on the wall, fringes on a rug, or articles on a desk. Obsessions can also include the fear of shouting obscenities or insults, and anti-religious or sexual thoughts (Foa et al., 1995). The obsessions are automatic because they come and go on their own accord. Although the person obsesses and may try to resist, ultimately they are unable to stop them from occurring.

Most types of OCD fall into the following five somewhat interrelated categories:

- *Aggression*, *morality*, *sinner*, or *religious doubters* fear terrible things will happen if they do not do everything perfectly.
- "*Washers*" fear contamination, usually of dirt or germs, and usually they clean in lieu of something bad happening.
- "*Hoarders*" cannot throw anything away because if they do something terrible will happen to them or to those they care about.
- "*Checkers*," "*counters*," and "*arrangers*" are generally ruled by magical thinking and superstitions that help fuel their strict need for orderliness and symmetry.
- *Sex* is seen as "indecent" or lewd acts.

Compulsions are "the doing." They are *repetitive behaviors*, such as hand washing or checking. They may also include physical or mental acts, such as praying, counting objects a precise number of times, or silently repeating words. The goal is to prevent or reduce anxiety or distress, not to provide the person with pleasure or gratification while performing the act. The lack of pleasure associated with compulsive behavior and the fact that it is performed in response to obsessional thoughts help differentiate OCD from other factors thought to be compulsive in nature, for example, gambling and/or substance abuse (Nietzel et al., 1998).

Compulsions may be manifested in a variety of ways; that is, the person may feel compelled to count, to touch, to check, to buy, to wash, to hoard (items like newspapers, mail, or string), and to have everything lined up in perfect symmetrical order (de Silva & Rachman, 1992; Jones & Menzies, 1998). Some compulsions are relatively simple, such as speaking or thinking a word or phrase to protect against an obsessive thought. Other times, compulsions are exceedingly elaborate, such as washing in a certain way, dressing in specific clothes, or placing items around the room in exact and complex patterns. These tasks may often take many hours to perform, and these rituals can be highly debilitating. Persons with a contamination obsession and its responding washing compulsion might in fact wash their hands 200 times a day. Hand washing, as shown in the case of Maddy Yarborough, had been known to continue even when her skin was rubbed raw.

If the person manages to resist performing a compulsion (even for a short time), they experience a great deal of anxiety that is relieved by "giving in" to the compulsion. Unfortunately, this becomes a never-ending revolving door consisting of obsessions/compulsions that force their way into the person's mind. The process becomes one of thinking = doing = action = relief = thinking = doing = action = relief (on and on and on). The individual experiences extreme distress, especially when these obsessions and compulsions interfere with their normal routine, occupation, and other interpersonal activities (Black et al., 1998).

Generally, the irrational aspect of the obsession is recognized by the person as they attempt to quell or suppress these intrusive and tormenting thoughts. In most cases, they recognize their obsessions as a product of their own mind and not externally imposed. It is an important distinction, in that persons with delusions do not recognize the irrationality of their thoughts and see them as being externally imposed.

Prevailing Pattern

Henin and Kendall (1997) point out that the disorder can occur in some rare cases as early as two years old, but the norm is closer to adolescence. Among adolescents, it occurs more often in boys. The mean age is approximately 20 years old, although men seem to have a slightly earlier onset.

The 1981 Epidemiologic Catchment Area (ECA) study conducted a five-center investigation into prevalence rates of a variety of psychiatric disorders in the United States (Robins & Regier, 1991). One of their most surprising findings was that the lifetime prevalence rate for obsessive-compulsive disorder ranged between 1.9 and 3.3 percent across the general population . Eighteen years later, Nestadt and associates (1998) followed up on more than half (1,920) of the original (3,481) study participants. They found that prevalence rates remained consistent, but the disorder now appeared in elderly women, 65 years of age and older. A recent study conducted by Riddle (1998) found most individuals experienced OCD before they were 18 years old.

According to Bebbington (1998), OCD causes considerable distress to those who suffer from it. They can also be affected by other medical conditions and/or mental disorders, which include body dysmorphic disorder (Phillips et al., 1998); depression (Jones & Menzies, 1998); substance abuse (Rothenberg, 1998); eating disorders (Aragona & Vella, 1998; Davis et al., 1998); bipolar disorder (Strakowski et al., 1998); personality disorders (Bejerot et al., 1998); anxiety disorders (Goisman et al., 1998; Hunt & Andrews, 1998); and Tourette's disorder (Leekman & Perner, 1994; Shapiro & Shapiro, 1992).

The Case of Maddy Yarborough

I had a message to return the call of Nelson Roberts, M.D., a board-certified dermatologist who often referred clients to me. Our telephone conversation follows:

"Hi Dr. Roberts, I got the message that you called."

"Hey, I'm really glad you called me back so quickly. The reason for my call is I have a very interesting patient I would like to refer to you. Your social work expertise is always right on target. Her name is Maddy Yarborough. She's a 22-year-old woman, who is a single parent and mother of two small children. I first saw her about a month ago for a severe case of excoriation (denuding the skin), which was complicated by a superficial infection. She had come in to see me complaining that her hands, knuckles, and elbows were raw and bleeding. Apparently, this young woman has been washing,…no I take that back, she wasn't washing, she was scouring her hands and arms with surgical soap and scrub brushes, sometimes more than 100 times a day. Maddy told me that she sometimes spends six hours a day washing. She's afraid of being contaminated by an antibiotic-resistant abhorrent 'skin eating bacteria' she'd heard about on television."

Dr. Roberts went on, "I treated her with a course of topical antiseptic ointment for a period of ten days, but that didn't really help. I saw her back in the office after that, and she had even more inflammation, with an early cellulitis. I started her on oral antibiotics and saw her back in the office about a week later, only to find a persistent and progressive cellulitis. I realized that if I didn't get her to stop washing her hands so excessively, she would continue to get even worse. So at that point, I applied an occlusive dressing to both of her hands. Finally, I saw signs of significant improvement by the next visit. Now she's returning to me once more with the same symptoms. That's the reason for my call to you. I don't think that medication alone is going to make a significant difference. I hope you can help her. She's going to need more assistance than I can provide."

I met with Maddy a few days later. She appeared to be in obvious distress about something. She blurted out, "I can't remember if I locked the front door of my house, and my two dogs are going to get out and run away." I asked if she ever had problems with locking her front door before. She answered, "Well, I haven't left the door unlocked yet, but I know I did this time. I can't stop worrying about it until I get home and can check on it." I asked her, "How does it feel when you have these worries?" She replied, "Oh, I can't stop thinking about getting diseases from people. That's why I wear a surgical mask and gloves all the time. That's why I wash my hands all the time, too. I can't stop worrying about germs. I know all about how antibiotics can't treat infections anymore because the germs are mutating so fast that everything is becoming resistant to bacteria. Pretty soon we are going have a plague on our hands, like the one that caused millions of deaths during the Middle Ages."

Maddy leaned over and began to straighten up some books lying on top of my desk, and moved on to tidying up my pencils and errant social work journals. Our eyes met, and she smiled sheepishly. "Sorry. I'm always doing that and I don't even realize it. My mom is always telling me our kitchen floor is cleaner than a hospital operating room." I asked her to tell me more about that. "Oh, ever since I was what, 15 or 16, I've been a cleaning nut. I just can't help it. I don't like it when anything is out of place. I guess I get carried away because I don't like to throw anything away. My mother is constantly nagging me to throw away my stacks of newspapers. She tells me they are causing a fire hazard in the house, but I just can't seem to throw them away."

I asked Maddy a series of questions to explore the difficulties she has been experiencing:

- What does she do to get rid of these thoughts in order to put them out of her mind?

- Does she try to ignore these thoughts?

- Are these her own thoughts, or does she believe they are put into her head by someone or something outside of herself?

- Does she ever worry about anything else?

Continuing our session, I asked if she was employed. Maddy replied, "I used to work as an aide at a nursing home, but that job only lasted a week. I guess because my hand washing and the scabs on my arms freaked out the administrator. I guess she was afraid I'd pass something dangerous onto the patients. Actually, I was the one afraid. I worried I'd get something from them, you know, changing bedpans and stuff like that. Man, I did not like that job at all [accentuating her tone of voice]." I asked whether her hand washing was a ritual that she always had to do in a particular order. I also explored what happened if the order of "washing" was changed. Would she have to start all over again? Maddy answered, "Why yes, that's exactly right. How did you know that?"

After a bit more discussion, I asked again about her employment status. She replied, "I once worked as a salesperson, but the manager wouldn't let me wear gloves when I handled money. The stupid manager told me [mimicking a singsong voice] 'Maddy, you spend entirely too much time rearranging the money drawer and all the clothes on display. You are supposed to sell clothes, not fuss over neatness.' After that, I looked for jobs that I didn't have to have direct public contact. The only one I've found so far is telemarketing. It meets all my needs, and I don't have to put up with anybody telling me what to do or when to do it. Hey, I'm not getting rich, but it's putting food on my table.

"I don't have much time or money to party with my friends. I'm really lucky that my best friend from high school, Melissa, still hangs out with me. Sometimes Melissa is a lot like my mother. She's constantly nagging me not to be so clean. Don't get me wrong. I think I'm a nice person, but people sometimes see me as strange. I used to have a boyfriend, but he got fed up when I spent more than half our date in the bathroom washing my hands."

I asked, "What do you think might happen if you didn't wash your hands?" Maddy replied, "Well, first of all something bad might happen to him. You see he didn't understand that if I didn't wash my hands I couldn't protect him. I know it probably sounds crazy to you, and in a way it sounds crazy to me, but I get so unstrung if I don't wash. Hey, like who am I hurting, huh?"

I asked if there were other areas in her life that caused her difficulties and what effect they had on her. She replied, "Did I tell you both of my babies were potty trained before they were a year old? I couldn't stand changing dirty diapers. I'm glad I live with my mother, because she took care of that job. Yuk! I had a hard time holding or touching my babies because if they didn't go through what my Mom called 'the cleansing ritual' I wouldn't hold or touch them. They were dirty, you know."

I asked if she knew why she felt compelled to wash her hands. Maddy looked pensive for a moment and answered, "I know it sounds really strange, but a part of me just has to wash all the time; otherwise, the pressure just builds up inside me until I *have to wash*. I wash I feel better, but it only lasts for a little while. Then the thoughts start up again, and well, you know, I end up at Dr. Roberts office."

Maddy denied depression, suicidal ideation, and eating or sleeping problems.

Assessment Summary

In Maddy's situation, she experienced some short-lived relief from obsessive tension but found no pleasure or gratification from the hand washing ritual itself. She recognized her obsessive thoughts as somewhat irrational and senseless, in contrast to most delusional thoughts found in persons with schizophrenia. For Maddy, her rigidity around washing seemed quite reasonable to her. While the terms obsessive-compulsive disorder and obsessive-compulsive personality disorder are similar,

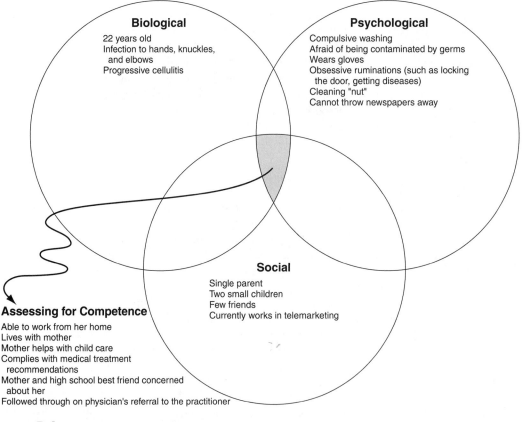

FIGURE 5-4

OBSESSIVE-COMPULSIVE DISORDER

The interactions of the biological, psychological, and social variables in Maddy Yarborough's life.

there are several notable distinctions between them. Persons with obsessive-compulsive personality disorder (refer to Chapter 9 for a more detailed discussion) rigorously defend following rules and regulations. Their rigid compulsive perfectionism gets in their way; things have to be done so correctly that they rarely get tasks completed to their total satisfaction. Although there once may have been a degree of perfectionism that was adaptive or encouraged by parents or teachers, the pattern now is self-defeating (Antony et al., 1998).

The person with obsessive-compulsive personality disorder shows behaviors that are punctual, precise, dependable, and conscientious. At the same time, their behavior often wears friendships thin because of the compulsive rigidity. In contrast, Maddy never attempted to justify her behavior, nor did she adhere to the rigidity that influences those with obsessive-compulsive personality disorders. The likelihood that Maddy has social or specific phobias must be considered because of her (almost phobic) concern about contamination. However, major differences occur with those having social phobias around humiliation, or specific phobias around avoiding particular things. This does not hold true in Maddy's situation.

The practitioner's struggle is how to shift the lens away from looking at Maddy's pathology to looking beyond her internal processes. The competency-based assessment considers all of the various environmental influences in Maddy's life. Despite what could be a potentially debilitating condition, she is coping relatively well. Maddy followed through on the physician's referral, and she complies with medical treatment recommendations. Similarly, she works cooperatively with the social worker. There are several supports to be found within her family system in that she lives with her mother, who is very supportive. Maddy found gainful employment working from home doing telemarketing, as a way to cope with her fear of germs in the workplace.

Maddy's five-axis diagnosis is as follows:

Axis I	300.3 Obsessive-Compulsive Disorder
Axis II	V71.09 (No diagnosis)
Axis III	682.9 Cellulitis
Axis IV	None
Axis V	GAF = 70 (at intake)

POSTTRAUMATIC STRESS DISORDER

The major reference points for *posttraumatic stress disorder* (*PTSD*) include the reaction to catastrophic events, such as witnessing a homicide (Miller, 1999); traffic accidents (Frommberger et al., 1998; Sprang & McNeil, 1998); combat (Beckham et al., 1998; Bremmer et al., 1996; Crowson et al., 1998; Dahl et al., 1998; Husain et al., 1998; Keane, 1998; Marshall et al., 1998; Lee et al., 1995; Schlenger et al., 1999); natural disasters (Wasserstein & La Greca, 1998); victimization (Acierno et al., 1999; Darves-Bornoz et al., 1998; Falk et al., 1997; Foa et al., 1991;

Kilpatrick et al., 1998; Schaaf & McCanne, 1998); holocaust survivors/families (Baranowsky et al., 1998; Yehuda et al., 1998); self-harming behavior (Chu, 1999); domestic violence (Kilpatrick, & Williams, 1998; Miller, 1999); and HIV (Howsepian, 1998; Kelly et al., 1998). PTSD is a specific set of symptoms developing after an individual experiences an "extreme traumatic stressor" (Barlow, 1988). The person reacts to the trauma in several different ways—namely, with unmitigated fear, feeling helpless, reliving the event, and/or trying to avoid being reminded of it (APA, 2000).

The development of symptoms subsequent to the event is the hallmark of PTSD. The features include exposure to some form of extreme trauma, the intrusive recollection and reexperiencing of the trauma, avoidance of the trauma, numbing of general responsiveness, hyper-arousal or hyper-vigilance, changes in aggression, and experiencing persistent symptoms, distress, and impairment in most areas of the person's life.

The competency-based assessment takes into account each person's individualized response to overwhelming stress. Some people can simply walk away from a terrible automobile accident in which they have been pried out with the "jaws of life." They never give the incident another thought other than the details about getting their car replaced. Others reexperience the automobile accident in their dreams and waking thoughts (daydreaming), endure a numbing responsiveness, and evade or shun everything that reminds them of the accident. Their life may become centered exclusively on the traumatic event, and accompanied by somatic complaints and chronic anxiety to the extent that difficulties arise in interpersonal functioning.

Those suffering from PTSD may not make the connection between feeling depressed and/or anxious, abusing substances, cognitive difficulties (memory problems or poor concentration), domestic violence, or marital problems and the traumatic event. The practitioner must incorporate into the competency-based assessment specific questions about either a traumatic event or a series of traumatic events experienced over time (King et al., 1999).

For PTSD to occur, symptoms must last for *more than one month* and significantly affect important interpersonal areas of the person's life such as family interaction and employment. The competency-based assessment should consider coping and adaptation to stressful life events. When there is a history of physical battering or child sexual abuse, the pain from the abusive experience may also later appear in adulthood as borderline personality disorder (Gunderson & Sabo, 1993; Weaver & Clum, 1993); addictive disorders (Brady et al., 1998; Brown et al., 1998; Dansky et al., 1998; Ruzek et al., 1998; Whitfield, 1998); severe mental illness (Bremmer et al., 1993; Mueser et al., 1998); depression (Shalev et al., 1998); or dissociative identity disorder (Brier & Runtz, 1991; Brier, 1997; Pelcovitz et al., 1994; Rodriguez et al., 1997).

Rodriguez and associates (1997) found 87 percent of women who had a history of sexual abuse history met the guidelines for PTSD, and 98 percent experienced PTSD at some point in their life since the abuse occurred. Although sexualized behaviors are more common among younger sexually abused children, they often reemerge later in life, particularly during the adolescent years and in the guise of acting out—sexual aggression, prostitution, runaway behavior, and victimization of others (Cauffman et al., 1998; Da Costa et al., 1992; Jumper, 1995; Kendall-Tackett et al., 1993; Zide & Cherry, 1992).

Prevailing Pattern

Interest in returning war veterans helped focus clinical research efforts on trauma leading to the emergence of the posttraumatic stress disorder diagnosis (King et al., 1999). Historically, social workers have recognized the impact of stressful life events and the challenges they place on a client's life (Germain & Gitterman, 1980; Maluccio, 1981). Longitudinal studies suggest PTSD can become a chronic mental health problem, often persisting for decades and sometimes lasting a lifetime (Fletcher, 1996). The relationship between gender and posttraumatic stress disorder suggests women tend to be more vulnerable to traumatic events than men (Berberich, 1998; Saxe & Wolfe, 1999).

The competency-based assessment explores the individual's multiple environmental interactions. Posttraumatic stress disorder can have long-range effects on "survivors," their families, significant others, and society as a whole (Figley, 1983). The plight of war veterans and the after–effects of their experience have suggested that certain types of war events are empirically connected with long-term dysfunction.

Often those exposed to a traumatic event may not exhibit PTSD features until months or years afterward as presented in the following case of Buddy Jackson. PTSD can occur at any time and to anyone. Prevalence rates are somewhere between 5 to 10 percent of adults in the United States (Kessler et al., 1996). The prevalence rates for those with a few symptoms would be obviously much higher (Shader, 1994). Often situations closely resembling the original traumatic event may trigger the onset of PTSD, as we will see in the following case.

The Case of Buddy Jackson

"I just don't know where to begin. I mean everything in our lives has been turned upside down. I'm at a loss of where to go from here," said a tearful Mrs. Jackson. I asked her to start at the beginning so I could understand what happened to bring her to my office.

"I guess I should start by telling you something about Buddy and me. We met in 1945, at the USO. I don't imagine you know what I'm talking about, because you seem much too young. But there were literally hundreds of these service 'clubs' in the States and around the world during the war. Servicemen went there for food, dancing, and you know, 'R & R.' I attended the club in 'Philly,' where I lived. My cousin Wynne and I went at least once a month. You know it's kinda funny, but I remember the night I met Buddy as if it were yesterday. I saw him from across the room; he was so handsome in his Navy uniform. So tall, so…I don't know, I guess it was love at first sight for me. Anyway, he was due to be discharged soon and one thing led to another. He found a job as a bookkeeper for a small company in 'Philly,' and the rest is history. We were married a year later, and then the kids started coming. I used laugh that our life was just like that cute rhyme, 'first comes love, then comes marriage, then comes Maggie Jackson with a baby carriage.'

"We had three boys. We named the boys after the saints, you know, Christopher, Patrick, and Anthony. Buddy thought the names would help keep the boys out of trouble, but it didn't work. I don't know, maybe Buddy was too strict with them. Oh, he didn't abuse them or anything like that, but he did have a heavy hand sometimes. Once in awhile he used to take a belt to keep them in line, but you can guess how much of a handful three boys can be. Looking back, I guess you might say he was isolated from the boys. Don't get me wrong or anything like that. He was always a good provider, husband, and father, but every once in a while he'd go on what I'd call a 'bender.' I kinda feel bad telling you this but Buddy really liked to 'tie one on.' He never missed much work or anything. He just had what I would call a lost weekend. I never saw him use drugs of any kind.

"Anyway, the boys are all grown now and out of the house. I guess they are doing as well as can be expected. Christopher, our oldest, has had his fair share of setbacks in his life. He's divorced twice and has a bunch of financial troubles. His ex-wife never cuts him slack about making child support payments. Did you know that Saint Christopher is the patron saint of travelers? Somehow our Christopher has gotten lost in life. Patrick, our middle son, unfortunately has been in and out of jail since he was a teenager. I don't know what Patrick's problem is. Buddy has just about stopped letting Patrick come visit me at the house. It's not Patrick's fault—his boss stole money and blamed the whole thing on him. Our youngest son, Anthony, is a good boy. He's never been married, and we call him the "playboy" of the family. He's got a good job, but he lives in California and we never see him. I'm still waiting to be a grandmother, but I don't think it's going to happen anytime soon.

"Anyway, this year Buddy and I have been married 50 years. One of our friends went to Hawaii to celebrate their anniversary, and they suggested we do the same. Buddy and I have never really traveled anywhere past Teaneck, New Jersey. I guess we're just two 'country bumpkins.' I know Buddy didn't want to go to Hawaii, but I told him the trip was 'free.' Actually, I lied and told him I won the trip in the San Pedro church raffle. I had some money set aside, and I really wanted to go."

Maggie asked me if she could have some water; after she was settled, she continued, "The trip was supposed to be the thing dreams are made of. You know, a second honeymoon?" I nodded my head encouragingly; she proceeded. "Hawaii in December, what could be better? Well, maybe I'm getting ahead of myself. I guess I should go back and tell you that Buddy was stationed in 1941 at Pearl Harbor, on December 7th. You know people call it 'the day of infamy,' but Buddy never talked to anybody about that day or about the war. It was an unwritten rule in our house; you just didn't talk about Pearl Harbor or his war experiences. Even when our boys were growing up, they weren't allowed to ask him any questions. If a documentary came on television about the war, Buddy either turned it off or walked out of the room. We just got used to the way he was about 'the war.' Buddy was hospitalized for a few weeks after Pearl Harbor for some kind of shrapnel injury. He has this big old scrape on the side of his body, but he won't talk about it. So I really don't know for sure what happened."

Maggie was quiet for what seemed like a long moment. I asked how she was doing. "Oh, I'm alright. It's just difficult to tell you about this part," she replied. "I can understand that," I said. She blew her nose and began to talk once more: "Well, there we were in Oahu. We couldn't have asked for a nicer flight over to Hawaii, nicer weather, or a nicer hotel. In fact, we met several couples flying to Hawaii for their wedding anniversaries on the airplane. Anyway, Buddy and I met this one couple, Gert and Abe, sitting next to us on the plane. Get this, Abe saw military action in Pearl Harbor as a gunnery officer. Gert told me about how Abe shot down several enemy airplanes and earned a Bronze Star. Gert said they planned this trip so Abe could have a reunion with some of the guys he served with. You can imagine how I felt when I realized that our trip coincided with the 55th anniversary of Pearl Harbor! Well, you could have knocked me over with a feather. Imagine, of all the lousy timing. I mean we weren't going to go to Pearl Harbor, but now with the anniversary how could we not?" Maggie reached for several more tissues and took another sip of water before continuing.

"I can't remember when I've talked so much about this. I can't seem to stop once the floodgates are opened. Are you sure you're OK listening to me go on and on?" I replied, "It sounds as if you have a lot to say." Maggie looked surprised and said, "Why, yes, I guess I do. Should I continue?" I answered, "Please."

"Well," she said, "we did some sightseeing and everything was fine. Or I should say I thought everything was fine. I found Buddy walking the floor at night at the hotel. When he did sleep, he seemed so restless and agitated, almost like he was having a bad dream. I figured he might be feeling the effects of jet lag, you know the difference in time? Me, I'm fine. No problems eating, sleeping, or anything. I'm soaking up the sun and having lots of fun. I'm in a real tourist mode and having a ball. Buddy was more quiet than usual, but I didn't think much of it. I noticed he took a few extra blood pressure pills, but he said not to worry about it.

"One day we met Abe and Gert leaving the hotel. They were on their way to visit the Pearl Harbor Naval Shipyard. On the spur of the moment, Abe asked us if we wanted to go with them to visit the memorial dedicated to the USS Arizona battleship. I said 'yes' immediately, but Buddy was quiet a long time. He asked Abe if he'd be willing to wait an extra minute so he could get something from our hotel room. Everybody got cozy in the taxicab, and we're waiting for Buddy to join us. Well, out of the front door of the hotel comes Buddy wearing a flak jacket I never saw before. It looked burned in several places and ripped up pretty good, too. In my mind, I thought the jacket could use a really good cleaning. Buddy settled into the taxi, and everything seemed to be all right until we got to the Memorial Visitor Center.

"Abe and Buddy sort of wandered off together and that was fine. Gert and I became interested in one of the National Park Service rangers detailing the battle that took place. We saw a 20-minute film documenting some of the actual footage of the attack, went through a small library, and found a few things to buy in the gift shop. I thought the memorial was a wonderful tribute to the men and women who died there, and it was done in really nice taste. Gert and I got to see some dioramas that explained exactly what happened that day. So many of our military personnel were killed, and so many ships and planes were destroyed. I remember thinking how the ex-servicemen were dealing with the Japanese visitors who were also there. I started to wonder what it must have been like that day for Buddy.

"Well, anyway, the 'boys' came back and we took a shuttle boat out to where the USS Arizona sunk after it was hit by enemy fire. The very nice folks tendering our launch pointed out some interesting areas such as 'Battleship Row' and Ford Island; that's where the beginning battle took place. Did you know that seven battleships were destroyed? I remember I kept peeking over at Buddy to see if he was okay. He didn't acknowledge me. He seemed like he was in his own world."

She went on, "One thing that impressed me was how quiet everyone was when we were riding over to the *USS Arizona*. It was so eerie. You could hardly tell there was a bustling city not more than ten minutes away. Anyway, we walked up the gangplank, and I have to tell you I had heard people complain about the memorial being 'too plain.' It wasn't. I thought it was a perfect balance between respect, serenity, and dignity. We were really lucky because when we got there the earlier crowds had already thinned out, and only about 30 people were walking around taking pictures. Buddy immediately walked away from me, and I guessed he wanted to be alone. I drifted over to the memorial railing, you know, to look over the side. It's true what they say, you can still see evidence of an oil slick floating on top of the water. Imagine that after all these years. Anyway, I was wearing one of those flower leis; the hotel gives them out when you first arrive. I was so touched about being there that I took the lei off my neck, dropped it in the water, and said a prayer for the dear souls who had died that day. I watched my lei float off among the oil slick and the current.

"I thought that it must be very hard for people to come back here and deal with what happened during the war. I started thinking that maybe I should be with Buddy and started looking around for him. Buddy was at the far end of the memorial, what's called the 'Shrine Room.' I could see he was reaching up to touch some of the names of military personnel who lost their lives. I started to walk over to him, when all of a sudden a loud commotion happened exactly where I last saw him. Oh, Lordy no! I felt it in my bones that something was terribly wrong. It could not have been more than 20 seconds, but by the time I got to Buddy I had to push my way through a small crowd of people. I found him laying on the floor, sort of wrapped into a tight ball. He was rocking side to side, and screaming, 'Get down, hurry up, and get over here! The planes are coming, hurry, hurry, hurry! John, Harry, Paul, Billy get over here. Help me with this. We've got to undo the ties on the airplanes or they'll be destroyed just sitting on the field. Hurry, hurry, hurry. No! No! No! Get away from there. No! No! Nooooooo! Oh, noooooooooo!'"

Mrs. Jackson added, "I can still hear Buddy's tormented screams. One of the Service Park rangers gently asked me if Buddy had seen military action here. I told him Buddy had been at 'Pearl.' The ranger said he'd seen this reaction lots of times over the years. He said it's called 'posttraumatic stress disorder.' Of course I'd heard of it, but wondered if it could still happen 50 years later. The ranger didn't know much about that, but said, 'Ma'am, your husband should seek some kind of counseling once you get him home.'"

Maggie reached for more tissues and said, "Somehow we got Buddy stabilized and started walking him off the *USS Arizona*. He pleaded that he had one more thing he had to do before he left the ship. I asked him what, and Buddy showed me two small boxes he carried in the pocket of his flak jacket. When he opened up the boxes I saw two beautiful Purple Heart medals nestled in the white silk lining. I started to ask him where he got them, but instead Buddy walked over to the railing of the memorial and silently dropped each medal into the water. I saw him salute, turn on his heel, and he never once looked back. We left for home the next day.

"He hasn't talked much about what happened at Pearl Harbor, except to say that he saw his four best friends die and he was stranded for several hours guarding their dead bodies. Apparently, he saved the lives of several people when he erected a temporary shelter from flying shrapnel. He also saved a man's leg by tying off a severed artery. You think you know somebody after 50 years, but it seems as if I really didn't. Buddy was a real war hero, and no one knew about it. I wonder how scared he felt being a 20-year-old boy in the middle of a raging battle. I tell you it's enough to break my heart. Do you think you can help him?"

Assessment Summary

In general, posttraumatic stress disorder must be differentiated from other mental disorders. The practitioner carefully asks about the presence of previous traumatic experiences. While the 50-year delay of Buddy's symptoms is quite atypical, his traumatic episode could be described as typical. The fact that Buddy experienced the severe trauma of combat and the death of several of his closest friends, coupled with his avoidance of talking about these experiences, contributes to making this diagnosis. There is no evidence to suggest Buddy was experiencing an anxiety or mood disorder, because his life history is not consistent with those symptoms. Adjustment disorder was not seen as a factor that could be troubling Buddy because it is more often associated with ordinary stressors, for example, the impending birth of a child, a divorce, or even going back to graduate school.

PTSD may go undetected, because sometimes substance abuse masks the debilitating symptoms seen in Buddy's situation (Kaplan & Sadock, 1998; Maxmen & Ward, 1995). Acute stress disorder can be considered when all of the elements of PTSD are present for less than one month. If symptoms persist, it is no longer considered as an acute stress disorder. The practitioner begins listening for the full spectrum of symptoms lasting much longer, as seen with Buddy Jackson. In Buddy's situation, a true war trauma occurred. He attempted to deal with his experiences by not talking about them. When Buddy and his wife visited the war memorial, his memories emerged.

In contrast, those with malingering disorder (see Chapter 6) "lose" their symptoms when there is no secondary material gain, for example, insurance or disability claims. In persons with phobias, their avoidant behavior may be similar to that seen in posttraumatic stress disorder. However, the person with phobias usually acknowledges the senselessness of their behavior, whereas Buddy's behavior was readily understandable. It is noteworthy that those with malingering disorder or a factitious disorder (Chapter 6) may present a history compatible with posttraumatic stress disorder.

Assessing Buddy's condition solely in terms of whether he meets the DSM criteria fails to appreciate the ways in which he has coped with life's challenges. **Competency-based practice** emphasizes the importance of investigating Buddy's competencies and focuses, instead, on assets rather than defects. Buddy has had a

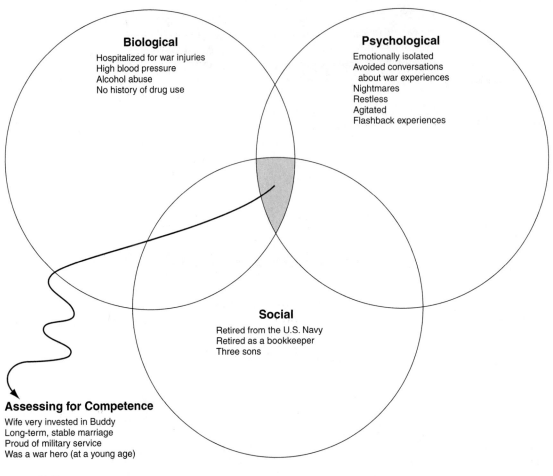

Biological

Hospitalized for war injuries
High blood pressure
Alcohol abuse
No history of drug use

Psychological

Emotionally isolated
Avoided conversations
  about war experiences
Nightmares
Restless
Agitated
Flashback experiences

Social

Retired from the U.S. Navy
Retired as a bookkeeper
Three sons

Assessing for Competence

Wife very invested in Buddy
Long-term, stable marriage
Proud of military service
Was a war hero (at a young age)

FIGURE **5-5**

POSTTRAUMATIC STRESS DISORDER

The interactions of the biological, psychological, and social variables in Buddy Jackson's life.

long-term and stable marriage with his wife, Maggie, who is very devoted to him. Additionally, he made an effort to be a parent to his sons and held long-term employment. Though troubled by the symptoms of PTSD, he is very proud of his military service record. In fact, he was a war hero at a very young age.

Buddy Jackson's complete diagnosis is:

Axis I   309.81 Posttraumatic Stress Disorder, with Delayed Onset

Axis II   V71.09 (No diagnosis)

Axis III   Rule Out Alcohol Abuse

402.90 Hypertensive Heart Disease Without Congestive Heart Failure

(continued)

History of War Injury

Axis IV   Problems with his children

Axis V   GAF = 70 (at intake)

GENERALIZED ANXIETY DISORDER

In contrast to the anxiety disorders previously discussed, those persons with *generalized anxiety disorder* (*GAD*) tend not to focus on any particular object, situation, or person. Rather, the anxiety they suffer significantly pervades their entire life and interferes in all aspects of life functioning. While it is generally understood that experiencing some worry is part of the normal human condition, those with generalized anxiety disorder are considered incessant "worrywarts"; that is, they worry about everything even when there is nothing obvious going on in their life to provoke their concerns (Dugas et al., 1998; Silverman & Ginsburg, 1995). This uncontrollable worry is the most salient feature (Chorpita et al., 1997).

Prevailing Pattern

GAD refers to what used to be termed *free-floating anxiety,* or the kind of anxiety experienced by a person not attached to any specific situation. The etiology of GAD is not clear, and unfortunately little is known about its history, cause, and predisposing features. In fact, there is some professional confusion whether GAD should be considered a viable and specific disorder or whether it is a residual category for anxiety disorders (Barlow & Wincze, 1998). A number of issues remain unresolved about this disorder. However, having said that (and with those reservations in mind), the lifetime prevalence ranges somewhere between 5 and 8 percent of the general population. GAD occurs in women about twice as often as in men (Robins & Regier, 1991; Wittchen et al., 1994), but diminishes with increasing age (Krasucki et al., 1998). Valid statistics on the prevalence of GAD are highly variable because the definition of this disorder has changed considerably in recent years (Nietzel et al., 1998). Individuals generally "tough it out"; if help is sought, they tend to turn to their own physician rather than to a social worker or other mental health practitioner. While GAD can occur at any age, it is most prevalent among those who are under the age of 30.

The following case vignette highlights generalized anxiety disorder.

The Case of Barbara "Barbie" Chapman

"Barbie" is a 34-year-old married woman, and the mother of two girls (ages 5 and 7). Barbie and her husband came for marital counseling because according to Mr. Chapman, "Barbie's excessive anxiety, worry, and physical complaints are destroying our 12-year marriage."

I saw the couple together and, typical of an initial session, asked what brought them to my office. Barbie began, "Jeffery overstates the problem. He thinks I worry too much, and calls me a 'worrywart,' and 'Mrs. Misgiving.' I guess I do tend to worry a little, but he calls me names, and well, it does cause tension between us."

Jeffery said, "Barbie understates the problem. She is in fact overly concerned about absolutely everything. Now I'm not just talking about being worried, for example, whether it will rain and whether she should take an umbrella to work. I'm talking about her being so worried that she's afraid she'll get the girls to school late, have an accident along the way, run a yellow light, run out of gas, or the windshield wipers won't work. I mean I could go on and on, but you get the picture."

Barbie broke in, "Hey, it's not a crime to take care of your family's safety, is it?" Jeffery responded, "Yeah, but you are always restless and edgy. You have trouble falling asleep, and when you wake up you're always tired. It's because you worry so much. You know, I could recite a litany of things that you worry about. You worry about something bad happening to you, to the girls or me, you worry about your job, you worry about driving, the weather, your mother's health, the Brazilian rain forest, and absolutely everything. You even call me ten times a day to make sure I'm okay. Your own mother put in caller identification just so she could screen your calls. You worry about things even before they occur. Do you remember that presentation you had to do at work? You worried about presenting your findings weeks beforehand."

I then asked whether Barbie was generally a nervous person. Barbie responded, "Well, I guess I do tend to ruminate about stuff, but I can't seem to stop, no matter how hard I try. I get so nervous. I guess I am just a 'worrywart' like Jeffery said. You know I try to maintain a tight control over all aspects of my life. If I can stay alert to anything that could go wrong, then I can prevent making a mistake." I inquired if Barbie ever experienced any physical problems. She replied, "Well, I do feel fidgety and jittery, you know, like I'm keyed up or something. I mean this has been going on for years. Sometimes my mind goes blank, and I have trouble concentrating. That's not so good when you're making a presentation in front of your boss. I sometimes worry so much that I can't fall asleep, and I wake up tired. I always seem to have neck and back aches, and I just about live on Tylenol because of muscle tension. I tried using a heating pad, you know, for the muscle aches. But then I worried the heating pad would short out and cause an electrical fire and burn the house down."

I then asked, "Barbie, how have these worries changed your life?" She replied, "Oh man, it's affected my job performance, my relationship with Jeffery and the girls, and our social life. Even with all my worrying, we still maintain our friendship with Kenny and Sue. We try to go to a movie with them at least once a month, but we hardly ever go out with any of our other friends anymore."

Assessment Summary

Generalized anxiety disorder is difficult to assess, because "worry" is a part of everyone's life. Although worry and physical tensions are very common experiences for most, the kind of severe anxiety experienced by Barbie is by far above and beyond what might be considered normal. Her worry is chronic and excessive, and it greatly diminishes the overall quality of her life.

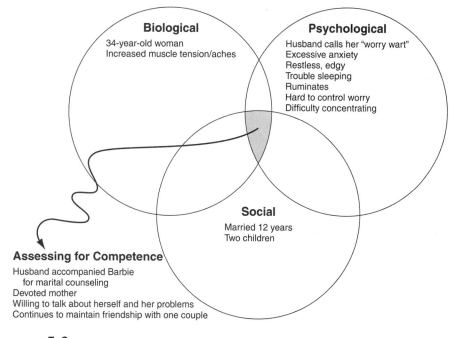

FIGURE **5-6**

GENERALIZED ANXIETY DISORDER

The interactions of the biological, psychological, and social variables in "Barbie" Chapman's life.

Unlike acute stress disorder that lasts about a month, generalized anxiety disorder is often pervasive and does not diminish over time. Individuals with phobias worry, but the quality of Barbie's worrying is very different. Those with panic disorder may develop anticipatory anxiety. The anxiety in panic disorder is over the anticipation of having another attack (Roy-Byrne & Cowley, 1998). The focus of Barbie's worries revolved around her husband, her children, and her job performance. If the target of her concerns revolved around a fear of becoming contaminated, the practitioner might begin thinking about obsessive-compulsive disorder (Wells & Papageorgiou, 1998). This vignette did not illustrate any struggles around depression, so a mood disorder would not be a viable consideration (Lydiard & Brawman-Mintzer, 1998). Barbie experienced no worries about her health or about having a serious illness. Therefore, the practitioner would not consider the presence of hypochondriasis or somatization disorders.

A competency-based assessment looked at the wide range of factors influencing Barbie's life. Among them, the practitioner inquired about medications or the drugs Barbie was taking. These may potentially produce side effects that might mimic generalized anxiety features; for example, taking certain antidepressants can cause similar symptoms. Generalized anxiety disorder is far more problematic than the symptoms found in an adjustment disorder; in the latter, symptoms tend to be milder. The practitioner distinguishes adjustment disorder from the normal reactions to psychosocial stressors that are not sufficient to cause clinically significant impairment and warrant a diagnosis of a mental disorder.

On the surface, Barbie's concerns about her family, husband, and job might not warrant professional intervention, but her husband described a much different scenario. He experienced Barbie's multiple excessive worries and her inability to control them as problematic. Additionally, her ongoing physical complaints have now become a burden for him. As illustrated in the vignette, family members tended to feel the brunt of Barbie's worries, but they remained supportive of her. In addition, this couple was able to maintain a relationship with another couple and socialized with them on a regular basis.

Barbie Chapman's full diagnosis would read:

Axis I	300.02 Generalized Anxiety Disorder (GAD)
Axis II	V71.09 (No diagnosis)
Axis III	Muscle Tension
Axis IV	None
Axis V	GAF = 75 (at intake)

SUMMARY

The core emotions of anxiety and fear serve as an alarm to escape danger or harm. They warn the person to take extra precautions or to galvanize protective behaviors; for example, a student who wants to pass a difficult test must study hard. The student's efforts are partially motivated by a fear of failure. Anxiety is a symptom found in almost all mental disorders. However, when it is the main symptom that requires the practitioner's help, it then is considered in a class by itself.

The behaviors a person uses to manage his or her anxiety will show in very different ways. The competency-based assessment helps the practitioner to tease out those critical differences. In sum:

- *The phobias*—Social phobias are those in which people fear they will embarrass themselves in front of others or attract negative attention, as in the case of Herb Wilks. Specific phobias show behaviors reflecting a persistent fear of objects or situations, as reflected by Ralph Tyler's fear of blood.

- *Panic disorder and agoraphobia*—Jada Wu's fear of flying and her concerns about being in places from which there is no escape cause her great distress. Panic disorders consist of intense attacks of panic and/or worries about experiencing a panic attack that are unexpected.

- *Agoraphobia without history of panic disorder*—As seen in Matilda Suarez's fears about leaving her home, she depends on others for her basic needs, is afraid to go out alone, and does not like being in crowded places. This disorder restricts the person's life, as they are severely impaired in almost all aspects of intrapersonal and/or interpersonal functioning.

- *Obsessive-compulsive disorder*—Maddy Yarborough illustrates the unwanted thoughts, images, and urges that compel her to engage in repetitive behaviors in order to help reduce her anxiety.

- *Posttraumatic stress disorder*—Buddy Jackson's earlier experiences in combat during World War II precipitated his traumatic reaction. His struggles around reexperiencing this early trauma were manifested by through flashbacks, insomnia, an increased heartbeat (physiological reactions), and feelings of detachment.

- *Generalized anxiety disorder*—GAD can overlap with other conditions, for example, panic disorder. However, the central feature, as in the case vignette of Barbie Chapman, is one of overriding worry and concern. Her complaints revolved around feeling restless and keyed up, trouble sleeping and waking up tired, difficulty concentrating, and increased muscle tension, all of which caused problems in the intrapersonal and interpersonal domains of her life.

PRACTITIONER REFLECTIONS

Most people function every day with some form or another of anxiety generated by life stresses, upheavals, or challenges. Anxiety is considered a normal part of one's internal signaling system that helps alert us to changes in our bodies and the world around us. Anxiety can be seen as either adaptive or maladaptive. Some degree of anxiety is experienced not only when things go wrong in life but also when things change or are unexpected. The purpose of this series of activities is to help the practitioner discern between normal anxiety versus anxiety disorders.

Activities

- Reflect back on the cases presented in this chapter. Select one of them, and find a partner to role-play the details of the case with you. Assume the role of either the client or the worker. At what point in the role-play exchange did you determine the presence of an anxiety disorder versus the feelings associated with "normal worry"?

- Rent the popular, award-winning film *As Good as It Gets* featuring the actors Jack Nicholson and Helen Hunt. Describe how his compulsive behaviors affected the everyday life of Nicholson's character. Pay particular attention to how he was able to cope, and notice those interpersonal and social factors in his environment that provided support.

- Discuss (with a group of colleagues) how superstitions are perceived in our society versus how compulsions are viewed.

REFERENCES

Acierno, R., Kilpatrick, D. G., & Resnick, H. S. (1999). Posttraumatic stress disorder in adults relative to criminal victimization: Prevalence, risk factors, and comorbidity. In P. A. Saigh & J. D. Bremner (Eds.), *Posttraumatic stress disorder: A comprehensive text*, pp. 44–68. Boston: Allyn & Bacon.

Albino, A. M., Chorpita, B. F., & Barlow, D. H. (1996). Childhood anxiety disorders. In E. J. Mash & R. A. Barkley (Eds.), *Child psychopathology*, pp. 196–241. New York: Guilford Press.

American Psychiatric Association [APA]. (2000). *Diagnostic and statistical manual of mental disorders* (4th ed.-TR). Washington, DC: APA.

Antony, M. M., Brown, T. A., & Barlow, D. H. (1997). Heterogeneity among specific phobia types in DSM-IV. *Behaviour Research and Therapy*, 35(12): 1089–1100.

Antony, M. M., Purdon, C. L., Huta, V., & Swinson, R. P. (1998). Dimensions of perfectionism across the anxiety disorders. *Behavior Research and Therapy*, 36(12): 1143–1154.

Aragona, M., & Vella, G. (1998). Psychopathological considerations on the relationship between bulimia and obsessive-compulsive disorder. *Psychopathology*, 31(4): 197–205.

Ballenger, J. C. (1998). Comorbidity of panic and depression: Implications for clinical management. *International Clinical Psychopharmacology*, 13(Suppl. 4): 13.

Baranowsky, A. B., Young, M., Johnson-Douglas, S., Williams-Keeler, L. (1998). PTSD transmission: A review of secondary traumatization in Holocaust survivor families. *Canadian Psychology*, 39(4): 247–256.

Barlow, D. H. (1988). *Anxiety and its disorders: The nature and treatment of anxiety and panic.* New York: Guilford Press.

Barlow, D. H., & Durand, V. M. (1995). *Abnormal psychology.* Pacific Grove, CA: Brooks/Cole.

Barlow, D. H., & Durand V. M. (1997). *Abnormal psychology.* (2nd ed.) Pacific Grove, CA: Brooks/Cole.

Barlow, D. H., & Wincze, J. (1998). DSM-IV and beyond: What is generalized anxiety disorder? *Acta Psychiatrica Scandinavica Supplementum*, 393: 23–29.

Bebbington, P. E. (1998). Epidemiology of obsessive-compulsive disorder. *British Journal of Psychiatry Supplement*, suppl. (35): 2–6.

Beckham, J. C., Moore, S. C., Feldman, M. E., Hertzberg, M. A., Kirby, A. C., & Fairbank, J. A. (1998). Health status, somatization, and severity of posttraumatic stress disorder in Vietnam combat veterans with posttraumatic stress disorder. *American Journal of Psychiatry*, 155(11): 1565–1569.

Bejerot, S., Ekselius, L., & von Knorring, A. L. (1998). Comorbidity between obsessive-compulsive disorder (OCD) and personality disorders. *Acta Psychiatrica Scandinavica*, 97(6): 398–402.

Berberich, D. A. (1998). Posttraumatic stress disorder: Gender and cross-cultural clinical issues. *Psychotherapy in Private Practice*, 17(2): 29–41.

Bienvenu, O. J., & Eaton, W. W. (1998). The epidemiology of blood-injection-injury phobia. *Psychological Medicine*, 28(5): 1129–1136.

Bierut, L. J. (1997). Anxiety disorder. In S. B. Guze (Ed.), *Adult Psychiatry*. St. Louis, MO: Mosby-Yearbook.

Beitchman, J. H., Zucker, K. J., Hood, J. E., Da Costa, G. A., Akman, D., & Cassavia, E. (1992). A review of the long term effects of child sexual abuse. *Child Abuse and Neglect*, 16: 101–118.

Black, D. W., Gaffney, G., Schlosser, S., & Gabel, J. (1998). The impact of obsessive-compulsive disorder on the family: Preliminary findings. *Journal of Nervous and Mental Disease*, 186(7): 440–442.

Brady, K. T., Dansky, B. S., Sonne, S. C., & Saladin, M. E. (1998). Posttraumatic stress disorder and cocaine dependence: Order of onset. *American Journal on Addictions*, 20(2): 212–224.

Bremmer, J. D., Steinberg, M., Southwick, S. M., Johnson, D. R., & Charney, D. S. (1993). Use of the structured clinical interview for DSM-IV dissociative disorder for systematic assessment of dissociative symptoms in posttraumatic stress disorder. *American Journal of Psychiatry*, 150: 1011.

Bremmer, J. D., Southwick, S. M., Darnell, A., & Charney, D. S. (1996). Chronic PTSD in Vietnam combat veteran's: Course of illness and substance abuse. *American Journal of Psychiatry*, 153: 369.

Brier, J. (1997). Treating adults severely abused as children: The self-trauma model. In D. A. Wolfe, R. J. McMahon, & R. Dev Peters (Eds.), *Child abuse: New directions in prevention and treatment across the life span*, pp. 178–205. Newbury Park, CA: Sage.

Brier, J., & Runtz, M. (1991). The long-term effects of sexual abuse: A review of synthesis. *New Directions in Mental Health Services*, 51: 3–13.

Brown, P. J., Stout, R. L., Gannon-Rowley, J. (1998). Substance use disorder–PTSD comorbidity: Patient's perceptions of symptom interplay and treatment issues. *Journal of Substance Abuse Treatment*, 15(5): 445–448.

Cauffman, E., Feldman, S. S., Waterman, J., & Steiner, H. (1998). Posttraumatic stress disorder among female juvenile offenders. *Journal of the American Academy of Child and Adolescent Psychiatry*, 37(11): 1209–1216.

Chorpita, B. F., Tracey, S. A., Brown, T. A., Collica, T. J., & Barlow, D. H. (1997). Assessment of worry in children and adolescents: An adaptation of the Penn State Worry Questionnaire. *Behaviour Research and Therapy*, 35: 569–581.

Chu, J. A. (1999). Trauma and suicide. In D. G. Jacobs (Ed.), *The Harvard Medical School guide to suicide assessment and intervention*, pp. 332–354. San Francisco: Jossey-Bass.

Coryell, W., & Winokur, G. (1991). *The clinical management in anxiety disorder*. New York: Oxford University Press.

Crowson, J. J., Jr., Frueh, B. C., Beidel, D. C., & Turner, S. M. (1998). Self-reported symptoms of social anxiety in a sample of combat veterans with posttraumatic stress disorder. *Journal of Anxiety Disorders*, 12(6): 605–612.

Dahl, S., Mutapcic, A., & Schei, B. (1998). Traumatic events and predictive factors for posttraumatic symptoms in displaced Bosnian women in a war zone. *Journal of Traumatic Stress*, 11(1): 137–145.

Dansky, B. S., Brady, K. T., & Saladin, M. E. (1998). Untreated symptoms of PTSD among cocaine-dependent individuals: Changes over time. *Journal of Substance Abuse Treatment*, 15(6): 499–504.

Darves-Bornoz, J. M., Lepine, J. P., Choquet, M., Berger, C., Degiovanni, A., & Gaillard, P. (1998). Predictive factors of chronic post-traumatic stress disorder in rape victims. *European Psychiatry*, 13(6): 281–287.

Davis, C., Kaptein, S., Kaplan, A. S., Olmsted, M. P., & Woodside, D. B. (1998). Obsessionality in anorexia nervosa: The moderating influence of exercise. *Psychosomatic Medicine*, 60(2): 192–197.

de Silva, P., & Rachman, S. (1992). *Obsessive-compulsive disorder: The facts*. Oxford, UK: Oxford University Press.

Dugas, M. J., Freeston, M. H., Ladouceur, R., Rheaume, J., Provencher, M., & Boisvert, J. M. (1998). Worry themes in primary GAD, secondary GAD, and other anxiety disorders. *Journal of Anxiety Disorders*, 12(3): 253–261.

Dunner, D. L. (1998). The issue of comorbidity in the treatment of panic. *International Clinical Psychopharmacology*, 13(Suppl. 4): S19–24.

Falk, B., Van Hasselt, V. B., & Hersen, M. (1997). Assessment of posttraumatic stress disorder in older victims of rape. *Journal of Clinical Geropsychology*, 3(2): 157–171.

Figley, C. R. (1983). Catastrophes: An overview of family reactions. In C. Figley & H. McCubbin (Eds.), *Stress and the family: Volume 2. Coping with catastrophe*, pp. 3–20. New York: Brunner/Mazel.

Fletcher, K. E. (1996). Childhood posttraumatic stress disorder. In E. J. Mash & R. A. Barkley (Eds.), *Child psychopathology*, pp. 242–276. New York: Guilford Press.

Foa, F. B., Roghbaum, B. O., Riggs, D. S., & Murdock, T. B. (1991). Treatment of posttraumatic stress disorder in rape victims: A comparison between cognitive-behavioral procedures and counseling. *Journal of Consulting Clinical Psychology*, 59: 715.

Foa, E. B., Steketee, G. S., & Azarow, B. J. (1995). DSM-IV field trial: Obsessive-compulsive disorder. *American Journal of Psychiatry*, 152: 90–96.

Fredrikson, M., Annas, P., Fischer, H., & Wik, G. (1996). Gender and age differences of specific fears and phobias. *Behavior Research and Therapy*, 34(1): 33–39.

Frommberger, U. H., Stieglitz, R. D., Nyberg, E., Schlickewei, W., Kuner, E., & Berger, M. (1998). Prediction of posttraumatic stress disorder by immediate reactions to trauma: A prospective study in road traffic accident victims. *European Archives of Psychiatry and Clinical Neuroscience*, 248(6): 316–321.

Fyer, A. J., Mannuzza, S., Chapman, T. F., Liebrowitz, M. R., & Klein, D. F. (1993). A direct interview family study of social phobia. *Archives of General Psychiatry*, 50: 286–293.

Germain, C., & Gitterman, A. (1980). *The life model of social work practice*. New York: Columbia University Press.

Goisman, R. M., Warshaw, M. G., & Steketee, G. S. (1995). DSM-IV and the disappearance of agoraphobia with a history of panic disorder: New data on a controversial diagnosis. *American Journal of Psychiatry*, 152: 1438.

Goisman, R. M., Allsworth, J., Rogers, M. P., Warshaw, M. G., Goldenberg, I., Vasile, R. G., Rodriguez, V., Mallya, G., & Keller, M. B. (1998). Simple phobia as a comorbid anxiety disorder. *Depression and Anxiety*, 7(3): 105–112.

Greist, J. H. (1995). The diagnosis of social phobia. *Journal of Clinical Psychiatry*, 56(Suppl. 5): 5.

Gunderson, J. G., & Sabo, A. N. (1993). The phenomenological and conceptual interface between borderline personality disorder and PTSD. *American Journal of Psychiatry*, 150: 19.

Harworth, E., Lish, J. D., Johnson, J., Hornig, C. D., & Weissman, M. M. (1993). Agoraphobia without panic: Clinical reappraisal of epidemiological findings. *American Journal of Psychiatry*, 150: 1496.

Henin, A., & Kendall, P. C. (1997). Obsessive-compulsive disorder in childhood and adolescents. *Advances in Clinical Child Psychology*, 19: 75–131.

Hofmann, S. G., Lehman, C. L., & Barlow, D. H. (1997). How specific are specific phobias? *Journal of Behavior Therapy and Experimental Psychiatry*, 28(3): 233–240.

Howsepian, A. A. (1998). Post-traumatic stress disorder following needle-stick contaminated with suspected HIV-positive blood. *General Hospital Psychiatry*, 20(2): 123–124.

Hunt, C., & Andrews, G. (1998). Long-term outcome of panic disorder and social phobia. *Journal of Anxiety Disorder*, 12(4): 395–406.

Husain, S. A., Nair, J., Holcomb, W., Reid, J. C., Vargas, V., & Nair, S. S. (1998). Stress reactions of children and adolescents in war and siege conditions. *American Journal of Psychiatry*, 155(12): 1718–1719.

Jefferson, J. W. (1996). Social phobia: Everybody's disorder? *Journal Clinical Psychiatry*, 57(6 Suppl.): 28.

Jones, M. K., & Menzies, R. G. (1998a). The relevance of associative learning pathways in the development of obsessive-compulsive washing. *Behaviour Research and Therapy*, 36(3): 273–283.

Jones, M. K., & Menzies, R. G. (1998b). Role of perceived danger in the mediation of obsessive-compulsive washing. *Depression and Anxiety*, 8(3): 121–125.

Judd, L. L. (1994). Social phobia: A clinical overview. *Journal of Clinical Psychiatry*, 55(Suppl. 6): 5.

Jumper, S. (1995). A meta-analysis of the relationship of child sexual abuse to adult psychological adjustment. *Child Abuse and Neglect*, 19: 715–728.

Kaplan, H. J., & Sadock, B. J. (1998). *Synopsis of psychiatry* (8th ed.). Baltimore, MD: Williams & Wilkins.

Katerndahl, D. A., & Realini, J. P. (1998a). Panic disorder in Hispanic patients. *Family Medicine*, 30(3): 210–214.

Katerndahl, D. A., & Realini, J. P. (1998b). Patients with panic attacks seeking care from family physicians compared with those seeking care from psychiatrists. *Journal of Nervous and Mental Diseases*, 186(4): 249–250.

Keane, T. M. (1998). Psychological effects of military combat. In B. P. Dohrenwend (Ed.), *Adversity, stress, and psychopathology*, pp. 52–65. New York: Oxford University Press.

Kearney, C. A., & Allan, W. D. (1995). Panic disorder with or without agoraphobia. In A. R. Eisen, C. A. Kearney, & C. A. Shaefer (Eds.), *Clinical handbook of anxiety disorders in children and adolescents*, pp. 251–281. Northvale, NJ: Jason Aronson.

Kelly, B., Raphael, B., Judd, F., Kernutt, G., Burnett, P., & Burrows, G. (1998). Posttraumatic stress disorder in response to HIV infection. *General Hospital Psychiatry*, 20(6): 345–352.

Kendall-Tackett, K. A., Williams, L. M., & Finkelhor, D. (1993). The impact of sexual abuse on children: A review and synthesis of recent empirical studies. *Psychological Bulletin*, 113: 164–180.

Kessler, R. C., McGonagle, S., Zhao, S., Nelson, C. B., Hughes, M., Eshelman, S., Wittchen, H., & Kendler, K. S. (1994). Lifetime and 12 month prevalence of DSM-III-R psychiatric disorders in the United States: Results from a national comorbidity survey. *Archives of General Psychiatry*, 51: 8–20.

Kessler, R. C., Sonnega, A., Bromet, E., Hughes, M., & Nelson, C. B. (1996). Posttraumatic stress disorder in the National Comorbidity Survey. *Archives of General Psychiatry*, 52: 1048–1060.

Kessler, R. C., Olfson, M., & Berglund, P. A. (1998). Patterns and predictors of treatment contact after first onset of psychiatric disorder. *American Journal of Psychiatry*, 155(1): 62–69.

Kilpatrick, K. L., & Williams, L. M. (1998). Potential mediators of post-traumatic stress disorder in child witnesses to domestic violence. *Child Abuse and Neglect*, 22(4): 319–330.

Kilpatrick, D. G., Resnick, H. S., Saunders, B. E., & Best, C. L. (1998). Rape, other violence against women, and posttraumatic stress disorder. In B. P. Dohrenwend (Ed.), *Adversity, stress, and psychopathology*, pp. 161–176. New York: Oxford University Press.

King, D. W., King, L. A., Keane, T. M., & Fairbank, J. A. (1999). Posttraumatic stress disorder in a national sample of female and male Vietnam veterans: Risk factors, war-zone stressors and resilience-recovery variables. *Journal of Abnormal Psychology*, 108(1): 164–170.

Krasucki, C., Howard, R., & Mann, A. (1998). The relationship between anxiety and age. *International Journal of Geriatric Psychiatry*, 13(2): 79–99.

Lecrubier, Y., & Ustun, T. B. (1998). Panic and depression: A world wide primary care perspectives. *International Clinical Psychopharmacology*, 13(April, Suppl. 4): 57–111.

Lee, K. A., Vaillant, G. E., & Torrey, W. C. (1995). A 50-year prospective study of the psychological sequelae of World War II combat. *American Journal of Psychiatry*, 152: 516.

Leekman, S., & Perner, J. (1994). Tic disorder. In M. Rutter, E. Taylor, & L. Herson (Eds.), *Child and adolescent psychiatry*. Oxford, UK: Blackwell Scientific Publications.

Lydiard, R. B., & Brawman-Mintzer, O. (1998). Anxious depression. *Journal of Clinical Psychiatry*, 59(Suppl. 18): 10–17.

Magee, W. J., Eaton, W. W., Wittchen, H. V., McGonagle, K. A., & Kessler, R. C. (1996). Agoraphobia, simple phobia, and social phobia in the National Comorbidity Survey, *Archives General Psychiatry*, 53: 159.

Maluccio, A. (1981). *Promoting competence in clients*. New York: Free Press.

Marshall, R. P., Jorm, A. F., Grayson, D. A., & O'Toole, B. I. (1998). Posttraumatic stress disorder and other predictors of health care consumption by Vietnam veterans. *Psychiatric Services*, 49(12): 1609–1611.

Maxman, J. S., & Ward, N. G. (1995). *Essential psychopathology and its treatment.* New York: W. W. Norton.

Merckelback, H., de Jong, P. J., van den Hout, M. A., & Marcel, A. (1996). The etiology of specific phobias: A review. *Clinical Psychology Review*, 16(4): 337–361.

Miller, L. (1999). Treating posttraumatic stress disorder in children and families: Basic principles and clinical applications. *American Journal of Family Therapy*, 27(1): 21–34.

Moore, D. P., & Jefferson, J. W. (1996). *Handbook of medical psychiatry*. St. Louis, MO: Mosby-Year Book.

Morrison, J. (1995). *The DSM-IV Made Easy*. New York: Guilford Press.

Mueser, K. T., Goodman, L. B., Trumbetta, S. L., Rosenberg, S. D., Osher, F., Vidaver, R., Auciello, P., & Foy, D. W. (1998). Trauma and posttraumatic stress disorder in severe mental illness. *Journal of Consulting and Clinical Psychology*, 66(3): 493–499.

Narrow, W. E., Regier, D. A., Rae, D. S., Marderschiend, R. W., & Locke, B. Z. (1993). Use of services by persons with mental and addictive disorders. *Archives of General Psychiatry*, 50(2): 95–107.

Nestadt, G., Bienvenu, O. J., Cai, G., Samuels, J., & Eaton, W. W. (1998). Incidence of obsessive-compulsive disorder in adults. *Journal of Nervous and Mental Disease*, 186(7): 401–406.

Nietzel, M. T., Speltz, M. L., McCauley, E. A., & Bernstein, D. A. (1998). *Abnormal psychology*. Boston: Allyn & Bacon.

Ollendick, T. H., & King, N. J. (1994). Fears and their level of interference in adolescents. *Behaviour Research and Therapy*, 32: 635–638.

Ost, L. G. (1992). Blood and injection phobia: Background and cognitive, physiological, and behavioral variables. *Journal of Abnormal Psychology*, 101(1): 68–74.

Overbeek, T., Rikken, J., Schruers, K., & Griez, E. (1998). Suicidal ideation in panic disorder patients. *Journal of Nervous and Mental Disease*, 186(9): 577–580.

Pelcovitz, D., Kaplan, S., Goldenberg, B., Mandel, F., Lehane, J., & Guarrera, J. (1994). Posttraumatic stress disorder in physically abused adolescents. *Journal of the American Academy of Child and Adolescent Psychiatry*, 33: 305–312.

Phillips, K. A., Gunderson, C. G., Mallya, G., McElroy, S. L., & Carter, W. (1998). A comparison study of body dysmorphic disorder and obsessive-compulsive disorder. *Journal of Clinical Psychiatry*, 59(11): 568–575.

Rees, C. S., Richards, J. C., & Smith, L. M. (1998). Medical utilization and costs in panic disorder: A comparison with social phobia. *Journal of Anxiety Disorders*, 421–435.

Riddle, M. (1998). Obsessive-compulsive disorder in children and adolescents. *British Journal of Psychiatry Supplement*, 1998(35): 91–96.

Robins, L. N., & Regier, D. A. (Eds.). (1991). *Psychiatric disorders in America: The Epidemiological Catchment Area study*. New York: Free Press.

Rodriguez, N., Ryan, S., Vande Kemp, H., & Foy, D. (1997). Posttraumatic stress disorder in female adult female survivors of childhood sexual abuse: A comparison study. *Journal of Consulting and Clinical Psychology*, 65: 53–59.

Rothenberg, A. (1998). Diagnosis of obsessive-compulsive illness. *Psychiatric Clinics of North America*, 21(4): 791–801.

Roy-Byrne, P. P., & Cowley, D. S. (1998). Search for pathophysiology of panic disorder. *Lancet*, 352(9141): 1646–1647.

Ruzek, J. I., Polusny, M. A., & Abueg, F. R. (1998). Assessment and treatment of concurrent posttraumatic stress disorder and substance abuse. In V. M. Follette & J. I. Ruzek (Eds.), *Cognitive-behavioral therapies for trauma*, pp. 226–255. New York: Guilford Press.

Saxe, H., & Wolfe, J. (1999). Gender and posttraumatic stress disorder. In P. A. Saigh & J. D. Bremmer (Eds.), *Posttraumatic stress disorder*, pp. 160–179. Boston: Allyn & Bacon.

Schaaf, K. K., & McCanne, T. R. (1998). Relationship of childhood sexual, physical, and combined sexual and physical abuse to adult victimization and posttraumatic stress disorder. *Child Abuse and Neglect*, 22(11): 1119–1133.

Schenier, F. R., Johnson, J., Hornig, C. D., Liebowitz, M. R., & Weissman, M. M. (1992). Social phobia: Comorbidity and morbidity in an epidemiological sample. *Archives of General Psychiatry*, 49: 282–288.

Schlenger, W. E., Fairbank, J. A., Jordan, K. B., & Caddell, J. A. (1999). Combat-related posttraumatic stress disorder: Prevalence, risk factors, and comorbidity. In P. A. Saigh & J. D. Bremner (Eds.), *Posttraumatic stress disorder: A comprehensive text*, pp. 69–91. Boston: Allyn & Bacon.

Shader, R. I. (1994). *Manual of psychiatric therapeutics*. Boston: Little, Brown & Company.

Shaner, R. (1997). *Psychiatry*. Baltimore, MD: Williams & Wilkins.

Shalev, A. Y., Freedman, S. P., Peri, B., Sahar, T., Orr, S. P., & Pitman, R. K. (1998). Prospective study of posttraumatic stress disorder and depression following trauma. *American Journal of Psychiatry*, 155(5): 630–637.

Shapiro, A. K., & Shapiro, E. (1992). Evaluation of the reported association of obsessive-compulsive symptoms or disorder with Tourette's disorder. *Comprehensive Psychiatry*, 33: 152–165.

Sheikh, J. I., Swales, P. J., King, R. J., Sazima, G. C., & Bail, G. (1998). Somatization in younger versus older female panic disorder patients. *International Journal of Geriatric Psychiatry*, 13(8): 564–567.

Silverman, W. K., & Ginsburg, C. S. (1995). Specific phobias and generalized anxiety disorder. In J. S. March (Ed.), *Anxiety disorders in children and adolescents*, pp. 151–180. New York: Guilford Press.

Sprang, G., & McNeil, J. (1998). Post-homicide reactions: Grief, mourning and post-traumatic stress disorder following a drunk driving fatality. *Journal of Death and Dying*, 37(1): 41–58.

Strauss, C. C., & Last, C. G. (1993). Social and simple phobias in children. *Journal of Anxiety Disorders*, 7: 141–152.

Starcevic, V., Djordjevic, A., Lotus, M., & Bogojevic, G. (1998). Characteristics of agoraphobia in female and males with panic disorder without agoraphobia. *Depression and Anxiety*, 8(1): 8–13.

Stein, M. B., Walker, J. R., & Forde, D. R. (1995). Public-speaking fears in a community sample: Prevalence, impact on functioning, and diagnostic classification. *Archives of General Psychiatry*, 53: 169.

Strakowski, S. M., Sax, K. W., McElroy, S. L., Keck, P. E., Jr., Hawkins, J. M., & West, S. A. (1998). Course of psychiatric and substance abuse syndromes co-occurring with bipolar disorder after a first psychiatric hospitalization. *Journal of Clinical Psychiatry*, 59(9): 465–471.

Turner, S. M., & Hersen, M. (1997). *Adult psychopathology and diagnosis* (3rd ed.). New York: Wiley and Sons.

Wasserstein, S. B. & La Greca, A. M. (1998) Hurricane Andrew: Parent conflict as a moderator of children's adjustment. *Hispanic Journal of Behavioral Sciences*, 20(2): 212–224.

Weaver, T., & Clum, G. (1993). Early family environments and traumatic experiences associated with borderline personality disorder. *Journal of Consulting and Clinical Psychology*, 61: 1068–1075.

Wells, A., & Papageorgiou, C. (1998). Relationships between worry, obsessive-compulsive symptoms and meta-cognitive beliefs. *Behaviour Research and Therapy*, 36(9): 899–913.

Whitfield, C. L. (1998). Internal evidence and corroboration of traumatic memories of child sexual abuse and addictive disorders. *Sexual Addiction and Compulsivity*, 5(4): 269–292.

Wittchen, H. V., Zhao, S., Kessler, R. C., & Eaton, W. W. (1994). DSM-III-R generalized anxiety disorder in the National Comorbidity Survey. *Archives of General Psychiatry*, 51: 355–364.

Wittchen, H. V., Reed, V., & Kessler, R. C. (1998). The relationship of agoraphobia and panic in a community sample of adolescent and young adults. *Archives of General Psychiatry*, 55(11): 1017–1024.

Unnewehr, S., Schneider, S., Florin, I., & Margraf, J. (1998). Psychopathology in children of patients with panic disorder or animal phobia. *Psychopathology*, 31(2): 69–84.

Yehuda, R., Schmeidler, J., Wainberg, M., Binder-Brynes, D., Duvdevani, T. (1998). Vulnerability to posttraumatic stress disorder in adult offspring of Holocaust survivors. *American Journal of Psychiatry*, 155(9): 1163–1171.

Yonkers, K. A., Zlotnick, C., Allsworth, J., Warshaw, M., Shea, T., & Keller, M. B. (1998). Is the course of panic disorder the same in women and men? *American Journal of Psychiatry*, 155(5): 596–602.

Zide, M. R., & Cherry, A. L. (1992). A typology of runaway youths: An empirically based definition. *Child and Adolescent Social Work Journal*, 9(2): 155–167.

SOMATOFORM, FACTITIOUS, AND MALINGERING DISORDERS

INTRODUCTION

The discussion about personality disorders (see Chapter 9) notes that the word *hysteria* dates back to Hippocrates, and the Egyptian era before him. "Hysteria" implied that the source of certain disorders, occurring primarily in women, could be traced to her "wandering uterus." Centuries later, Greek physicians believed the event of a "wandering uterus" resulted from the uterus being displaced (or wandering about the body) and dislocated vital organs, resulting in the development of multiple physical symptoms. The treatment consisted of attracting and redirecting the wayward uterus to its proper place in the womb, by using aromatic substances placed near the vagina (Smith, 1990).

In the ninth century, "hysteria" was considered a purely physical disorder. During the Middle Ages, the perspective shifted away from thinking of hysteria as a medical condition to that of a spiritual disorder emerging from evil and demonic possession, as in the case of witchcraft (Fabrega, 1991). In the seventeenth century, Thomas Sydenham, an English physician, observed that hysteria could disguise almost any medical disease (North & Guze, 1997). A century later, Dr. William Cullen adapted the term *neurosis* to describe a type of "nervous energy" or "nervous force" that he thought played an important part in the etiology of certain illnesses having medical, neurological, or psychiatric underpinnings (Fabrega, 1991).

In 1859, a noted French physician, Pierre Briquet, studied 430 of his patients for over a decade and provided the first formal description of the somatoform disorders. Briquet described people who had seemingly endless lists of complaints, but did not have a supporting medical basis (APA, 1980). His observations advanced the notion that individuals were usually afflicted early in life, and their symptoms were manifested by recurrent, unexplained, somatic complaints noted in many organ sites. Women were primarily affected. The disorder seemed to be incurable; individuals would return time and again with a new batch of symptoms. The more common complaints noted by Briquet's patients included vomiting, aphonia (inability to create sounds or speak), painful limbs, muscle weakness, dizziness, painful menstruation, a burning sensation in reproductive organs, and paralysis. Because of his initial observations, this "hysterical" disorder became known as Briquet's syndrome, and remained so for over 100 years. In 1980, the disorder was renamed **somatization disorder**, and it was included, for the first time, in the DSM-III (APA, 1980).

During the later part of the nineteenth century, the emerging field of psychiatry began to become more differentiated, and so did certain disorders including hypochondriasis, hysteria, and neurasthenia (unexplained fatigue and lassitude) that came to be regarded more as psychological disorders than organic disorders.

THE ESSENTIAL FEATURES OF SOMATOFORM DISORDERS

Somatoform disorders are a cluster of "illnesses" that comprise physical symptoms with no acceptable medical explanation (Kaplan et al., 1994). These somatic complaints are serious enough to cause the person significant emotional distress or diminish their interpersonal functioning, especially in social or occupational roles. The social worker should not underestimate the genuine discomfort experienced by their client (Maxmen & Ward, 1995).

When considering the various etiologic factors applicable to the somatization process, one must also appreciate the distinction between the concepts of illness and disease. *Disease* is defined as "a pathological condition of the body that presents a group of clinical signs, symptoms, and laboratory findings peculiar to it and setting the condition apart as an abnormal entity differing from other normal or pathological conditions" (Thomas, 1997, p. 552). In addition, there exist objectively measurable anatomic deformations and pathophysiologic states presumably caused by such varied factors as degenerative processes, traumas, toxins, and infectious agents. *Illness* refers to those experiences associated with disease that ultimately affect the person's state of being and social functioning. When describing illness, most would agree that it includes more than just the notion of a state of being sick. The practitioner takes into account the uniquely personal nature of each individual's suffering, their inability to fully participate in activities, and the decreased capacity for interpersonal relationships, all of which significantly affect their quality of life. The major distinction between disease and illness is that illness is highly individual. A person may have a serious disease, for example, hypothyroidism, but experience no feelings of pain or suffering, and thus no illness. Conversely, a person may be extremely ill as with a somatization disorder, but have no evidence of disease as measured by pathological changes in their body.

It is important to acknowledge that people who have somatoform disorders are not faking their symptoms, as would be in the case of factitious disorder, nor are they consciously pretending to be ill, as would be in the case of malingering disorder. The person with somatoform disorder really believes they have something seriously wrong with them, and this often causes enormous anxiety, distress, and impairment.

There are five somatoform disorders: *somatization disorder*, *conversion disorder*, *pain disorder*, *hypochondriasis*, and *body dysmorphic disorder* (BDD). This chapter will briefly address two additional categories. The first is undifferentiated somatoform disorder; this includes those persons who do not "fit" or fall below threshold somatization disorder behaviors because their symptoms are perceived as less severe. The second is somatoform disorder not otherwise specified; this is considered a catchall category for those who do not meet specific criteria for any of the somatoform disorders listed above.

When considering the presence of somatoform disorders, the central feature involves the individual who is pathologically concerned about the functioning or appearance of their body. These somatoform disorders are divided into three different groups based on the specific focus of the individual's beliefs or concerns regarding their physical symptoms, physical illness, and/or physical appearance:

- When the focus of attention and/or concern is on the individual's physical symptoms, somatization disorder, undifferentiated somatoform disorder, pain disorder, and conversion disorder should be considered.

- When focus is on the belief that the individual has a serious or life-threatening physical illness, hypochondriasis should be considered.

- When the individual believes and is convinced they have a serious defect in their physical appearance (while appearing normal to others), body dysmorphic disorder should be considered.

All of the somatoform disorders share two important features; namely, they involve predominately somatic complaints (or bodily preoccupation), and they are based on the idea that the focus on the body cannot be fully explained by any known medical disease or substance use. Kirmayer and Taillefer (1997) suggest, "as illness behavior, somatoform disorders can be best typified and understood in terms of dimensions rather than categories, processes rather than symptoms and signs, and social contexts rather than isolated behaviors" (p. 334). They further note, "this social approach not only fits the research data better than the individual psychopathology oriented perspective, it also has very useful implications for clinical assessment and treatment" (p. 334). The authors agree and suggest the competency-based assessment model is a way to help practitioners rethink the category of somatoform disorders. The model encourages the practitioner to avoid some of the invalidating, negative attitudes and stigmatization that affect clients with somatoform disorders. This approach to assessment pays attention to the client's biological domain, and the practitioner should consider the presence of four pain symptoms, two gastrointestinal symptoms, one sexual symptom, and one pseudoneurological symptom when assessing for somatoform disorders. We will review each of the major somatoform disorders and provide an illustrative example for each in this chapter. The first discussed is somatization disorder.

SOMATIZATION DISORDER

Somatization represents a polysymptomatic disorder that begins early in life, affects mostly women, and is characterized by recurrent, multiple bodily or physical somatic complaints (Stoudemire, 1994). Among women, estimates of the lifetime prevalence range from 0.2 to 2 percent (Moore & Jefferson, 1996). Unlike most of the other groups of disorders we have discussed so far, somatoform disorders are not anchored together by common etiologies, family histories, or other associated factors (Morrison, 1995; Yutzy et al., 1995). Somatization disorder is rarely seen in males, and some doubt that it ever occurs in males.

Certainly most of us have endured annoying physical symptoms or ailments at one time or another. We have all suffered from headaches, nausea, muscle aches, or just feeling "blah." However, much of the time we try to "tough it out" or ignore the discomfort. For the individual with somatization disorder, this is generally not true. They will seek medical attention for almost every ache or pain. This may include an office visit to a physician, with a workup that might involve extensive laboratory tests, X rays, or other diagnostic medical procedures, and from which they leave with several prescriptions in hand that will "cure" their medical complaint (Maxmen & Ward, 1995; Smith, 1994). It is incumbent upon the practitioner to be mindful of the client who describes a pattern of recurring, multiple, clinically significant physical complaints.

The practitioner should listen carefully when the person talks about their medical history. The individual tends to be somewhat inaccurate, vague, and uncertain about when symptoms first started. In addition, the person may tend to exaggerate or dramatize their symptoms. For example, a backache is never described as a mild ache that "will pass." Their backache, as noted by one of the authors' clients, is described as "the worst backache anyone in the entire world could possibly have which feels like red-hot pokers jammed up inside my spine." Some individuals may assume an opposite emotional stance, or show inappropriate indifference in the face of seemingly tragic and overwhelming medical events. This is known as *la belle indifference*. For example, a person might describe "vomiting buckets of blood until passing out with no trace of emotional concern" (North & Guze, 1997, p. 271). However, either the presence or absence of *la belle indifference* should not be considered an accurate measure of whether the individual has somatization disorder (Kaplan & Sadock, 1998).

After repeatedly recounting descriptions of complaints, the individual might begin to reinvent or create "changes" regarding the intensity, duration, severity, or the level of impairment in their health and medical problems. These symptoms become a never-ending way of life. If the person manages to gain some relief, there are always new complaints waiting to emerge. "In fact, physical complaints seem to be the one constant that these people depend on, almost as if their complaints give meaning and organization to their otherwise chaotic lives" (Nietzel et al., 1998, p. 275).

Certain red flags in a client's medical history should begin to alert the practitioner to beginning an assessment for the presence of a somatization disorder. Often, the first clue is a complicated medical history that is fraught with multiple diagnoses, failed treatments, and voluminous medical records (North & Guze, 1997). Hardly a year will pass without the person experiencing some intense physical discomfort. In addition, their medical "story" is complicated by a number of other features, for example, a history of multiple allergies or medication intolerance (Gothe et al., 1995; Simon et al., 1990). None of these are pathognomonic (indicative of a disease) by themselves. However, they are important to consider when combined with other signs and symptoms. They include complaints for which no well-integrated structural or pathophysiologic (the study of how normal physiological processes are altered by disease) models are known, or for which the individual does not fit the definition of the syndrome (North & Guze, 1997). Examples include irritable bowel syndrome (Talley, 1991; Thompson & Pigeon-Ressor, 1990); burning tongue or burning mouth (Jerlang, 1997; Van Houdenhove & Joostens, 1995); bodily sensations (Steptoe & Noll, 1997); nonanginal chest pain (with normal angiogram) (Eifert, 1991); pseudoseizures (Griffith et al., 1998; Harden, 1997; Kalogjera-Sackellares & Sackellares, 1997; Savard, 1990); pseudocyesis (false pregnancy) (Small, 1986; Starkman et al., 1985); dysphagia (difficulty swallowing) (Kim et al., 1996); chronic fatigue syndrome (Abbey & Garfinkel, 1991; Fischler et al., 1997; Lawrie et al., 1997); fibromyalgia (Hadler, 1997; Ostensen et al., 1997); myofascial pain syndrome (Merskey, 1993); interstitial cystitis (Ratliff et al., 1994); dyspareunia (painful coitus) (Meana & Binik, 1994); dysmenorrhea (painful menses) (Whitehead et al., 1986); "hysterical paralysis" (Marshall et al., 1997); tension headache (Blanchard, 1992); syncope (fainting) (Kapoor et al., 1995); and premenstrual syndrome (Kuczmierczyk et al., 1995).

An important area to explore is the extent to which a person who is suffering from a somatoform disorder wants to get better versus what it would entail to give up their physical symptoms. People with somatization disorder sometimes use their symptoms to control, manipulate, hold on to a relationship, or divert attention away from other problematic aspects of their lives. Other individuals may experience *alexithymia*; that is, the inability to identify and articulate their feelings and needs, or to experience and express emotions except through physical symptoms.

Based on current research, somatization criteria are greatly simplified by requiring the presence of at least eight symptoms (Cloninger, 1996). For those reporting fewer than eight somatic complaints, undifferentiated somatization disorder may apply. We will discuss assessment differentiation in greater detail later in the chapter.

When considering somatization disorder, the assessment includes:

- The onset starts before the age of 30, and the individual has a history of having many physical complaints occurring over several years.

- The individual sought treatment for these symptoms, or they experienced significant impairment in social, occupational, or other important areas of interpersonal functioning.

- *Each of the following* must have been met, with individual symptoms occurring at any time during the course of the disturbance. (These symptoms do not have to be concurrent.)

    Pain symptoms (four or more) that are related to different sites or functions, such as the head, abdomen, back/spine, joints, extremities, chest, rectum, or related to bodily functions, such as during sexual intercourse, menstruation, or during urination.

    Gastrointestinal symptoms (two or more, excluding pain), such as nausea, bloating, vomiting (other than during pregnancy), diarrhea, or intolerance of certain foods.

Sexual symptoms (at least one, excluding pain), including indifference to sex, difficulties with erection or ejaculation, irregular menses, excessive menstrual bleeding, or vomiting throughout an entire pregnancy.

Pseudoneurological symptoms (at least one), a history suggesting a neurological condition, including poor balance or poor coordination, paralysis or localized weakness, difficulty in swallowing or feeling a lump in the throat, loss of voice, urinary retention, hallucinations, loss of touch or pain sensation, double vision, blindness, deafness, or seizures or other dissociative symptoms, such as amnesia or loss of consciousness (other than fainting). None of these are limited to pain; in other words, pain in itself is not enough to assess the presence of a pseudoneurological symptom.

- For each of the symptoms noted above, *one of the following* additional conditions must also be met:

    Appropriate physical or laboratory examination determines that symptoms cannot be fully explained by a general medical condition or by the use of substances (for example, a drug of abuse or a medication); *or*

    When there is a related general medical condition, the impairment or physical complaints experienced exceed what would generally be expected, based on the history, physical examination, or laboratory findings.

- The individual does not consciously feign or intentionally produce the symptoms, as in factitious disorder (for example, maintaining the sick role for their secondary gain) or as in malingering (achieving some material gain) (APA, 1994, 2000).

Prevailing Pattern

Although somatization is a discrete (or single) disorder, the practitioner may also recognize it as a continuum of physical disturbances. Individuals with this disorder have a number of both medical and physical complaints. Katon and associates (1993) studied a group of individuals considered to be primarily emotionally distressed and found they frequently utilized medical services instead of using mental health services. Their study suggests a fine line exists between those who have psychologically related concerns and those who struggle with somatic complaints. Those with somatization disorder tend to be shuffled back and forth between medical and mental health settings. A thorough physical examination helps to distinguish those physical symptoms that cannot be explained by the accompanying physical findings (Frances et al., 1995).

For women in the United States, the prevalence of somatization disorder ranges somewhere between 0.5 and 2 percent, but the percentage may be even higher when undifferentiated somatoform disorders are included. Cultural factors and beliefs (Piccinelli & Simon, 1997) may also affect the prevalence rate and the kind of symptoms reported. While somatization disorder is rarely seen in men (less than 0.2 percent) within the United States (APA, 1994, 2000; Golding et al., 1991), other studies support finding somatization disorder in men living in Puerto Rico (Canino et al., 1997), Latin America, India, Africa, and Greece (Gureje et al., 1997; Maxmen & Ward, 1995).

In the United States, unmarried, poorly educated women of color are most likely to be assessed as having somatization disorder (Ford, 1995). Kaplan and

Sadock (1996) suggest that somatizing may be the primary way some disenfranchised women express their discontent or feelings of disappointment with their social situation without having to deal with some of the more negative consequences of acting out in other inappropriate ways. Ford (1995) posits that those who lack social support may be driven to seek out medical or clinical attention as a substitute for the lack of a social network. Although these individuals tend to focus on their physical complaints, they also report many other psychological symptoms. In addition to these physical complaints, individuals with somatization disorder commonly suffer from a wide spectrum of psychological symptoms, and mood and anxiety disorders are often assessed (Wetzel et al., 1994). Katon (1993) suggests that both a prior or current episode of major depression can be found in approximately 90 percent of somatizing individuals. Phobias, panic, and anxiety disorders are often present, as is a history of suicide attempts (Barbee et al., 1997; Bhui & Hotoph, 1997).

The competency-based assessment provides insight into the somatization disorder by directing the practitioner's attention to a better understanding of biopsychosocial factors. Several findings point to a *biological predisposition* (Wilson et al., 1996). Of the few studies that have examined somatization disorder, most found strong evidence that it tends to run in families and has an element of inheritance (Andreasen & Black, 1995; Katon, 1993). Somatization disorder is strongly correlated to a familial predisposition for antisocial personality disorder. (Refer to Chapter 9 for a more detailed discussion of personality disorders.) Sigvardsson et al. (1984) note that somatization disorder was more common in women whose biological parents were diagnosed with antisocial personality disorder. This was later confirmed in a study by Lilienfeld (1992), who found high rates of antisocial personality disorder in first-degree relatives of individuals with somatization disorder.

Researchers have suggested that familial association between somatization disorder and antisocial personality disorder represents a different gender-based expression of the same underlying biological predisposition. Specifically, somatization occurs chiefly in women, while antisocial personality disorder occurs primarily in men (Lilienfeld, 1992). These two disorders are linked through several distinctive and overlapping features. Both begin early in life, follow a chronic course, and are complicated by marital discord, substance abuse, and suicidal behavior (Lilienfeld, 1992). On the face of it, these disorders seem to be quite different. While all of the answers are not known just yet, the current thinking about the influence of gender differences (Lilienfeld, 1992) is a compelling argument for using the competency-based assessment. Empirical data is needed that builds on the competency-based assessment perspective while exploring the interplay among the social and interpersonal aspects of a person's life, the illness experience, and the stigma of medically unexplained symptoms (Fritz et al., 1997).

Individuals with an antisocial personality disorder (mostly males) do not seem to experience anxiety, although they may experience panic on occasion (Fowles, 1993). Instead, they are overly responsive to short-term impulsive rewards, even if the pursuit of these rewards eventually gets them into serious trouble. There is accumulating evidence that impulsive and aggressive intrapersonal tendencies are common themes for those with antisocial personality disorder. It is quite possible that gender roles and societal attitudes toward gender socialization play a large role in the profound differences found between men and women in the expression of the same biological vulnerability. This raises an interesting point to consider. Could these gender differences suggest that while society is more "forgiving" of men for being aggressive, society does not accept a woman's similar response? Those behavioral characteristics of antisocial personality disorder that include problems with law enforcement, persistent lying, problems with money and finances, poor interpersonal relationships, occupational difficulties, and physical aggression toward others are seen as more "acceptable" behaviors for men. Consequently, if women exhibit these same behaviors, they are viewed as being more "disturbed." On the other hand, the frequent development of new somatic symptoms, the lack of aggression, and notable dependence among women often gains them immediate sympathy and attention, even though this eventually dissipates. Kirmayer and Robbins (1991) suggest women with a somatization disorder exhibit a variety of somatic complaints and psychological problems in lieu of being aggressive.

Stern et al. (1993) note that over 70 percent of those with somatization disorder also have coexisting personality disorders. It is inaccurate to view persons who somatize as having predominately physical symptoms. While somatization disorder has historically been linked to the histrionic personality disorder (Slavney, 1990), the most commonly associated personality disorders include avoidant, paranoid, and obsessive-compulsive (Smith et al., 1991).

The competency-based assessment considers interpersonal variables in a person's life. Those with somatization disorder often describe their childhood experiences that include pain or serious illness in a family member (Hartvig & Sterner, 1985). Women with somatization disorder are more likely to report a history of childhood sexual and/or physical abuse than other females who have somatic complaints (Pribor et al., 1993; Slavney, 1994). Interestingly, it may be that women who suffered childhood abuse establish some sort of paradoxical communication patterns that include hiding their feelings and reality on one hand, while seeking acknowledgment of their current suffering from medical intervention on the other hand (Morse et al., 1997). Brodsky's (1984) earlier work identified six important family factors that one should consider when assessing for somatization disorder:

- Raised in a family that has a history of multiple physical complaints
- Raised by parent(s) who were seen as demanding and unrewarding when the child was healthy, but seen as caring and loving when the child was sick
- A home environment where one or both parents suffered from multiple illnesses
- An environment where other coping mechanisms for handling or dealing with psychosocial crisis were unavailable
- Developing a repertoire of reactions that are used to withdraw from usual life activities or to engage, manipulate, or punish others
- Knowingly fabricating and inventing an illness in order to obtain something of value, gain a benefit, or avoid punishment.

Somatization disorder begins before the person is 30 years old. Furthermore, Swartz et al. (1991) found that 55 percent of cases they studied had an onset before the age of 15. This finding suggests that somatization disorder might develop earlier in childhood or adolescence than was previously thought. The most common symptoms associated with somatization disorder include chest pain, palpitations, feeling bloated, shortness of breath (without exertion), dizziness, headaches, feelings of weakness, and fatigue (North & Guze, 1997; Smith et al., 1986). The following vignette illustrates how the practitioner might encounter someone who has a somatization disorder.

The Case of Helene Martin

Helene Martin, is a 24-year-old single, attractive African-American woman. She came into the emergency room with her best friend, Jessica Leah, because she was "having trouble breathing," and wondered whether she was starting to have a heart attack. Helene and Jessica have been friends since grade school. They have shared many "troubles" together, and Helene values their mutual friendship. She also complained to the emergency room physician that she was experiencing "terrible swelling in my knees."

Upon physical examination, Helene related that she had many health problems over the years. She always considered herself to be a "sickly" child. However, she started having physical problems when she was a teenager. She related that she was raised in a family who were demanding and critical. When she was ill, the story changed; that is, her parents seemed to be loving and caring. She stated that her mother tended to be "sickly" as a child, too. As a part of taking her medical history, Helene revealed that her father tended to rule the family "with an iron hand and a heavy belt." The physician noted in the medical history that Helene was overly dramatic when talking about her self, had a strong need to be the center of attention, and that her expression of emotion was shallow and shifted rapidly. In addition, she described an excessive concern with her physical appearance and that her relationships with men were fraught with sexually provocative behavior.

The physician considered Helene to be very bright, but noted that she never finished high school. Helene stated that she wants to go back to night school to earn her GED. Her lack of formal education seemed to keep her locked into low paying and menial jobs, causing feelings of discontent and disappointment. Before the physician could go further in her examination, Helene took out a large sheaf of papers, and handed them over. She stated, "Here, I think that instead of me rattling off all the problems I've had, I'll give you a copy of what's been wrong with me, and save you some time figuring everything out."

Helene's personal 300-page "health diary" documented ten years of her past medical history. The following highlights a partial and limited illustration of her more current problems:

January 10   (3:30 P.M.) I had a terrible period, with lots of horrible cramps and bleeding. I stayed in bed four days; had to miss work. I saw Dr. Able, and she gave me a prescription, but it didn't help very much.

January 31 (3:00 A.M.) I had pain during intercourse (again).

I went to see Dr. Baker today but she wasn't very helpful. She told me to "relax more." What a joke!

February 9 I had a urinary tract infection, and it burned a lot when I tried to pee. I saw Dr. Carter, but he wouldn't give me a prescription (said it wouldn't help). He said that I've complained about urinary burning three times last year, and didn't have anything wrong then, and I didn't have anything wrong today. I won't go back to him again!

March 7 I had another seizure (again). I was admitted to the hospital, but the EEG didn't show anything. I was hospitalized at Mercy Baptist for two days and had lots of tests. Dr. Dankin said, "There was really good news, you don't have a brain tumor." I told him that I felt really dizzy a lot this week and lost my balance four times. He told me not to worry about anything and said my problems would probably disappear if I forgot about them.

April 11 (8:00 P.M.) My knee and hip joints are really painful and swollen. I lost three days of work because I can hardly sit or walk. Mom came over to cook dinner. Dr. Evans was on vacation, but her associate (I don't know her name) was on emergency call. The doctor said that since she didn't know me well enough, she couldn't give me a prescription over the telephone. She told me to go the emergency room and she would meet me there to examine me. I don't think I'm gonna use Dr. Evans anymore.

May 21 I had several really bad incidents of diarrhea, bloating, and vomiting the past few days. I went in for an appointment with Dr. Frankel, and he admitted me to the hospital. He said that I needed a complete workup. I had every test you could think of (upper and lower barium enema, sigmoidoscopy, colonoscopy, X rays to my stomach, MRI, and lots of blood work). Dr. Frankel called it the "VIP treatment." He said, "Absolutely nothing is wrong with you," and suggested that maybe "it was just an upset stomach." Dr. Frankel added that I should watch my diet for a couple of days after I got home. He also suggested that I make an appointment to see a social worker. I think he wants to blame this on a mental condition, but he's wrong.

May 25 I had terrible diarrhea again at midnight; and also think I'm allergic to eggs, because I had a serious case of heartburn.

June 1 The diarrhea is finally gone, but now I'm so constipated I feel very bloated. My rectum is swollen and it hurts to have a bowel movement. Being constipated has irritated my hemorrhoids into acting up. I called Dr. Graystone, but she's no longer in practice, so I guess I'll find another doctor (someone who can finally help me). I went to the emergency room and they agreed with me that I was constipated. I wanted a prescription for my condition, but they told me to go out to the drug store and buy "Milk of Magnesia." They promised it would work.

June 15   I have both a terrible headache and backache, but I don't have the money to go see a doctor, so I used some of the medicine I once got from Dr. Carter, but it didn't help. I'm in a tremendous amount of pain. I have to miss work again.

June 17   (2:00 A.M.) My headache and backache continue to cause me terrible pain. I finally went to the emergency room, and they admitted me for observation. I had several tests, but the doctors think that whatever I had went away, and that I shouldn't have anymore trouble. The ER doctor gave me the name of some social worker, but I told him, "I'm not a head case." They are just trying to pass me off because they can't find out what's wrong with me.

July 15   I'm having a lot of trouble swallowing. I saw a new doctor, Dr. Herrold, and he referred me to Dr. Isaac, an ear, nose, and throat specialist. Dr. Isaac stuck some tubes down my throat, and said he couldn't find anything wrong. He told me not to think about it, and that it would go away. I got a peek at my insurance form, and saw that the doctor called my swallowing trouble, "Globus hystericus." I looked up that diagnosis as soon as I got home. I think that Dr. Isaac doesn't know what he's talking about. Globus hystericus doesn't sound like "nothing" to me. In the meantime, Mom prepares soft foods and milkshakes for me to eat.

August 13   I can't tolerate eating any dairy products because I have had lots of stomach bloating recently. I found out from my mom that when I was a teenager I had lots of "intolerances to foods and certain medications."

September 22   I'm having burning when I urinate. I went to see Dr. Jankowski and she told me, "Helene, you don't have any evidence of a urinary tract infection. There is nothing to treat you for." I don't agree with her. Later, that day, I made an appointment to see Dr. Kaye, who came highly recommended by another secretary who used her. Dr. Kaye said she thought I might have a bladder problem. I had all sorts of "procedures" done. She told me, "my laboratory tests were unremarkable and didn't support any findings that would lead her to believe that I had any kind of urinary or bladder problem going on right now." Dr. Kaye told me that I should try to drink more fluids.

October 5   (11 P.M.) I'm feeling really very, very nauseous. I know that I'm not pregnant (have my period, too). I threw up lots of times. I don't know what's wrong. Fred, my boyfriend, went to get me something from the drug store. I didn't work yesterday or today.

November 15   I went to see Dr. Baker (again). My period is causing me a lot of discomfort. She said that if I still have problems by tomorrow, she'll do a D&C. She said she was not happy to be performing a fourth D&C on me. She said I should go to a specialist after this.

November 22 Today, I went to the outpatient facility for a D&C. The doctor said that maybe I should seek out some counseling. I told her I'd think about it, but I really won't. How come they don't realize how much pain I'm in?

December 15 (6:00 A.M.) I'm really having problems breathing. I can't catch my breath or take a deep breath. I'm worried that I might be having a heart attack because my heart feels like its fluttering. I'm going to go to the emergency room, and maybe they can help me.

On December 16, Helene was hospitalized because of her cardiac symptoms and breathing complaints. During the current hospitalization, she had both a comprehensive physical and medical examination, and laboratory tests (to rule out any viable medical condition). Helene was given a clean bill of health and subsequently referred to a social worker for counseling and support.

Assessment Summary

Irrespective of the underlying motives, all possible explanations for somatization encourage a thorough medical examination and an inquiry into Helene's biopsychosocial history. Helene's behavior should be explored in the context of existing medical complaints and the extent to which these symptoms could help serve to resolve her life problems or represent psychological conflicts (Folks et al., 1994). The extent of Helene's complaints, the degree to which she suffers, and her inability to engage in her usual level of activities is noteworthy.

While those with major depressive disorder, generalized anxiety disorder, and schizophrenia might present somatic complaints, eventually their symptoms override the somatic complaints (Kaplan et al., 1994). Although there is a strong association between panic attacks and somatization disorders, the person is generally not bothered by somatic symptoms between panic attacks (Furer et al., 1997). In factitious disorder, the person derives great satisfaction from being considered ill. In malingering disorder, the symptoms are intentionally produced to avoid some task, legal action, or obtain material and/or financial goods for their own "gain." In contrast, Helene's physical discomfort is "genuine" to her; that is, she truly believes she is ill. Helene also exhibits a long-standing pattern of excessive emotionality and attention seeking behaviors that seeps into all areas of her life. She needs to be the center of attention in two main ways. Her interests tend to be at the forefront of all of her relationships, and her behavior, including speech, constantly calls attention to herself. This supports an Axis II diagnosis of histrionic personality disorder.

In beginning to understand Helene's total functioning, the practitioner must first make an assessment that includes all aspects of her life history and life experiences. Helene's worker, first and foremost, must rule out nonpsychiatric medical conditions that may offer an alternative explanation of her symptoms. Unlike the individual with hypochondriasis, who excessively "doctor shops" (Barsky et al., 1998; McCahill, 1995) and who is more preoccupied with the false belief that they have a specific disease or have a *fear of a specific disease*, Helene's focus is more on the

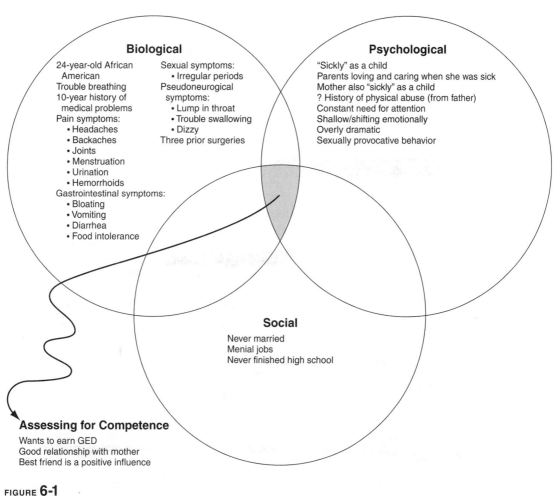

Biological

24-year-old African
   American
Trouble breathing
10-year history of
   medical problems
Pain symptoms:
   • Headaches
   • Backaches
   • Joints
   • Menstruation
   • Urination
   • Hemorrhoids
Gastrointestinal symptoms:
   • Bloating
   • Vomiting
   • Diarrhea
   • Food intolerance

Sexual symptoms:
   • Irregular periods
Pseudoneurogical
   symptoms:
   • Lump in throat
   • Trouble swallowing
   • Dizzy
Three prior surgeries

Psychological

"Sickly" as a child
Parents loving and caring when she was sick
Mother also "sickly" as a child
? History of physical abuse (from father)
Constant need for attention
Shallow/shifting emotionally
Overly dramatic
Sexually provocative behavior

Social

Never married
Menial jobs
Never finished high school

Assessing for Competence

Wants to earn GED
Good relationship with mother
Best friend is a positive influence

FIGURE **6-1**

SOMATIZATION DISORDER

The interactions of biological, psychological, and social variables in Helene Martin's life.

symptoms of disease. In conversion disorder, symptoms are usually limited to only one, typically involving the central nervous system—for example, the individual becomes "blind," "paralyzed," or "mute" (Poyner & Pritty, 1997). Pain disorder is limited to one or two complaints of pain symptoms, such as low back pain. In contrast, Helene's "health diary" reveals a wide variety of symptoms occurring over a period of time (Hiller et al., 1997). Once one complaint is addressed, another one emerges. The competency-based assessment provides a framework for assessing Helene's strengths. In particular, an assessment of interpersonal factors notes that she has a good relationship with her mother. She also has a "best friend" who is supportive of her. Additionally, Helene wants to return to school for her GED.

Helene Martin's current diagnosis is:

Axis I	300.81 Somatization Disorder
Axis II	301.50 Histrionic Personality Disorder
Axis III	None
Axis IV	None
Axis IV	GAF = 60 (at time of examination)

CONVERSION DISORDER

Conversion symptoms have been described since antiquity and represent a type of somatoform disorder. The individual experiences a loss or change in physical functioning that suggests the presence of a physical disorder but cannot be explained on the basis of any known physiologic mechanism. In other words, this loss or change does not exist outside the individual's own personal experience.

Freud believed that the anxiety resulting from unconscious conflicts needed to find expression and was somehow "converted" into physical symptoms. He believed that this transformation, or conversion, allowed the individual to "get rid" of some of their anxiety without actually having to experience it (Barlow & Durand, 1997). Freud was given credit for coining the term *conversion* in conjunction with his famous work with his patient, Anna O. However, he was not the actual originator of the term, but borrowed it from the Middle Ages (Mace, 1992).

Conversion disorder is one of the most intriguing examples of an individual's behavior that the practitioner will probably encounter in professional practice. What could possibly account for a person going blind when their optic functions are perfectly normal, or experiencing a seizure when there is no viable neurological explanation (Barlow & Durand, 1995; Lesser, 1996)? Consider the following case that is an interesting historical account from the 1677 Bargarran witchcraft trial:

> Seven people were condemned in Paisley, Ireland for allegedly using witchcraft against Christina, favored daughter of the powerful Laird of Bargarran. As the story unfolds, seven months after several disgruntled servants placed a "spell" on Christina, she began having bizarre seizures. During these episodes she claimed to "see the devil." She believed that invisible assailants forced strange and foreign materials into her mouth and she had no real understanding why she experienced fits [seizures] or why she ate strange things. The notable Glasgow physician, Matthew Brisban, was consulted, and he later gave evidence at the trial against the servants. Dr. Brisban admitted he could find no natural explanation for Christina's seizures or her eating strange substances.
>
> Christina subsequently recovered, and later married a minister from Kilmours. After her husband's untimely death (no information is known about what happened), Christina established a highly prosperous spinning business that later led to the beginning of the famous Paisley cotton industry. (McDonald & Thom, 1996)

The case of Christina is a good example of pseudoneurological symptoms. Her conversion symptoms resemble genuine sensory or motor symptoms that do not conform to anatomical patterns expected for a condition with a well-defined physical cause, and they developed suddenly after a stressful event (being cursed by disgruntled servants).

Prevailing Pattern

Given similar circumstances, it is highly likely that Christina would be considered as someone with a conversion disorder. Criteria for conversion disorder are:

- One or more symptoms affecting voluntary motor or sensory function suggesting a neurological or another general medical condition
- Psychological factors are considered to be associated with the symptoms, because interpersonal conflicts or other social stresses precede the onset (or exacerbation) of the symptoms
- The individual does not consciously produce or feign the symptoms, as in factitious or malingering disorder
- A neurological condition, medication, the effects of a substance, or culturally sanctioned behaviors cannot fully explain these symptoms
- Symptoms are not limited to pain or sexual dysfunction
- It does not occur solely during somatization disorder, and no other medical disorder better explains it
- Symptoms are serious enough to produce at least one of the following:
    It causes distress that is clinically important; or
    It warrants medical evaluation; or
    It impairs social, occupational, or personal functioning.

It is important to *specify* among four types of symptoms or deficits. They are:

- *Motor deficits*, including difficulties such as swallowing (lump in throat), poor balance or gait, paralysis or feeling weakness in arms or legs, loss of voice, and urinary retention
- *Seizure-like symptoms*
- *Sensory deficits*, such as losing the sensation of touch or pain, blindness, double vision, and deafness
- *With a mixed presentation* (APA, 1994, 2000).

Although the symptoms of conversion disorder are temporarily disabling, they differ significantly in a number of ways from those disabilities caused by actual neurological disorders. In conversion disorder, the symptoms ebb and flow depending on the person's activity level. The symptoms typically do not conform to known anatomical pathways, disease processes, or physiological mechanisms. Conversion disorder is characterized by the occurrence of certain signs and symptoms that are clearly inconsistent with what is actually known about human anatomy and pathophysiology (Moore & Jefferson, 1996). In other words, the individual's understanding and their own conceptualization, however faulty, of anatomy, diseases, and physiology help shape the symptoms they present (APA, 1994, 2000; Andreasen & Black,

1995). The individual who is actually paralyzed cannot move certain parts of their body, whereas in conversion disorder the individual is able to move their "paralyzed" arm if, for example, they need to scratch an annoying itch (Nietzel et al., 1998). However, they do not realize it. "People with conversion symptoms can usually function normally, but they seem truly and honestly unaware of this ability or of the sensory input they are receiving. An individual with conversion symptoms of blindness can usually make their way around and avoid objects in their visual field, but they can't tell you they saw the objects" (Barlow & Durand, 1995, p. 214). This is not to say that these symptoms are consciously constructed or intentionally faked. For the individual who suffers from conversion disorder, the intent and construction of symptoms are an unconscious process.

Conversion symptoms are called pseudoneurological because they resemble actual sensory or motor symptoms. They usually do not correspond to the anatomical pattern that would be expected for a condition with a well-defined physical cause. Actual manifestations of symptoms are quite varied. In some cases, the disorder mimics neurological problems, where symptoms presented range among poor balance, poor coordination, paralysis, or an inability to see. Others experience symptoms of weakness in their limbs or have difficulty swallowing. Sometimes conversion disorders appear as tics or tremors. At other times, there may be sensory symptoms or deficits that include double vision, tunnel vision, blindness, deafness, hallucinations, or the absence of touch or pain sensation. When the practitioner explores a person's medical history, most individuals with conversion disorder will describe only one motor or neurological symptom, such as blindness, paralysis, seizures, tunnel vision, coordination disturbances (previously known as astasia-abasia), **ataxia** (defective muscle coordination), **globus hystericus** (lump in throat), **syncope** (fainting), **dyskinesia** (inability to perform voluntary movements), **paresthesia** (sensation of numbness, prickling, or tingling), **tonic-clonic pseudoseizures** (muscular spasms), **anosmia** (absent sense of smell), **hemiplegia** (paralysis on one side of the body), deafness, anesthesia (absence of feel), or **akinesia** (complete or partial loss of muscle movement).

When conversion "anesthesia" occurs in a hand (or foot), the syndrome might accompany the so-called *stocking-glove distribution*. The individual experiences the loss of sensation or numbness in their hand (or foot), in an area typically covered by a glove (or stocking) and ending abruptly in a sharply demarcated line like a bracelet around the wrist. The actual disbursement pattern of the nerves (or "wiring" that occurs in the hand or foot) is, in reality, very different. If a true paralysis occurred, it would run the entire length of the hand or foot and not end in such a sharply demarcated line (Martin, 1992; Morrison, 1995; Neitzel et al., 1998).

Although conversion disorder can appear at any age, most individuals experience their first symptoms during adolescence or early adulthood. In most cases, the actual onset is abrupt and typically follows a major stress event in a person's life (Moore & Jefferson, 1996).

It is important to be aware of other important features associated with conversion disorder. They are:

• *Primary gain*—Individuals can achieve primary gain by keeping internal conflicts outside of their awareness, and they have low levels of insight about what is going on in their lives.

- *Secondary gain*—Individuals accumulate discernable advantages from their symptoms and behaviors as a result of being in the sick role. For instance, they may be excused from confronting or dealing with difficult life situations, control other people, or receive support and help that might not otherwise be given.

There is some risk associated with actual physical and long-term impairment if certain conversion symptoms persist over an extended period of time. Those who do not regularly use their muscles often experience muscle atrophy (or damage). This disuse of muscles may also result in causing the demineralization of the skeletal system. The vignette below, about Jenny Webber, illustrates how someone may experience conversion disorder.

Differential Assessment

Until recently, conversion disorder was thought to be primarily psychological in origin. Parobek (1997) raises the possibility that conversion disorder is actually an early disruption in the functioning of the nervous system in certain predisposed individuals. Conversion disorders have an uncanny resemblance to neurological problems. Formulating a differential assessment is critical, and the practitioner should refer the client to a physician in order to rule out neurological diseases.

The Case of Jenny Webber

Jake Webber rushed his wife, Jenny, to the emergency room of a rural hospital that was two towns away from their home. During the 75-mile drive, he was extremely worried about his wife. Jenny Webber is 34 years old and the mother of three children. She has been employed as a secretary for the past eight years at a local accounting firm. She is involved in her church, where she teaches Sunday school. Through work and church she has cultivated many friends.

In the emergency room, Jake told the resident physician on duty, "We were just standing in line buying some soda at Duncan's General Store when all of a sudden some guy pulls out a gun and tells everybody, 'This is a hold-up,' and then he tells us to get down on the floor." He continued, "The robber grabs some money out of the cash register, runs into the a waiting car, and heads for the hills. I mean, the whole thing didn't take more than 15 seconds. The next thing I know, the police are all over the place and they're asking people to describe the thief. One of the cops comes over to Jenny and me and asks us if we'd come downtown to the station and go through some 'mug shots.' The next thing I know, Jenny stumbles and falls, yelling at me that she can't see."

The physician began his physical examination. He noted that while Mrs. Webber complained of blindness, her pupils constricted when his flashlight illuminated her eyes. When he made a sudden movement toward her face, she blinked rapidly as if to involuntarily protect her eyes from harm.

Mrs. Webber was examined for signs of neurological or other general medical conditions that may explain her "blindness." Her laboratory results indicated that she was not under the influence of drugs or alcohol. The physician consulted the other doctor in town, who suggested using a treatment that included a placebo. The emergency room physician assured Mrs. Webber that she would receive a "special shot" intended to bring her vision back to normal. Within ten seconds of having this "special shot," Mrs. Webber's vision returned, much to her delight. She was discharged from the hospital with a referral for counseling at the North Bismark Mental Health Center.

Assessment Summary

In contrast to somatization disorder, which is chronic and polysymptomatic (involving many organ systems), Jenny's conversion disorder included features that are sporadic and monosymptomatic (Kent et al., 1995). Her frightening experience observing the general store hold-up set the foundation for a symbolic relationship between the underlying psychological struggle to cope with her fears and the associated loss of sight. A pivotal point in this vignette is that Jenny's blindness occurred suddenly when the police officer asked her to come to the station to look at mug shots of potential suspects.

While Jenny was an unwilling participant in this criminal activity, she manifested none of the features of posttraumatic disorder as discussed earlier (see Chapter 5), for example, flashbacks of the event or nightmares. While Jenny claimed she

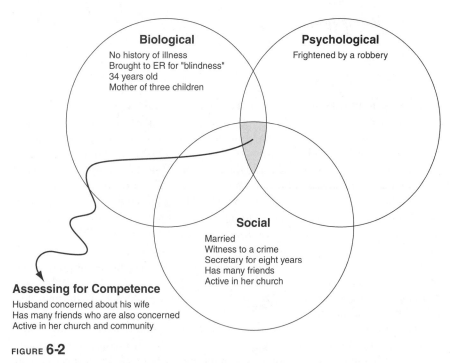

Biological
No history of illness
Brought to ER for "blindness"
34 years old
Mother of three children

Psychological
Frightened by a robbery

Social
Married
Witness to a crime
Secretary for eight years
Has many friends
Active in her church

Assessing for Competence
Husband concerned about his wife
Has many friends who are also concerned
Active in her church and community

FIGURE **6-2**

CONVERSION DISORDER

The interactions of biological, psychological, and social variables in Jenny Webber's life.

could not see, her eyes reacted to light. When the physician moved toward her, she blinked reflexively in response to his sudden movement.

When given the "special shot" (a placebo), Jenny experienced a spontaneous remission of her blindness and a complete recovery. In fact, prompt recovery is usually the rule, and few individuals need long-term care (Silver, 1996; Speed, 1996). It is not uncommon for the practitioner to see someone similar to Jenny in an ambulatory or emergency room setting where the individual responds to almost any therapeutic intervention that offers the suggestion of a "cure."

While the relevant information in this case focuses on "deficits" and "blindness," the practitioner looks at the whole person and takes into consideration Jenny's strengths as an integral part of the assessment. She is very active in her rural community and committed to church functions. A number of friends care about Jenny. She has worked in the same position for eight years, and lastly, her husband, Jake, is very devoted to her.

Jenny Webber's overall diagnosis would be considered:

Axis I	300.11 Conversion Disorder		
Axis II	V71.09 (No diagnosis)		
Axis III	None		
Axis IV	None		
Axis V	GAF =	60 (on admission)	
		90 (at discharge)	

UNDERSTANDING PAIN DISORDER

The assessment of pain disorder can be made when a person's predominant clinical complaint is pain that is "the predominant focus of clinical attention" *and* when psychological factors that may play a significant role in causing or maintaining the pain are present. This disorder has been known by a number of different names in the past including somatoform pain disorder, psychogenic pain disorder, idiopathic pain disorder, and atypical pain disorder.

Pain disorder is assessed when both psychological and medical factors are present; for example, when someone sustains a hand injury, they may suffer from excessive pain and seek a disproportionate amount of medical treatment. Sometimes pain disorders are diagnosed only on the basis of psychological features, identified by history, evidence of past somatization, prominent guilt, or a history of physical or emotional abuse by either a parent or spouse. However, these "soft" findings together with negative laboratory or physical findings do not automatically imply that the pain presented is attributable to psychosocial factors.

To make the assessment, pain must occur in one or more anatomic sites, with psychological factors believed to play a very important role in its etiology. The defining feature is the preoccupation with pain that cannot be accounted for by any known medical or neurological condition. Pain disorder shares a noteworthy feature with conversion disorder, in that both are the only two conditions noted in the

DSM-IV-TR whose criteria require an assessment for those intrapersonal factors playing an important role in the development or maintenance of symptoms (APA, 1994, 2000). This can be problematic because it becomes purely subjective; that is, what may be important to one practitioner may seem irrelevant to another. A second problem is that pain is also subjective, and difficult to measure with any validity. It is commonly agreed that people experience pain differently (Morrison, 1995). For that reason it becomes important for the practitioner to separate out emotional reactions associated with chronic or excruciating pain through the competency-based assessment.

Pain disorder can occur at anytime, but most often it becomes apparent during adolescence or early adulthood. Symptoms usually emerge after an unexpected acute stressor, and they can last weeks or months, though symptoms generally subside after the initial stress disappears. However, because of envisioned or anticipated secondary gain, the pain might persist long after the tension has diminished, or it might worsen under stress and continue to persist indefinitely. These persons are known to "physician shop," undergo unnecessary examinations, procedures, and tests, become ingrained in maintaining the sick role, restrict their social and occupational functioning (often because they are bedridden), and abuse medications, especially analgesics (Maxmen & Ward, 1995).

The sick role was first examined by Parson (1951), who suggested that the process of "being sick" helps to release individuals from their usual personal and family obligations while also absolving them from any blame for their sick condition. The sick role also functions as a way to obtain love, punishment for failures, a way to compensate for guilt, or atonement for an innate sense of badness (Kaplan & Sadock, 1998).

While pain can assume many forms, it is most frequently manifested in three major areas: the head, pelvis, and lower back. The pain presented can be evidenced through posttraumatic, neuropathic (disease of nerves), neurological, or/and iatrogenic conditions (adverse mental or physical condition caused by side effects from surgical or medical treatment). Pain complaints are the chief reason motivating people to seek out medical attention. While some people can "grin-and-bear" their pain, others can become severely immobilized and incapacitated.

Pain disorder is a fairly common condition among the adult population in the United States. Estimates are that between 15 and 33 percent of individuals aged 25 to 74 suffer from some form of chronic musculoskeletal pain (Magni et al., 1990, 1993). Groth-Marnat and Edkins (1996) calculate that both the direct and indirect costs of pain medication in the United States amounts to somewhere in the neighborhood of $90 billion a year, and Americans alone consume as much as 20 million pounds of aspirin annually.

Prevailing Pattern

The assessment for pain disorder includes the following features:

- Pain that occurs in more than one anatomical site is the presenting problem and the predominant focus for seeking clinical attention; the pain is severe enough to warrant clinical attention

- The pain causes distress that impairs social, occupational, or social functioning

- Intrapersonal factors are considered important in the onset, severity, and exacerbation of pain (or supports maintaining the pain)

- The individual does not consciously feign the pain symptoms, as seen in malingering or factitious disorder
- The pain is not explained by a mood, anxiety, or psychotic disorder, and it does not meet the criteria for dyspareunia (pain that occurs during or after sexual intercourse).

If the duration of the person's pain is less than six months, it is considered acute. If longer, it is considered chronic. It is important to consider not only intrapersonal factors but also medical or biological conditions when exploring onset, intensity, exacerbation, and maintenance of pain (APA, 1994, 2000). The following discussion illustrates Aleta Austin's pain disorder.

The Case of Aleta Austin

Aleta is a 26-year-old woman who was seen by the social worker during her first clinic visit. When asked what brought her to our clinic, Aleta stated, "I work as an aide in a nursing home and I was lifting a patient up from a chair to her wheelchair. Well, anyhow, all of a sudden I felt this terrible and very painful 'snap' in the back of my neck. I lost my balance and fell on the floor. As I was falling, I hit my arm real bad, too. The next thing I knew I was in the hospital, and they were doing some X–rays and an MRI. The doctors said I sprained my neck, and I might have a hairline fracture of my arm. They put some kind of neck brace on me and said I had to wear it for two weeks. I didn't need to have a cast on my arm, but I was supposed to be real careful."

Aleta continued, "I wasn't allowed to work for six weeks. I collected Workmen's Compensation benefits, but the checks stopped when the doctors said I could go back to work. The doctor's said four months was too long to have the pain for the injury I got. I don't care what they said, I still hurt."

She further notes, "After being discharged by those doctors, I went to see several new ones. I thought that maybe the first group of doctors didn't know what they were talking about. Over the past three months, I saw two orthopedic surgeons, one neurologist, two chiropractors, and a massage therapist. I was given lots of different medicines and treatments, but I still didn't get much relief. One of the doctors even suggested that I make an appointment to see a social worker. He thought my problems were all in my head. Can you beat that? Doesn't he realize that I really want to go back to work, and see all my friends again? Does he think I like being in constant pain? Does he think I like not getting any relief from any of the medicine?"

Aleta was asked about medications she was currently using. She stated, "In the beginning they gave me some pain pills, and they helped some, but the doctors won't prescribe anything for me now. They think I'm getting too used to all the pills. Now I'm limited to taking over-the-counter stuff, you know, like Aleve, Tylenol, and aspirin, but they don't do much good. Nothing seems to help nowadays."

When asked how she spent her days, she replied, "I pretty much stay inside the house all day long. I have a hard time finding a comfortable place to sit or lay down.

My brother, Chad, brought over his favorite recliner chair for me to use, and that does help some. Most of the time I watch TV, sleep, or play with my dogs." Aleta volunteered that she and her husband, Bill, were "in the middle of getting a divorce after being married five years." She stated, "It's all for the best. During the time we were married, I realized that I was a lesbian. I always felt different from other women and a little confused about this. I tried to bury these feelings 'cause my family made it clear that it's bad for a woman to love another woman. It was so hard to come to terms with this. I can't believe he wants a divorce after all the time we've been together. He told me that there wasn't someone else. Anyhow, Bill said he was tired of me being sick all the time. I don't believe him. Well, maybe it's for the best, 'cause he's absolutely no use to me now."

Three months ago, Aleta's parents moved into her home "so they could help out while I was recovering. My dad works full-time, as a barber, but he finds the time to mow the grass, run errands, and keep my house in good repair." Aleta repeatedly stated she wanted to go back to work; however, she also said, "It's kinda nice to have Mom and Dad around the house right now. Mom fixes my favorite foods, and I know I'm gonna gain ten pounds before she leaves to go back home [laughing]!"

"You know, my mom told me that when she was younger, she had problems like me. She said as a teenager she had problems with pain in her back for a really long time. Isn't that weird? Mom said when she was around 20 years old she had 'trouble with painful headaches and breathing' but she doesn't like to talk about it much." Aleta once asked her Aunt Dolly, her mother's oldest sister, who told her, "It's just something the Walker women get when they are young'uns."

Aleta was asked if she had experienced any previous psychological problems such as hallucinations, delusions, depression, suicidal ideation, or anxiety. She noted that aside from her neck and arm pain, her physical and emotional health has been somewhat good. She described herself having frequent bouts of low back pain, headaches, and "sometimes my jaw hurts real bad off and on," but overall denies any serious medical problems. When Aleta was relating her past medical history to this worker, it was apparent that her trend of thought changed in midstream, as she interrupted herself, and said, "You know, I've been thinking about the question you just asked, the question about psychological problems. Does sibling rivalry count as a psychological problem?" She continued, "When Chad, my brother, and I were growing up, we fought like we were mortal enemies. I mean we hated each other. I always felt that Chad was Mom's favorite child, and I grew up feeling like a 'secondhand Rose.' That was awful."

Our session continued along these lines for another 15 minutes or so. While walking out of our session, Aleta leaned over to this worker and said, "You know, it's really very nice to have all my mother's attention right now because I'm in so much pain."

Assessment Summary

The dramatic presentation of Aleta's pain might sound extreme to the practitioner, but this symptom alone does not qualify for making the assessment of having a pain disorder. In Aleta's situation, the pain not only impaired her ability to work but caused problems with interpersonal relationships with her husband, family, and coworkers. The pain must be distinguished from other somatoform disorders,

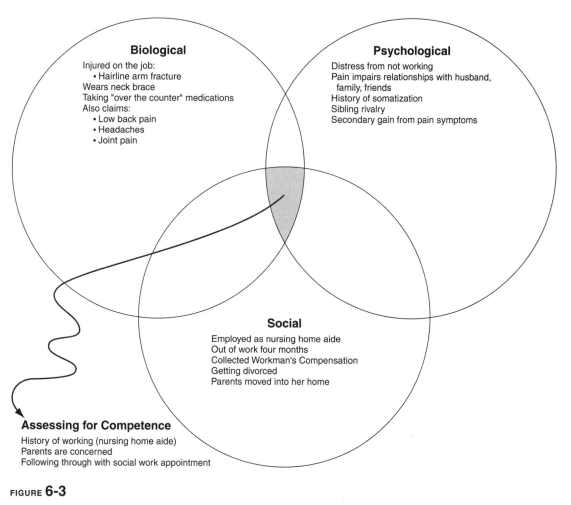

Biological

Injured on the job:
    • Hairline arm fracture
Wears neck brace
Taking "over the counter" medications
Also claims:
    • Low back pain
    • Headaches
    • Joint pain

Psychological

Distress from not working
Pain impairs relationships with husband,
    family, friends
History of somatization
Sibling rivalry
Secondary gain from pain symptoms

Social

Employed as nursing home aide
Out of work four months
Collected Workman's Compensation
Getting divorced
Parents moved into her home

Assessing for Competence

History of working (nursing home aide)
Parents are concerned
Following through with social work appointment

FIGURE **6-3**

PAIN DISORDER

The interactions of biological, psychological, and social variables in Aleta Austin's life.

although some can and do coexist. Pain complaints may be discernible in those persons with conversion disorder. However, by definition, conversion disorder includes other symptoms along with pain, and the associated discomfort is seen as short-lived. Those with hypochondriasis are always preoccupied with concern, fear, or worry about having a serious illness; they have many more fluctuating symptoms than do individuals with pain disorder (Salkovskis & Clark, 1993). Malingering is connected with clearly recognizable benefits and advantages, for example, in litigation where the individual falsifies symptoms in order to receive ill-gotten financial gain. Aleta's suffering was real to her and gives no indication that her pain changes whether she is at home or at work. A differential assessment needs to separate out those who falsify their symptoms versus someone like Aleta, who truly believes her pain is genuine despite the gains received through Workman's Compensation or attention from her family. Recognizing the factors involved in Aleta's pain appears to be uncomplicated by any secondary gain.

There may be a temptation for the practitioner to prematurely diagnose first and then ask questions to support this clinical picture. Typically, the competency-based assessment encourages an exploration of the multiple influences in Aleta's life, for example, intrapersonal issues (distress caused by not working), patterns of interpersonal relationships (close relationship with parents, conflictual relationship with her brother, Chad), social context (getting a divorce), and support networks (concerned friends).

Aleta Austin's five-axis diagnosis would be as follows:

Axis I	307.89 Pain Disorder Associated with Psychological Factors and a General Medical Condition, Acute
Axis II	V71.09 (No diagnosis)
Axis III	Hairline Fracture of Arm
Axis IV	Divorce
	Unemployed four months
	Financial problems
Axis V	GAF = 65 (current)

UNDERSTANDING HYPOCHONDRIASIS

"The term hypochondriasis has carried multiple meanings in modern as well as historical cultures, and therefore it is an imprecise term that may encompass a wide variety of contexts" (North & Guze, 1997, p. 277). Barsky (1992) suggests hypochondriac individuals experience what he calls *somatosensory amplification;* that is, the tendency to experience their own bodily sensations as being unusually intense, aversive, and distressing. The individual has an overwhelming and unrelenting preoccupation with physical symptoms that is deeply rooted in unrealistic apocalyptic interpretations of their symptoms.

The person not only strongly suspects but actually believes he or she is suffering from a very serious and life-threatening condition. Often the hypochondriasis process begins when the person notices a lump, bruise, or blemish, from which they begin to assume, with a great degree of certainty and considerable anxiety, that they have contracted a serious illness. As the process unfolds, the individual begins to constantly fret about "the illness," often to the point where their normal occupational activities and relationships with others are dramatically disrupted. Their world becomes filled with unrealistic and dire interpretations of disease symptoms and their subsequent reactions to it (Maxmen & Ward, 1995). They remain steadfast in their concern for themselves, and they are convinced that something is very wrong with them.

A central feature of this disorder is the person's faulty interpretation of physical signs and sensations as evidence of having an actual physical illness. According to Barsky et al. (1990), hypochondriasis should be considered a "disorder of cognition or perception" with strong intrapersonal contributions. In a recent study, those with hypochondriasis routinely reported experiencing more distress and discomfort when describing what were seemingly benign bodily sensations (Haenen et al., 1997). At times, these beliefs approach delusional proportions, and the boundary between whether this should be considered a delusional disorder is unclear and arbitrary. More often the individual experiences extreme anxiety, which they view as irrational. However, they cannot rid themselves of these bodily preoccupations and catastrophizing thoughts (Turner & Hersen, 1997). Any relief from reassuring the person about their medical "condition" is generally short-lived. In time, they once more begin to ruminate about their "symptoms," and the cycle of worry begins anew (Warwick & Salkovskis, 1990). This preoccupation with minor symptoms, the persistent conviction that they suffer from a deadly disease, and the futile inadequacy of medical reassurance can cause friendships to wear thin, especially when every ache or pain is recounted in minute detail.

Prevailing Pattern

While we know very little about the prevalence of hypochondriasis, Barsky et al. (1990) suggest between 4 and 9 percent of those seeking medical treatment have this disorder. The true prevalence rate in the general population currently remains unknown; however, what is known that men and women are equally at risk (Katon, 1993). Hypochondriasis may begin anytime between the adolescent years straight through to older adulthood. Peak onset occurs during the 20s and 30s. It appears to be found more in the older adult population; perhaps this is due to their seeking medical attention more often (Barsky et al., 1994).

The clinical course is seen as lifelong and chronic, and symptoms tend to wax and wane over months or years. Often symptoms flare up during times of stress. The individual's concern is always related to having a grave, life-threatening condition versus a transient or minor disease.

Hypochondriasis includes the following features:

- Because of misinterpreting bodily symptoms, the individual becomes preoccupied with the fear or idea of having a serious or grave illness.

- The individual's preoccupation persists despite receiving appropriate medical investigation, examination, and/or reassurance.

- These ideas are not considered delusional (as would be seen in delusional disorder), and the ideas are not restricted to circumscribed concern about their appearance, as seen in body dysmorphic disorder.

- This preoccupation causes clinically significant distress or impairment in the performance of occupational, social, or interpersonal functioning.

- Symptoms have persisted for at least six months.

- This preoccupation of ideas cannot better be explained by generalized anxiety disorder, obsessive-compulsive disorder, major depressive episode, panic disorder, separation anxiety, or other somatoform disorders (APA, 1994, 2000).

During most of the episode, the individual does not realize that their preoccupation is excessive or unreasonable. The following case description illustrates how someone with hypochondriasis typically presents in social work practice.

The Case of Carl Beacher

Carl is a 53-year-old white male. He married his high school sweetheart, Sally, 30 years ago. While they have no children, the couple is involved actively in the lives of their many nieces, nephews, and godchildren.

Carl initially complained of anxiety and stress resulting from his high-pressured job as a manager in used car sales. During our first contact, it soon became apparent that his principal concerns revolved around health issues. Whenever he experienced some minor physical problem, such as a cough or headache, Carl would become "immediately frightened that the coughing symptoms meant I had a serious medical illness." A cough to him was, "I had lung cancer. If I have a headache, it means I probably have an undiagnosed malignant brain tumor." When experiencing other (benign) physical sensations, he quickly transformed them into severe or life-threatening medical diseases. "Going to all these doctor appointments cuts into my commissions and vacation time," he added. Carl went on, "I really can't afford to lose any more time away from work. As it is now, the 'big bosses' are looking at me kinda funny. I don't know how long I can keep taking time off."

Carl relates that his wife Sally calls him "my disease-of-the-month husband." He adds with some irritation in his voice, "You know, I don't appreciate the way Sally treats my medical concerns." He admits that his worrying about having a serious disease has caused a great deal of tension in his relationship with Sally and other family members, and that "they don't want to listen to me anymore." Carl says he finds himself absorbed by reading medical books or medical journals. In fact, he admits to subscribing to several of them. He related, "Sometimes when I have a problem I look up my physical symptoms, and then I start worrying about when I'll get these diseases." His wife says, "He lives in fear of being diagnosed. For example, in the last six months, Carl complained of chest pain, stomach problems, dizziness, muscle spasms, and bruises on his arm. I could go on and on." Carl adds somewhat defensively, "Even hearing about a friend or family member's illness is enough to incapacitate me for days." Interestingly, he brags about having an extensive and valuable collection of vintage medical books and antique surgical instruments that he bought at a local flea market.

Carl's fears developed about five years ago, "around the time I was trying to start up a new trucking business. I had a bad cough that just wouldn't go away." At first, he went to the family physician, Dr. Vasquez, who could not find anything wrong with him. Carl was referred to a specialist for an in-depth evaluation, "but they couldn't find anything wrong with me either." Carl continued to see a succession of physicians despite their reassurances that he is in excellent health. When asked how it feels to be constantly reassured that no medical condition exists, Carl answers, "I know the doctors just keep missing what's really wrong, and they just haven't diagnosed me yet, but they will." When asked whether he ever felt a sense of relief when reassured that he didn't have cancer, Carl said, "At first, I feel some relief, but it only lasts a few days. When my symptoms would start up again, I start to worry all over again." When the social worker asked what got in his way when he didn't believe the reassurance of his doctors, he responded, "You know laboratories are always making mistakes, and they aren't infallible. Suppose they mixed up my results with somebody else's? Can you absolutely tell me that that doesn't happen? Well, I say it's hard to reassure somebody when so many people have the opportunity to mess up."

The social worker probed further and asked if it was possible that he didn't have cancer. He replied, "Absolutely not!" The worker then asked, "Why do you think your doctors haven't diagnosed you yet?" He replied, "Because they have to do a few more tests. The last time I had a workup was six months ago. I'm sure between then and now something has had time to develop." The social worker asked Carl about his car sales job. He responded that his concerns about his medical "condition" sometimes take his mind away from the business at the office. "I get so distracted that once in a while I lose business when I'm not attentive to my customers. Things could be better in the money department," he said.

Carl denies thoughts about suicide, or delusions, hallucinations, or symptoms of a major depressive episode. His appetite and sleep habits are no cause for concern, except "when I can't stop worrying about my cancer." He denies a history of problems related to alcohol or recreational drug use. Although he has experienced quite a lot of anxiety about having cancer, he has never had symptoms that are suggestive of a panic disorder.

Assessment Summary

The distinction between hypochondriasis and somatization disorder essentially rests on age at onset and the number of symptoms individuals are likely to report. Carl's complaints are more typical of the person experiencing hypochondriasis. That is, his initial concerns started when he was 48; those who experience somatization tend to be 10 to 15 years younger. The individual with hypochondriasis readily seeks out constant medical attention since they truly believe they are afflicted with a serious disease despite a lack of supportive findings. In this case, Carl continues to question his physicians' expertise. His world is filled with anxiety and constant worry. It is more than just the matter of "if" he is going to be diagnosed with cancer, a tumor, or a serious disease, but "when" he is going to be diagnosed. To Carl, every symptom is the precursor of a life-threatening condition.

The individual with somatization disorder will complain that when they cough it hurts. However, when Carl coughs, he concludes this is another "sign" that he has cancer; this time it may be lung cancer. Phobic individuals who are afraid they might develop a disease usually take steps to avoid being in situations exposing them to risks. People with panic disorders might fearfully overreact to physical symptoms, but their reaction is generally confined to the experience of having a panic attack,

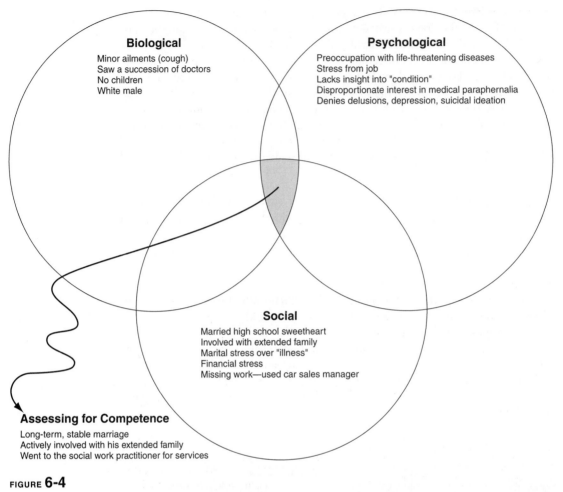

FIGURE 6-4

HYPOCHONDRIASIS

The interactions of biological, psychological, and social variables in Carl Beacher's life.

and they do not consult physicians to verify or disprove their health status (Nietzel et al., 1998). In contrast, Carl consults physicians until he can find the right one who will confirm his "disease." Carl truly believes he experiences these physical symptoms rather than inventing or maintaining them as found in persons with factitious and malingering disorders. Figure 6-4 summarizes the biopsychosocial features in Carl's life.

In contrast to Carl's preoccupation with "illness," it is important to discern adaptive coping skills. Paying attention to such skills serves a preventive function in that Carl learns to anticipate and thereby prevent further problems from arising. He has a long-term and stable marriage with his wife, Sally; is actively involved the lives of extended family members; and is seeking counseling.

A full diagnosis in this case is as follows:

Axis I	300.7 Hypochondriasis
Axis II	V71.07 (No diagnosis)
Axis III	None
Axis IV	Financial problems
Axis V	GAF = 70 (at intake)

UNDERSTANDING BODY DYSMORPHIC DISORDER

The initial formulation of the clinical category of dysmorphophobia (which literally means fear of being ugly) resulted from a term coined by Enrico Morselli during the late nineteenth century. Dysmorphophobia referred to specifiable behaviors that described having an "attitude" toward parts of oneself and/or one's body (Berrios & Kan, 1996). Dysmorphophobia disorder has been depicted for more than a century and has been reported to occur around the world (Phillips, 1996). It was commonly referenced in European literature during the 1960s and 1970s, but it was not formally introduced in the United States until its appearance in DSM-III-R (APA, 1987). As an interesting aside, the DSM-IV editors felt the term *dysmorphophobia* would inaccurately suggest the presence of phobic avoidance, and so they consequently made the decision to relabel dysmorphophobia as body dysmorphic disorder (BDD) in order to avoid any clinical confusion.

A central feature to remember about body dysmorphic disorder is the person's preoccupation about some *imagined defect* in their body. Virtually any body part can be the focus of concern. The individual is greatly preoccupied with the notion that something is very wrong with the shape, size, or appearance of some part of their body. If there happens to be some slight physical defect present, the concern is grossly exaggerated and in excess of what would be considered normal. While the individual's appearance causes them a great deal of distress, they appear normal to others. Their preoccupation with physical appearance includes extreme self-consciousness and embarrassment, excessive importance given to appearance in self-evaluation, avoidance of activities, body camouflaging, and a pattern of constant body checking (Rosen & Reiter, 1996).

Prevailing Pattern

Body dysmorphic disorder includes the following features:

- The individual is preoccupied with an imagined defect in their appearance, or is excessively concerned about a slight physical anomaly.

- This preoccupation causes significant distress or impairs several important areas of interpersonal functioning, such as in family or social relationships or at work.

- Another disorder, for example, anorexia nervosa, does not better explain the individual's preoccupation (APA, 1994, 2000).

The more common symptoms of body dysmorphic disorder that the social worker will encounter in practice involve facial flaws such as wrinkles; spots and/or texture of the skin; excessive facial hair; and the shape of the nose, jaw, mouth, eyes, or eyebrows. On average, individuals generally have concerns about four different body areas, but sometimes the particular "flawed" body part will change from one site to another (Cotterill, 1996; Phillips, 1991; Phillips et al., 1993). At times, the individual excessively checks their appearance in a mirror, or they might avoid reflective surfaces altogether. They may also exhibit strenuous attempts to camouflage a "flawed" appearance using excessive amounts of makeup, clothing, or hats. In sum, their lives are significantly affected, as they tend to withdraw from most social and occupational activities. In some severe cases, they may become housebound to hide their "deformity."

Differential Assessment

Recent research suggests that individuals with body dysmorphic disorder share a wide range of comorbid disorders that run the gamut from obsessive-compulsive disorder, to social phobia, generalized anxiety disorder, or panic disorder (Hanes, 1998; Perugi et al., 1998; Phillips et al., 1993, 1995; Simeone et al., 1995; Wilhelm et al., 1997). The practitioner carefully assesses the person's perceptions about themselves and the interplay with how this influences interpersonal relationships.

Gender differences occurring in body dysmorphic disorder are just beginning to emerge, and several studies have noted some interesting findings about the way these defects are viewed (Biby, 1998; Perugi et al., 1997). Women were seen as more preoccupied with the size of their hips and the texture of their skin, and evidenced lifetime comorbidity with bulimia nervosa. Women also paid significant attention to their breast size and shape of their legs, and they had higher lifetime comorbidity with developing panic disorder and generalized anxiety disorder. Men have significantly higher body preoccupations about their genitals, body height or build, and excessive body hair or thinning hair, along with higher lifetime comorbidity with bipolar disorder. Men also tended to experience problems with alcohol abuse or dependency (Phillips & Diaz, 1997; Veale et al., 1996). Most often, both men and women seek out plastic surgery or dermatological interventions, but these procedures, while physically successful, were not able to change perceptions about the "defect" (Fink, 1992; Phillips, 1996).

Another relatively unexplored and underinvestigated variation of body dysmorphic disorder is known as "muscle dysmorphia" (Pope et al., 1997) and is found in men and women who are preoccupied with the degree of their muscularity. The individual is highly obsessive and "hyperfocused" on the appearance of their body (Sarwer, 1997; Sarwer et al., 1998). While rarely recognized, this disorder may afflict a substantial number of individuals. This condition often causes severe subjective distress, and it creates the potential for abusing anabolic steroids or other body-building substances. The person may spend many hours in the gym working out in lieu of social and occupational pursuits.

The following case presentation of Barry Roger and his concern about his thinning hair can better distinguish the pathologic state associated with body dysmorphic disorder.

The Case of Barry Roger

"Oh, please whoever you are, just shut that door, you're letting in all the light."

I started to poke my head inside my office, when the voice once again demanded, "Please, just come on in and close that door." I said to the voice, "I think I'm in the right room, because this is my office." The voice said, "Who are you looking for?" I replied, "I have an appointment to see Barry Roger. Is that you?" The voice answered somewhat wearily, "Yeah, that's me all right. I guess the staff was pretty freaked out when they saw me walk into the waiting room." I responded, "Why is that?" Mr. Roger replied, "Well, you have to admit I'm pretty ugly looking. Hey, I don't blame anybody getting grossed out when they see my ugly and grotesque baldness. I mean, come on, I can't even look. Yuk! Anyway, that's why your staff hustled me in your office real quick because they didn't want me scaring the other clients. Don't get me wrong or anything. They were real nice to me, but I could see 'that look' in their eyes."

By a bit of dim light afforded me from a small separation between the window shades, I was able to see Mr. Roger sitting on a chair in the corner of my office. When I approached, he turned his face away and appeared to want to hide from my gaze. I was able to see that he had covered the top part of his head with something that looked like a cross between a baseball cap and something worn by the French Foreign Legion.

I asked Mr. Roger why he had made an appointment to come see me. He replied, "I want to have another hair transplant." When I asked him to clarify what coming in for an appointment to see a social worker had to do with having a hair transplant, he responded, "I used to use old Doc Connolly, but he retired last year. So I found this new plastic surgeon Dr. Frick. He told me that I wasn't bald, and he refused to do any more surgery because he said I didn't need it. I don't know what his problem is. He told me that I was lucky because I had a nice full head of hair. Dr. Frick said I might have the slightest bit of thinning present, but this was normal for a guy 27 years old. Personally, I think he needs glasses, that's all I can say." I noted that Mr. Roger's overall health was excellent except for episodic hemorrhoid inflammation.

I gently reminded him that he hadn't answered my question about his reasons for coming to the agency, and he said, "Dr. Frick told me I didn't have a hair problem, but a problem about the way I see myself. He said he absolutely wasn't going to do a hair transplant, and that I should go and talk to a professional."

I asked, "Could you describe for me what you think you look like." He responded with a deep sigh, "Yeah, it's obvious that I look gross, ugly, and disfigured. I mean look at this [he took his hat off]. What do you think about this, huh?" I was a bit startled and said, "Well, actually I see a very full head of hair." He responded, "That's what everyone says."

After a moment of silence, I continued, "I was wondering how much time you think about your hair?" He said, "All the time. I can't seem to get my mind off my baldness. If only I didn't have this problem, everything else would be terrific." I asked, "Have you discussed this with anyone in your family or perhaps with your friends?" He replied, "Yeah, but all they do is say the same thing that you just did. They don't see what I'm talking about. You know, its funny, well not really funny, but my girlfriend, Sharron, broke up with me a few months ago. She told me she was damn tired of always hearing about my hair all the time. I mean what's her problem? If she doesn't love me enough, well good riddance to her. It just proves how ugly I really am without much hair."

I asked how long he's been troubled by his "baldness." He said, "I can't really say exactly when I started worrying about my hair. Maybe it started three years ago when I was 24. I began to notice that I was picking out a greater number of hairs from my hairbrush." At that time, Mr. Roger asked family and friends whether they noticed he was beginning to become bald. He said, "They just told me I had enough hair on my head for three people."

When asked about the difficulties his "baldness" caused, he responded, "I can't leave my house or do anything outside. I know I disgust people because I can see it in their eyes. I notice it more when I don't wear my hat, because people point at me and laugh. I hate to live like this. I'm a salesman and need to constantly interact with people, but I can't do it as a bald man."

Mr. Roger admitted that he felt unhappy but denied feeling depressed or having any thoughts about suicide. He stated he was eating and sleeping well and felt no loss of energy. I asked if there were other parts of his body that concerned him. He reported when he was a teenager he had a few plastic surgeries including a rhinoplasty, his ears flattened, and a "huge" mole removed from the right side of his nose. He continued, "I had a hard time convincing my parents to let me have those surgeries. You know how parents are. They always think their child looks perfect even when they are ugly and deformed."

He admitted to regularly working out at a gym near his home. Last year he opted to have bilateral chest muscle implants put in "because my chest looked so sunken in." He admits, "I know my life would be absolutely perfect if I could only get another hair transplant. Is that so terrible?"

Assessment Summary

Figure 6-5 summarizes the biopsychosocial factors in Barry Roger's life. Hypochondriac individuals, as seen in the case of Carl Beacher, might be overly concerned about having blotches or blemishes on their body. However, Carl's concern is not over being unattractive but centers on his fear of having a severe underlying disease that is so far undiagnosed. Those with a narcissistic personality disorder always have excessive concerns about maintaining a flawless appearance.

On the other hand, Barry Roger is generally satisfied in other aspects of his life with the exception of his thinning hair. By contrast, those with anorexia nervosa are characterized by a pervasive concern with the shape and size of their body. Their goal is to be successful in the absolute pursuit of thinness rather than the quest of maintaining a normal weight (Rosen et al., 1995). A notable difference for Barry is that he sees himself as ugly in an interpersonal world that views him as unremarkable. The imagined ugliness causes him a great deal of distress.

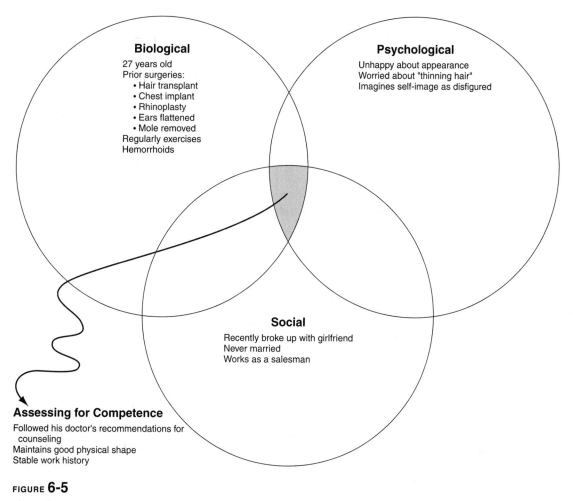

FIGURE **6-5**

BODY DYSMORPHIC DISORDER

The interactions of biological, psychological, and social variables in Barry Roger's life.

The individual with monohypochondriacal paranoia (delusional disorder, somatic type) has a delusional belief where their bodies play a part, such as their eyes are grossly deformed or distorted. In the body dysmorphic disorder, the individual is not seen as being delusional but is unwilling to acknowledge the possibility that the perceived defect is minimal.

Focusing on deficiencies is not a helpful approach for the practitioner. Concentrating on negative characteristics often encourages clients in picking out their own negative qualities in themselves, their lives, and in significant others. It is of utmost importance that Barry be helped to identify and focus on his positive assets, which include following up on the referral for counseling and maintaining a healthy lifestyle.

According to the case vignette, Barry's full diagnosis is:

Axis I	300.7 Body Dysmorphic Disorder
Axis II	V71.09 (No diagnosis)
Axis III	455.6 Hemorrhoids
Axis IV	Recently broke up with girlfriend
Axis V	GAF = 75 (at intake)

UNDERSTANDING OTHER SOMATOFORM DISORDERS

Understanding the somatoform disorders requires the practitioner to appreciate the biological or medical aspects of the individual's symptomatic behavior. Referrals to the social worker are generally made to provide support for the emotional underpinnings. The category of undifferentiated somatoform disorder is included in this chapter in order to help the practitioner carefully assess those client behaviors that do not quite meet the categories described earlier and to avoid stigmatizing or stereotyping clients. Abbey and Garfinkel (1991) point out that cultural influence plays an important role in understanding a person's manifestation of physical illness. Vague complaints, often labeled as an unconscious psychological conflict, may in fact be culturally acceptable and adaptive behavior (Fabrega, 1991). For example, *neurasthenia* is more commonly recognized in eastern Asia (Jorge & Goodnick, 1997). Wessley and Lutz (1995) note that headaches, insomnia, and related vague somatic complaints comprising neurasthenia are considered related to stress rather than to pathology.

Additionally, the category of somatoform disorder not otherwise specified (NOS) is included in this chapter to help the practitioner consider those persons with characteristics suggestive of somatoform disorder but who do not meet the assessment criteria for intensity or duration. There may be some instances where making an assessment is not clear-cut. It is during those times when the practitioner must be especially savvy about the multiple factors influencing the client's life.

Understanding Undifferentiated Somatoform Disorder

Unfortunately, minimal published data is available on the following two somatoform disorders to be addressed in this chapter, and therefore little can be said about their history, genetic composition, familial patterns, epidemiology, and treatment predictability (North & Guze, 1997). The diagnostic criteria of undifferentiated somatoform disorder is an appropriate category for those persons:

- With one or more physical complaints that cannot be explained by any known general medical condition or pathophysiologic mechanism, or that grossly exceeds the expected complaints of a medical condition; and
- Who are below the threshold for meeting the diagnostic criteria for a specific somatoform disorder (APA, 1994, 2000).

Often with the passage of time some individuals will develop more somatic complaints. If they eventually meet the specific criteria for somatization disorder, they can be reclassified. Individuals experiencing isolated somatic symptoms do not really predict very much of anything. In order to consider the presence of an undifferentiated somatoform disorder, the symptoms must be present for at least six months, and they must cause significant emotional distress or seriously impair the person's social or occupational functioning. Additionally, undifferentiated somatoform disorder includes neurasthenia ("nervous exhaustion") or chronic fatigue syndrome, as well as other functional somatic symptoms and syndromes that are without widely accepted medical explanations (Turner & Hersen, 1997).

There are two types of symptom patterns that are seen in those individuals with undifferentiated somatoform disorder: those involving the autonomic nervous system or having complaints involving the respiratory, gastrointestinal, and/or urogenital systems; and those involving sensations of fatigue, weakness, or being unable to perform everyday activities due to symptoms of exhaustion.

Undifferentiated somatoform disorder includes the following features:

- The individual has at least one physical complaint, including painful urination, fatigue, or gastrointestinal complaints.
- In order for a symptom to be considered, one of the following two conditions must be met:
    After an appropriate investigation, the symptoms presented cannot be fully explained by the presence of a recognized general medical condition or by the use of substances (including medications and alcohol).
    When a general medical condition is present, the physical complaints or resulting social or occupational impairment far exceeds what would typically be expected from a person, based on history, physical examination, or laboratory findings.
- The symptoms cause clinically significant distress or affect work (or school), or social or interpersonal functioning.
- The disturbance lasts longer than six months.
- Another mental disorder, such as somatoform, mood, anxiety, sleep, or psychotic disorder or the diagnosis of a sexual dysfunction does not better explain the disturbance.
- The individual does not intentionally produce or fake symptoms for material gain (malingering) or willingly seek secondary gain from occupying the sick role (factitious disorder) (APA, 1994, 2000).

Kroenke et al. (1997) suggest that using the DSM criteria for the undifferentiated somatization category may be too conditional or restrictive, and they suggest an alternative classification described as a "multisomatoform disorder." This comprehensive look at the individual's interpersonal world supports the competency-based assessment that looks at the different ways individuals cope and adapt to a particular set of circumstances.

Because of its close resemblance to somatization disorder, we have decided not provide case presentations for undifferentiated somatoform disorder or for somatoform disorder not otherwise specified. However, the following discussion of somatoform disorder not otherwise specified is provided to help the practitioner understand the complete picture of somatoform disorders. With this information, the practitioner will be better able to discern among the various clusters of symptoms and better grasp their impact on the individual's life picture.

Understanding Somatoform Disorder Not Otherwise Specified

This residual or catchall category includes persons who have some symptoms suggestive of a somatoform disorder but who do not meet the specific diagnostic criteria for any of the other specific somatoform disorders, including the undifferentiated type (APA, 1994, 2000). This category primarily addresses clusters of symptoms that include:

- Pseudocyesis is a false belief of being pregnant without supporting objective physical signs and clinical manifestations of pregnancy, such as an enlarged abdomen, nausea, amenorrhea (absence of menstruation), breast engorgement, fetal movements, and labor pains at the approximate "due date." While there may be evidence of endocrine changes, a general medical condition cannot be found that causes these endocrine conditions (as in a hormone-secreting tumor).

- Transient hypochondriac states (nonpsychotic) present symptoms that include conditions that would meet criteria for hypochondriasis except that they do not last for the required six months.

- Environmental illness (or total environmental allergy syndrome) is a relatively new phenomenon. It is a polysymptomatic disorder that some consider to be associated with immune system dysfunction and allergy-like sensitivity to many compounds found in chemicals, food, clothing, perfumes, and airborne substances (Neligh, 1996). These individuals claim to be allergic to almost everything they come in contact with. Sometimes they isolate themselves from these chemical toxins by staying indoors, whereas at other times they may use extreme measures such as wearing a gas mask out in public.

- A disorder involving unexplained physical symptoms that last less than six months and are not caused by another psychological disorder may be categorized here (APA, 1994, 2000).

RELATED DISORDERS: FACTITIOUS AND MALINGERING

There are two notable conditions that are seen as related to the somatoform or somatic disorders; that is, people with these conditions exhibit symptoms having no evidentiary physical cause, and their symptoms are collectively viewed as being manifested unconsciously. We will briefly discuss them in this chapter because, historically, practitioners have thought of them as involving common threads, with similar symptoms and processes.

Understanding Malingering Disorder

Malingering involves a pattern of behavior similar to that seen in someone who has a genuine medical disorder. It occurs mostly frequently in males, but it can also occur in women. Instead of actually having a medical problem, the person deliberately and consciously pretends to be ill or suffering from "something" that is nonexistent in order to arouse sympathy, avoid criminal prosecution or military duty, obtain drugs, or receive financial rewards. An example of malingering would be those individuals who pretend to make a slow recovery from an illness or a previously sustained work-related injury in order to continue receiving benefits from an insurance settlement or Workman's Compensation. The "illness" may also provide opportunities for a temporary escape from harsh situations such as being incarcerated, or other unpleasant settings (Dembe, 1998; Schmand et al., 1998). The following case discussion provides a transcript of a "conversation" between a client and the social worker that illustrates the kind of questioning that may be helpful when considering an assessment of malingering disorder.

The Case of Brad Jones

"Ow, ow, that hurts, oh my gosh, ow my neck hurts something terrible," said Mr. Jones as he was attempting to sit down. Mr. James Martino, a well-known personal injury attorney, referred Mr. Jones to our clinic. When asked what brought him here, Mr. Jones stated he was involved in a rear-end collision and subsequently missed a great deal of work. He added, "You know, I'm enduring a tremendous amount of pain. I have constant neck pain and terrible headaches. I feel dizzy most all the time, and I don't sleep a wink most nights. If that isn't bad enough, my chest hurts when I try and take a deep breath and I really feel lousy. You know, I'm not asking for anything special. I just want to reclaim damages I got from the woman who rear-ended me, destroyed my car, ruined my health, and cost me my job."

The following is an illustration of the questions the practitioner may integrate into the competency-based assessment when malingering is suspected.

Worker: Mr. Jones, can you tell me about what is currently going on for you?

Mr. J: I can't begin to tell you how much pain this accident has caused me. I mean I can't do anything for myself anymore. I had to move into a limited nursing care facility. Do you know anything about what they are like?

Worker: Could you tell me?

Mr. J: Well, it's a place you live where they cook your meals, do your laundry, and clean your room. I didn't want to move into a place like that, but

Mr. Martino, that's my lawyer, told me that I wouldn't have to strain myself having to do all this stuff for myself. He thought it would be best especially since I'm in so much pain.

Worker: Where did you live before the accident?

Mr. J: I lived here and there. You know, sometimes with friends, and sometimes with family members. Hey, aren't we here to talk about how much pain I'm having?

Worker: Yes, could you tell me more about that?

Mr. J: Well, yeah, I ran up a lot of financial costs as a result of that nitwit smashing into my car. Now I'm taking lots of medicine, but none of it seems to help. I was wondering if maybe one the docs here could give me something to help relax, you know, for my muscle spasms and all?

Worker: Mr. Jones, have you ever been involved in any kind of lawsuit before this one?

Mr. J: What do you mean, like a slip and fall accident or something like that?

Worker: Well, yes, or something like that.

Mr. J: You probably won't believe this but I did fall down once when I was walking out of a department store. It was really storming something fierce, the exit ramp was very slippery. I broke my glasses, hurt my back, and wore a neck brace, and walked with a cane for six months. Oh, wait a minute. I just remembered there was one other time. I worked at some diner, as a short-order cook, you know? My arm got burned when I was cooking some eggs in hot grease. But it was really nothing like this.

Worker: What do you make of what has happened?

Mr. J: Hey, are you gonna be like all the rest of them social workers?

Worker: What do you mean?

Mr. J: You know, suggesting that I just want to make some money out of this accident?

Worker: Has someone accused you of that?

Mr. J: Yeah. It's not like I'm trying to get away with something. Why does everybody think I'd try to do a thing like that? Listen, I'm outta here. Send the bill to my lawyer.

Prematurely ending our session, Mr. Jones abruptly stood up. Interestingly, he showed no indication of having the debilitating physical pain so much in evidence earlier.

Assessment Summary

Malingering is very often confused with factitious disorder. The single most notable difference between these two disorders is the impetus or incentive for maintaining symptoms. In malingering disorder, symptom continuance is externally motivated; that is, the individual obtains something they want or desire, such as money, drugs, or shelter. In factitious disorder, these external incentives are not present, but the individual maintains the sick role.

Distinguishing malingering from conversion disorder is often difficult. The person with malingering exhibits the same pattern of behavior as is characterized by someone with conversion disorder, but someone with malingering disorder deliberately and intentionally produces symptoms in order to obtain appreciable rewards or incentives, or avoid some unpleasant situation. The person with conversion disorder, as in the case of Aleta Austin, did not intentionally produce her symptoms. The "malingerer" can voluntarily control the symptoms of illness, often switching back and forth between normal and abnormal physical behavior. In addition, they are able to stop their symptoms when considered no longer profitable or when the danger of being "discovered" becomes too great a risk. In our case vignette, Mr. Jones chose to abruptly leave the interview session. As a postscript, the social worker followed up with a letter inviting Mr. Jones to return. To date, there has been no further communication.

While malingering is easy to suspect, it is much harder to prove even in the face of overt documentation, such as surveillance videos. The practitioner should strongly suspect malingering if any combination of the following is noted:

- There is legal litigation or a medical context that overshadows the symptoms presented, especially when there is an opportunity for financial gain, such as receiving money, or free hospital room and board (Yates et al., 1997).

- The client's history suggests the presence of an antisocial personality disorder (APA, 1994, 2000).

- The lack of client cooperation is noted during diagnostic efforts and evaluation, and there is a lack of compliance with a prescribed medical regimen.

- There is evidence of marked discrepancies between the person's claimed clinical presentation and objective findings (Morrison, 1995).

Careful documentation is essential to accurately assess the presence of malingering, prevent iatrogenic conditions, and rule out actual medical disorders. In some situations the individual diagnosed with malingering disorder may have a history of substance abuse.

Understanding Factitious Disorder

Factitious disorder is "[a] disorder that is not real, genuine or natural" (Thomas, 1997, p. 559). The person displays physical and psychological symptoms that are intentionally produced, under their voluntary control, and deliberately used to pursue a desired goal, such as assuming the sick role and requiring hospitalization. As a part of the competency-based assessment, it is helpful to explore the person's level of social and occupational functioning. In addition, hospitalizations, medical appointments, and being "sick" may impair relationships and job performance. Often these individuals have distorted perceptions of justice and a sense of entitlement, which further justify their sick role. Further, they may tend to see themselves as the "victim" (Bellamy, 1997).

A prototypical factitious disorder is Munchausen syndrome, named after the eighteenth-century Baron Karl Friedrich Hieronymous von Munchausen, who made his appearance in Raspe's (1948) book, *Baron Munchausen's Narrative of His Marvelous*

Travels and Campaigns in Russia. The Baron, a German calvary officer, had a reputation for being a colorful raconteur who spun outrageous stories and wandered about the countryside to find audiences. There is no evidence that the real Baron von Munchausen ever believed the stories he fabricated, tried to deceive his listeners, or sought out unneeded medical treatment. Nevertheless, his name continues to remain linked to the term used to represent this syndrome. Munchausen syndrome is considered the most extreme example of factitious disorder. In 1951, Asher borrowed Munchausen's name, and applied it to people who demonstrated a triad of features involving the recurrent simulation of disease, pathological lying (pseudologia fantastica), or wandering (peregrination). The individual has been known to travel extensively in order to receive medical care where their previous medical history is unknown. The disorder has been called various names, including polysurgical addiction, hospital addiction, and professional patient syndrome (Kaplan & Sadock, 1998).

The available literature in understanding this disorder is still evolving. According to Guze (1997), the key issues include understanding the conceptualization of the disorder; changing descriptions of "typical client" profiles; infrequent case identification; difficulties in distinguishing among other comorbid conditions; the lack of significant follow-up studies; and a lack of family studies. In addition, clients often provide misleading information about themselves (Guze, 1997). The available literature suggests this disorder is far more common than was once generally believed. There is some data to suggest that young female adults who are likely to be employed in medically related occupations such as nursing, medicine, and medical technology have a higher incidence of factitious disorder (Andreasen & Black, 1995; Stoudemire, 1994).

Munchausen by proxy is a variant of the factitious disorder. This disorder occurs within the context of a relationship between the parent and child. It is briefly presented here to complete the discussion of factitious disorder. This disorder occurs when the parent or caregiver deliberately falsifies their child's medical history and subjects the child to unnecessary medical procedures and unneeded hospitalizations. Similar to the goal of assuming the sick role in fictitious disorder, the motivation for this behavior is the psychological need for the parent to assume the sick role, albeit indirectly. The deception often involves contaminating laboratory samples, providing a false medical history, or initiating injury and ill health toward the child. Munchausen by proxy is considered a form of child abuse and is mandated by law reportable if suspected (Iezzi & Adams, 1993). It is extremely difficult to detect (North & Guze, 1997; Shaner, 1997).

The following vignette describes how clients with factitious disorder will present their concerns to the practitioner. Nan Finkelhorn's feelings of victimization and "righteous indignation" are underscored in the following case discussion.

The Case of Nan Finkelhorn

Nan Finkelhorn is a 27-year-old female who is currently in her 35th hospital admission. She works as a nurse in the dialysis unit of the hospital, and her supervisor is wondering if Nan may have some kind of rare infection. Lately, Nan's job performance has been sporadic since a recent diagnosis of "chronic fatigue." It has been difficult for the supervisor to know how to respond, because Nan is vague about the details of her "condition." It seems that when the unit is hectic and there is much work to be done, Nan loudly announces to her coworkers that she needs a coffee break. As a result, there is growing tension between Nan and her supervisor around performance expectations. Nan's presenting problem during this current admission includes chronic headaches, fevers, "lupus like" symptoms, vomiting, the inability to walk, and numbness in her left hand and her right foot. She came to the emergency room last evening asking for narcotic medication "for pain." While being examined by the attending physician on duty, Nan stated she felt "a terrible, terrible pain in my left kidney area," and then she doubled over. The physician felt it was prudent to admit Ms. Finkelhorn for observation. Nan stated, "I hate hospitals, especially this one, because my mother died here and no one ever bothered to take care of her."

After complete laboratory and physical examinations, she was been given a clean bill of health. Just a few minutes after she was discharged and declared fit to return to her full responsibilities at work, Ms. Finkelhorn began to loudly complain that her doctors were incompetent and she was going to report her supervisor to the hospital's employee assistance program to "finally get some justice." Ms. Finkelhorn felt that it was too soon to be discharged, and that she was "a very ill woman." She stated, "If the doctors can't see that, then I'll end up dead, and it's all their fault."

SUMMARY

This chapter has reviewed the various somatoform disorders with a focus on the most prevalent diagnoses. Somatization disorders have earned a reputation of being very difficult to assess. Even though the client is faking an "illness," they are still ill. It is important to consider the client's concerns rather than to dismiss them as "playing games, simulating, and pretending illness that they do not have" (North & Guze, 1997, p. 277). The competency-based assessment considers the following:

- Symptom presentation should be evaluated in the context of both current and past interpersonal, social, cultural, and environmental factors.
- During each session the practitioner should include a conversation about how well the client is functioning in terms of their interpersonal relationships and their social and family support systems.
- New signs or symptoms are carefully assessed, but the focus is on intrapersonal, interpersonal, and/or social problems, not the physical or somatic symptoms. It is important to remember that for the client their symptoms are real and quite distressing.
- The need for a comprehensive medical evaluation is recognized early, especially for those individuals who have chronic symptoms, severe psychological consequences, or morbid types of illness behavior.

Kathol (1997) suggests:

- Question the client thoroughly about their medical history.
- Provide reassurance to the client that he or she does not have a serious illness.
- Suggest to the client that their symptoms will eventually resolve themselves.
- Encourage the client to return to their normal activities.
- Closely follow the client for a period of time and inquire about their medical status on subsequent visits.

PRACTITIONER REFLECTIONS

This chapter outlines the primary features found in somatoform, factitious, and malingering disorders. Central to the development of somatoform disorders are individuals who are overly preoccupied with their health and have no identifiable medical conditions to support their complaints. Factitious disorders are characterized by the intentional feigning of physical symptoms to assume the sick role. This contrasts to the malingering disorder, which includes external motivations for sustaining such behavior, for example, seeking economic gains through litigious actions. The following reflections are intended to help the practitioner better understand these disorders.

Activities

- This activity focuses on understanding the individual with hypochondriasis. Keep a log of your bodily sensations for three or four days. Be as detailed as you can in your recording. Include, for example, headaches, backaches, muscle aches, stomach grumblings, perspiration, fatigue, and so forth. Reflect back on your log and compare how your own body sensations differ from the case of Carl Beacher. Be a specific as you can. Imagine for a moment that you are having a conversation with Carl Beacher. How would he respond to your listing of your body sensations?
- Remember the last time you had a "common cold." Write down your experiences. Be sure to include how you felt, how long it lasted, and what you did to minimize your discomfort. Look over this list, and imagine how a person diagnosed with hypochondriasis would describe their own experience with having a cold. Describe a person with a factitious disorder and what their experiences would be like having the common cold.
- Develop a list of the advantages and disadvantages of undergoing plastic surgery. Imagine how a person with body dysmorphic disorder would critique your listing?
- Develop a list of the ethics related to having a "perfect" body. Considering the increase of cosmetic surgeries, how do you feel about individuals who have multiple surgical procedures to improve "defects" that no one else can see?

- In many instances, the practitioner's first contact with their client is over the telephone. This activity is designed to help you to focus, as sharply as possible, on the client's concerns. Review the case of Barry Roger. With a colleague or your supervisor, role-play how you would proceed in the first five minutes of conducting a telephone interview. Imagine this is your first contact. The major difference in conducting this "session" is to screen out all visual stimuli. You may decide to sit in a darkened room, agree (as the worker) to be blindfolded, or sit with your back to your partner. After you have completed this exercise, exchange with each other those "cues" that helped you to discern that you were speaking with someone with body dysmorphic disorder. Ask yourself the following questions:

  At what point did you begin to consider that Mr. Roger is someone with body dysmorphic disorder?

  When did you decide that he met the criteria for body dysmorphic disorder?

  How does he cope?

  What strengths does Mr. Roger have?

- Persons with body dysmorphic disorder tend to focus their attention on the defects found on their breasts, face, neck, or genitals. Using the format described above, conduct a role-play of someone who is concerned about a mole on their chin (or use another example), but does not have a body dysmorphic disorder.

REFERENCES

Abbey, S. E., & Garfinkel, P. E. (1991). Neurasthenia and chronic fatigue syndrome: The role of culture in the making of a diagnosis. *American Journal of Psychiatry*, 148: 1638–1646.

American Psychiatric Association [APA]. (1980). *Diagnostic and statistical manual of mental disorders* (3rd ed.). Washington, DC: APA.

American Psychiatric Association [APA]. (1987). *Diagnostic and statistical manual of mental disorders* (3rd rev. ed.). Washington, DC: APA.

American Psychiatric Association [APA]. (1994). *Diagnostic and statistical manual of mental disorders* (4th ed.). Washington, DC: APA.

American Psychiatric Association [APA]. (2000). *Diagnostic and statistical manual of mental disorders* (4th ed.-TR). Washington, DC: APA.

Andreasen, N. C., & Black, D. W. (1995). *Introductory textbook of psychiatry* (2nd ed.). Washington, DC: American Psychiatry Press.

Asher, R. (1951). Munchausen's syndrome. *Lancet*, 1: 339–341.

Barlow, D. H., & Durand, V. M. (1997). *Abnormal Psychology* (2nd ed.). Pacific Grove, CA: Brooks/Cole.

Barbee, J. G., Todorov, A. A., Kucznuieczyk, A. R., Mancuso, D. M., Schwab, J. J., Maddock, R. J., Hoehn-Saric, R., Kelley, L. A., & Davidson, J. R. (1997). Explained and unexplained medical symptoms in generalized anxiety and panic disorders. *Annuals of Clinical Psychiatry*, 9(3): 149–155.

Barsky, A. J. (1992). Amplification, somatization, and the somatoform disorders. *Psychosomatics*, 33: 28–34.

Barsky, A. J., Barnett, M. C., & Cleary, P. D. (1994). Hypochondriasis and panic disorder. *Archives of Psychiatry*, 51: 918–925.

Barsky, A. J., Fama, J. M., Bailey, E. D., & Ahem, D. K. (1998). A prospective 4- to 5-year study of DSM–III–R hypochondriasis. *Archives of General Psychiatry*, 55(8): 737–744.

Bellamy, R. (1997). Compensation neurosis: Financial reward for illness. *Clinical Orthopaedics and Related Research*, March (336): 94–106.

Berrios, G. E., & Kan, C. S. (1996). A conceptual and quantitative analysis of 178 historical cases of dysmorphophobia. *Acta Psychiatrica Scandinavica*, 94(1): 1–7.

Bhui, K., & Hotoph, M. (1997). Somatization disorder. *British Journal of Hospital Medicine*, 58(4): 145–149.

Biby, E. L. (1998). The relationship between body dysmorphic disorder and depression, self-esteem, somatization and obsessive compulsive disorder. *Journal of Clinical Psychology*, 54(4): 489–499.

Blanchard, E. B. (1992). Psychological treatment of benign headache disorders. *Journal of Consulting and Clinical Psychology*, 60(4): 537–551.

Brodsky, C. M. (1984). Sociocultural and interactional influences on somatization. *Psychosomatic*, 25: 673–680.

Canino, G., Bird, H., Rubio-Stipec, M., & Bravo, M. (1997). The epidemiology of mental disorders in the adult population of Puerto Rico. *Puerto Rico Health Sciences Journal*, 16(2): 117–124.

Cloninger, C. R. (1996). Somatization disorder. In T. A. Widiger, A. J. Frances, H. A. Pincus, M. R. Ross, & W. W. Davis (Eds.), *DSM-IV sourcebook*, Vol. 2, pp. 885–892. Washington, DC: American Psychiatric Press.

Cotterill, J. A. (1996). Body dysmorphic disorder. *Dermatologia Clinica*, 14(3): 457–463.

Dembe, A. E. (1998). The medical detection of simulated occupational injuries: A historical and social analysis. *International Journal of Health Services*, 28(2): 227–239.

Eifert, G. (1991). Cardiophobia: A paradigmatic behavioral model of heart-focused anxiety and nonanginal chest pain. *Behavior Research and Therapy*, 30(4): 329–345.

Fabrega, H. (1991). Somatization in cultural and historical perspective. In L. J. Kirmayer, & J. M. Robbins (Eds.), *Current concepts of somatization and clinical perspectives*, pp. 181–199. Washington, DC: American Psychiatric Press.

Fink, D. (1992). Surgery and medical treatment in persistent somatizing patients. *Journal of Psychosomatic Research*, 36: 439.

Fischler, B., Cluydts, R., De-Gucht, Y., Kaufman, L., & De-Meirleir, K. (1997). Generalized anxiety disorder in chronic fatigue. *Acta Psychiatrica Scandinavica*, 95(5): 405–413.

Folks, D. G., Ford, C. V., & Houck, C. A. (1994). Somatoform disorders, factitious disorder, and malingering. In A. Stoudemire (Ed.), *Clinical psychiatry for medical students* (2nd ed.), pp. 274–305. Philadelphia: J. B. Lippincott.

Ford, C. V. (1995). Dimensions of somatization and hypochondriasis. *Neurologic Clinics*, 12: 241–253.

Fowles, D. C. (1993). A motivational theory of psychopathology. In W. Spaulding (Ed.), *Nebraska symposium on motivation: Integrated views of motivation, cognition, and emotion*, Vol. 41, pp. 181–238. Lincoln: University of Nebraska Press.

Frances, A., First, M. B., & Pincus, H. A. (1995). *DSM-IV guidebook*. Washington, DC: American Psychiatric Press.

Freud, S. (1894). The neuro-psychoses of defense. In J. Strachey (Ed.), *The complete psychological works*, Vol. 3, pp. 45–62. London: Hogarth Press (1962).

Fritz, G. K., Fritsch, S., & Hagino, O. (1997). Somatoform disorders in children and adolescents: A review in the past 10 years. *Journal of the American Academy of Child and Adolescent Psychiatry*, 36: 1329–1338.

Furer, P., Walker, J. R., Chartier, M. J., & Stein, M. D. (1997). Hypochondriacal concerns and somatization in panic disorder. *Depression and Anxiety*, 6(2): 78–85.

Golding, J. M., Smith, R., & Kashner, M. (1991). Does somatization disorder occur in men? Clinical characteristics of women and men with multiple unexplained somatic symptoms. *Archives General Psychiatry*, 48: 231.

Gothe, C. J., Molin, C., & Nilsson, C. G. (1995). The environmental somatization syndrome. *Psychosomatics*, 36(1): 1–11.

Griffith, J. L., Polles, A., & Griffith, M. E. (1998). Pseudoseizures, families and unspeakable dilemmas. *Psychosomatics*, 39(2): 144–153.

Groth-Marnat, G., & Edkins, G. (1996). Professional psychologist's in general health care settings: A review of the financial efficacy of direct treatment interventions. *Professional Psychology: Research and Practice*, 27: 161–174.

Gureje, O., Simon, G. E., Ustun, T. B., & Goldberg, D. P. (1997). Somatization in cross-cultural perspective: A World Health Organization study in primary care. *American Journal of Psychiatry*, 154(7): 989–995.

Guze, S. B. (1997). *Adult psychiatry*. St. Louis, MO: Mosby-Year Book.

Hadler, M. (1997). Fibromyalgia, chronic fatigue, and other iatrogenic diagnostic algorithms. Do some labels escalate illness in vulnerable patients? *Postgraduate Medicine*, 102(2): 161–162.

Haenen, M. A., Schmidi, A. J., Schoenmakers, M., & van den Hout, M. A. (1997). Tactual sensitivity in hypochondriasis. *Psychotherapy and Psychosomatic*, 66(3): 128–132.

Hanes, K. R. (1998). Neuropsychological performance in body dysmorphic disorder. *Journal of the International Neuropsychological Society*, 4(2): 167–171.

Harden, C. L. (1997). Pseudoseizures and dissociative disorder: A common mechanism involving traumatic experiences. *Seizures*, 6(2): 151–155.

Hartvig, P., & Sterner, G. (1985). Childhood psychological environmental exposure in women diagnosed somatoform disorder. *Scandinavian Journal of Social Medicine*, 13: 153–157.

Hiller, W., Rief, W., & Fichter, M. M. (1997). How disabled are patients with somatoform disorder? *General Hospital Psychiatry*, 19(6): 432–438.

Iezzi, A., & Adams, H. E. (1993). Somatoform and factitious disorders. In P. B. Sutker & H. E. Adams (Eds.), *Comprehensive handbook of psychopathology* (2nd ed.), pp. 167–201. New York: Plenum.

Jerlang, B. B. (1997). Burning mouth syndrome (BMS) and the concept of alexithymia—a preliminary study. *Journal of Oral Pathology Medicine*, 26(6): 249–253.

Jorge, C. M., & Goodnick, P. J. (1997). Chronic fatigue syndrome and depression: Biological differentiation and treatment. *Psychiatric Annuals*, 27: 365.

Kalogjera-Sackellares, D., & Sackellares, J. C. (1997). Personality profiles of patients with pseudoseizures. *Seizure*, 6(1): 1–7.

Kaplan, H. I., & Sadock, B. J. (1996). *Pocket handbook of clinical psychiatry* (2nd ed.). Baltimore, MD: Williams & Wilkins.

Kaplan, H. I., & Sadock, B. J. (1998). *Synopsis of psychiatry* (8th ed.). Baltimore, MD: Williams & Wilkins.

Kaplan, H. I., Sadock, B. J., & Grebb, J. A. (1994). *Synopsis of psychiatry* (7th ed.). Baltimore, MD: Williams & Wilkins.

Kapoor, W. N., Fortunato, M., Hanusa, B. H., & Schulberger, H. C. (1995). Psychiatric illnesses in patients with syncope. *American Journal of Medicine*, 99(5): 505–512.

Kathol, R. G. (1997). Reassurance therapy: What to say to symptomatic patients with benign or non-existent medical disease. *International Journal of Psychiatry in Medicine*, 27(2): 173–180.

Katon, W. (1993). Somatization disorder, hypochondriasis, and conversion disorder. In D. L. Dunner (Ed.), *Current Psychiatric Therapy*, pp. 314–320. Philadelphia: W. B. Saunders.

Kent, D., Tomasson, K., & Coryell, W. (1995). Course and outcome of conversion and somatization: A four-year follow-up. *Psychosomatics*, 36: 138.

Kim, C. H., Hsu, J. J., Williams, D. E., Weaver, A. L., & Zinsmeister, A. R. (1996). A prospective psychological evaluation of patients with dysphagia of various etiologies. *Dysphagia*, 11(1): 34–40.

Kirmayer, L. J., & Robins, J. M. (1991). Three forms of somatization in primary care: Prevalence, co-occurrence, and sociodemographic characteristics. *Journal of Nervous and Mental Disease*, 179: 647–655.

Kirmayer, L. J., & Taillefer, S. (1997). Somatoform disorder. In S. M. Turner & M. Hersen (Eds.), *Adult psychopathology and diagnosis* (2nd ed.), pp. 333–383. New York: John Wiley & Sons.

Kroenke, K., Spitzer, R. L., de Gruy, F. V., Hahn, S. R., Linzer, M., Williams, J. B., Brody, D., & Davies, M. (1997). Multisomatoform disease. An alternative to undifferentiated somatoform disorder for the somatizing patient in primary care. *Archives of General Psychiatry*, 54(4): 352–358.

Kuczmierczyk, A., Labrum, A. H., & Johnson, C. C. (1995). The relationship between mood, somatization, and alexithymia in premenstrual syndrome. *Psychosomatics*, 16: 213–223.

Lawrie, S. M., Manders, D. N., Geddes, J. R., & Pelosi, A. J. (1997). A population-based incidence study of chronic fatigue. *Psychological Medicine*, 27(2): 343–353.

Lesser, R. P. (1996). Psychogenic seizures. *Neurology*, 46: 1499.

Lilienfeld, S. O. (1992). The association between antisocial personality and somatization disorder: A review and integration of theoretical models. *Clinical Psychology Review*, 12: 641–662.

Mace, C. J. (1992). Hysterical conversion II: A critique. *British Journal of Psychiatry*, 161: 378–389.

Magni, G., Caldieron, C., Rigatti-Luchini, S., & Mersky, H. (1990). Chronic musculoskeletal pain and depressive symptoms in the general population. An analysis of the first National health and nutrition examination survey data. *Pain*, 43: 299–307.

Magni, G., Marchetti, M., Moreschi, C., Mersky, H., & Rigatti-Luchini, S. (1993). Chronic musculosketal pain and depressive syndrome in the National health and nutrition examination: I. Epidemiologic follow-up study. *Pain*, 53: 163–168.

Martin, R. L. (1992). Diagnostic issues for conversion disorder. *Hospital Community Psychiatry*, 43: 771.

Maxmen, J. S., & Ward, N. G. (1995). *Essential psychopathology and its treatment* (2nd ed.). New York: W. W. Norton.

Marshall, J. C., Halligan, P. W., Fink, G. R., Wade, D. J., & Frackowiak, R. S. (1997). The functional anatomy of a hysterical paralysis. *Cognition*, 64(1): 1–8.

McCahill, M. E. (1995). Somatoform and related disorders: Delivery of diagnosis as first step. *American Family Physician*, 52(1): 193–204.

McDonald, S. W., & Thom, A. (1996). The Bargarran witchcraft trial—a psychiatric reassessment. *Scottish Medical Journal*, 41(5): 152–158.

Meana, M., & Binik, Y. M. (1994). Painful coitus: A review of female dyspareunia. *Journal of Nervous and Mental Disease*, 182(5): 264–272.

Merskey, H. (1993). *The classification of fibromyalgia and myofacial pain*, pp. 191–194. New York: Elsevier.

Moore, D. P., & Jefferson, J. W. (1996). *Handbook of medical psychiatry*, pp. 198–207. St. Louis, MO: Mosby-Year Book.

Morrison, J. C. (1995). *DSM-IV made easy*. New York: Guilford Press.

Morse, D. S., Suchman, A. L., & Frankel, R. M. (1997). The meaning of symptoms in 10 women with somatization disorder and a history of childhood abuse. *Archives of Family Medicine*, 6(5): 468–476.

Neligh, G. L. (1996). Somatoform and associated disorders. In J. H. Scully (Ed.), *Psychiatry*, pp. 167–189. Baltimore, MD: Williams & Wilkins.

Nietzel, M. T., Speltz, M. L., McCauley, E. A., & Bernstein, D. A. (1998). *Abnormal psychology*. Needham Heights, MA: Allyn & Bacon.

North, C. S., & Guze, S. B. (1997). Somatoform disorders. In S. G. Guze (Ed.), *Adult psychiatry*. St. Louis, MO: Mosby-Year Book.

Ostensen, M., Rugelsjoen, A., & Wigers, S. H. (1997). The effect of reproductive events and alterations of sex hormone levels on the symptoms of fibromyalgia. *Scandinavian Journal of Rheumatology*, 26(5): 355–360.

Parobek, U. M. (1997). Distinguishing conversion disorder from neurologic impairment. *Journal of Neuroscience Nursing*, 29(2): 128–134.

Parson, T. (1951). Social structure and dynamic process: The case of modern medical practice. In T. Parson (Ed.), *The social system*, pp. 428–479. New York: The Free Press.

Perugi, G., Akiskal, H. S., Giannotti, D., Di Vaio, S., & Cassano, G. B. (1997). Gender-related differences in body dysmorphic disorder (dysmorphophobia). *Journal of Nervous and Mental Disease*, 185(9): 578–582.

Perugi, G., Akiskal, H. S., Lattanzi, L., Cecconi, D., Mastrocinque, C., Patronelli, A., Vignoli, S., & Bemi, E. (1998). The high prevalence of "soft" bipolar (II) features in atypical depression. *Comprehensive Psychiatry*, 39(2): 63–71.

Phillips, K. A. (1991). Body dysmorphic disorder: The distress of imagined ugliness. *American Journal of Psychiatry*, 148, 1138.

Phillips, K. A. (1996). Body dysmorphic disorder: Diagnosis and treatment of imagined ugliness. *Journal of Clinical Psychiatry*, 57(Suppl. 8): 61–64.

Phillips, K. A., & Diaz, S. F. (1997). Gender differences in body dysmorphic disorder. *Journal of Nervous and Mental Disease*, 185(9): 570–577.

Phillips, K. A., Mc Elroy, S. L., Keck, P. E., Pope, H. G., & Judson, J. I. (1993). Body dysmorphic disorder: 30 cases of imagined ugliness. *American Journal of Psychiatry*, 150: 302.

Phillips, K. A., Kim, J. M., & Hudson, J. I. (1995). Body image disturbance in body dysmorphic disorder and eating disorder. Obsessions or delusions? *Psychiatric Clinics of North America*, 18(2): 317–334.

Piccinelli, M., & Simon, G. (1997). Gender and cross-cultural differences in somatic symptoms associated with emotional distress. An international study in primary care. *Psychology Medicine*, 27(2): 433–444.

Pope, H. G., Gruber, A. J., Choi, P., Olivardia, R., & Phillips, K. A. (1997). Muscle dysmorphia. An under recognized form of body dysmorphic disorder. *Psychosomatics*, 38(6): 548–557.

Poyner, F. E., & Pritty, P. E. (1997). Conversion disorder presenting as a head injury. *Journal of Accident and Emergency Medicine*, 14(4): 263–264.

Pribor, E. F., Yutzy, S. H., Dean, J. T., & Wetzel, R. D. (1993). Briquet's syndrome, dissociation, and abuse. *American Journal of Psychiatry*, 150: 1507–1511.

Raspe, R. E. (1948). *Singular travels, campaigns and adventures of Baron Munchausen*. London: Cresset Press.

Ratliff, T. L., Klutke, C. G., & McDougall, E. M. (1994). The etiology of interstitial cystitis. *Urologic Clinics of North America*, 21(1): 21–30.

Rosen, J. C., & Reiter, J. (1996). Development of the body dysmorphic disorder examination. *Behaviour Research and Therapy*, 34(9): 755–766.

Rosen, J. C., Reiter, J., & Orosan, P. (1995). Assessment of body image in eating disorder with the body dysmorphic examination. *Behaviour Research and Therapy*, 33(1): 77–84.

Salkovskis, P. M., & Clark, D. M. (1993). Pain disorder and hypochondriasis. *Advances in Behavior Research and Therapy*, 15: 23–48.

Sarwer, D. B. (1997). The "obsessive" cosmetic surgery patient: A consideration of body image dissatisfaction and body dysmorphic disorder. *Plastic-Surgical-Nursing*, 17(4): 193–197.

Sarwer, D. B., Wadden, T. A., Pertschuk, M. J., & Whitaker, L. A. (1998). Body image dissatisfaction and body dysmorphic disorder in 100 cosmetic surgery patients. *Plastic and Reconstructive Surgery*, 101(6): 1644–1649.

Savard, G. (1990). Convulsive pseudoseizures: A review of current concepts. *Behavioral Neurology*, 3(3): 133–141.

Schmand, B., Lindeboom, J., Schagen, S., Heijt, R., Koene, T., & Hamburger, H. L. (1998). Cognitive complaints in patients after whiplash injury: The impact of malingering. *Journal of Neurology, Neurosurgery and Psychiatry*, 64(3): 339–343.

Shaner, R. (1997). *Psychiatry*. Baltimore, MD: Williams & Wilkins.

Silver, F. W. (1996). Management of conversion disorder. *Journal of Physical Medicine and Rehabilitation*, 75(2): 134–140.

Sigvardsson, S., von Knorring, A. L., Bohman, M., & Cloninger, C. R. (1984). An adoption study of somatization disorder. *Archives of General Psychiatry*, 41: 853–859.

Simon, G. E., Katon, W. J., & Sparks, P. J. (1990). Allergic to life: Psychological factors in environmental illness. *American Journal of Psychiatry*, 147(7): 901–908.

Simeone, D., Hollander, E., & Stein, D. J. (1995). Body dysmorphic disorder in the DSM-IV field trial for obsessive-compulsive disorder. *American Journal of Psychiatry*, 152: 1207.

Slavney, P. R. (1990). *Perspectives on hysteria*. Baltimore, MD: John Hopkins University Press.

Slavney, P. R. (1994). Pseudoseizures, sexual abuse, and hermeneutic reasoning. *Comprehensive Psychiatry*, 35(6): 471–477.

Small, C. W. (1986). Pseudocyesis: An overview. *Canadian Journal of Psychiatry*, 31: 452–457.

Smith, G. R. (1990). *Somatization disorders in the medical setting*. Rockville, MD: National Institute of Mental Health.

Smith, G. R. (1994). The course of somatization and its effects on utilization of health care resources. *Psychosomatics*, 35: 263–267.

Smith, G. R., Manson, R. A., & Ray, D. C. (1986). Patients with multiple unexplained symptoms: Their characteristics, functional health, and health care utilization. *Archives of Internal Medicine*, 146: 69–72.

Smith, G. R., Golding, J. M., Kashner, T. M., & Rost, K. (1991). Antisocial personality in primary care patients with somatization disorder. *Comprehensive Psychiatry*, 32(4): 367–372.

Speed, J. (1996). Behavioral management of conversion disorder: A retrospective study. *Archives of Physical Medicine and Rehabilitation*, 77(2): 147–154.

Starkman, M. N., Marshall, J. C., La Ferla, J., & Kelch, R. P. (1985). Pseudocyesis: Psychological and neuroendocrine interrelationships. *Psychosomatic Medicine*, 47(1): 46–57.

Steptoe, A., & Noll, A. (1997). The perception of bodily sensations, with special reference to hypochondriasis. *Behaviour Research and Therapy*, 35(10): 901–910.

Stern, J., Murphy, M., & Bass, C. (1993). Personality disorder in patients with somatization disorder: A controlled study. *British Journal of Psychiatry*, 363: 785–789.

Stoudemire, A. (Ed.) (1994). *Clinical psychiatry for medical students* (2nd ed.). Philadelphia: J. B. Lippincott.

Swartz, M., Landerman, R., George, L. K., Blazer, D. G., & Escobar, J. (1991). Somatization disorder. In L. N. Robins & D. A. Regier (Eds.), *Psychiatric disorder in America: The epidemiologic catchment area study*, pp. 220–257. New York: Free Press.

Talley, N. J. (1991). Diagnosing an irritable bowel: Does sex matter? *Gastroenterology*, 110: 834–837.

Thomas, C. L. (Ed.). (1997). *Taber's cyclopedic medical dictionary*. Philadelphia: F. A. Davis.

Thompson, W. G., & Pigeon-Ressor, H. (1990). The irritable bowel syndrome. *Seminars in Gastrointestinal Disease*, 1(1): 57–73.

Turner, S. M., & Hersen, M. (1997). *Adult psychopathology and diagnosis*. New York: John Wiley & Sons.

Van Houdenhove, B., & Joostens, P. (1995). Burning mouth syndrome: Successful treatment with combined psychotherapy and pharmacotherapy. *General Hospital Psychiatry*, 17: 385–388.

Veale, D., Gournay, K., Dryden, W., Boocock, A., Shah, F., Willson, R., & Walburn, J. (1996a). Body dysmorphic disorder: A cognitive behavioural model and pilot randomized controlled trial. *Behaviour Research and Therapy*, 34(9): 717–729.

Veale, D., Boocock, A., Gournay, K., Dryden, W., Shah, F., Willson, R., & Walburn, J. (1996b). Body dysmorphic disorder: A survey of fifty cases. *British Journal of Psychiatry*, 169(2): 196–201.

Warwick, H. M. C., & Salkovskis, D. (1990). Hypochondriasis. *Behaviour Research and Therapy*, 28: 105–117.

Wessley, S., & Lutz, T. (1995). Neurasthenia and fatigue syndromes. In G. E. Berrios & R. Porter (Eds.), *A history of clinical psychiatry: The origin and history of psychiatric disorders*, p. 509. New York: New York University Press.

Wetzel, R. D., Guze, S. B., Cloninger, C. R., & Martin, R. L. (1994). Briquet's syndrome (hysteria) is both a somatoform and a "psychoform" illness: A Minnesota Multiphasic Personality Inventory Study. *Psychosomatic Medicine*, 56(6): 564–569.

Whitehead, W. E., Busch, C. M., Heller, B. R., & Costa, P. T. (1986). Social learning influences on menstrual symptoms and illness behavior. *Health Psychology*, 5: 13–23.

Wilhelm, S., Otto, M. W., Zucker, B. G., & Pollack, M. H. (1997). Prevalence of body dysmorphic disorder in patients with anxiety disorders. *Journal of Anxiety Disorders*, 11(5): 499–502.

Wilson, T., Nathan, P. E., O'Leary, K. D., & Clark, L. A. (1996). *Abnormal psychology*. Boston: Allyn & Bacon.

Yates, B. D., Nordquist, C. R., & Schultz-Ross, R. A. (1997). Feigned psychiatric symptoms in the emergency room. *Psychiatric Services*, 47(9): 998–1000.

Yutzy, S. H., Cloninger, C. R., Guze, S. B., Pribor, E. F., Martin, R. L., Kathol, R. G., Smith, G. R., & Strain, J. J. (1995). DSM-IV field trial: Testing a new proposal for somatization disorder. *American Journal of Psychiatry*, 152(1): 97–101.

DISSOCIATIVE DISORDERS

INTRODUCTION

When the DSM-I was first published in 1952, only one dissociative disorder, the dissociative psychoneurotic reaction, was described. Fifteen years later, the second edition noted two dissociative disorders: depersonalization neurosis and dissociative type of hysterical neurosis (mentioning multiple personality disorder as a symptom). The DSM-III (APA, 1980) and the later revised version DSM-III-R (APA, 1987) included four dissociative disorders: psychogenic amnesia, psychogenic fugue, depersonalization disorder, and multiple personality disorder. In the DSM-IV (APA, 1994), all of these dissociative categories underwent a name change and the role dissociation plays in each disorder was highlighted. The existing categories are dissociative amnesia, dissociative fugue, depersonalization disorder, and dissociative identity disorder.

The dissociative disorders are controversial. Most practitioners find them difficult to understand and may wonder whether a person could be faking these symptoms or pretending to be more troubled than they really are (Slovenko, 1995). This is particularly relevant in situations where a person is charged with a serious crime and they plead "not guilty by reason of insanity" (Slovenko, 1995). What causes these puzzling conditions is not really known, and understanding the disorder is complicated by practitioners wanting to prove its authenticity by searching for "alters" (Chitalkar et al., 1996).

Most theorists agree that unexpected trauma or severe emotional threats are the immediate triggers for some dissociative experiences. However, the majority of people who have experienced some form of trauma do not suffer a dissociative disorder, and so the importance of a competency-based assessment that avoids coming to premature conclusions about what happens in the client's life is underscored. As the practitioner explores the client's life history, perhaps what is more important is what is *not* said. The person may have large gaps of time which they cannot account for, or they may relate many inconsistencies about their past. Rather than acknowledge these discrepancies, the person may try to make up the details or change the subject away from a conversation about him- or herself. As the practitioner explores interpersonal relationships, the following questions can be helpful to add to the competency-based assessment when considering the presence of a dissociative disorder:

- Do others seem to know you and yet you do not know them?
- Are you unable to figure out how you got from one place to another?

The following questions may provide additional insight about the client's social environment:

- Have you ever found things and not known how you happened to have them?
- Have you ever had things missing and you have no idea how this happened?

After the therapeutic relationship has been established and the practitioner begins to suspect the presence of alters, the following questions may be helpful in understanding the intrapersonal domain in the client's life:

- Are you unable to remember significant periods of time?
- Are there periods of time in your life (especially during early childhood) that you cannot remember?
- Do you sometimes hear voices and when no one else is physically present?
- Are there other people who are inside of you and who take charge of you at times?
- Do you think that one of the individuals (inside of you) takes charge for any particular period of time?
- Do any of these people have a special occupation, behavior, or social relationship that the others (inside of you) do not?
- Are all of the persons (inside of you) of the same age or gender?
- Do these people have names?
- How often do you notice these changes in your personality?

Dell (1998), Frischholz et al. (1992), Rauschenberger and Lynn (1995), and Spiegel and Vermutten (1994) isolated three variables that tend to produce a vulnerability to dissociative disorders. They are:

- Imaginative involvement, absorption, or fantasy proneness—The tendency to fantasize increases recollection of past negative experiences and/or a tendency to exaggerate the potential negative aspects of future events. The exact nature of this intrapersonal process in a person's life and its relationship to the etiology of dissociative disorders remains unclear.
- Hypnotizability—This refers to the ease with which someone can be hypnotized, differences in hypnotic suggestibility, and increased risk of using hypnotic-like dissociation in anxiety-provoking situations.
- Childhood trauma—A history of physical and/or sexual abuse is involved.

Note / Grief Recovery text Steve Moeller
Losses back to childhood

Dissociation is defined as a "disruption in the usually integrated functions of consciousness, memory, identity, or perception of the environment" (APA, 1994, p. 477), that is distressing or impairs an individual's basic areas of functioning. The term is generally used to describe an alteration of consciousness characterized by estrangement from the self or the environment, and a mechanism of defense to ward off the emotional impact of traumatic or abusive events and memories (Cardena, 1997). To qualify as a dissociative experience, such discrepancies cannot be the product of other forms of conscious deception, for example, malingering. In other words, the person's ability to function on his or her own is disrupted, and their normal process of consciousness, memory, and singular personal identity becomes splintered.

Dissociation occurs when one group of normal mental processes becomes separated from the rest; that is, the person's sense of identity changes along with their memories, feelings, and perceptions. The individual experiences a loss in connections, and parts of their identity are relegated to a separate "compartment" (or buried), which may suddenly and unexpectedly emerge. Some individuals may experience a sudden onset with temporary symptoms, whereas others may experience a gradual onset and a chronic course.

There has been a resurgence of interest in dissociative disorders, especially in view of its association with posttraumatic stress disorder and its correlation with severe childhood sexual abuse. Unfortunately, the field has advanced largely on anecdotal experience, poorly conceived studies (suffering from lack of adequate controls, selection bias, and/or unwarranted conclusions from data), and polemical arguments that form the bulk of the published literature (North and Yutzy, 1997). While studies have grown exponentially in the recent decade, there appears to be no actual consensus about what "dissociation" really means. It is our contention that a competency-based assessment, which considers all the systems affecting the client's life, is most helpful in understanding the client's experience with traumatic life events while looking for strengths as they cope with these difficulties.

Not all dissociative experiences are viewed as pathological, and to some extent, most of us have experienced "dissociative events" at one time or another. Daydreaming is one example of how people can switch states of consciousness. To do this, a person's sets of memory and attitudes must also switch. From time to time, many of us have experienced boredom while listening to a lecture or presentation, and "daydream" or "tune out" the content of what is being said. On the surface it appears that the person is listening intently, while in actuality he or she is not actually aware of what is being said. Rather, the person is listening while on "automatic pilot" (Nietzel et al., 1998). Usually the incident is brief, and it does not interfere or cause any problems with normal functioning.

The dissociative disorders entail a more complicated process wherein people forget who they are, where they are, and what they have been doing. One might begin to think of these disorders as the "elsewhere disorders"; that is, part of the person's present memory or identity is elsewhere and not available (Maxmen & Ward, 1995). In dissociative states, the person "loses" their identity. For example, they may wander away from their home, as seen in a fugue state; lose their memory without wandering away from their home, as seen in amnesia. In extreme cases of dissociation, people acquire more than one distinct identity, typically referred to as **alters**. Each represents a cohesive character with its own unique memories, attitudes, habits, facial expressions, gestures, and personal histories that are clearly different and apart from the "host" individual they share. Typically, these "personalities" differ from each other along other dimensions including race, gender, age, and intelligence. As the alter emerges, the individual appears to become a different person.

The normal end of the dissociative continuum includes daydreaming and culture-specific manifestations, while the more dysfunctional end of the spectrum is represented by the dissociative disorders. The essential feature of dissociative disorders is a disruption in the client's intrapersonal domain—and specifically of the mental functions of consciousness, identity, perception of the environment, and memory. The dissociative disorders share several common features: they generally end suddenly; a profound disturbance of memory is noted (except in depersonalization disorder); and episodes are precipitated by psychological conflicts. Steinberg (1994) identifies five key symptoms found in most dissociative disorders:

- *Amnesia*—This is considered more than simple forgetfulness, such as where the car was parked at the mall after a busy day shopping. This manifestation of amnesia includes the loss of memory of a person's identity or the loss of periods of time in a person's past.

- *Depersonalization*—The person feels detached from themselves as if another person were observing them.

- *Derealization*—The person senses that objects in their world are strange, unreal, or have suddenly changed dimension, appearance, or location. For example, a person's home may feel unfamiliar to them.

- *Identity confusion*—The person is unsure of their own identity and who they are.

- *Identity alteration*—The person's behavior suggests they have assumed a new identity.

While dissociative disorders were previously thought to be extremely rare, they are now considered to occur more frequently (Dallam & Manderino, 1997). When the dissociative episode does occur, it is transient in nature and disappears within a few hours or days. As a result, most practitioners have few opportunities to witness an episode firsthand. Relying on client accounts of their experiences complicates the understanding of dissociative disorders. The two most common dissociative disorders are dissociative amnesia and depersonalization disorder. Dissociative identity disorder (DID), formerly known as multiple personality disorder (MPD), attracts the most research and clinical attention. On the dissociative continuum, dissociative identity disorder is considered the most severe (Brenner, 1996; Ellason et al., 1996).

CULTURAL PERSPECTIVES AND DISSOCIATION

It is important for the practitioner to take into account the individual's social and cultural context when considering dissociative disorders. Throughout history and across many cultures, examples of dissociation have been described (Putnam, 1989). Dissociative experiences such as trance states, "speaking in tongues," or spirit possession are widely accepted and practiced in many present-day cultures, and they are not considered as being a "disorder" within the culture. Specific characteristics are generally determined by the culture. They include dissociative symptoms, but the personality "changes" are attributed to the spirit or state recognized by the particular culture. Within the environmental or cultural context, trance or possession states are culturally sanctioned and seen as normative and adaptive. For example, in regions of Thailand, Phii Poh (a common type of spirit possession) temporarily "takes over" a person's body. Afterward, there is no memory of what took place during the event (Spanos, 1994). Other cultures have *shamans* or healers who induce trancelike states in order to communicate with "spirits" or the "other world" (Ferracuti et al., 1996; Gleaves, 1996; Kirkmayer, 1994). In the highland region of Papua, New Guinea, dissociative states are an intrinsic part of religious ceremonies. Only men participate in ceremonies in the "spirit house" (a place of worship), where they "speak" with their ancestor's through an intermediary known as the "crocodile spirit" who intercedes between and interprets ancestor responses. Women are expressly forbidden to enter a spirit house or practice any form of "ancestor" religion.

Another culturally accepted dissociative experience is **Ataque de Nervios**, a commonly noted response to acute stress in Latin American and Hispanic cultures (APA, 1994, 2000; Comas-Diaz, 1981; Lewis-Fernandez, 1994). Features include uncontrollable crying, screaming, shouting, seizurelike behaviors, and a failure to remember the episode afterward. The event is usually brief, leaves no evidence of any residual difficulties, and is perceived within the culture to be a beneficial and adaptive way to cope and relieve distress. A competency-based assessment takes into account the individual's cultural context and may find situations of "dissociation" considered adaptive.

DISSOCIATIVE IDENTITY DISORDER

Dissociative identity disorder (DID) is considered the most severe of all the dissociative disorders, because the most common and fundamental alteration includes the presence of more than one discrete identity. In spite of all the stories seen on television talk shows or read in tabloid headlines, most research studies indicate the median number of an individual's personalities ranges from five to ten (Kluft, 1996; Ross, 1989; Sackeim & Devanand, 1991). Once the disorder is established, it tends to last a lifetime (in the absence of treatment). It is generally considered chronic, and it typically involves traumatic events that occurred during childhood.

A competency-based assessment that pays attention to life circumstances will uncover environmental factors that help set the stage for the development of dissociative identity disorder. The client's life history, in at least one aspect, contains terrible and frequently indescribable instances of physical or sexual abuse, most often incest (Waites, 1993). In the authors' combined practice experiences, it was not uncommon for clients to relate childhood incidents of being locked in basements or closets, brutally tortured, burned, cut, beaten, or tormented in a variety of ways far too horrible to recount in detail here. The important thing to remember is that the individual, as a young child, learns to survive this "ordeal" by fleeing into the dissociative process. This process includes a psychobiological mechanism that allows the mind to escape what the body is experiencing; the child exists in a fantasy world where these brutal experiences are blunted (Solomon, 1997). Each time the child endures the abusive episode, they "learn" to re-create the haven of safety by escaping or "switching" into their fantasy world. On some level, the child learns there is no limit to the variety of "identities" they can construct for protection from the abusive situation.

The process of "switching" seems to decrease with age, and there is some evidence to suggest that one of the personalities becomes more dominant (Sackeim & Devanand, 1991). Although the use of dissociation as a defense mechanism begins in childhood, the presence of a dissociative identity disorder is often undetected until adulthood. By this time, the dissociation is well entrenched as a way of coping (Barker & Herlache, 1997).

The developmental disruptions that accompany child sexual abuse and neglect help set in motion a series of events that increase the likelihood of impending future maladaptation (Marsh & Wolfe, 1999). It should be pointed out that not all children who experience maltreatment will later develop serious problems in living. However, there is evidence to suggest they are at a much greater risk for problems (Cicchetti & Lynch, 1995; Jumper, 1995)—for example, aggression and violence (Malinosky-Rummell & Hansen, 1993); chronic impairment in self-concept and self-esteem; emotional and behavioral self-regulation (Putnam & Trickett, 1993), and including depression and posttraumatic stress disorder (Shader, 1994). In adulthood, the developmental impairments stemming from those childhood experiences often lead to more pervasive and chronic intrapersonal and interpersonal difficulties and including panic disorders, eating disorders, personality disorders, and sexual problems (Wolfe & Jaffee, 1991; Wolfe & McGee, 1994; Wolfe et al., 1994; Garnefski & Diekstra, 1997; Rodriguez et al., 1997).

There is emerging opinion suggesting dissociative identity disorder is a very extreme subtype of posttraumatic stress disorder (PTSD). In both conditions, strong emotional reactions are commonly associated with experiencing a severe trauma (Bremner et al., 1993). When posttraumatic stress disorder was first identified, the specific reference points were catastrophic events, for example, war, rape, torture, natural disasters (hurricanes or floods), and disasters of human origin (airline or train crashes) (Acierno et al., 1999; Weathers & Keane, 1999). A distinction should be made between trauma and other extremely stressful life events such as a family breaking up due to a divorce. The traumatic experiences associated with posttraumatic stress disorder are likely to exceed and overwhelm the person's abilities in coping. It has been found that children who experience sexual abuse show many of the same symptoms previously identified in adults who experienced combat situations, torture, or natural disasters; that is, what they share in common is nightmares, fears, and panic attacks for many years following the traumatic experiences (Husain et al., 1998; Weathers & Keane, 1999; Yule, 1994). In South Florida, as many as 30 percent of the children who experienced Hurricane Andrew in 1992 reported having severe levels of PTSD symptoms for almost two years afterward (La Greca et al., 1996).

Prevailing Pattern

Most persons with dissociative identity disorder are generally not forthcoming about their various personalities, even when they learn that they have them. They often fear they will be regarded as an exhibitionist or worse, as a "freak." The various "personalities" tend to be distinctive and dominate or control the behavior of the person; often there is a sense of struggle for dominance among the alters. Sometimes there may be a shifting importance to the role of each personality over time and the amount of the time spent in each identity.

The "host" identity, that is, the person who comes in (or is referred) for counseling, is usually overwhelmed by efforts to hold various fragments of these personalities together. The person may not be aware of the presence of these alters and may be confused about what is happening to them. A prevailing question remains as to whether these fragmented identities are real, or the individual is just faking "symptoms" to avoid some responsibility or relief from stress. Similar to the conversion disorder (discussed in Chapter 6), this question is very difficult to answer for several reasons.

First, evidence suggests that persons with dissociative identity disorder are highly suggestible (Bliss, 1984, 1986). Second, there is empirical evidence to support that some persons could easily simulate and fake dissociative experiences (Spanos et al., 1985; Spanos, 1994), and that the *enactment* of multiple identities usually serves specific personal goals. Spanos (1994) suggests during the last 20 years in the United States, dissociative identity disorder has become a socially acceptable way to "express failures and frustrations as well as a covert tactic by which to manipulate others and attain succor and other rewards" (p. 143). Third, if people have been abused as children, the chances are they will more than likely have been given information about enacting multiple "personalities" as a way to deal with abuse and the associated trauma (Bowers & Farvolden, 1996).

Finally, practitioners who believe having a history of childhood abuse is a primary cause of dissociative identity disorder (Lewis et al., 1998) are more likely to ask clients leading questions and to use interview techniques that often encourage a report of symptoms that might not otherwise appear (Chitalkar et al., 1996; Crothers, 1995). While some individuals may enact dissociated identities, and some practitioners reinforce these enactments, this is not enough to corroborate that *all* cases of dissociated identity disorder are fabrications (Gleaves, 1996; Kluft, 1996). It is probably best for the practitioner to complete a competency-based assessment that carefully explores the intrapersonal, interpersonal, and sociocultural domains of the client's life, and to remain open-minded to all manner of possibilities that explain client behavior.

Differential Assessment

Dissociative disorder must be differentiated from other general medical conditions, particularly neurological conditions, and the effects of psychoactive substances that can lead to impaired memory. Individuals with certain neurological disorders, particularly seizure disorders, experience an increase of dissociative features (Cardena et al., 1996). In an alcoholic blackout, the person may behave in very uncharacteristic ways and have no memory of events, but he or she maintains the same identity. A neurological examination is essential to rule out other factors. With malingering disorder, it is difficult to rule out reasons for inventing other personalities, and the practitioner should look for any type of gain, financial or otherwise, that a person might obtain by virtue of having these symptoms.

The dissociative disorder is often misconstrued as being a thought disorder, for example, as in the case of schizophrenia. However, dissociative identity disorder is the result of "switching" back and forth between one personality entity and another. The symptoms are usually transient and related to a cycling of personality entities as they struggle for control over the person's core identity versus being the result of delusions, hallucinations, bizarre behavior, or disorganized speech. Dissociative amnesia, fugue, and depersonalization are not characterized by the experience of multiple, discrete identities. People suffering from dissociative identity disorder may be initially misdiagnosed as having an affective disorder. (Refer to Chapter 4 for a more in-depth discussion.) The reason for this is because of the mood swings found in affective disorders. However, the person usually does not feel depressed for any length of time, and if mood swings exist they are frequently of short duration.

The following case represents an example of someone with dissociative identity disorder.

The Case of Emily Samuels

Emily Samuels was referred by one of the authors' colleagues for a consultation who called and said, "Susan, I've seen Emily three times, and I'm more confused than ever. While she presents herself in sessions with some depression, I'm not sure what is going on for this young woman. I only know it might be something very serious. Could you please see her for me?"

The first thing I noticed about Emily was how she entered my office. She was very subdued and approached the session in a tentative, hesitant manner. I felt she was watching me to make the "first move." Her voice was barely above a whisper as she introduced herself. Once she became settled, I asked her why she thought she was referred to me. Emily responded, "Well, I don't want you to think I'm crazy or anything, but sometimes I get into trouble using my MasterCard." I asked her to elaborate on what she meant by that. "Well, I know it sounds really strange, but if you believe the MasterCard Company, they claim I've charged over $22,000 this year on three different cards. I don't know anything about that. I think they are a bunch of crooks trying to rip me off. I wanna know one thing. If I spent that much money, where is all the stuff I'm supposed to have bought? They don't want to tell me anything. They are taking me to court in two months. They said I applied for three different credit cards in three different names and now I have to pay up. Where would I get that kinda money? Besides, I can prove I didn't spend that money. Those cards aren't in my name, and on top of it all the handwriting on the charge receipts isn't mine either."

I asked her, "Has anything else happened like this before where you didn't remember things?" She responded, "Sometimes, people I don't even know call me by other names. For instance, I was shopping in Wal-Mart last week and this strange lady called me 'Harriet.' To top it off, this lady just about ran me down yelling, 'You hoo, Harriet, Harriet where are you going?' Then she had the nerve to yell at me for not answering her. Don't that beat all? Who the hell did she think I was? I'm me, not some Harriet."

I asked Emily, "What did you think about that?" She shrugged her shoulders to indicate she was not sure, and looked slightly uncomfortable. I thought I saw a momentary look of fear in her eyes, but then she averted her gaze away from mine. I continued, "Has this ever happened to you before?" She responded, "Well, yeah. Now that you mention it, some guy I didn't know before called me 'Beth Ann' when I was grocery shopping. I thought this guy was a 'nut job,' you know a stalker or something. I went and complained to the store manager, and told him to tell the weird guy 'to get lost.' Can you believe the manager came back and told me that the 'weird guy' was my husband? I guess that's why Mary Jo [the worker requesting the consultation] called you. Personally, I think its 'cause she's never heard of anything like this happening to people before."

I asked Emily, "What do you think happened to you [when you were] in the grocery store?" She laughed saying, "The lighting musta been bad, and I didn't recognize my husband, that's all." She refused to answer any further questions along that line of inquiry.

I asked Emily a series of questions regarding her interpersonal experiences as a child, specifically school, and whether she had any difficulties with her peer group or with her family. She acknowledged problems with poor grades, truancy, and having few friends. She also mentioned her parents were very strict with her; she was their only child. She denied being hospitalized for anything more significant than "having my tonsils out." Emily denies currently taking any medication.

She appeared at this point in the interview to be concentrating for a moment, and then asked me, "Is being hospitalized the same as being in a mental institution?" I explored what she meant, and she continued, "Well, my parents put me in a mental hospital a coupla times when I was a kid 'cause I used to have terrible nightmares all the time. I would try to stay awake all night. I guess I was afraid to go to sleep." When Emily was asked about what happened at this time in her life, she replied, "I don't really remember much 'cept I had these terrible, terrible dreams that somebody was really hurting me." Emily recounted that the nightmares usually had a pattern that were connected to her father coming into her room at night and touching her in "secret places" and how much it hurt. She continued, "I told my mother about this, but she laughed and told me, 'Emily, you have such a vivid imagination. You know I'd never let anybody hurt you.' She used to tell me, 'that's why we put you in a mental institution because you remembered things that never happened.' I wish she would have believed me." Emily denied currently feeling depressed or suicidal.

Emily was asked if she ever found items of clothes, jewelry, or other possessions and did not know where they came from. She replied, "Yeah, once I found some motorcycle stuff in my closet at home. It was really weird stuff, too." Gently, I asked her to elaborate. "Well, you know, some of the stuff looked like they shoulda belonged to a guy. They sure didn't belong to me. [She sounded a bit scared and uncertain at this point.] I mean, what would I be doing with a pair of black leather pants, boots, and some bracelets with nail studs? The only thing I can think of is, I musta found them and brought them home or something," she replied twisting in her chair.

I then inquired, "Have you ever experienced gaps of time that you could not account for?" and, "Have there been large periods of time when you were growing up that you could not remember?" Quite abruptly, Emily sat up and began to stare at me in a way that she had not done before. I observed almost immediately that her posture, facial expressions, and mannerisms also changed. Her "voice" while soft at the beginning of the session had changed into a gruff tone. She began to talk to me in an entirely different manner than that of "Emily."

"Hey, bitch, you leave the kid alone. You hear what I'm saying? She's had enough trouble from you 'shrinks,' so cool it." I responded that I had been asking questions about gaps of time in Emily's life, and wondered out loud, "What did I say that brought about such a change?" **"Well, first of all, I ain't Emily, I'm Rick. I bet you weren't expecting me, huh?"** Emily responded. I began to wonder about several inconsistencies around what Emily had told me. I replied, "I wonder if you could tell me something about who you are."

"Emily doesn't know about us, but we know all about her. We don't get in her face too often, but every once in awhile we like to get out and have fun. She's much too fussy, you know what I mean? Anyway, there are four of us and ...," she continued.

"Hey, Bozo, you don't have to talk for me, I can talk for myself. I'm Frenchy, and I love to have sex. That Emily girl was always such a rigid little piece of work. She used to really hate it when her father would come into her room and 'make her give him sex.' She would just cry and cry, you know, 'boo hoo,' and beg for him to stop and leave her alone. So I take over for her 'cause if you love to have sex and it don't bother you, then it doesn't hurt, right?" The interview continued.

"Where was I?" continued Rick, **"Oh yes, I was telling you that we protect Emily and always have. So butt out."**

At this point, Emily flexed her neck and head from side to side, and looked at me in the way I first remembered meeting her. She shyly smiled, raised her eyes and asked, "Did something happen I should know about?" Before answering her, I immediately remember thinking that I needed to call Mary Jo and discuss this interesting event.

Assessment Summary

The most striking feature about Emily is her sudden shift, while in session with the social worker, among three distinct personalities: Emily (the host), Rick, and Frenchy. It should be pointed out to the reader that the phenomenon of "switching" is rare and a relatively unusual occurrence in practice. Each distinct personality state struggles for dominance. This shift can initially confuse the practitioner. As Emily's "story" unfolds, she relates to the worker as a shy, soft-spoken and demure young

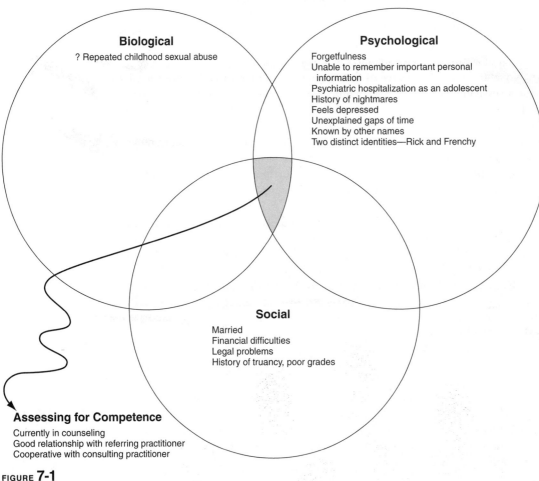

Biological

? Repeated childhood sexual abuse

Psychological

Forgetfulness
Unable to remember important personal
  information
Psychiatric hospitalization as an adolescent
History of nightmares
Feels depressed
Unexplained gaps of time
Known by other names
Two distinct identities—Rick and Frenchy

Social

Married
Financial difficulties
Legal problems
History of truancy, poor grades

Assessing for Competence

Currently in counseling
Good relationship with referring practitioner
Cooperative with consulting practitioner

FIGURE **7-1**

DISSOCIATIVE IDENTITY DISORDER

The interactions of the biological, psychological, and social variables in Emily Samuels' life.

woman. The session continues and the worker is confronted with indications of other personalities. In this case, we find Rick, who is a different gender and seemingly quite protective of "Emily." He is brusque and controlling. Rick emerges in the interview at a time when the worker begins to explore potentially sensitive material, specifically whether Emily had ever experienced blocks of time she could not explain. Frenchy emerged as the worker attempted to understand Rick and his relationship to Emily. This personality functioned as Emily's protector, and the interview content of childhood sexual abuse was again introduced. The first reference to abuse was made when Emily talked about being institutionalized in a mental hospital.

These personalities were aware of each other. However, only one at a time came forth during the interview. The transition from one personality to another occurred during stressful points in the session. Both personalities conveyed to the worker a sense of protection during stressful times in Emily's life.

Emily's history of childhood sexual abuse by her father set the stage for the development of her dissociative identity disorder. This fantasy world is, in fact, very closely associated with posttraumatic stress disorder in that both are strong reactions to the experience of childhood trauma. Emily's escape into the dissociative realm blunted her physical and emotional pain.

No matter what the source of the referral, it is important to involve the client in the assessment conversation. During the initial meeting, the practitioner encouraged Emily to share personally relevant material, and helped her to explore situations of concern, their meanings, and related feelings. Sometimes people will immediately bring up topics for discussion, and at other times, like Emily, they are reserved and hesitant.

Emily's overall diagnosis is as follows:

Axis I	300.14 Dissociative Identity Disorder
Axis II	V71.09 (No diagnosis)
Axis III	None
Axis IV	? Childhood sexual abuse
Axis V	GAF = 55 (at interview)

DISSOCIATIVE AMNESIA DISORDER

Dissociative amnesia disorder was formerly known as psychogenic amnesia. This is a completely reversible amnesia that is associated with some form of emotional, traumatic, or psychological stress. While the person's generalized fund of life knowledge remains intact, they cannot remember important personal information, such as their name, age, or marital status. This cannot be attributed to ordinary forgetfulness or absentmindedness.

There are several different patterns of dissociative amnesia:

- *Localized amnesia* (or "circumscribed" amnesia)—The person is unable to recall events that occurred during a particular time or following a profoundly disturbing event, such as combat (Lowenstein, 1991).

- *Selective amnesia*—The person can bring to mind patchy recollections of an event, but other portions of time are forgotten; for example, a woman might not remember giving birth to her child, but she might remember various aspects of being in labor before or remember events after the actual birth.

There are three types of amnesia considered less common. They are generalized, continuous, and systematized amnesia.

- *Generalized amnesia*—This is a disorder that encompasses all the experiences during the person's entire lifetime. The person cannot remember anything from infancy to the present time; for example, they are unable to recall their name and who they are.

- *Continuous amnesia*—This includes the person's inability to remember all events from a given time up to and including the present time.

- *Systematized amnesia*—The person loses memory pertaining only to certain categories of information, such as relating to their family or to work.

The behaviors found in these latter three types of dissociative amnesia may eventually lead to a more complex diagnosis of dissociative identity disorder.

Dissociative amnesia has been poorly studied, and not much is known about family prevalence, demographic data, or etiology. However, what is known is that it is more commonly reported in young women, usually preceded by severe stress, and can occur at any age. The symptoms disappear as suddenly as they appear; amnesia events can range from minutes to years. In rare instances, the amnesia can recur. In dissociative amnesia, the person may remember what they have eaten for breakfast but not recall their name. In contrast, for those with Alzheimer's-type dementia, the person usually remembers their name, but they are unable to recall what they have eaten for breakfast (Kaplan & Sadock, 1998). The clinical features are not limited to amnesia that occurs in the course of dissociative identity disorder and are not the result of ingesting a substance (illicit or prescribed) or a general medical condition such as seizures (Cardena et al., 1996).

Prevailing Pattern

A single episode of dissociative amnesia is the most common pattern. Multiple episodes are possible if there are repeated experiences of extreme stress or trauma, for example, being the victim of a crime (Shader, 1994). The person experiences at least one episode where they are either partially or completely unable to retrieve important memories and personal information. The information usually is about trauma or stress, and it is more extensive than what could be explained by ordinary forgetfulness. These symptoms cause significant distress and interpersonal difficulties including, for example, problems with employment and in social relationships. They do not occur solely during dissociative fugue, acute stress disorder, posttraumatic stress disorder (PTSD), dissociative identity disorder, or somatization disorder. The symptoms are *not caused* by a general medical condition, the use of alcohol, and/or drugs (including prescribed medications).

The assessment is not made if the loss of recall is only around childhood memories; it must involve events that are more current, usually those following a psychologically traumatic event. Interestingly, a study conducted by Pope et al. (1998) failed to demonstrate the association between dissociative amnesia and traumatic events. This suggests a note of caution to the practitioner to evaluate the association between a traumatic event in the client's life with the onset of dissociative amnesia. Looking at biological vulnerability in reaction to a trauma is indicated (Durand & Barlow, 1997). A competency-based assessment that thoroughly explores the biological, psychological, and social factors in a person's life and their interrelationships decreases the possibility of coming to the wrong conclusion about how a person copes with and adapts to traumatic life events.

Differential Assessment

In contrast to transient global amnesia, persons with dissociative amnesia usually experience their first difficulty with amnesia at a young age, rather than in middle age. Most important, they are able to eventually recall what happened. Dissociative fugue requires unexpected travel and confusion about personal identity; dissociative amnesia is *not* assessed if the person's memory gaps occur exclusively during dissociative fugue states. Malingering and factitious disorders are characterized by amnesia that is feigned.

The Case of Margarethe Jean-Baptiste

"Paging Doctor Gray. Doctor Susan Gray, please call operator number three." Hurrying to the telephone, I asked for "operator three." I began, "This is Susan Gray, can I help you?" The voice on the other end of the line responded, "Hi, Susan, it's Terry in the emergency room. Look, I don't have time to go into a lot of detail, but could you please come down here right away?" I replied, "Sure, I'm on my way."

"Terry, what's up?" I asked. "Well, we have a 'situation' here. Did you hear about the group of 'rafters' the Marathon Police picked up this morning?" I shook my head no. She continued, "Well, the police found five men and two women beached in what's left of some homemade wooden raft out near the Seven Mile Bridge. The story I heard from one of the men is originally ten of them fled from Haiti eight days ago, but the raft ran into problems almost right away. They encountered a terrible sudden storm. Three people in their boat died when they were swept overboard during the storm. To make matters worse, most of their water and supplies were lost, too. It's nothing short of a miracle that everyone was in as good shape as they are. I mean, other than maybe being a bit exhausted and sunburned.

"Anyway, the reason I wanted you to come down here is to talk with a young woman; they call her Margarethe Jean-Baptiste. She seems unable to recall the last eight days. We asked her the usual questions, you know, 'Who are you? Where are you? What's today's date? yah dee yah dah' ...; anyway, she was unable to recount any subsequent events since she left Haiti. It's like time just seemed to stop for her. Margarethe does not remember what happened to the other people, and it's my guess she experienced some pretty bad emotional stuff on that raft. You know, like she had to have seen her raft-mates die. She doesn't know where she is, even though I've reminded her several times that she's safe and sound in the hospital here in the Florida Keys."

I asked Terry, "What about her physical exam?" She responded, "Everything checks out fine. Margarethe doesn't appear to be suffering from any kind of problem other than being sunburned and having some mild dehydration. She's some lucky lady considering what she's been through. Just to cover all my bases, I brought in Malcolm Renaldo. Do you know him? No? Well, he just started his neurology rotation here from the University of Miami and seems like a sharp fellow. Anyway, I spoke to him before I called you. On his physical exam he found no evidence of any head trauma or problems that could explain her memory loss. Margarethe's 'labs' just came back and nothing remarkable there either. You know, drugs or unusual stuff. So it appears medically she's all right. I guess, the next 'look see' is in your department. I'll be waiting to hear from you."

I introduced myself to Margarethe through an interpreter who spoke Creole and asked what I could do to be of help. Her English was pretty good, but I used the interpreter as a backup. I also wanted to reduce any additional stresses in our conversation since English was Margarethe's second language. She replied, "I want to call my family back home and let them know I'm all right. They will be worried about me." I sensed that Margarethe was a bit uneasy at this point and gently inquired about how she managed to survive the last few days. Tears welled up in her eyes as she spoke to me. She said (sobbing softly), "I remember leaving my country to make a new life. Since the storm, I, I, I, … I do not know the rest." I reassured Margarethe that I would try to help.

After a few days in the hospital, Margarethe was discharged with a referral to the Middle Keys Guidance Clinic and to legal aid to address her immigration status.

Assessment Summary

Margarethe Jean-Baptiste's amnesia was the chief concern for hospital staff. Aside from being sunburned and dehydrated, she was in good overall medical condition. She was under a great deal of physical exhaustion and emotional stress coupled with a tortuous boat trip, which could have provided the stimulus for her dissociative amnesia. When found, Margarethe was brought to the local hospital, where she received a complete medical evaluation. The findings of her tests and examination were all within normal limits and provided no basis to support any biological cause for her state of amnesia. There was no indication of head trauma, epilepsy, or substance abuse, and it would seem that Margarethe's health was generally good even before the boat trip. Ultimately, her dissociative amnesia was attributed to the traumatic experience of leaving her country and the resulting voyage.

The competency-based assessment looks at environmental factors as well as intrapersonal ones that include thoughts and feelings. In Margarethe's case, her immigration from Haiti was complicated by a perilous boat journey that ended in the death of several of her companions. This traumatic incident was the capstone of events causing her memory loss.

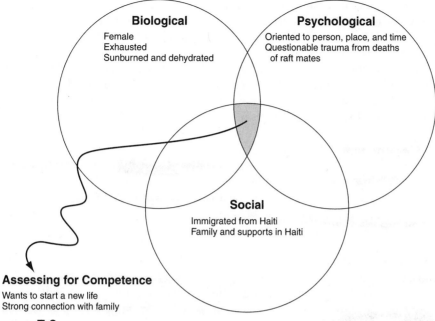

Biological
Female
Exhausted
Sunburned and dehydrated

Psychological
Oriented to person, place, and time
Questionable trauma from deaths
of raft mates

Social
Immigrated from Haiti
Family and supports in Haiti

Assessing for Competence
Wants to start a new life
Strong connection with family

FIGURE **7-2**

DISSOCIATIVE AMNESIA DISORDER

The interactions of the biological, psychological, and social variables in Margarethe Jean-Baptiste's life.

According to the DSM-IV-TR, Margarethe's five-axis diagnosis is as follows:

Axis I	300.12 Dissociative Amnesia
Axis II	V71.09 (No diagnosis)
Axis III	Sunburn
	Dehydration
Axis IV	Illegal immigrant
	No social support
	Death of friends
Axis V	GAF = 55 (on admission)
	70 (on discharge)

DISSOCIATIVE FUGUE DISORDER

Persons with *dissociative fugue disorder*, formerly called psychogenic fugue, experience sudden, unexpected travel away from their home or work, suffer an inability to recall their past, assume a new identity, and cannot remember important personal details about their past. Mostly, the person with this curious disorder just takes off and loses the ability to recall their entire previous identity. While in a fugue state, the person does not remember their prior life. After the fugue, the episode may or may not be remembered. Usually the person leaves behind some very difficult and troubling situation on some level they find intolerable; for example, traumatic memories, financial crises, and/or marital problems (Kaplan et al., 1994) have triggered fugue states. In some, cases they assume an entirely new identity along with traveling to another geographical location.

Prevailing Pattern

Fugue states usually do not appear until early adolescence, and more commonly they occur in adulthood. They rarely appear for the first time after the age of 50 (Cardena, 1997; Sackeim & Devanand, 1991). The duration of the fugue state is a few hours or several days, and it ends abruptly. Once the person returns home, they may recall some of what happened to them.

Differential Assessment

Dissociative fugue is far more commonly seen in movies and television programs than in clinical practice. The person with this disorder usually comes to the practitioner's attention as someone who is lost or confused about who he or she is or where he or she comes from. Typically, this is the "John Doe" who wanders the streets with no personal identification. A competency-based assessment is helpful to avoid being overly vigorous in assigning "pathology" and helps to discern more serious conditions such as dissociative identity disorder, dementia, delirium, substance-related disorders, or schizophrenia.

The symptoms associated with dissociative fugue are the same as those for dissociative amnesia except for sudden travel. Other diagnostic categories to consider are manic or schizophrenic episodes accompanied by traveling, organic, nonepileptic factors such as brain tumors, and alcohol- and drug-related loss of memory and wandering. In addition, an assessment for the possibility of delirium, dementia, or substance use should be considered. Before making an assessment of dissociative fugue, the practitioner should also consider malingering, factitious disorder (discussed in Chapter 6), and dissociative identity disorder.

The following case vignette provides an example of someone with dissociative fugue.

The Case of "Elvis Garfield Lancaster Smith"

"I'll tell you boys once again, my name is Elvis Garfield Lancaster Smith, but my friends call me 'Elvis.' Now that we've gotten through that, I'd like to get back to the shelter and get something to eat. That is, if y'all don't mind."

"Mr. Smith" was brought to the emergency room after he got into a physical scuffle with another man also seeking a meal and a shower at the Salvation Army Shelter.

The police brought "Mr. Smith," a gentleman who appeared to be middle-aged, to the hospital because he sustained a head wound during the physical altercation. When the emergency room physician asked "Mr. Smith" for some identification or insurance papers, "Mr. Smith" was unable to provide any of the necessary documentation. He carried no personal papers or identification of any kind on him.

On physical examination, the physician noted, "The patient has very recently sustained severe body trauma, and shows evidence of multiple slash-type wounds. "Mr. Smith" commented when viewing his injuries, "Man, I sure look like someone musta beat me up pretty bad. The strange thing is, I just don't remember nothing." As the interview progressed, "Mr. Smith" offered that he was new to the Miami area, and he could not recall where he had worked or lived before he came here. He was unable to provide the names of friends or family members who could be contacted to help. The police began an investigation to see if they could find out any thing further about "Mr. Smith," who was kept overnight for observation.

During the night, the police were able to piece together his identity and what had happened to him. "Mr. Smith," as it turned out, was really Mr. Edgar Edelstein, who lived in Orlando. Three days before the physical altercation at the homeless shelter, Mr. Edelstein was involved in an automobile accident that killed his wife, Margie, and his mother-in-law, Sheila. The Orlando police had been looking for Mr. Edelstein, who apparently wandered away from the scene of the accident.

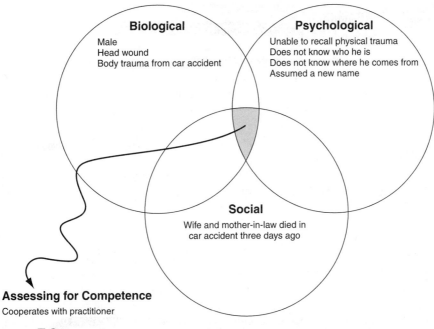

Biological
Male
Head wound
Body trauma from car accident

Psychological
Unable to recall physical trauma
Does not know who he is
Does not know where he comes from
Assumed a new name

Social
Wife and mother-in-law died in
car accident three days ago

Assessing for Competence
Cooperates with practitioner

FIGURE **7-3**

DISSOCIATIVE FUGUE DISORDER

The interactions of the biological, psychological, and social variables in "Mr. Smith's" life.

Assessment Summary

The competency-based assessment serves as a tool to organize the data collected. The case vignette is a classic example of dissociative fugue in that "Mr. Smith" Edelstein was confused about his identity. He traveled away from home and set about seeking shelter. There is no evidence that Mr. Edelstein switched between other personality entities, which would rule out making the assessment of dissociative identity disorder. Dissociative fugue and dissociative identity disorder cannot coexist. There is no evidence in Mr. Edelstein's history of a cognitive disorder that would support an assessment of dementia, other than the obvious amnesia.

Mr. Edelstein's presentation suggests:

Axis I	300.13 Dissociative Fugue Disorder	
Axis II	V71.09 (No diagnosis)	
Axis III	Sustained severe body trauma	
Axis IV	Death of wife and mother-in-law three days ago	
	Police investigation of accident	
Axis V	GAF = 60 (current)	

DEPERSONALIZATION DISORDER

The person with *depersonalization disorder* experiences themselves as "strange or unreal" in some way. They feel detached from their surroundings, as if someone else is "in control" (Simon et al., 1995) or as if they are living in a dream or moving in "slow motion." The depersonalization experience is highly subjective. The individual reports feeling detached from their own body. While they remain in touch with reality, making an assessment of depersonalization disorder should not be considered unless symptoms are persistent, recurrent, or seriously impair functioning.

Depersonalization seems to be one of those disorders that often captures the imagination of filmmakers and tabloid headline writers. In reality, it remains poorly studied and is rarely seen in clinical practice (Simon et al., 1997, 1998). We have included it in this chapter to remind the practitioner that while they more than likely will not work with a client who has these experiences, a competency-based assessment will avoid jumping to premature conclusions about the person's biopsychosocial history.

Prevailing Pattern

Often the first episode occurs during late adolescence or early adulthood. An episode will generally begin without warning, and the person will find himself or herself "detached" though they might continue to do what they already were doing, that is, eating, working, or talking. They seem to be observing these things without actually participating in them. It has been described in a client's words as, "I'm on automatic pilot and watching myself looking at seeing myself from outside my body." The following case discussion illustrates how these symptoms may emerge in the therapeutic conversation.

The Case of Jean "Redhorse" Osceola

"Listen, I don't want to be here. I want to go home. I don't want somebody to lock me up and tell me that I'm crazy or something," Jean Redhorse cried. She had come to the attention of the school social worker when it was reported that the 17-year-old Native American told one of her teachers she "felt like a robot," and "I can see myself standing outside my body." Jean Redhorse's mother was called at work, and she was asked to come to the school immediately.

Mrs. Osceola said, "My daughter had this 'thing' several times before, but it doesn't amount to much of anything. It's just her 'crazy talk.' Listen, I have way too much to do to waste my time coming down to school when she gets into one of her 'spells.' I just wish she would eat a good breakfast, ya know?" The social worker replied, "Can either you or Jean Redhorse tell me anything more about this"? Jean Redhorse replied, "Well, sometimes it looks like my arms and legs get really big, or really small. Sometimes I even feel like I'm floating up in the air. You know, like floating outside my body and above my head. You know, it's not like I'm crazy or anything, because I know it's happening, but the first time it was so weird. Now it's getting a little scary. I feel like I have no control over it. It just sorta happens."

Jean Redhorse denied any periods of time that she experienced blackout spells, convulsions, headaches, dizziness, or trauma to her head. She also denied hearing voices or having hallucinations. She denied feeling other people plotted against her, and never felt suicidal or depressed. She claimed she was alcohol and drug free, and while some friends tried pot once or twice, she never did. Mrs. Osceola stated with a note of pride in her voice, "It is unacceptable for us Navajos to drink." Jean Redhorse just had a physical examination by their family physician, and "other than these 'spells' nothing is wrong."

Assessment Summary

Jean Redhorse appears to be a typical teenager in every way with the exception of the "spells" she experiences. These episodes illustrate the typical depersonalization experience wherein Jean Redhorse reports feeling as if a part of her body is detached from the rest of her. There are no physical or neurological "explanations" for these sensations. While her mother dismisses them as teenage exaggerations, Jean Redhorse seems to be becoming increasingly concerned by their recurrence.

The practitioner is not Native American. To make a competency-based assessment, the worker needs to have an understanding of culturally competent practice. The assessment begins with understanding the dimensions of culture and the cultural social environment. For instance, when Mrs. Osceola comments that her tribe does not drink, the worker recognizes that this statement reflects her culture's beliefs about drinking. When considering depersonalization disorder, the practitioner should not be confused by the presence of their client's culture and its interplay with coping behaviors.

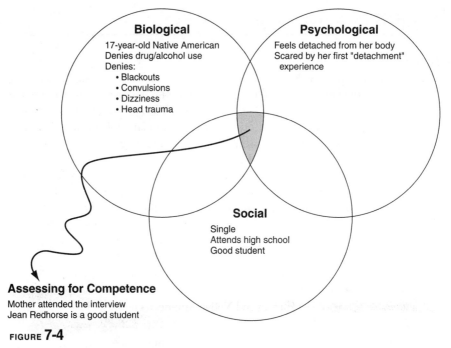

Biological

17-year-old Native American
Denies drug/alcohol use
Denies:
- Blackouts
- Convulsions
- Dizziness
- Head trauma

Psychological

Feels detached from her body
Scared by her first "detachment" experience

Social

Single
Attends high school
Good student

Assessing for Competence

Mother attended the interview
Jean Redhorse is a good student

FIGURE **7-4**

DEPERSONALIZATION DISORDER

The interactions of the biological, psychological, and social variables in Jean Redhorse Osceola's life.

According to the above criteria, Jean Redhorse Osceloa's diagnosis would be:

Axis I	300.6 Depersonalization Disorder
Axis II	V71.09 (No diagnosis)
Axis III	None
Axis IV	None
Axis V	GAF = 70 (current)

SUMMARY

The competency-based approach to assessment explores the full spectrum of a client's life. In this way, the practitioner considers not only the overt, troublesome, or difficult behaviors but also pays attention to the influence of interpersonal and sociocultural factors that underlie the dissociative experience. The dissociative disorders continue to be mired in controversy. On a positive note, empirical inquiry is gradually replacing the uninformed speculation that characterized earlier versions of the DSM (Ganaway, 1995). We can say with a great degree of confidence that dissociative disorders are more common than they used to be (Ferracuti et al., 1996).

PRACTITIONER REFLECTIONS

Depersonalization is a common phenomenon and is not necessarily considered pathological. The practitioner must listen carefully to the client's story, especially when the individual experiences alterations in their perception and a temporary loss of reality, which is generally viewed as pathological. Paying close attention to the client's symptoms, the practitioner can recognize dissociative disorders from other less serious disorders or normal behavior.

Activities

- Practitioners often encounter clients who come from different cultural backgrounds, as evidenced in the cases of Margarethe Jean-Baptiste and Jean Redhorse Osceola. This exercise is aimed at helping you begin increasing your sensitivity to a client's cultural background while, at the same time, fully understanding their presenting concerns. Imagine that you are the social worker assigned to Margarethe or Jean Redhorse. Briefly summarize your knowledge about the language, customs, and values found in the Haitian and Native American cultures.

- Additionally: What could be some of Margarethe's motives for coming to the United States illegally? What immigration problems will she encounter? What difficulties might she have in locating other family members who live here while she gets settled?

- Describe some of the residuals of either Margarethe's or Jean Redhorse's culture that they may try to maintain, such as family traditions, religious ceremonies, or folklore sayings.

- Sometimes dissociation is a normal experience; for example, one may find themselves involved in a boring conversation and "tune out." Reflect back on those situations where this may have happened to you. How does your experience compare with someone who has a dissociative disorder?

- Rent the video (or read the book) *The Three Faces of Eve.* How closely does this portrayal fit the classification of dissociative identity disorder?

REFERENCES

Acierno, R., Kilpatrick, D. G., & Resnick, H. S. (1999). Post traumatic stress disorder in adults relative to criminal victimization: Prevalence, risk factors, and comorbidity. In P. A. Saigh & J. D. Bremner (Eds.), *Post traumatic stress disorder: A comprehensive text*, pp. 44–68. Boston: Allyn & Bacon.

American Psychiatric Association [APA]. (1952). *Diagnostic and statistical manual of mental disorders.* Washington, DC: APA.

American Psychiatric Association [APA]. (1980). *Diagnostic and statistical manual of mental disorders* (3rd ed.). Washington, DC: APA.

American Psychiatric Association [APA]. (1987). *Diagnostic and statistical manual of mental disorders* (3rd rev. ed.). Washington, DC: APA.

American Psychiatric Association [APA]. (1994). *Diagnostic and statistical manual of mental disorders* (4th ed.). Washington, DC: APA.

American Psychiatric Association [APA]. (2000). *Diagnostic and statistical manual of mental disorders* (4th ed.-TR). Washington, DC: APA.

Barker, M. S., & Herlache, M. (1997). Expanding the view of treatment with an MPD client and her family. *Journal of Systematic Therapies*, 16(1): 47–58.

Bliss, E. L. (1986). *Multiple personality allied disorders and hypnosis.* New York: Oxford University Press.

Bowers, K. S., & Farvolden, P. (1996). Revisiting a century-old Freudian slip—from suggestion disavowed to the truth repressed. *Psychological Bulletin*, 119: 355–380.

Bremner, J., Steinberg, M., Southwick, S. M., Johnson, D. R., & Charney, D. S. (1993). Use of the structured clinical interview for DSM-IV dissociative disorder for systematic assessment of dissociative symptoms in post traumatic stress disorder. *American Journal of Psychiatry*, 150: 1011.

Brenner, I. (1996). The characterological basis of multiple personality. *American Journal of Psychotherapy*, 50(2): 154–166.

Cardena, E. (1997). Dissociative disorder: Phantoms of the self. In M. Hersen & S. M. Turner (Eds.), *Adult psychopathology and diagnosis* (2nd ed.), pp. 384–408. New York: John Wiley & Sons.

Cardena, E., Lewis-Fernandez, R., Bear, D., Pakianathan, I., & Spiegel, D. (1996). Dissociative disorders. In T. Widiger, A. J. Frances, H. Pincus, M. R. Ross, M. First, & W. W. David (Eds.), *DSM-IV sourcebook*, Vol. 2, pp. 973–1005. Washington, DC: American Psychiatric Association.

Chitalkar, Y., Pande, N., & Shetty, J. (1996). Collusion and entanglement in the therapy of a patient with multiple personalities. *American Journal of Psychotherapy*, 50(2): 243–251.

Cicchetti, D., & Lynch, M. (1995). Failures in the expectable environment and their impact on individual development: The case of maltreatment. In D. Cicchetti & D. J. Cohen (Eds.), *Developmental psychopathology: Vol. 2, Risk, disorder, and adaptation*, pp. 32–71. New York: John Wiley & Sons.

Comas-Diaz, L. (1981). Puerto Rican espiritismo and psychotherapy. *American Journal of Orthopsychiatry*, 51(4): 636–645.

Crothers, D. (1995). Vicarious traumatization in the work with survivors of childhood trauma. *Journal of Psychosocial Nursing and Mental Health Services*, 33(4): 9–13.

Dallam, S., & Manderino, M. A. (1997). "Free to be" peer group supports patients with multiple personality disorder/dissociative identity disorder. *Journal of Psychosocial Nursing and Mental Health Services*, 35(5): 22–27.

Dell, P. F. (1998). Axis II pathology in outpatients with dissociative identity disorder. *Journal of Nervous and Mental Disease*, 186(6): 352–356.

Durand, M. V., & Barlow, D. H. (1997). *Abnormal psychology.* Pacific Grove, CA: Brooks/Cole.

Ellason, J. W., Ross, C. A., & Fuchs, D. L. (1996). Lifetime axis I and II comorbidity and childhood trauma history in dissociative identity disorder. *Psychiatry*, 59(3): 255–266.

Ferracuti, S., Sacco, R., & Lazzari, R. (1996). Dissociative trance disorder: Clinical and Rorschach findings in ten persons reporting demon possession and treated by exorcism. *Journal of Personality Assessment*, 66(3): 525–539.

Ganaway, G. K. (1995). Hypnosis, childhood trauma, and dissociative identity disorder: Toward an integrative theory. *Internal Journal of Clinical and Experimental Hypnosis*, 43(2): 127–144.

Garnefski, N., & Diekstra, R. F. W. (1997). Child sexual abuse and emotional and behavioral problems in adolescents: Gender differences. *Journal of American Academy of Child and Adolescent Psychiatry*, 36: 323–329.

Gleaves, D. H. (1996). The sociocognitive model of dissociative identity disorder: A reexamination of the evidence. *Psychological Bulletin*, 120: 42–59.

Husain, S. A., Nair, J., Holcomb, W., Reid, J. C., Vargus, V., & Nair, S. S. (1998). Stress reactions of children and adolescents in war and siege conditions. *American Journal of Psychiatry*, 155(12): 1718–1719.

Jumper, S. (1995). A meta-analysis of the relationship of child sexual abuse to adult psychological adjustment. *Child Abuse and Neglect*, 19: 715–728.

Kaplan, H. I., & Sadock, B. J. (1998). *The synopsis of psychiatry* (8th ed.). Baltimore, MD: Williams & Wilkins.

Kaplan, H. I., Sadock, B. J., & Grebb, J. A. (1994). *Synopsis of psychiatry: Behavioral sciences, clinical psychiatry.* Baltimore, MD: Williams & Wilkins.

Kirkmayer, L. J. (1994). Pacing the void: Special and cultural dimensions of dissociation. In D. Spiegel (Ed.), *Dissociation: Culture, mind and body*, pp. 91–122. Washington, DC: American Psychiatry Press.

Kluft, R. P. (1996). Treating the traumatic memories of patients with dissociative identity disorder. *American Journal of Psychiatry*, 153(Suppl. 7): 103–110.

La Greca, A. M., Silverman, W. K., Vernberg, E. M., & Prinstein, M. J. (1996). Symptoms of posttraumatic stress in children after Hurricane Andrew: A prospective study. *Journal of Consulting and Clinical Psychology*, 64: 712–723.

Lewis, D. O., Yeager, C. A., Swica, Y., Pincus, J. H., & Lewis, M. (1998). Objective documentation of child abuse and dissociation in 12 murderers with dissociative identity disorder. *American Journal of Psychiatric*, 154(12): 1703–1710.

Lewis-Fernandez, R. (1994). Culture and dissociation: A comparison of Ataque de Nervios among Puerto Ricans and possession syndrome in India. In D. Spiegel (Ed.), *Dissociation: Culture, mind and body*, pp. 123–170. Washington, DC: American Psychiatric Press.

Lowenstein, R. J. (1991). Psychogenic amnesia and psychogenic fugue: A comprehensive review. *Annual Review of Psychiatry*, 10: 223–247.

Malinosky-Rummell, R., & Hansen, D. J. (1993). Long-term consequences of childhood physical abuse. *Psychological Bulletin*, 114: 68–79.

Marsh, E. J., & Wolfe, D. A. (1999). *Abnormal child psychology*. Belmont, CA: Wadsworth.

Maxmen, J. S., & Ward, N. G. (1995). *Essential psychopathology and its treatment* (2nd ed.). New York: W. W. Norton.

Nietzel, M. T., Speltz, M. L., McCauley, E. A., & Bernstein, D. A. (1998). *Abnormal psychology*. Boston: Allyn & Bacon.

North, C. S., & Yutzy, S. H., (1997). Dissociative and factitious disorder. In S. B. Guze (Ed.), *Adult psychiatry*, pp. 285–299. St Louis, MO: Mosby-Year Book.

Pope, H. G., Hudson, J. I., Bodkin, J. A., & Oliva, P. (1998). Questionable validity of dissociative amnesia in trauma victims. Evidence from prospective studies. *British Journal of Psychiatry*, 172: 210–217.

Putnam, F. W. (1989). *Diagnosis and treatment of multiple personality disorder*. New York: Guilford Press.

Putnam, F. W., & Trickett, P. K. (1993). Child sexual abuse: A model of chronic trauma. *Psychiatry*, 56: 82–95.

Rauschenberger, S. L., & Lynn, S. J. (1995). Fantasy proneness, DSM-III-R Axis I psychopathology, and dissociation. *Journal of Abnormal Psychology*, 104: 373–380.

Rodriguez, N., Ryan, S., Vande Kemp, H., & Foy, D. (1997). Post traumatic stress disorder in adult female survivors of childhood sexual abuse: A comparison study. *Journal of Consulting and Clinical Psychology*, 65: 53–59.

Ross, C. A. (1989). *Multiple personality disorder: Diagnosis, clinical features and treatment.* New York: John Wiley & Sons.

Sackeim, H. A., & Devanand, D. P. (1991). Dissociative disorder. In M. Hersen & S. M. Turner (Eds.), *Adult psychopathology and diagnosis* (2nd ed.), pp. 279–322. New York: John Wiley & Sons.

Shader, R. I. (1994). Dissociative, somatoform, and paranoid disorder. In R. I. Shader (Ed.), *Manual of psychiatric therapeutics* (2nd ed.), pp. 15–23. Boston: Little, Brown & Company.

Simon, D., Stein, D. J., & Hollander, E. (1995). Depersonalization disorder and self-injurious behavior. *Journal of Clinical Psychiatry*, 56(Suppl. 4): 36–39.

Simon, D., Gross, S., Guralnik, O., Stein, D. J., Schmeidler, J., & Hollander, E. (1997). Feeling unreal: 30 cases of DSM-III-R depersonalization disorder. *American Journal of Psychiatry*, 154(8): 1107–1113.

Simon, D., Guralnik, O., Gross, S., Stein, D. J., Schmeidler, J., & Hollander, E. (1998). The detection and measurement of depersonalization disorder. *Journal of Nervous and Mental Diseases*, 186(9): 536–542.

Slovenko, R. (1995). Multiple personality: Perplexities about the law. *Medicine and Law*, 14(7–8): 623–629.

Solomon, H. M. (1997). The not-so-silent couple in the individual. *Journal of Analytical Psychology*, 42(3): 383–404.

Spanos, N. (1994). Multiple identity enactments and multiple personality disorder. *Psychological Bulletin*, 116: 143–165.

Spanos, N., Weeks, J. R., & Bertrand, L. D. (1985). Multiple personality: A social psychological perspective. *Journal of Abnormal Psychology*, 94: 362–376.

Spiegel, D., & Vermutten, E. (1994). Psychological correlates of hypnosis and dissociation. In D. Spiegel (Ed.), *Dissociation: Culture, mind and body*, pp. 185–210. Washington, DC: American Psychiatric Press.

Steinberg, M. (1994). Systemizing dissociation: Symptomatology and diagnostic assessment. In D. Spiegel (Ed.), *Dissociation: Culture, mind and body*, pp. 59–90. Washington, DC: American Psychiatric Press.

Waites, E. A. (1993). *Trauma and survival.* New York: W. W. Norton.

Weathers, F. W., & Keane, T. M. (1999). Psychological assessment of traumatized adults. In P. A. Saigh & J. D. Bremner (Eds.), *Post traumatic stress disorder: A comprehensive text*, pp. 219–247. Boston: Allyn & Bacon.

Wolfe, D. A., & Jaffe, P. (1991). Child abuse and family violence as determinants of child psychopathology. *Canadian Journal of Behavioral Science*, 23: 282–299.

Wolfe, D. A., & McGee, R. (1994). Dimensions of child maltreatment and their relationships to adolescent adjustment. *Development and Psychopathology*, 6: 165–181.

Wolfe, D. A., Sas, L., & Wekerle, C. (1994). Factors associated with the development of post traumatic stress disorder among child victims of sexual abuse. *Child Abuse and Neglect*, 18: 37–50.

Yule, W. (1994). Post traumatic stress disorder. In T. H. Ollendeck, N. J. King, & W. Yule (Eds.), *International handbook of phobic and anxious disorders in children and adolescents: Issues in clinical psychology*, pp. 223–240. New York: Plenum.

EATING DISORDERS

INTRODUCTION

Eating disorders have been recognized throughout history beginning with the ancient past, through the early Christian era, the Dark and late Middle Ages, early Renaissance, and the twentieth century continuing to the present time. Each historical period has influenced the frequency and appearance of eating disorders (Bemporad, 1998; Hudgens, 1997; Robertson & Palmer, 1997). For example, incidents of bingeing and purging (vomiting) of food were considered socially acceptable during the Roman era. At that time, banquets serving 20 or more different courses were a common occurrence (Giannini, 1993). Societal, cultural, or religious influences also affected eating patterns. During the Dark Ages, a person could rid themselves of sin and/or sexual desire through acts of purging. During the Middle Ages, according to well-documented accounts, women known as "the sainted women" starved themselves for their religious beliefs; these episodes of starvation are referred to as *anorexia mirabilis*.

In 1689, Dr. Richard Morton described a self-starving 18-year-old woman who looked like a "skeleton only clad with skin" and referred to her condition as "nervous consumption" (Maxmen & Ward, 1995; Turner & Hersen, 1997). Other examples of starvation involved the notorious "fasting girls" of the sixteenth and seventeenth centuries (Yager, 1994). This eating pattern was a visible demonstration of their virtuous lifestyle and zealous commitment to the church. While starvation occurred in some societies, others encouraged women to have a well-fed or plump appearance. This was often seen as an indication that a father or husband was a good provider and could afford to feed his family well (Abraham & Llewellyn-Jones, 1992).

Anorexia nervosa, as it is currently recognized, was first described in the early 1860s and 1870s by the French physicians Marcé (1860) and Lasegué (1873) and by the English physician Sir William Gull (1873). Gull characterized this disorder of eating as a "want of appetite," which he saw as being characteristic of a "morbid mental state." Marcé (1860) eloquently describes the ravages of starvation and the curious mental state that often accompanied it:

Whatever the duration of their abstinence, they experience a distaste for food which the most pressing want is unable to overcome…. Deeply impressed, whether by the absence of appetite or by the uneasiness caused by digestion, these patients arrive at a delirious conviction that they cannot or ought not to eat. In one word, the gastric nervous disorder becomes cerebro-nervous. (pp. 264 & 266)

Lasegué (1873) notes the frustration encountered by families and caregivers:

The delicacies of the table are multiplied in the hopes of stimulating the appetite, but the more the solicitude increases, the more the appetite diminishes. What dominates in the mental condition of the hysterical patient is, above all, the state of quietude…. Not only does she not sigh for recovery, but she is not ill-pleased with her condition. (pp. 385 & 403)

AN OVERVIEW OF THE EATING DISORDERS

Because of the pandemic extent of eating disorders over the last century, the DSM-IV (APA, 1994) included them, for the first time, as a separate group. There are two major eating disorders. The first is *anorexia nervosa*, wherein the individual severely limits food intake, resulting in substantial weight loss and dangerously low body weight. The second is *bulimia nervosa*, where the individual's "diet" results in out-of-control binge eating episodes followed by purging behaviors where food is eliminated by vomiting or other means. Although anorexia and bulimia are the most thoroughly studied eating disorders, the most common eating disorder is *binge eating disorder* (*BED*) (APA, 1994, 2000). This disorder is characterized by recurrent binge eating, but it is without the inappropriate weight control behaviors that are part of the bulimic picture.

Anorexia nervosa and bulimia nervosa are characterized by the individual's overemphasis on their body image, but there are several important distinctions between these two disorders. The individual with anorexia nervosa must have an abnormally low body weight; and in the case of women, they must miss at least three consecutive menstrual cycles (amenorrhea). The person with bulimia nervosa generally has a normal or slightly above-normal weight. They exhibit a pattern of sequential binge eating in addition to inappropriate compensatory weight loss responses that include self-induced purging (vomiting), misuse of laxatives or enemas, and excessive exercise. Individuals with anorexia nervosa may binge or purge to a level that would met criteria for bulimia nervosa; however, bulimia nervosa should be considered a coexisting diagnosis if the binge eating or purging is restricted to episodes of anorexia nervosa.

While the majority of eating disorders are first noticed during late childhood and early adolescence, they often continue well into adulthood. The authors exclude an in-depth examination of childhood eating disorders. However, we suggest an excellent resource on childhood psychopathology by E. J. Marsh and D. A. Wolfe (1999), *Abnormal childhood psychology*, published by Wadsworth Publishing Company, Pacific Grove, California.

The Essential Features of Anorexia Nervosa

Individuals with eating disorders manifest abnormal attitudes about their body shape (Schaaf & McCanne, 1994), and maladaptive attempts to control their body weight. The assessment criteria for anorexia nervosa include:

- The individual's refusal to maintain their weight at or above a minimally normal weight for age and height. (For example, a woman who should weigh 100 pounds weighs less than 85 pounds.)
- Even though the person is severely underweight, they continue to be desperately fearful of gaining weight or becoming "fat."
- There is a disturbance in the way individuals perceive their body weight or body shape, or they may deny the seriousness of their present low weight.
- In women who are of postmenarche status, they must have an absence of at least three or more consecutive menstrual cycles (amenorrhea).

Anorexia nervosa is divided into two subtypes, based on the method used to limit calorie intake. They are:

- *Restricting type*—During the current episode, the individual severely limits caloric intake, and they *do not* regularly engage in binge eating or purging behavior.
- *Binge eating/purging type*—During the current episode, the individual regularly engages in binge eating or purging behavior, for example, self-induced vomiting, or misuse of laxatives, enemas, or diuretics.

The two subtypes of anorexia nervosa have significantly different clinical presentations and characteristics:

- Those individuals who have the restricting subtype are described as highly controlled, rigid, and obsessive. They use various techniques that help enhance their control over food intake; for example, they might eat very slowly, make their food less attractive, or garnish their food with unappetizing spices. The individual often feels a great deal of satisfaction about controlling or regulating their calorie intake.
- The individual with binge eating/purging subtype alternates between periods of perfectionism and rigid control, or impulsive eating behavior (APA, 1994, 2000; Szabo & Terre Blanche, 1997). Binge eating is defined as an eating episode where the individual is eating "out of control" and is unable to resist the temptation to consume certain foods.

Fairburn and Cooper (1998) define a *binge* as ingesting a much larger amount of food than most people would eat under similar circumstances. Although there can be a wide variation in the quantity of calories ingested, a very large amount of food is consumed during a binge episode. Some binges occur in time-limited situations; others can take most of the day, where the individual eats small amounts of food almost continuously. The latter is sometimes referred to as *grazing* (Agras,

1994). Binge eating is usually performed in private because the individual does not want to be discovered or interrupted.

A binge episode should be distinguished from those overeating incidents that occur during special occasions such as a birthday celebration or holiday events. Perhaps the most notable culturally sanctioned time for overeating is the Thanksgiving holiday dinner. Binge eating is often followed by depressive moods, feelings of guilt, and self-deprecating thoughts. When overeating is more culturally sanctioned (along with very little long-lasting guilt associated with eating a large meal), the person does not have the sense of "losing control." In those instances, the amount of food eaten more closely resembles a normal meal than the quantity of food consumed during a binge.

Purging is defined as any activity aimed at ameliorating the perceived negative effects of a binge on body shape and weight (Agras, 1994; Kinder, 1997). This includes self-induced vomiting, the misuse of laxatives, enemas, or diuretics, or excessive exercise. When exercise and diet are used for weight loss rather than to counteract the effects of a particular episode of excessive bingeing, these should be regarded as *compensatory behaviors*. With eating disorders, the individual continues to use weight loss techniques, or purging, in the desperate hope that they will somehow "work."

There are several significant coexisting disorders associated with eating disorders (Wonderlich & Mitchell, 1997), including major depressive disorders and obsessive tendencies (Kaye et al., 1993); anxiety disorders (Bulik, 1995; Halmi et al., 1991); personality disorders; substance abuse (Wilson, 1993; Lilienfeld & Kaye, 1996; Grilo et al., 1997; Wiederman & Pryor, 1997); and suicide (Hsu, 1990; Scocco & De Leo, 1995; Strober, 1995; Favaro & Santonastaso, 1996; Gleaves & Eberenz, 1993).

Prevailing Pattern

The development of eating disorders seems related to several factors, with no single identifiable event that could be considered as the cause of the person's eating difficulties (Austrian, 1995; Buddeberg, 1997). Although many women diet to control their weight, few individuals will go on to develop the extreme weight loss and clinical symptoms of anorexia (Kaye, 1997). When assessing for the presence of anorexia nervosa, the primary intrapersonal characteristics include an unreasonable fear of gaining weight, perceptual disturbance regarding the person's body shape or size, and the relentless pursuit of wanting to be thin no matter what consequence (APA, 2000; Schlundt & Johnson, 1990; Heatherton et al., 1997).

According to Agras (1994), the individual with an eating disorder has two faulty perceptions regarding their own body. The first is the way they view their body, or *body image distortion (BID)*. The second faulty perception deals with body image concerns that are viewed as involving a delusional misperception, which Agras (1994) refers to as "body dysmorphobphobia." (Refer to Chapter 6 for a more in-depth discussion.) In both areas, misperception of body size and shape is the central feature. Agras (1994) underscores the concept that body image is primarily a perceptual phenomenon.

Studies suggest that the individual's judgments about their body image are influenced by cognitive, affective, cultural and attitudinal variables (Agras, 1994; Castillo,

1997; Wilfley et al., 1996). This underscores the importance of a competency-based assessment that considers a thorough examination of all aspects of an individual's life. Some of the broader, social factors for the practitioner to consider that can potentially influence eating disorders include a cultural emphasis on the desirability of being thin; and youthful concerns with attractiveness, self-concept, body concept, and sexuality. The practitioner also carefully evaluates the coexistence of other mental disorders (for example, anxiety, affective, or personality disorders).

Differential Assessment

Anorexia is most often seen in adolescent girls (APA, 2000). Between 90 and 95 percent of all reported cases are females who start to diet in the belief that they are excessively fat, whether in reality this is true or not. In general, most individuals with an eating disorder do not exhibit any actual prodromal period. They are usually characterized as being "a normal healthy girl" prior to the actual onset of the eating disorder. Occasionally, a major life cycle event will immediately precede the onset, such as going off to college or a death in the family. At other times, the precipitating factor may be so integrated into a decision to begin dieting that the onset seems almost immaterial; for example, following the case discussion about Joy Walker illustrates her motivation to lose weight so she could fit into her prom dress. Joy begins to diet simply by reducing her total daily food intake, and later, she begins to restrict all high-calorie foods. Eventually, her eating pattern is severely limited, and Joy ingests very few foods. She dreaded being "fat," and her weight loss did not alleviate this fear. As part of this picture, she underestimated the extent of her thinness, believing herself to be "fat and ugly." In reality, she appeared skeletal to her family and friends.

The most striking feature of anorexia is the marked distortion in the way the individual experiences their body size and shape (Stein & Hedger, 1997). Often they have no concept of how they appear to others, and distort what they want to see. They are generally dissatisfied with their weight; losing weight every day and for months on end is seen as satisfactory. Although the person is usually hungry and preoccupied with thoughts of food, they will not eat because of their relentless obsession to be thinner.

Grigg et al. (1996) studied 869 adolescent girls between the ages of 14 and 16 to determine the prevalence of disordered eating behaviors, unhealthy dieting practices, and distorted body image. Their study indicated motivating factors for eating disorders include peer pressure, media influence, and the perception that extreme dieting strategies were harmless. These findings underscore the importance of looking at the whole person and exploring variables in their social context. The competency-based assessment expands the practitioner's thinking and considers the influence of social and environmental factors found in a person's life.

Although the DSM criteria specifies body weight that is at least 15 percent below what is normally expected (APA, 2000), individuals with anorexia nervosa usually weigh less than this by the time they come to the attention of the practitioner. Hsu (1990) suggests that when these individuals seek help, they often weigh somewhere between 25 and 30 percent below their normal weight. Unfortunately, there is no clear boundary between the "thinness" of anorexia nervosa and an individual who is considered naturally slender, so it is important to carefully evaluate the multiple influences in a person's life when considering an eating disorder. Many individuals are naturally thin, others diet to remain slim, while still others are in occupations where low body weight is a mandated requirement, for example, a jockey, model, or ballet dancer (Hamilton et al., 1985). The difference between someone who is of low weight and someone with anorexia nervosa revolves around intrapersonal factors where the individual *refuses* to maintain a "normal body weight" and is *extremely fearful* of becoming fat.

Anorexia nervosa is seen about 15 times as often in women as in men (Abraham & Llewellyn-Jones, 1992); and conservative figures estimate that the prevalence in women ranges between 0.1 and 0.8 percent (Hoek, 1993). According to the DSM-IV, "There is limited data concerning the prevalence of this disorder in males" (APA, 1994, p. 543). In a recent study, Kinzel et al. (1997) examined the possible correlation between a childhood characterized by sexual abuse, physical abuse, or a dysfunctional family background and the development of eating disorders in males. They studied 307 men, and found no significant correlations between those who experienced sexual or physical abuse during childhood and the development of eating disorders. However, they did find a significant increased incidence of eating disorders in men who experienced negative familial relationships while growing up. It may be possible that there is a greater prevalence of anorexia nervosa in men than has generally been documented; however, it should be noted there is no relevant corresponding criterion for amenorrhea in men (Andersen, 1992; Frances et al., 1995; Carlat et al., 1997). Males represent approximately 10 percent of eating disorders, an extreme gender discrepancy. Explaining these differences presents a challenge for future research (Andersen & Holman, 1997).

Anorexia nervosa typically develops during adolescence; the average age of onset ranges between 14 and 18, with a mean of 17 (APA, 2000). The DSM suggests that the onset of this disorder in females is relatively rare after the age of 40. Beck et al. (1996) studied three university hospital eating disorder programs and examined the experiences of women who had their first onset of eating disorders occurring after age 40 and met the DSM-IV-TR criteria. They found that approximately 1 percent of all cases of eating disorders seen at the university programs had a clinical presentation after the age of 40; the average age of onset was 57, but some individuals had their initial onset as late as age 77. Their study challenges current etiological theories that stipulate a younger age of onset (adolescence), premenopausal endocrine functioning, or intrapersonal adolescent conflicts. Eating disorders can occur late in a person's life, and the practitioner should pay attention to those associated intrapersonal factors as a part of their competency-based assessment, in particular, bereavement issues or perceptions about body image.

Hsu (1988) studied a variety of causal factors associated with anorexia nervosa and concluded that a woman's perception regarding ideal body size is greatly influenced by television commercials, magazines, and/or beauty pageants. For reasons that are unclear, the incidence of anorexia nervosa has increased substantially in North America during the last half of the twentieth century (APA, 2000). The media, which promotes being thin as the ideal standard for beauty, can partially explain this rise in anorexia nervosa. As a corollary, many impressionable young women (and men) hold unreasonable expectations about how thin they should be in order to be attractive (Harrison & Cantor, 1997; Schulken et al., 1997).

Biological Factors Associated with Anorexia Nervosa

One of the unfortunate aspects of this eating disorder is that it is entirely possible for an individual to starve to death in the midst of plenty. As the person stops eating, their body tries to conserve resources, and amenorrhea occurs (monthly menstruation stops). This is considered perhaps the most characteristic medical complication. Abnormally low levels of the estrogen hormone are found, which in turn diminish pituitary secretions of follicle-stimulating hormone (FSH) and luteinizing hormone (LH); diminished levels of FSH and LH turn off the mechanism for generating the menstrual cycle, causing amenorrhea. When considering an assessment of anorexia nervosa, one should keep in mind that amenorrhea is a significant requirement of, and a defining feature for, this eating disorder. The biological component, an integral part of the competency-based assessment, helps serve as an objective physical index of the degree of food restriction.

Pirke et al. (1987) studied the correlation between ovulation, menstruation cycle, and weight. Their study concluded that endocrinological difficulties were a *consequence* of the effects of semistarvation rather than the *cause*. Other biological problems associated with starvation include osteoporosis caused by loss of calcium from the bones; constipation (Mehler, 1997); mild anemia; and swollen joints.

There is a secretive nature to anorexia nervosa, and it behooves the practitioner to look for "clues" to disturbances in eating patterns. Persons with anorexia nervosa often exhibit dry or scaly (yellowed) textured skin; lanugo ("peach fuzz" or baby fine hair found on the trunk, face, and extremities); and intolerance of cold temperatures. It is not uncommon to find a person wearing a heavy sweater on a hot summer day. Extensive weight loss can also affect the skeletal structure. There is a tremendous loss of body fat and muscle mass, and the individual takes on a stooped or hunched-over appearance. In practice, the practitioner will often see someone with dull, lifeless hair, a pale complexion, poor posture, and who is extremely thin but covers their appearance by wearing loose, baggy clothing.

Purging behaviors may cause fatigue and weakness, a mild cognitive disorder, or seizures (Yager, 1994). Other purging complications include infection of the parotid or salivary glands, which sometimes gives the face a puffy or "chipmunk" appearance. Frequent vomiting also takes a tremendous toll on teeth, causing severe dental erosion and tooth decay (Rytomaa et al., 1998). The front teeth are especially vulnerable and may look "moth-eaten." Most who purge become quite adept at inducing vomiting "at will" and can do so without any extraneous methods such as the use of emetics. However, there are those who consume large amounts of ipecac (solution that induces vomiting); this practice occasionally causes death from overdose toxicity (Agras, 1994).

As a part of the competency-based assessment, biologically oriented areas the practitioner might consider exploring include what the individual wants to weigh; dieting, nutritional, or exercise patterns; and the use of laxatives. The worker should pay careful attention to nonverbal communication when asking about eating habits, since the individual may withhold information or minimize the extent of their eating behaviors. The practitioner should be courteous but direct, and more specifically the questions should explore some of the following:

- Has there ever been a time when people (either friends or others) have given you a hard time about being too thin or losing too much weight?
- Have you ever weighed a lot less than others thought you should weigh?

If the answer is *yes* to either question, follow with:

- How old were you when this first happened?
- Is this still true?
- What was the lowest amount you have ever weighed?
- What do you weigh right now? How do you feel about that?
- What do you think about your body size and shape?
- What do you think about how much you weigh?
- Are you on a diet right now?
- Do you ever feel the urge to binge or purge? What happens when you do?
- How often do you diet?
- Have either you or anyone in your family ever had a history of anorexia, bulimia, or obesity?

The practitioner should be mindful of a number of cardiovascular or renal problems that include hypotension (chronically low blood pressure); bradycardia (slow heartbeat) (Hsu, 1990); cardiac arrhythmia (irregular heartbeat); and an increased risk of renal (kidney) failure. Purging behaviors often deplete essential body sustaining minerals including potassium, sodium, magnesium, phosphate, and chloride, often causing concern for hypokalemic alkalosis.

The course and outcome of anorexia nervosa varies; some individuals recover after a single episode, whereas others continue to vacillate between trying to restore their normal weight and/or relapsing. Those who struggle with a fluctuating pattern may require hospitalization to reinstate their weight and address fluid and electrolyte imbalances. Anorexia nervosa is considered a potentially fatal disease, with a mortality rate that ranges somewhere between 5 to 10 percent (APA, 1994, 2000). The cause of death is usually associated with starvation, suicide (Favaro & Santonastaso, 1997; Kaplan et al., 1994), infection, or electrolyte imbalance.

The following vignette describes Joy Walker's struggle to lose weight and illustrates some of the eating patterns "typical" of someone with anorexia nervosa.

The Case of Joy Walker

Joy Walker started with a diet to lose weight, but almost lost her life instead. At the age of 17, she weighed 130 pounds (considered normal for her height and build). She was asked to go to the senior prom by her boyfriend, Kenneth, but he warned her in advance, "You'd better lose some weight, because I don't want to be seen dancing with a fat blimp."

Joy made up her mind to lose some weight and started by skipping breakfast. A few days later, she stopped eating lunch. Dinner time with her family became problematic, because she did not eat anything. She was served regular portions, but ended up moving the food around on her plate to appear as if she was eating. She told her parents that she ate "a huge lunch" so she was not very hungry.

Most of the time Joy secretly dropped food to the dog sitting under the table. Other times, she managed to hide food in her pockets only to throw it away later. Within a month, Joy lost almost 30 pounds. She began to receive a lot of positive attention, especially from her boyfriend, and compliments on how nice she looked. By now her daily food intake included eating some lettuce leaves or an apple, but nothing more. Her hair began to thin and then started falling out in clumps. Her fingernails started to split, and she began to have problems with constipation, cold intolerance, and painful swelling of her fingers, knees, and elbows.

After five months of dieting, Joy weighed 85 pounds. She had gone from a size nine to a size zero. When her friends told her that she looked "like a skeleton" and was "way too thin," Joy responded, "I just want to lose a few more pounds because my thighs are 'way too fat,' and my stomach 'pouches out' too much." She added, "I'm so disgusting." Joy has not had a normal menstrual period for the past three months, and this pleased her.

While dancing with Kenneth at the senior prom, Joy fainted. She was taken by ambulance to a nearby emergency room. The attending physician was shocked at the state of Joy's physical condition and emaciation. The physician immediately contacted Joy's parents and explained that their daughter was in serious trouble. Joy was admitted to the hospital and diagnosed with anorexia nervosa. The hospital social worker spoke to Joy and referred her and her family to the eating disorder clinic.

Assessment Summary

The differential assessment of anorexia nervosa is complicated by Joy's denial of symptoms and her unwillingness to seek help. In addition, she was extremely secretive about her eating pattern and methods of weight control. Joy's caloric intake, consisting of an apple or lettuce leaves, is a typical eating pattern. Even though Joy was 35 percent underweight, she continued to express unrealistic concerns about being "fat." She had a distorted view of her body, also characteristic of those with anorexia nervosa, seeing her thighs as too fat and her stomach as bulging.

Some individuals are humiliated or embarrassed when seen eating food in public (Brewerton et al., 1993; Wiederman, 1996), as in *social phobia*. While Joy obsessed about her food intake, she did not show obsessions and compulsions in other areas of her life as is commonly seen in persons with obsessive-compulsive disorder (Chapter 5). The latter may be considered if Joy had shown obsessions and compulsions unrelated to food, such as repeatedly washing her hands (Thornton & Russell, 1997; Hollander & Benzaquen, 1997). Those with body dysmorphic disorder are preoccupied with an imagined defect in their body appearance (Cash & Deagle, 1997; Gillespie, 1996). This assessment should only be considered if the

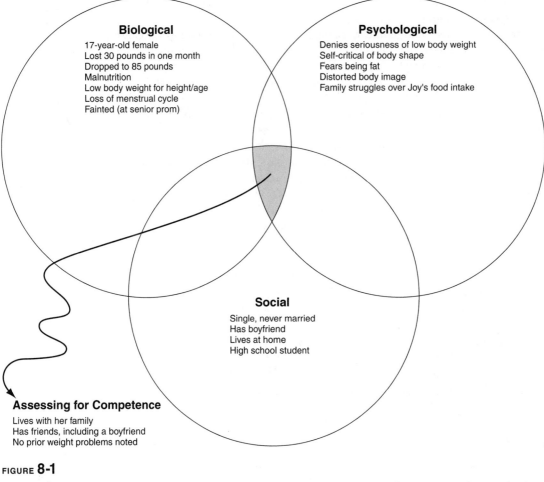

Biological

17-year-old female
Lost 30 pounds in one month
Dropped to 85 pounds
Malnutrition
Low body weight for height/age
Loss of menstrual cycle
Fainted (at senior prom)

Psychological

Denies seriousness of low body weight
Self-critical of body shape
Fears being fat
Distorted body image
Family struggles over Joy's food intake

Social

Single, never married
Has boyfriend
Lives at home
High school student

Assessing for Competence

Lives with her family
Has friends, including a boyfriend
No prior weight problems noted

FIGURE **8-1**

ANOREXIA NERVOSA

The interactions of the biological, psychological, and social variables in Joy Walker's life.

details of the person's "distortion" are unrelated to body size and shape. Joy's main concerns revolved around her body image.

Weight fluctuations, vomiting, and eccentric food handling might occur in some somatization disorders (Chapter 6). Further, these behaviors are not considered as severe as Joy Walker's eating habits. Further, those with somatization disorder do not have the morbid fear of becoming "fat" (Silverstein & Blumenthal, 1997). Schizophrenia (Chapter 3) might look very similar to anorexia, especially if the person refuses to eat. However, upon closer examination, the person with schizophrenia is rarely concerned about caloric content, although they might exhibit bizarre eating patterns. Additionally, they rarely are preoccupied with the fear of becoming "fat" nor do they have the same body distortions. Those with major depressive disorder (Chapter 4), in the absence of anorexia, may eat very little and profess to have little or no appetite. However, peculiar attitudes about eating (such as Joy's tendency to push food around her plate, feed it to the dog, or hide it in her pockets, the pursuit of being thin, and the increased level of physical activity) are absent.

It is important that a referral be made to a physician who can appropriately determine whether there are other processes going on that can better account for the weight loss, for example, hyperthyroidism, diabetes mellitus, Crohn's disease, acquired immunodeficiency syndrome (AIDS), neoplasms, or tuberculosis. The important distinction between the eating disorder illustrated in the Joy Walker vignette versus a general medical condition is that individuals with general medical conditions usually do not have a *distorted body image (DBI)*, or the desire for further weight loss. Figure 8-1 illustrates the interplay of the biological, psychological, and social factors in Joy Walker's life.

The case vignette does not address Joy's familial picture and related interpersonal processes. However, the competency-based model would look at the full range of factors affecting Joy's life, how she copes with life challenges, and supports that are available. This perspective suggests that the person is not the problem, but the problem is the problem. What is known is that Joy lives at home with her family who are concerned about her, she has many friends, and she has not experienced prior eating difficulties.

Based on Joy's current history, and this typical presentation, her diagnosis would read as follows:

Axis I	307.1 Anorexia Nervosa, Restricting Type
Axis II	V71.09 (No diagnosis)
Axis III	263.0 Malnutrition, Moderate
Axis IV	None
Axis V	GAF = 55 (on admission)

THE ESSENTIAL FEATURES OF BULIMIA NERVOSA

Bulimia nervosa is characterized by repeated dietary restriction alternating with uncontrollable binge eating and desperate measures to prevent weight gain. Individuals with purging type bulimia counteract the effects of eating either by vomiting or using compensatory methods in the struggle to control their weight; for example, the person uses large amounts of laxatives to purge their bowels. Those who use excessive exercise and fasting to control their weight are considered nonpurging types. The use of fasting is often a misguided method for controlling a binge—the process usually backfires, causing increased hunger and leading to greater overeating.

Bulimia nervosa is a comparatively recent eating disorder, having first been introduced in the DSM-III (APA, 1980). It occurs more frequently than anorexia nervosa (APA, 1994, 2000) but tends to be underassessed, perhaps because the symptoms are less obvious and discernible than the starving symptoms of anorexia or because most individuals are normal to slightly overweight in appearance (Hudgens, 1997). Bulimia nervosa is known to occur among individuals considered moderately or morbidly obese, but this is an uncommon pattern.

An important distinction between anorexia nervosa and bulimia nervosa is that the person with bulimia does not have the extreme distortion of self-image characteristic of those with anorexia. A majority of individuals with bulimia never have had anorexia. However, it is not uncommon to find a past history of many anorexic features (Yager, 1994; Sullivan et al., 1996).

The assessment criteria for bulimia nervosa include:

- Recurrent episodes of binge eating, which is characterized by *both* of the following:

    Eating occurs during a discrete period of time; for example, within two hours the amount of food eaten is definitely larger than most other individuals would eat during a similar period of time and under similar circumstances.

    The individual experiences a lack of control over eating during the episode. They cannot stop eating or control what they are eating.

- Recurrent, inappropriate compensatory methods are used to prevent weight gain; for example, self-induced vomiting, fasting, excessive exercise, and misuse of laxatives, enemas, diuretics, or other medications.

- Both the binge eating and inappropriate compensatory methods must occur, on average, at least twice (or more) a week for three months.

- Body shape and weight unduly influence the way a person sees her- or himself.

- The disturbance does not occur exclusively during an episode of anorexia nervosa.

In addition, bulimia nervosa is divided into two subtypes based on the method the individual employs to limit weight gain:

- *Purging type*—During the current episode the individual regularly engages in self-induced vomiting or the misuse of laxatives, diuretics, or enemas.

- *Nonpurging type*—During the current episode the individual has used other inappropriate compensatory behaviors, such as fasting or excessive exercise, but has *not* regularly engaged in vomiting or misused laxatives, diuretics, or enemas (APA, 1994, 2000).

Prevailing Pattern

Typically, the person with bulimia nervosa is a young woman. The lifetime prevalence of women who meet the criteria ranges between 1 and 3 percent (APA, 1994, 2000; Fairburn et al., 1993a), and the rate of occurrence in males is approximately one-tenth of that found in females (APA, 1994, 2000). Bulimia may or may not begin in the context of another disorder, for example, depression, obsessions, or substance abuse (Myers, 1995; Hay & Fairburn, 1998). The onset of symptoms occurs fairly innocuously during late adolescence or up until the early 20s when an attempt to diet is closely followed by purging behaviors (Hsu, 1990; Bulik et al., 1997). While purging may serve as a convenient method to overeat without gaining the resultant weight, it often quickly becomes a destructive process that cannot be easily controlled. Over time, the binge/purge cycle escalates and becomes more dominant in the individual's thoughts and behaviors, often causing a multitude of difficulties—

for example, impaired interpersonal relationships, leading to isolation, shame, help-lessness, and lowered self-esteem.

Bulimia appears to run a chronic and episodic course whereby the occurrence of binge eating may either have a gradual or acute presentation. Sometimes the individual can sense a binge starting, whereas other times they have no forewarn-ing. They may or may not report feeling hungry preceding a binge; and a binge is often precipitated by the simple presence of something to eat. Yager (1997) sug-gests that psychologically stressful circumstances often trigger a binge, because food becomes a temporary "fix" to sooth and reduce emotional tensions.

The individual often reports episodes where they eat large amounts of food in a short period of time, once or twice a week or several times a day. Generally, high-calorie sweets are the food of choice, but once a binge begins it is very difficult to control and the person eats everything within their reach. Most often binges last upward of one hour, and the individual eats well past the point when their sensa-tion of being hungry should have been quelled.

An episode of binge eating is followed by the physical discomfort of abdomi-nal distension (bloating) caused by the amount of food eaten or the emotional dis-tress of how much was consumed. The person often feels helpless, disgusted, depressed, and fearful about becoming fat. They usually feel very guilty and anx-ious about the amount of food they have eaten and immediately begin planning to quickly get rid of it. The most common and favored "action" is vomiting (whereby the individual sticks their finger or fingers down their throat to bring about regur-gitation). Some individuals become so proficient at vomiting they do not need any other catalyst measures, and vomit at will.

Like anorexia nervosa, the individual with bulimia is very secretive about their eating behaviors. It is helpful for the practitioner to look for telltale visual signs of repeated purging behaviors. These perceptible clues consist of skin lesions, abra-sions, small lacerations, or raised calluses found on the dorsal (top) surface of fin-gers and knuckles. These dorsal lesions, known as *Russell's signs*, are the by-products of repeated and constant friction of fingers being scraped back and forth across incisor teeth to induce vomiting (Daluiski et al., 1997). Not all individ-uals use finger manipulations to generate vomiting, instead using emetics or specif-ically ipecac, an agent that produces vomiting. Sometimes diuretics are used, for example, furosemide, as a cathartic for weight control (Gerstein & Woodside, 1997). Other maneuvers used for purging include using laxatives or enemas (used less often) that empty the bowel. Still other techniques involve using coat hangers, wadded paper, or pens that are stuck down the throat.

Biological Factors Associated with Bulimia Nervosa

As noted in the previous discussion of anorexia nervosa, purging behaviors can pro-duce serious negative health complications. The chemical stimulation of vomiting by ingesting ipecac can lead to serious heart damage. Excessive laxative abuse often causes constipation or permanent damage to the colon. Perhaps one of the most serious medical complications is caused by electrolyte abnormalities (low potassium levels), which can disrupt signals to the heart causing irregular conduction, as well as causing kidney failure.

Differential Assessment

It has been reported that persons with bulimia nervosa are more likely to engage in impulsive behaviors such as shoplifting (Mitchell & Pyle, 1985) and substance abuse (Walfish et al., 1992). In addition, co-occurrence of eating disorders and borderline personality disorder or avoidant personality disorder have been reported in a number of studies; however, the results of this research were noted to be inconsistent at best (Skodal et al., 1993). According to Striegel-Moore (1993), depression can also co-occur with bulimia. Further, Schwalberg and colleagues (1992) found a high incidence of anxiety disorders associated with bulimia.

Bulimia has been associated with a history of sexual or physical abuse (Yegidis & Morgan, 1994). Wonderlich et al. (1997) reviewed the literature from 53 empirical studies dating from 1987 through 1994 that examined the relationship between childhood sexual abuse and eating disorders. They found some indication that childhood sexual abuse was more strongly associated with bulimic disorders than with the restricting type of anorexia. This history of abuse did not correlate with the severity of the bulimia. In addition, the researchers identified several factors that may mediate the relationship between childhood sexual abuse and eating disorders, including family variables, interpersonal skills, and emotional reactions following sexual abuse.

According to Waller et al. (1993), women who report more recent abuse show greater body image disturbance. Schaaf and McCanne (1994), who found no such association between abuse and body image disturbance, found conflicting evidence. Waller et al. (1994) suggest a strong correlation between prior sexual abuse and purging behavior. Sexual abuse does not appear to be a risk factor specific to eating disorders, but rather a risk factor for intrapersonal difficulties in general (Welch & Fairburn, 1994). Rorty et al. (1994) offer that it is helpful to consider the possibility of prior sexual or physical abuse when assessing the presence of eating disorders.

The tragic pull of a binge/purge episode is presented in the following vignette as Mary McDaniel struggles with her eating disorder. The full range of intrapersonal, interpersonal, and sociocultural variables are not included, as the vignette focuses on a typical day of bingeing and purging.

The Case of Mary McDaniel

"I eat a tremendous amount of food and I don't care what the food is. You know, like milk and orange juice usually sours the stomach? I don't care when it comes to anything like that. I eat whatever is in the pantry. The best way I can explain it is that it's sorta like a 'feeding frenzy.' I gulp food down, and most of the time I don't even taste it."

Mary continues, "A typical day for me starts after my kids go off to school and my husband leaves for work. I usually have an extra hour before I have to leave the house. During this time I usually eat anything I can stuff in my mouth. I start with some ice cream, and when I'm done with that I munch on bags of cookies. They are much easier to put in mouth and eat when I'm getting dressed. I always try and eat soft things, because they're easier to vomit up. I don't like to eat stuff like pretzels or hard candies. I also don't like to eat spicy stuff, you know, hot peppers, garlic, and onions. They are terrible to bring up!

"Before I leave for work, I have just enough time to vomit up everything I already ate. I'm pretty good at that, and I don't usually need to stick my fingers down my throat anymore. All I have to do is just start thinking about throwing up, and the next thing I know I start gagging and then I just vomit. I usually vomit within 20 minutes of eating because after that I've already started digesting the food and it's too late. The food is already being absorbed.

"When I'm driving to work, I always have a bag of M&Ms or cookies in the car; or else I stop and buy a dozen Dunkin Donuts. You know, it's stuff I can eat, but I don't have to take my eyes off the road. Usually I throw up before I get to work, and I always keep a couple of mason jars under the front seat of my car for that purpose. I don't usually like to do that because vomiting smells up everything, and I can't rinse my mouth out right afterward. I do keep a can of air freshener in the glove compartment, and that keeps the smell down.

"When I'm at work, I don't eat much in front of others. They mean well, but I feel they are always so critical of me. They'll say things like 'you eat like a bird, but you never lose any weight on all your different diets.' I always eat lunch alone, and most of the time, I go out. I either get a couple of hamburgers, fries, and a large shake, or I'll find a drive-in fast-food place to get something. I always eat in my car, and I always throw up before I go back to work. If things are rushed at work and I don't have a long lunch hour, I'll grab a bunch of laxatives. Only problem is going to the bathroom all afternoon. Good thing my office is away from everybody and down the hall near the restrooms.

"After work, I eat stuff in the car on the way home, but as soon as I get home I'll eat whatever I can find. I have secret 'stashes' of food hidden all over the house. I have food hidden in the bottom of the laundry hamper. Nobody is going to find the food, because nobody but me washes the clothes. I have candy stuffed deep inside my shoes and shoeboxes. I have food inside the pockets of my winter clothes, and under my mattress. I used to hide food under the kid's cribs, but they sleep in beds now. Once I hid food in my dogs' dry food bin, but my husband found out and I had a hard time explaining how M&Ms got inside the dog food container. So I stopped using that place. Now I have to get real creative, sometimes like when I wrap up ice cream bars in aluminum foil so they look like frozen hamburger patties. I'm always saving empty cereal boxes so I can put food back inside them and then place them back on the pantry shelf. My husband really complains about our food bills, but he doesn't know why we go through so much money at the grocery store. I hope he never finds out. I tell him that prices are really terrible, but most of the time I clip coupons to help defray the cost. During dinner I eat like everybody else, but as soon as dinner is over I start eating again right up until the time I go to bed. I usually can put away half of an apple pie and a quart of ice cream, but I have to be quiet when I throw up because everybody is home and they might hear me. Sometimes, when it's late at night and everyone is in bed, I'll treat myself to a nice enema.

"Most of the time when I eat, I'll eat in the bathroom, because it's the only place that offers me any privacy. The hard part is throwing up so no one hears me. I usually run the shower to hide my gagging noises. I used to pride myself on what a nice person I was, but now I'm nothing but a horrible pig. I feel terrible, but I don't know how to stop. I've tried stopping so many times. I just can't give up the food, but if I don't vomit, use laxatives, or enemas I start putting on the pounds. This is no way to live."

Assessment Summary

Consistent with bulimia nervosa, Mary McDaniel's behaviors leave little doubt concerning her pattern of this eating disorder. She has all the salient features including binge/purge cycles, use of laxatives, diuretics, and enemas, and no control over how much she eats. Despite feeling unhappy about herself, Mary is unable to stop her eating pattern; in fact, she believes she has no control over this behavior. For Mary, her struggles around food are never ending. It is an all or nothing perspective; that is, she is either completely in control or completely out of control. Likewise, food is seen as either all good or all bad. With this pattern, the practitioner might begin pay attention to presenting somatic complaints.

THE ROLE OF OBESITY

> Obesity is *not* considered a psychiatric disorder (APA, 2000); however, it is generally lumped together with "eating or weight disorders." Unfortunately, this only serves to stigmatize those who are portly. As researchers continue to examine the role of biological influences (particularly neurotransmitters and genetic predisposition), perhaps society will begin to view obesity differently; that is, as a complex metabolic disorder, rather than as an emotional or behavioral problem (Garner & Wooley, 1991; Wilson, 1993).

The term obesity does not appear in the DSM-IV-TR because it has not been established that it is consistently associated with a psychological or behavioral syndrome (APA, 2000). The DSM continues, "when there is evidence that psychological factors are of importance in the etiology or course of a particular case of obesity, this can be indicated by noting the presence of Psychological Factors Affecting Medical Condition" (APA, 1994, p. 539). The DSM (2000) notes obese individuals *may* develop eating disorders; a small percentage of individuals with bulimia nervosa are obese; and still more obese individuals engage in binge eating behaviors. Binge eating has two main characteristics: first, the consumption and the amount of food eaten is unquestionably greater than most people would eat during a similar period of time or under the same circumstances; and second, the individuals feel they are eating "out of control" and cannot stop (Fairburn et al., 1993b).

THE MAJOR FEATURES OF BINGE EATING DISORDER

Binge eating disorder (BED) has been called by a variety of other names, including bulimia, nonpurging bulimia nervosa, and compulsive overeating. The syndrome is most similar to that of bulimia, except there is no self-induced vomiting or laxative misuse. Therefore, no medical complications attributable to purging behaviors are present.

Although binge eating disorder is characterized by recurrent binge eating, it is not considered an "official disorder" in the DSM-IV-TR (APA, 2000). This, in part, is because the individual does not regularly engage in purging (Marcus, 1993), and the criteria do not specify any weight range. However, in contrast to findings about bulimia, early studies indicate that BED occurs predominately in individuals who are obese (Spitzer et al., 1991). Similar to the eating pattern of bulimia, the individual alternates between episodes of binge eating and efforts to restrict their food intake. Interestingly, although the presentation appears comparable to that of bulimia, there are two distinctive differences. One is that the person comes for treatment later in life, and second, the individual usually seeks methods of weight reduction. In a study conducted by Marcus (1993), not only do people with BED consume large quantities of food, they also report disorganized and even chaotic eating habits.

The criteria for binge eating disorder include:

- Recurrent episodes of binge eating must occur. In these episodes:
  Eating occurs during a discrete period of time, for example, within a two-hour interval. The amount of food is considered definitely much larger than most people would eat in similar circumstances and in the same amount of time.
  The individual has a lack of control over their eating, and feels they cannot stop what or how much they eat.

- The binge eating episode is usually affiliated with *three or more* of the following:
  Consuming food more rapidly than would be considered "normal"
  Eating food until one feels uncomfortably full or overstuffed
  Eating large quantities of food even when not physically hungry
  Eating alone because they are usually embarrassed about the quantity of food they eat
  Feeling disgusted with themselves or guilty after they overeat

- Marked distress regarding binge eating is present.

- The binge eating occurs, on average, at least twice a week over a period of at least six months.

- Binge eating is not combined with the regular use of inappropriate alleviative behaviors, for example, fasting, and does not occur solely during the course of either anorexia or bulimia (APA, 1994, 2000).

Current investigative clinical trials are being conducted to determine whether binge eating disorder should eventually become a DSM category (Cooke et al., 1997; Schwitzer et al., 1998; Walsh & Kahn, 1997; Tanofsky et al., 1997); however, this proposal is seen as controversial (Wilson et al., 1998). Some critics note it may be somewhat premature to single out a particular subgroup of eating disorders, not otherwise specified (EDNOS). There has been concern expressed among researchers about the lack of rigorous and methodological accuracy in some earlier studies using self-report questionnaires (Spitzer, et al., 1992, 1993), which yielded unreliable estimates about binge eating. (Binge eating might not be as common as first identified.)

Individuals with BED seem to differ in a variety of ways from people with other eating disorders and from obese people who do not engage in binge behaviors. For example, the ratio of females to males is 3:1, lower than for any other eating disorder (Bruce & Agras, 1992); individuals are older on average and experience increased psychosexual dysfunction (Schwalberg et al., 1992); and they experience increased mood and anxiety disorders (Marcus et al., 1990, 1992; Kirkley et al., 1992). "For all these reasons, BED has found its way into the appendix of DSM-IV as a potential new disorder requiring further study" (Durand & Barlow, 1997, p. 264). To date, most studies have continued to rely on self-report rather than interviews and direct field observation. It is anticipated that this category will generate a great deal of research in the years to come.

Referring back to Mary McDaniel's vignette, individuals with an eating pattern referred to as binge eating disorder would exhibit different eating behaviors. In this latter category, the person does not attempt to compensate for gaining weight by vomiting, using laxatives, or excessive amounts of exercise. While no weight range is noted, research suggests these individuals tend to be obese (Spitzer et al., 1992; Yanovski & Sebring, 1994).

SUMMARY

Individuals with anorexia nervosa differ in one very important way from those with bulimia—they are, much to their detriment, extremely successful at losing weight. The individual with bulimia is not trying to achieve low weight. The motivating force here seems to be the avoidance of becoming fat rather than the desire to be extremely thin (Nietzel et al., 1998). Although these two conditions frequently co-exist, the individual with bulimia usually does not have the minimum 15-percent weight loss found in those with anorexia. While binge eating may occur in persons with anorexia, some confusion can center around when the collateral assessment of bulimia should apply. The practitioner begins by evaluating how often the individual uses the purging/bingeing behaviors. Important "rules of thumb" include:

- An individual assessed with anorexia who experiences only a few binges scattered throughout a year should not be considered for bulimia.

- On the other hand, the individual with anorexia who binges several or more times a week would appear to have both disorders concurrently (Moore & Jefferson, 1996).

During the past 20 years there has been an increase in the clinical arena regarding eating disorders, and research efforts have scrambled to keep up with this burgeoning attention. Unfortunately, there are some serious methodological problems in many of the studies referenced in the literature; namely, diagnostic criteria vary greatly, there are low numbers of individuals included in the studies, and there are inadequate comparison groups. Nevertheless, some tentative conclusions can be drawn:

- Eating disorders are primarily conditions found in females between the ages of 15 and the early 20s.
- Medical complications associated with both anorexia and bulimia are often serious and potentially life threatening without appropriate intervention.
- Individuals with anorexia and bulimia show evidence of significant cognitive distortions about themselves and their body image, and a variety of other psychological problems, such as depression.
- The literature finds limited support for theories concerning the etiology of eating disorders.

Future research, it is hoped, will lead to a significant increase in the factual knowledge concerning these eating disorders. Table 8-1 summarizes the major features of anorexia nervosa and bulimia nervosa.

PRACTITIONER REFLECTIONS

This chapter outlined the major characteristics of the eating disorders, including anorexia nervosa, bulimia nervosa, and binge eating disorder (BED). Anorexia nervosa refers to an individual's refusal to eat anything but minimal amounts of food, resulting in extremely low body weight. Those with bulimia nervosa engage in uncontrolled binge eating episodes followed by self-induced purging. Both disorders involve an overwhelming desire to be thin. Individuals with binge eating disorder, while experiencing marked distress due to their binge eating, do not engage in extreme compensatory behaviors. In each of these eating disorders, because of the individual's tendency to hide their patterns of eating, it becomes important for the practitioner to initially listen for "clues."

Activities

- There are some differences found among cultures about attitudes concerning "ideal" body weight. Identify cultures where a heavier body type is valued. Discuss how this compares with your own cultural beliefs.
- Negative stereotypes are often perpetuated in the media. Browse through a popular magazine and identify the number of advertisements that portray individuals who you consider "thin" and those with a heavier body frame. How many are portrayed as thin and how many have more body weight? Next, identify how many are female and how many are male. Finally, identify how many are ethnic minorities. What implications can be drawn from this exercise?
- Keep a diary for one week and record everything that you eat and include the time of day you ate, whether you were hungry (or not), whether the food satisfied you (or not), whether you had cravings for certain foods, and whether you thought about food more often than you regularly do. In addition, weigh yourself every time you eat something. This activity is designed to begin to sensitize

TABLE 8-1   AN OVERVIEW OF THE MAJOR FEATURES OF ANOREXIA NERVOSA AND BULIMIA NERVOSA

Anorexia	Bulimia
Ego syntonic	Ego dystonic
Malnutrition-starvation	Binge/purge cycle
Refusal to maintain minimal weight	Purging: self induced vomiting, laxatives, diuretics, exercise
Intense fear of gaining weight	Weight fluctuation
Loss of menstrual cycle	Fear of being fat
Distorted body image	Fear of loss of control
Perfectionism	
Somatic complaints	***Medical complications***
Denial about weight condition	"Chipmunk" cheeks
Compliant and accommodating	Teeth yellow, eroded ("moth-eaten")
Very deceptive	Sore throat from purging
Infantile, demanding, negative	Knuckles (callous formation), Russell's signs
Manipulative	Acute electrolyte imbalance
Hair loss and/or lanugo	Abnormalities of renal and reproductive systems
	Kidney failure
Medical complications	Gastrointestinal systems (heartburn, abdominal pain, cramps & bloating)
Loss of normal muscle and fat	Esophageal tears
Low insight/misinterprets body image	Irregular menstrual cycle
Secondary gain about appearance	Constipation (rebound from laxatives)
Decreased sexual interest	Poor hair texture
Irregular heartbeat	Dehydration
Osteoporosis	
Digestive-gastrointestinal problems	
Sudden death	

you to what it might be like to have an eating disorder and how all-consuming eating food and weighing oneself can be.

- Review the case of Joy Walker. Which of the following questions do you think she would feel comfortable discussing with you? Which topics do you imagine would be the most difficult for her to talk about? Explain your conclusions.

    Feelings about her appearance
    Things she likes to eat and what she does not like
    Her "ideal" appearance and what that would look like

Concerns that she may have had with her appearance in the past

Current health problems, for example, feeling weak or dizzy, heart palpitations, sore throat, hair loss, and so on

Possible long-range worries about health issues

Past medical problems

Attempts to keep healthy, fit, and attractive, for example, her exercise regimen and diet.

REFERENCES

Agras, W. S. (1994). Disorders of eating: Anorexia nervosa, bulimia nervosa, and binge eating disorder. In R. I. Shader (Ed.), *Manual of psychiatric therapies* (2nd ed.), pp. 59–67. Boston, MA: Little, Brown and Co.

American Psychiatric Association [APA]. (1980). *Diagnostic and statistical manual of mental disorders* (3rd ed.). Washington, DC: APA.

American Psychiatric Association [APA]. (1993). Practice guidelines for eating disorders. *American Journal of Psychiatry*, 150(2): 212–228.

American Psychiatric Association [APA]. (1994). *Diagnostic and statistical manual of mental disorders* (4th ed.). Washington, DC: APA.

American Psychiatric Association [APA]. (2000). *Diagnostic and statistical manual of mental disorders* (4th ed.-TR). Washington, DC: APA.

Andersen, A. E. (1992). Males with eating disorders. In J. Yager, H. E. Gwirtsman, & C. K. Edelstein (Eds.), *Special problems in managing eating disorders*, pp. 87–118. Washington, DC: American Psychiatric Press.

Andersen, A. E., & Holman, J. E. (1997). Males with eating disorders: Challenges for treatment and research. *Psychopharmacology Bulletin*, 33(3): 391–397.

Beck, D., Casper, R., & Andersen, A. (1996). Truly late onset of eating disorders: A study of 11 cases averaging 60 years of age at presentation. *International Journal of Eating Disorders*, 20: 389–395.

Bemporad, J. R. (1998). Self-starvation through the ages: Reflections on the pre-history of anorexia nervosa. *International Journal of Eating Disorders*, 19: 217–237.

Brewerton, T. D., Lydiard, R. B., Ballenger, J. C., & Herzog, D. B. (1993). Eating disorders and social phobias. *Archives of General Psychiatry*, 50: 70.

Bruce, B., & Agras, W. S. (1992). Binge eating in females: A population based investigation. *International Journal of Eating Disorders*, 12(4): 365–373.

Buddeberg, F. B. (1997). Disorders of eating behavior—early detection and treatment possibilities in general practice. *Schweizerische Rundschay fur Medizin Praxis*, 86(31–32): 1209–1212.

Bulik, C. M. (1995). Anxiety disorders and eating disorders: A review of their relationship. *New Zealand Journal of Psychology*, 24(2): 51–62.

Bulik, C. M., Sullivan, P. F., & Carter, F. A. (1997). Initial manifestations of disordered eating behavior: Dieting versus bingeing. *International Journal of Eating Disorders*, 22: 195–201.

Carlat, D. J., Camargo, C. A., & Herzog, D. B. (1997). Eating disorders in males: A report on 135 patients. *American Journal of Psychiatry*, 154(8): 1127–1132.

Cash, T. F., & Deagle, E. A. (1997). The nature and extent of body-image disturbances in anorexia nervosa and bulimia nervosa: A meta-analysis. *International Journal of Eating Disorders*, 22(2): 107–125.

Castillo, R. J. (1997). *Culture and Mental Illness: A Client-Centered Approach*. Pacific Grove, CA: Brooks/Cole.

Cooke, E. A., Guss, J. L., Kissileff, H. R., & Devlin, M. J. (1997). Patterns of food selection during binges in women with binge eating disorder. *International Journal of Eating Disorders*, 22(2): 187–193.

Daluiski, A., Rahbar, B., & Means, R. A. (1997). Russell's sign. Subtle hand changes in patients with bulimia nervosa. *Clinical Orthopaedics and Related Research*, Oct.(343): 107–109.

Durand, V. M., & Barlow, D. H. (1997). *Abnormal psychology*. Pacific Grove, CA: Brooks/Cole.

Fairburn, C. G., & Cooper, Z. (1998). The schedule of the eating disorder examination. In C. G. Fairburn & G. T. Wilson (Eds.), *Binge eating: Nature, assessment and treatment*. New York: Guilford Press.

Fairburn, C. G., Hay, P. J., & Welch, S. L. (1993a). Binge eating and bulimia nervosa: Distribution and determinants. In C. G. Fairburn & G. T. Wilson (Eds.), *Binge eating: Nature, assessment and treatment*. New York: Guilford Press.

Fairburn, C. G., Welch, S. L., & Hay, P. J. (1993b). The classification of recurrent overeating: The "binge eating disorder" proposal. *International Journal of Eating Disorders*, 13: 155.

Favaro, A., & Santonastaso, P. (1997). Suicidality in eating disorders and psychological correlates. *Acta Psychiatrica Scandinavica*, 95(6): 508–514.

Frances, A., First, M. D., & Pincus, H. A. (1995). *DSM-IV Guidebook*. Washington, DC: American Psychiatric Press.

Garner, D. M., & Wooley, S. C. (1991). Confronting the failure and dietary treatment for obesity. *Clinical Psychology Review*, 11: 729–780.

Gerstein, F., & Woodside, B. (1997). Diuretic abuse in eating disorders: Treatment protocol and case report. *Eating Disorders: The Journal of Treatment and Prevention*, 5(3): 184–190.

Giannini, A. J. (1993). A history of bulimia. In J. A. Gianni & A. E. Salby, (Eds.), *The eating disorders*, pp. 18–21. New York: Springer Verlag.

Gillespie, J. (1996). Rejection of the body in women with eating disorders. *Arts in Psychotherapy*, 23(2): 153–161.

Gleaves, D. H., & Eberenz, K. P. (1993). Eating disorders and additional psychopathology in women: The role of prior sexual abuse. *Journal of Child Sexual Abuse*, 2(3): 71–80.

Grigg, M., Bowman, J., & Redman, S. (1996). Disordered eating and unhealthy weight reduction practices among adolescent females. *Preventive Medicine: An International Journal Devoted to Practice and Theory*, 25(6): 748–756.

Grilo, C. M., Walker, M. L., Becker, D. F., Edell, W. S., & McGlashan, T. H. (1997). Psychiatric comorbidity differences in male and female adult psychiatric inpatients with substance use disorders. *Comprehensive Psychiatry*, 38(3): 155–159.

Gull, W. W. (1873). Anorexia Hysterical (Apepsia hysteria). *British Medical Journal*, 2, 527.

Halmi, K. A., Eckert, E., Marchi, P., Sampugnaro, V., Apple, R., & Cohen, J. (1991). Comorbidity of psychiatric diagnosis in anorexia nervosa. *Archives of General Psychiatry*, 48, 712–718.

Hamilton, L., Brooks-Gunn, J., & Warren, M. P. (1985). Sociocultural influences on eating disorders in professional female ballet dancers. *International Journal of Eating Disorders*, 4(4): 465–477.

Harrison, K., & Cantor, J. (1997). The relationship between media consumption and eating disorders. *Journal of Communication*, 47(1): 40–67.

Hay, P., & Fairburn, C. (1998). The validity of the DSM-IV scheme for classifying bulimic eating disorders. *International Journal of Eating Disorders*, 23: 7–15.

Heatherton, R. F., Mahamedi, F., & Striepe, M. (1997). A 10-year longitudinal study of body weight, dieting, and eating disorder symptoms. *Journal of Abnormal Psychology*, 106: 117–125.

Hoek, H. W. (1993). Review of the epidemiological studies of eating disorders. *International Review of Psychiatry*, 5: 61–74.

Hollander, E., & Benzaquen, S. (1997). The obsessive-compulsive spectrum disorders. *International Review of Psychiatry*, 9(1): 99–110.

Hudgens, R. W. (1997). Eating disorders. In S. B. Guze (Ed.), *Adult psychiatry*. St. Louis, MO: Mosby-Year Book.

Hsu, L. K. G. (1988). The etiology of anorexia nervosa. In B. J. Blinder, B. F. Chaitin, & R. Goldstein (Eds.), *The eating disorders*, pp. 239–246. PMA Publishing.

Hsu, L. K. G. (1990). *Eating disorders*. New York: Guilford Press.

Hudgens, R. W. (1997). Eating disorders. In S. B. Guze (Ed.), *Adult psychiatry*, pp. 257–268. St. Louis, MO: Mosby-Year Book.

Kaplan, H. I., Sadock, B. J., & Grebb, J. A. (1994). *Synopsis of psychiatry* (7th ed.). Baltimore, MD: Williams & Wilkins.

Kaye, W. H. (1997). Anorexia nervosa, obsessional behavior, and serotonin. *Psychopharmacology Bulletin*, 33(3): 335–344.

Kaye, W. H., Weltzin, T., & Hsu, L. K. G. (1993). Relationship between anorexia nervosa and obsessive compulsive behaviors. *Psychiatric Annals*, 23: 365–373.

Kinder, B. N. (1997). Eating disorders. In S. M. Turner & M. Hersen (Eds.), *Adult psychopathology and diagnosis* (3rd ed.), pp. 465–482. New York: John Wiley & Sons.

Kinzel, J. F., Mangweth, B., & Traweger, C. M. (1997). Eating-disordered behavior in males: The impact of adverse childhood experiences. *International Journal of Eating Disorders*, 22: 131–138.

Kirkley, B. A., Kolotkin, R. L., Hernandez, J. T., & Gallagher, P. N. (1992). A comparison of binge-purgers, obese binge eaters and obese non-binge eaters on the MMPI. *International Journal of Eating Disorders*, 12(2): 221–228.

Lasequé, C. (1873). L'anorexia hysterique, *Archives generales de medicine*, 1: 385–403.

Lilienfeld, L. R., & Kaye, W. H. (1996). The link between alcoholism and eating disorders. *Alcohol Health and Research World*, 20(2): 94–99.

Marcé, L. V. (1860). On a form of hypochondriacal delirium occurring consecutive to dyspepsia, and characterized by refusal of food. *Journal of Psychology Medical Mental Pathology*, 13: 264–266.

Marcus, M. D. (1993). Binge eating in obesity. In C. F. Fairburn & G. T. Wilson (Eds.), *Binge eating: Nature, assessment, and treatment*, pp. 77–96. New York: Guilford Press.

Marcus, M. D., Wing, R. R., Ewing, L., Keern, E., Gooding, W., & McDermott, M. (1990). Psychiatric disorders among obese binge eaters. *International Journal of Eating Disorders*, 9: 69–77.

Marcus, M. D., Smith, D., Santelli, R., & Kaye, W. (1992). Characterization of eating disordered behavior in obese binge eaters. *International Journal of Eating Disorders*, 12: 249–255.

Marsh, E. J., & Wolfe, D. A. (1999). *Abnormal childhood psychology*. Pacific Grove, CA: Wadsworth.

Maxmen, J. S., & Ward, N. G. (1995). *Psychotropic drugs fast facts* (2nd ed.). New York: W. W. Norton.

Mehler, P. S. (1997). Constipation: Diagnosis and treatment in eating disorders. *Eating Disorders: The Journal of Treatment and Prevention*, 5(1): 41–46.

Mitchell, J. E., & Pyle, R. L. (1985). Characteristics of bulimia. In J. E. Mitchell (Ed.), *Anorexia nervosa and bulimia: Diagnosis and treatment*, pp. 29–47. Minneapolis: University of Minnesota Press.

Moore, D. P., & Jefferson, J. W. (1996). *Handbook of medical psychiatry.* St. Louis, MO: Mosby-Year Book.

Myers, L. L. (1995). Bulimia nervosa: What social workers need to know. *Journal of Applied Social Sciences*, 20(1): 63–75.

Nietzel, M. T., Speltz, M. L., McCauley, E. A., & Bernstein, D. A. (1998). *Abnormal psychology.* Boston: Allyn & Bacon.

Pirke, K. M., Schweiger, V., & Fichter, M. M. (1987). Hypothalamic-pituitary-ovarian axis in bulimia. In J. J. Hudson & H. G. Pope (Eds.), *The psychobiology of bulimia*, pp. 15–28. Washington, DC: American Psychiatric Press.

Robertson, D. N., & Palmer, R. L. (1997). History of obesity. *International Journal of Eating Disorders*, 22(3): 323–327.

Rorty, M., Yager, J., & Rossotto, E. (1994). Childhood sexual, physical, and psychological abuse in bulimia nervosa. *Journal of Psychiatry*, 151: 1122–1126.

Rytomaa, I., Jarvinen, V., & Heinonen, O. P. (1998). Bulimia and tooth erosion. *Acta-Odontologica-Scandinavica*, 56(1): 36–40.

Schaaf, K. K., & McCanne, T. R. (1994). Child abuse, body image disturbances and eating disorders. *Child Abuse and Neglect*, 18(8): 607–615.

Schlundt, O. G., & Johnson, W. G. (1990). *Eating disorders: Assessment and treatment.* Boston: Allyn & Bacon.

Schulken, E. D., Pinciaro, P. J., Jensen, J., & Hoban, M. T. (1997). Sorority women's body size perceptions and their weight-related attitudes and behaviors. *Journal of American College Health*, 46(2): 69–74.

Schwalberg, M. D., Barlow, D. H., Alger, S. A., & Howard, L. J. (1992). Comparison of bulimics, obese binge eaters, social phobics and individuals with panic disorder or comorbidity across DSM-III-R anxiety. *Journal of Abnormal Psychology*, 101: 675–681.

Schwitzer, A. M., Bergholz, K., Dore, T., & Salimi, L. (1998). Eating disorders among college women: Prevention, education, and treatment responses. *Journal of American College Health*, 46(5): 199–207.

Scocco, P., & De Leo, D. (1995). Patologia psichiatrica e comportamenti suicidari (Psychiatric disorders and suicidal behavior: An overview). *Giornale Italiano di Suicidologia*, 5(2): 102–126.

Silverstein, B., & Blumenthal, E. (1997). Depression mixed with anxiety, somatization, and disordered eating: Relationship with gender-role-related limitations experienced by females. *Sex Roles*, 36: 709–724.

Skodal, A. E., Oldham, J. M., Hyler, S. E., Kellman, H. D., Doidge, N., & Davies, M. (1993). Comorbidity of DSM-III-R eating disorders and personality disorders. *International Journal of Eating Disorders*, 14: 403–416.

Spitzer, R. L., Devlin, M. J., Walsh, B. T., Hasin, D., Wing, R., Marcus, M. D., Mitchell, J., & Nonas, C. (1991). Binge-eating: To be or not to be in DSM-IV. *International Journal of Eating Disorders*, 10: 627–629.

Spitzer, R. L., Devlin, M. J., Walsh, B. T., Hasin, D., Wing, R., Marcus, M., Stunkard, A., Wadden, T., Yanovski, S., Agras, S., Mitchell, J., & Nonas, C. (1992). Binge eating disorder: A multisite field trial of the diagnostic criteria. *International Journal of Eating Disorders*, 11: 191–203.

Spitzer, R. L., Yanovski, S., Wadden, T., Wing, R., Marcus, M., Stunkard, A., Devlin, M., Mitchell, J., Hasin, D., & Horne, R. L. (1993). Binge eating disorder: Its further validation in a multisite study. *International Journal of Eating Disorders*, 13: 137–153.

Stein, K. F., & Hedger, K. M. (1997). Body weight and shape self-cognitions, emotional distress, and disordered eating in middle adolescent girls. *Archives of Psychiatric Nursing*, 11(5): 264–275.

Striegel-Moore, R. H. (1993). Etiology of binge eating: A developmental perspective. In C. G. Fairburn & G. T. Wilson (Eds.), *Binge eating: Nature, assessment and treatment*, pp. 144–172. New York: Guilford Press.

Strober, M. (1995). Family genetic perspectives on anorexia nervosa and bulimia nervosa. In C. G. Fairburn & K. Brownell (Eds.), *Comprehensive textbook of eating disorders and obesity*, pp. 212–218. New York: Guilford Press.

Sullivan, P. F., Bulik, C. M., Carter, F. A., & Gendall, K. A. (1996). The significance of a prior history of anorexia in bulimia nervosa. *International Journal of Eating Disorders*, 20(3): 253–261.

Szabo, C. P., & Terre Blanche, M. J. (1997). Perfectionism in anorexia nervosa. *American Journal of Psychiatry*, 154(1): 132.

Tanofsky, M. B., Wilfley, D. E., Spurrell, E. B., Welch, R., & Brownell, K. D. (1997). *International Journal of Eating Disorders*, 21(1): 49–54.

Thornton, C., & Russell, J. (1997). Obsessive compulsive comorbidity in the dieting disorders. *International Journal of Eating Disorders*, 21(1): 83–87.

Turner, S. M., & Hersen, M. (1997). *Adult psychopathology and diagnosis* (3rd ed.). New York: John Wiley & Sons.

Walfish, S., Stennmark, D. E., Sarco, D., Shealy, J. S., & Krone, A. M. (1992). Incidence of bulimia in substance misusing women in residential treatment. *International Journal of the Addictions*, 27: 425–433.

Waller, G., Hamilton, K., Rose, N., Sumra, J., & Baldwin, G. (1993). Sexual abuse and body image distortion in the eating disorders. *British Journal of Clinical Psychology*, 32: 350–352.

Waller, G., Halek, C., & Crisp, A. H. (1994). Childhood abuse, body image disturbance, and eating disorders. *Child Abuse and Neglect*, 18: 607–615.

Walsh, B. T., & Kahn, C. B. (1997). Diagnostic criteria for eating disorders: Current concerns and future directions. *Psychopharmacology Bulletin*, 33(3): 369–372.

Welch, S. L., & Fairburn, C. G. (1994). Sexual abuse and bulimia nervosa: Three integrated case control comparisons. *Journal of Psychiatry*, 151: 402–407.

Wiederman, M. W. (1996). Women, sex and food: A review of research on eating disorders and sexuality. *The Journal of Sex Review*, 33(4): 301–311.

Wiederman, M. W., & Pyror, T. (1997). The relationship between substance abuse and client characteristics among adolescent girls with anorexia nervosa or bulimia nervosa. *Journal of Child and Adolescent Substance Abuse*, 6(2): 39–47.

Wilfley, D. E., Schreiber, G. B., & Pike, K. M. (1996). Eating disturbance and body image: A comparison of a community sample of adult black and white women. *International Journal of Eating Disorders*, 20: 377–387.

Wilson, G. T. (1993). Binge eating and addictive disorder. In C. G. Fairburn & G. T. Wilson (Eds.), *Binge eating: Nature assessment and treatment*. New York: Guilford Press.

Wilson, G. T., Nathan, P. E., O'Leary, K. D., & Clark, R. (1998). *Abnormal psychology*. Boston: Allyn & Bacon.

Wonderlich, S. A., & Mitchell, J. E. (1997). Eating disorders and comorbidity: Empirical, conceptual, and clinical implications. *Psychopharmacology Bulletin*, 33(3): 381–390.

Wonderlich, S. A., Brewerton, T. D., & Jocic, Z. (1997). Relationship of childhood sexual abuse and eating disorders. *Journal of the American Academy of Child and Adolescent Psychiatry*, 36: 1107–1115.

Yager, J. (1994). Eating disorders. In A. Stoudemire (Ed.), *Clinical psychiatry for medical students*. Philadelphia: J. B. Lippincott.

Yanovski, A. Z., & Sebring, N. G. (1994). Recorded food intake of obese women with binge eating disorders before and after weight loss. *International Journal of Eating Disorders*, 15: 135–150.

Yegidis, B. I., & Morgan, S. (1994). Sexual abuse and eating disorders. *Arete*, 18(2): 22–30.

THE PERSONALITY DISORDERS

INTRODUCTION

Hippocrates (460–377 B.C.), traditionally considered the father of medicine, suggested that disease, mainly brain disease, was responsible for mental problems. He believed that most were due to an imbalance in four essential fluids, or "humors," that circulated throughout the body. These humors, "blood, black bile, yellow bile and lymph," were somehow responsible for characterizing an individual's worldview. "Hippocrates' theory of imbalance in the body's chemistry foreshadowed the discovery of biological components of mental disorders made centuries later by modern science" (Wilson et al., 1996, p. 13). Centuries ahead of his time, Hippocrates described several mental disorders that are familiar to contemporary practitioners, including mania, melancholia, and paranoia.

Two thousand years later, DSM-I described 27 "personality disorders" and organized them into five specific headings that included personality pattern disturbance, personality trait disturbance, sociopathic personality disturbance, special symptom reactions, and transient situational personality disorders (APA, 1952). When DSM-II made its appearance, the subheadings were subsequently eliminated and the number of personality disorders was reduced from 27 to 12 categories (APA, 1968). The professional community did not endorse these as positive changes, because they were considered too limited (Sperry, 1995). The next round of diagnostic revisions began in 1974, leading to the publication of the DSM-III in 1980 (APA, 1994). This manual introduced the concept of Axis II; for the first time, the personality and developmental disorders were separated from the clinical syndromes noted on Axis I. This Axis II stipulation ensured the personality disorder designation would not be overlooked (Rapoport & Ismond, 1996). DSM-III-R, published in 1987, described 11 personality disorders subdivided into three "clusters."

While there are many schools of thought, Freudian psychodynamic theory has historically influenced the way practitioners conceptualized personality and pathology. An in-depth discussion of psychoanalytic theory is beyond the scope of this book. For a more thorough review, the reader is directed to Goldstein (1984, 2000) and Teyber (1996). Briefly, adult personality is viewed as the accumulation of early childhood experiences. Individuals generally learn to solve their own emotional problems during various stages of childhood development. These characteristic ways of interacting help determine adult personality traits. According to Freud, the emotional problems of childhood are resolved by the development of defense mechanisms aimed at decreasing anxiety. Defenses were conceptualized as unconscious processes originating within the "ego," or the executive function of the individual's personality structure.

The term *personality* implies the manner in which a person interacts with their environment and other people. *Personality disorder* characterizes those individuals who usually respond poorly to changes, exhibit deficiencies in their capacity to form relationships, and have interpersonal problems in a variety of arenas, such as employment or school. Problems occur when traits, or those features that make up a personality, remain inflexible, thus impairing the individual's ability to interact within their social environment and with others.

Each person has a unique and individualized repertoire of defense mechanisms geared to maintaining balance between their internal drives and the external world. This repertoire is seen as personality; that is, a set of characteristics defining the behaviors, thoughts, and emotions of each individual. These characteristics become ingrained and usually dictate the person's worldview, lifestyle, and life choices (Scully, 1996). An individual's personality can be defined as those emotional and behavioral traits that characterize day-to-day living under normative conditions; an individual's personality is relatively predictable (Kaplan & Sadock, 1996; Widiger & Costa, 1994).

A personality disorder is seen as a variant of character traits going far beyond the normative range found in most people. When these traits are extremely inflexible and maladaptive, and cause significant functional impairment or subjective distress, they constitute a personality disorder. Individuals characterized by a personality disorder exhibit deeply ingrained, inflexible, rigid, problematic, and maladaptive patterns of relating to others and in perceiving themselves (Kaplan & Sadock, 1996). While the individual's interactional style generally creates no distress for them, it may adversely affect others; that is, the person's behavior is considered ego-syntonic. This might present a major problem for the practitioner, especially when trying to foster the therapeutic relationship and develop collaborative efforts aimed at change.

The DSM-IV defines a personality disorder as "enduring pattern[s] of perceiving, relating to, and thinking about the environment and oneself [that] are exhibited in a wide range of important social and personal contexts, [and] are inflexible and maladaptive, and cause either significant functional impairment or subjective distress" (APA, 1994, p. 630). The competency-based assessment expands this definition by considering the influence of the full range of biological, psychological, sociocultural, and environmental factors that affect the individual's life.

TY DISORDERS

Juan, for instance, can be described as "gre-
ichard as "quiet and introspective." In fact,
e *think* or *behave.* Each of us has probably
eristics construed as "gregarious," "fun-lov-
avior is seen as being part of a person's per-
tions and events (Barlow & Durand, 1995).
e ways of behaving as they relate specifically
rs develop in early childhood, and continue

THE CLUSTERS

The DSM-IV noted ten distinct personality disorders, and one other, nonspecific category "which warrant(s) additional future investigation" (DSM-IV, 1994 pp. 732–733). They are grouped into three clusters referred to as A, B, and C:

- *Cluster A*—Individuals are seen as "odd and eccentric" and include the paranoid, schizoid, and schizotypal personality disorders.
- *Cluster B*—Individuals appear highly emotional, dramatic, or erratic and include antisocial, histrionic, borderline, and narcissistic personality disorders.
- *Cluster C*—These individuals are seen as anxious and fearful and include avoidant, dependent, and obsessive-compulsive personality disorders.

Table 9-1 shows the major characteristics of each personality disorder organized by cluster.

The DSM-IV (APA, 1994) acknowledged that "the clustering system ... has serious limitations and has not been consistently validated" (p. 630). Nonetheless, this method of organization is a helpful framework for the competency-based assessment that looks at the influence of the wide range of factors affecting client behavior and attempts to identify their impact on the client's biopsychosocial world. The important distinction is that the personality disorders are long-term, stable patterns of unusual and inflexible personality characteristics leading to pervasive impairment or interpersonal distress throughout a person's life (Barlow & Durand, 1995; Frances et al., 1995; Scully, 1996; Kaplan & Sadock, 1996; APA, 2000). This pattern is evident in two (or more) of the following areas:

- *Cognition*—Ways of perceiving and interpreting one's self, other people, and events
- *Affectivity*—The range, intensity, and appropriateness of emotional response(s)
- *Interpersonal functioning*—The instability of and inability to maintain relationships; poor self-image or self-esteem

St. Anthony of Padua

ERVIEW OF **PERSONALITY DISORDERS**

nd eccentric

		Schizoid	*Schizotypal*
ustful of other's t	Socially restricted	Perceptual disturbances; interpersonal deficits
rm them	• No desire for close friendships	• Ideas of reference
unjust doubts	• Chooses solitary activities	• Odd beliefs
	• No interest in sex	• Unusual perceptions
de in others	• Takes little pleasure in activities	• Odd thinking and speech
anings	• Lacks friends	• Suspicious or paranoid ideation
	• Indifferent to praise or criticism	• Behavior appears odd, eccentric
reacts angrily	• Cold, detached, or flat affect	• Inappropriate affect
n about fidelity		

nal, dramatic, or erratic

	Borderline	*Histrionic*	*Narcissistic*
ard sent ust d	Unstable relationships; poor self-image; marked impulsivity	Excessive emotionality; attention seeking	Requires excessive admiration
	• Frantic efforts to avoid being abandoned	• Uncomfortable when not center of attention	• Grandiose
		• Provocative behavior	• Fantasizes about unlimited success, power
rofit	• Unstable chaotic relationships	• Uses physical attraction to draw attention to self	• Striking sense of entitlement
	• Impulsive spending, sex, substance abuse	• Self-dramatization	• Lacks empathy
	• Suicidal	• Rapidly changes shifting emotions	• Believes self "special" and others ordinary
	• Feeling "empty"	• Highly suggestible	• Interpersonal relationships exploited; others manipulated
	• Inappropriate, intense, or difficulty controlling anger		• Envious of others and thinks others jealous of them
	• History of mutilating		• Arrogant
• Lack of remorse			

Cluster C: Anxious, fearful

Avoidant	*Obsessive-Compulsive*	*Dependent*
Inhibited; feels inadequate	Order; perfection; inflexible	Needs to be taken care of; clinging behavior
• Avoids meaningful relationships with others	• Preoccupied with rules, regulations	• Difficulty making everyday decisions
• Unwilling to get involved unless "guaranteed" they will be liked	• Perfection interferes with completion of tasks	• Desires others to assume responsibility for them
• Shows restraint because they fear shame or ridicule	• Over-conscientious	• Lacks initiative
• Preoccupied with criticism or rejection	• Hoardes objects	• Excessive lengths to obtain support from others
• Feels inadequate	• Rigid and stubborn	• Feels uncomfortable or helpless
• Views self as inept, inferior	• Reluctant to delegate tasks	• Preoccupied with fears of being left alone
• Reluctant to take risks, might be embarrassed		

- *Poor impulse control*—The individual has difficulty anticipating the repercussions of their behavior, learning from undesirable consequences of their previous behaviors, or delaying an action (appropriately).

Typically, most individuals adapt their behavior to a variety of different situations; for example, those persons characterized as talkative are able to be quiet during an important speech or a religious service. Individuals with a personality disorder exhibit personality traits so out of proportion or inflexible that they often cause problems for themselves and those around them. These difficulties continue over an extended period of time (Barlow & Durand, 1995; Wilson et al., 1996). In earlier stages of life, these traits might have been effective ways to cope in the person's family of origin.

To identify the presence of a personality disorder, the individual must exhibit *four or five* of the following behaviors:

- Almost always inflexible across a wide range interpersonal and intrapersonal situations
- Leads to significant distress or impairment in social, occupational, or other important areas of interpersonal functioning
- Is stable and of long duration; onset can usually be traced back at least to early adolescence (or earlier)
- Is not the result of another mental disorder
- Is not due to the direct physiological effects of a substance (for example, a drug of abuse) or a general medical condition (APA, 1994, 2000).

The ten personality disorders described in this chapter are certainly not the "final word," but they do arise from historical traditions of dividing the domain of personality disorders (Frances et al., 1995). These categories can cause assessment dilemmas when an individual's behavior pattern comes very close to what is considered "normal" behavior versus "abnormal" behavior. Identifying the boundary between one specific personality disorder and another also poses a challenge. The main point for the practitioner to recognize is that these personality disorders are considered no more than behavioral prototypes with indistinct boundaries (Frances et al., 1995; Gabbard, 1995).

The competency-based assessment underscores the uniqueness of each individual. In addition, when the influence of biopsychosocial factors is considered, an individual's life "story" is certainly far more complex than any listing of behavior patterns. The DSM should not serve as a "recipe" for understanding behavior. However, an awareness of the DSM's guidelines for differential assessment will help the practitioner to approach the competency-based assessment process in a systematic way. The competency-based framework is intended to enhance, not to replace, the central role of the practitioner's clinical judgment, empirical evidence to formulate a clinical diagnosis, and the wisdom of accumulated practice experience. Merging the DSM format with the competency-based assessment model helps the practitioner to fully explore the client's life history and the impact of biological, psychological, and social variables.

In what follows, descriptions of the ten personality disorders noted in the DSM-IV-TR will be provided. While these descriptions tap into the basic features of each personality disorder, it is important to understand that these are only abbreviated characterizations. In practice, the social worker attends to the whole person and their unique life history.

CLUSTER A PERSONALITY DISORDERS

PARANOID PERSONALITY DISORDER

In *paranoid personality disorder*, the individual's behavior is characterized by pervasive, groundless suspiciousness and an inherent distrust of others. This person is often described as hostile, irritable, or angry, and he or she refuses to take responsibility for their own actions and feelings. As the name suggests, these individuals generally interpret insults or threats made from innocent remarks. They often believe their personal character and reputation are being attacked when, in fact, these "injuries" are unintended. Because of the fear of exploitation, they generally do not confide in or trust others.

Central characteristics include:

- *Suspicion*—Although the individual has no real basis or evidence of another person's malfeasance, they tend to be preoccupied assuming others are somehow being unfaithful or betraying them.

- *Holding grudges*—These individuals do not forgive insults, slights, or injuries. They are predisposed to blame others for their problems, and often have a history of being litigious.

- *Paranoia*—They are distrustful and suspicious of others; they are inclined to view the motives of others as malevolent. These individuals have a tendency to be chronically tense, and constantly mobilize themselves against perceived threats from others in their social environment. This worldview generally begins by early adulthood.

- *Problems around intimacy*—The individual has difficulty being intimate with others, and is apprehensive about trusting people.

- *Centrality*—These individuals often believe they are somehow the focus of other people's interest or attention.

- *Censure*—The person has a strong tendency to blame others, and believe others are generally ill intentioned or hostile toward them. They spend a great deal of time and effort being hypervigilant against what they perceive as hurtful intentions of others (Gabbard, 1995). The individual is supersensitive to issues regarding rank, class, and power; the person resents others who have things they do not.

These individuals are prone to see insult where none exists, and quick to take offense when none was intended (Moore & Jefferson, 1996; Kaplan & Sadock, 1996). Their personality can be described as chronically sarcastic, argumentative, angry, irritable, querulous, and having a "chip on their shoulder" (Stoudemire, 1994; Wilson et al., 1996). It is not unusual for them to bear grudges for a long period of time, and they pursue "insults" with a righteous, moralistic tenacity. Relationships with neighbors or coworkers can be described as tense. For example, a neighbor's barking dog is seen as a deliberate attempt to annoy them. There exists a profound negativistic, bitter, and cynical attitude, which often pervades their perception of life. Often they are cold and humorless (Moore & Jefferson, 1996), extremely self-protective of their own interests, jealous, controlling, and possessive in whatever relationships they secure (Stoudemire, 1994). "It is not unusual to see such individuals fascinated with weapons, survivalist organizations, or with extremist political groups" (Stoudemire, 1994, p. 184).

Prevailing Pattern

According to Kaplan and Sadock (1996), the prevalence of paranoid personality disorder ranges between 0.5 and 2.5 percent of the general population. These individuals rarely seek help on their own, but rather are referred to treatment by others in their social environment such as a spouse or an employer. This disorder appears to be more common in men and does not seem to have a familial pattern. Currently, there have been no systematic long-term studies conducted (Gabbard, 1995; Kaplan & Sadock, 1996); what is known is these individuals have lifelong problems in living and working with others.

Differential Assessment

Paranoid schizophrenia may *mimic* many aspects of paranoid personality disorder. For those persons with schizophrenia, the practitioner notes the presence of chronic delusions or hallucinations and also notes a greater degree of incoherence and illogical speech. These characteristics are not in found in persons with a paranoid personality disorder (Moore & Jefferson, 1996). The persecutory subtype of delusional disorder may resemble paranoid personality disorder. However, the major distinction is the delusions for the persecutory subtype are chronic. Delusions experienced by those with a paranoid personality disorder are transient or may not occur at all (Moore & Jefferson, 1996). Individuals with delusional disorder do not display the constant hypervigilance or pervasive mistrust seen in paranoid personality disorder. On closer examination, those with a paranoid personality disorder desperately want a relationship with others. In contrast, relationships are difficult for persons with the borderline personality disorder as they are characterized as chaotic, fractured, and difficult.

The following vignette illustrates the characteristics of someone with a paranoid personality disorder.

The Case of Ben Rogers

Ben Rogers, a 77-year-old retired pharmacist, is seen by a social worker at a senior citizens center for an evaluation of health care needs for himself and his 75-year-old bedridden wife, Franne. Mr. Rogers states that he is a relatively healthy individual, except for angina and high blood pressure. He has been the sole caretaker for his wife and was recently urged by their only child, Myra Schwartz, to seek help because his wife's condition is deteriorating and his responsibility for her care has become more of a physical drain.

Since the daughter was instrumental in getting her father involved with the senior citizens center, the social worker set some time aside to gather collateral information about what was happening in the Rogers' home. Ms. Schwartz reported that her parents had been married for 55 years. She went on to add that her father had a moderately successful business as a pharmacist, and he retired a little over 15 years ago to take care of her mother full-time. Her parent's relationship was characterized as "rough," and, "Mother was the only one father had very tender feelings for."

Ms. Schwartz further revealed that except for her mother, "My father never trusted anyone." She continued, "Father's attitude is that people shouldn't be trusted because they are always out to get you," and "He refuses offers of help from family and friends because he believes they want to find 'something on him' that will expose him later." Ms. Schwartz added, "My father never ever forgave an insult," and jokingly stated, "He probably has earned a place in the *Guinness Book of World Records* for holding a grudge longer than anyone else on earth." When asked if her father ever exhibited evidence of mood swings or psychosis, she responded, "He's not crazy or anything like that, he's just nasty."

She stated her father's "personality problems" have been fairly stable, and she noted that he behaved "that way" for as long as she could remember. "You know, now that I look back on my relationship with my father, I don't really know him much at all. He's a very difficult man to have a relationship with, or even try to love. Hey, don't get me wrong, I do love my father, but it's like I always have to walk on eggshells whenever I try to talk with him. I mean, he questions my every motive."

Assessment Summary

Exploring the interaction of the biopsychosocial factors in Ben Rogers' life, his wife's deteriorating health conditions seem to intensify his paranoid beliefs. Ben's wife continues to physically decline, and his ability to care for her becomes increasingly demanding and emotionally draining. This sets the stage for Ben, a man who usually refuses help, to reach out to others and to depend on them for assistance. His daughter notes, "Father has a long history of not trusting people." He is suspicious of everyone and is known to hold a grudge for a long time. He always thinks other people will take advantage of him, and sometimes he reads hidden meanings from innocent remarks.

The competency-based assessment considers strengths and positives in the client's situation. Ben has had a moderately successful career as a pharmacist. In that capacity, it was necessary for him to interact with others. Despite evidence of interpersonal difficulties, he maintained a 55-year marriage and professes "tender feelings" for his wife. While Ben is in relatively good health, the physical demands of being the sole caretaker for his wife may adversely affect his own health status; he is currently taking medication for hypertension and angina. Though one might

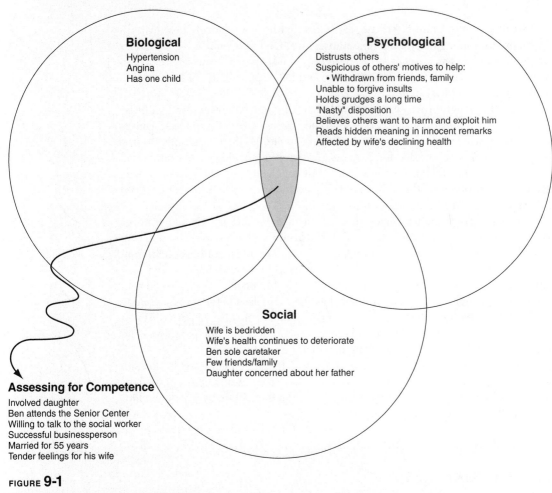

Biological
Hypertension
Angina
Has one child

Psychological
Distrusts others
Suspicious of others' motives to help:
 • Withdrawn from friends, family
Unable to forgive insults
Holds grudges a long time
"Nasty" disposition
Believes others want to harm and exploit him
Reads hidden meaning in innocent remarks
Affected by wife's declining health

Social
Wife is bedridden
Wife's health continues to deteriorate
Ben sole caretaker
Few friends/family
Daughter concerned about her father

Assessing for Competence
Involved daughter
Ben attends the Senior Center
Willing to talk to the social worker
Successful businessperson
Married for 55 years
Tender feelings for his wife

FIGURE **9-1**

PARANOID PERSONALITY DISORDER

The interactions of the biological, psychological, and social factors in Ben Rogers' life.

suspect it is difficult, Ben has been attending the senior citizens center once or twice a week after being urged by his daughter to seek help.

From the information available in this case presentation, Ben has come to the practitioner's attention because of interpersonal family issues, and he has not sought help on his own. This pattern of access to services is not inconsistent with persons who experience intense interpersonal conflicts. Further, Ben lacks the insight to understand that his behavior creates relational difficulties with others; personality traits that produce such behavior are considered ego-syntonic. It is important for the practitioner to be attentive to the features of this personality disorder, as this characteristic way of relating will influence the helping relationship.

Ben Rogers' overall diagnosis is as follows:

Axis I	V71.09 (No diagnosis)
Axis II	301.0 Paranoid Personality Disorder
Axis III	413.9 Angina Pectoris
	402.91 Hypertensive Heart Disease, with Congestive Heart Failure
Axis IV	Wife bedridden and in poor health
Axis V	GAF = 70 (on intake)

SCHIZOID PERSONALITY DISORDER

Persons with *schizoid personality disorder* display a lifelong pattern of social withdrawal; that is, they tend to be introverted, and remain isolated from others by choice. Often, their lifestyles are described as bland and solitary (Austrian, 1995), with very little human interaction. Eccentric, lonely, and ill at ease in the company of others are typical ways to describe their behaviors; however, the individual does not exhibit the disordered thinking so apparent in those persons with schizophrenia. Gathering childhood information may reveal a history of having been a "loner," or sensitive to the teasing of other children during early school years.

The major characteristics include:

- *No penchant for social relationships*—While some may form stable relationships with family members (or others), they lack the ability to *sustain close* relationships.

- *Little or no sex drive*—They rarely date or marry; men are more likely to remain single than women (perhaps due to problems around initiating courtship).

- *Preference for solitary activities*—Typically, the individual retains low-level jobs requiring limited interpersonal contact; for example, they are employed as a night security worker, janitor, or computer technician. Interestingly, they often succeed at solitary jobs others might find difficult to endure.

- *Limited range of emotions*—They have a confined range of emotions in social settings and are often described as "cold and detached." The person appears indifferent to both compliments and/or criticisms, and takes little or no pleasure in life. Their discomfort with relationships is noteworthy.

Do you know someone you consider a "loner"? Someone who would rather stay home to watch television than accept an invitation to join a party? Magnify this preference for isolation many times over, and you begin to grasp the impact on someone with a schizoid personality disorder. These individuals give the impression of being reserved, indifferent, or detached from everyday events. They lead quiet, distant, reclusive, and unsociable lives, usually maintaining their own lives with remarkably little need or desire for emotional ties to others (Gabbard, 1995). The person is characterized as eccentric, isolated, detached, or lonely (Kaplan & Sadock, 1996). "They may daydream excessively, become attached to animals, and often do not marry or even form long-lasting romantic relationships" (Morrison, 1995, p. 467). Beneath the surface of their indifference often exists a deep loneliness and a desire for close relationships (Stoudemire, 1994; Gabbard, 1995).

Prevailing Pattern

Knowledge about this disorder remains incomplete (Barlow & Durand, 1995). However, over the past several decades research has pointed to the role of biological influences in combination with poor family socialization and early learning or relationship problems (Barlow & Durand, 1995). The onset typically occurs during early childhood years, and the disorder may affect up to 7.5 percent of the general population in the United States (Kaplan & Sadock, 1996). Review of the individual's biopsychosocial history may reveal solitary interests and noncompetitive, remote or secluded types of employment such as working the "graveyard shift." Additionally, they seem not able to express their anger directly.

Differential Assessment

Many similarities are shared between individuals with the schizoid personality disorder and those with paranoid personality disorder. What differentiates persons with the paranoid personality is that they are more socially connected, and they show a greater tendency to project their feelings onto others (Kaplan & Sadock, 1996). Those with avoidant personality disorders are also characterized by isolation, but these individuals want very much to participate in activities, something that is absent in persons with the schizoid personality disorder. The chief distinction between schizotypal personality disorder and schizoid personality disorder is that the individual with schizotypal personality disorder shows a greater similarity to the person with schizophrenia in terms of oddities of perception, thought, behavior, and communication (Kaplan & Sadock, 1996).

The following case discussion of Tyrone White, a young man brought to a mental health clinic by a concerned relative, illustrates what the life of someone with schizoid personality disorder might look like.

The Case of Tyrone White

His cousin, Sabrina, referred Tyrone White to the XYZ Mental Health Clinic. With concern in her voice, she expressed, "Tyrone is such a lonely boy and needs someone to talk to about his troubles."

As I entered the waiting room, the first thing I noticed about Tyrone was that he seemed oblivious to those around him, as his face was hidden in a movie star magazine. I went over greet him and invite him into my office. When Tyrone entered my office, it was quite apparent to me that he did not regard the appointment as much of an event. His physical appearance sort of said the same thing; his shorts were torn, and he wore a tattered T-shirt and no shoes. My initial impression was that he was dressed for washing his car instead of going to an office appointment.

Throughout most of the interview, Tyrone continued to leaf through his magazine. I waited for about a minute for him to say something, but he did not even seem to notice that I was sitting there. The interview began:

"Hello, I'm Marilyn Zide, one of the social workers here. I understand your name is Tyrone. Is that what other people call you?"

He nodded his head in agreement.

"Most people call me Marilyn, and if you'd like, you can also. May I call you Tyrone?"

He nodded affirmatively.

"How are you doing?" I asked.

"Fine," he replied.

"Do you know why you are here today?" I asked.

"Nuh huh," he replied. (I waited again.)

"Well, what I know about why you are here is that your cousin Sabrina is worried about you and thought you might need someone to talk to. What do you think?"

"I'da know," he replied (still reading his magazine).

I asked (trying again), "Did Sabrina tell you why she was so worried about you?"

"Nuh huh," he replied. (Most of Tyrone's interview followed this same pattern.)

In the interest of saving time, this worker will provide a brief overview of the session. If I asked Tyrone a direct question, he answered but did not elaborate or volunteer additional data. He sat quietly (reading his magazine) throughout the interview, and I noticed no evidence of abnormal or eccentric behavior. When asked, he was appropriately oriented to time, place, and date, and he denied any drug or alcohol use. I asked whether he had ever heard any voices (that other people did not hear) or saw things (that other people did not see). He generally replied, "Nuh huh," to my inquiries.

Tyrone is a 27-year-old African American, and the youngest of eight children. Somehow through our convoluted session, he revealed that his father died ten years ago from some kind of surgical complications. He volunteered no other details. His mother recently remarried, and, he added, "I don't see my family very often." He lives alone in a small apartment in the same neighborhood as his cousin, Sabrina. He supports himself as a movie projectionist. Tyrone did not finish high school, and he has held this job for the past seven years. He has gotten several raises over the years, and although asked to become a manager, Tyrone replied that he does not want to "attend all those meetings with all those people." He stated, "I like my job a lot because I can look at movie stars all day, and nobody bothers me." He considers himself to be an "average guy" and doesn't really want friends or family around because he "likes my own good company." Tyrone does not have a history of dating nor has he been sexually active.

In speaking with his cousin, Sabrina, after the session, she commented that Tyrone has always been "a loner," even when he was a child. Tyrone corroborated this, saying, "I was a street kid." He never spent much time with his family and does not remember very much time spent doing "family things." Tyrone stated that the neighborhood kids "picked on me because I was so small," but he insists, "I never cared." In school, his progress was noted as "nothing special."

When asked, "What makes you happy?" he replied, "I just like being left alone." When the session was over, Tyrone stood up, carefully turned down the corner of the page he had been reading, tucked the magazine under his arm, and walked out of my office without a backward glance, never to return.

Assessment Summary

Tyrone relates to the practitioner in a stilted but passively cooperative manner. While he responds to the interviewer, he provides little information beyond superficial data. Tyrone seems more comfortable answering questions than initiating conversation. He presents an appearance of being poorly prepared for our session, reflected by his casual, almost shabby attire and his insistence that he is unaware of his cousin Sabrina's concerns about him. Tyrone appears to be oriented to his surroundings (time, place, and date) and denies hearing voices and seeing things that others do not.

Tyrone's affect during the interview, while seeming appropriate on the surface, has an underlying detached quality. Tyrone shows a greater interest in reading a magazine than in talking to the social worker. He denies any problems, giving the impression that he would not seek counseling on his own.

Tyrone is in good health and denies alcohol or drug use. The quality of family interaction seems limited; his father died ten years ago, and his mother remarried giving the impression she plays no part in Tyrone's current life. Tyrone's social context is constricted, and he has few environmental resources; that is, he lives alone and professes he does not want friends or family around. Working as a movie theater projectionist further limits any opportunity for developing social contacts.

Tyrone's biopsychosocial history reveals a pattern of being a "loner" from early childhood and being singled out for ridicule because of his small size while growing up. While he is the youngest of eight children, very little is known about his older siblings. His academic performance was not exceptional, and he did not complete high school. Being left alone seems to be a source of pleasure for Tyrone; he is single, does not date, lives alone, and works alone. Tyrone does not seem interested in job promotions, primarily because this would create added opportunities to interact with others, such as going to meetings or being with "all those people."

Tyrone White tends to turn inward, and he moves away from interpersonal connections with the outside world. This inner-directed reality does not exhibit the disordered pattern of thinking commonly associated with persons with schizophrenia. His responses in the interview reveal a constricted emotional range. What is seen is a man who is unsociable, distant or indifferent, and reclusive. Based on the characteristic way that Tyrone approaches interpersonal relationships, the practitioner can expect him to relate more like an observer rather than an active participant in the therapeutic relationship.

The medical model might accentuate the negatives in looking at Tyrone's behavior. The competency-based assessment pays attention to the associations between behaviors and the various positive external factors. Tyrone has worked steadily for the past seven years; he is self-sufficient; he pays his own rent; he receives routine raises; and he has been offered opportunities for job advancement.

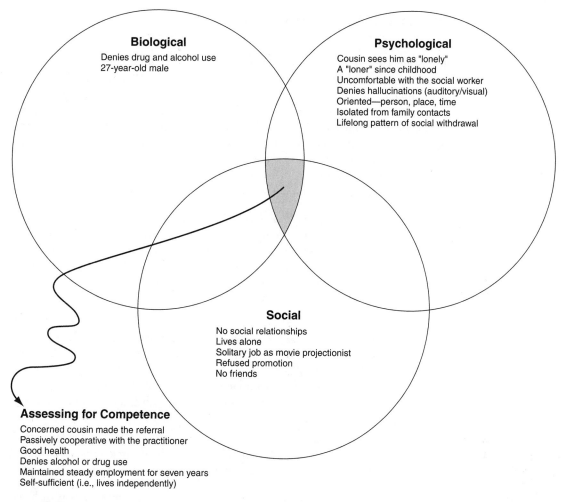

Biological
Denies drug and alcohol use
27-year-old male

Psychological
Cousin sees him as "lonely"
A "loner" since childhood
Uncomfortable with the social worker
Denies hallucinations (auditory/visual)
Oriented—person, place, time
Isolated from family contacts
Lifelong pattern of social withdrawal

Social
No social relationships
Lives alone
Solitary job as movie projectionist
Refused promotion
No friends

Assessing for Competence
Concerned cousin made the referral
Passively cooperative with the practitioner
Good health
Denies alcohol or drug use
Maintained steady employment for seven years
Self-sufficient (i.e., lives independently)

FIGURE **9-2**

SCHIZOID PERSONALITY DISORDER

The interactions of the biological, psychological, and social factors in Tyrone White's life.

Although Tyrone is socially isolated, his cousin Sabrina seems concerned enough to bring him to the clinic for help.

Tyrone's diagnosis at this point would be as follows:

Axis I	V71.09 (No diagnosis)	
Axis II	301.20 Schizoid Personality Disorder	
Axis III	None	
Axis IV	None	
Axis V	GAF =	65 (highest level past year)

SCHIZOTYPAL PERSONALITY DISORDER

Individuals with *schizotypal personality disorder* exhibit strikingly odd or strange mannerisms in addition to having a very active fantasy life. This may include "magical thinking," illusions, derealization, and ideas of reference in which everything everyone else does somehow relates back to them (Moore & Jefferson, 1996). Interpersonally, they, much like Tyrone White who was described in the previous vignette and diagnosed with a schizoid personality disorder, are described as loners. However, their solitary pursuits and social isolation may stem more from strained social anxiety that does not diminish with familiarity (Sperry, 1995).

Summarizing the major characteristics:

- *Extreme discomfort in social relationships*—The individual is extremely uncomfortable in close relationships, even when people are familiar to them. They are rarely able to form intimate relationships, and employment that requires extended social contact is generally not possible. When left alone, they may be able to perform simple tasks; however, the peculiarities of their thoughts often sidetrack them.

- *Restricted close relationships*—They often do not have close friends or confidants.

- *Odd appearance and thinking*—They have unusual perceptual experiences, namely, illusions sensing the presence of a "force" or person not actually there. Generally described as being unkempt, they also show unusual mannerisms or they may talk to themselves (without loosening of association). Their speech is characterized by vagueness, digressions, excessive abstractions, limited vocabulary, or an unusual pattern of words (Morrison, 1995).

- *Paranoid ideas*—They are very suspicious and believe others are talking about them. However, their affect is more likely to be characterized as anxious rather than hostile. They may perceive references to themselves in others' conversations.

Schizotypal personality disorder in the DSM evolved from attempts to clarify the boundary between schizophrenia and borderline personality disorder. Siever et al. (1991) suggest that this personality disorder is related to schizophrenia in a number of important ways. Individuals with schizotypal personality disorder experience subtle distortions of their environment similar to those experienced by individuals with schizophrenia; but the latter have the fully developed syndrome that includes hallucinations or delusions, and have lost contact with reality (Stoudemire, 1994). Under stress, individuals with schizotypal personality disorder may decompensate and display psychotic-like symptoms, but these are usually of brief duration. In severe instances, anhedonia and severe depression may also be present (Kaplan & Sadock, 1996).

The notion that there is a relationship between schizotypal personality disorder and schizophrenia arises in part from how people with these two disorders behave. For example, ideas of reference, illusions, and paranoid thinking are described as similar, and yet persons with schizotypal personality disorder have somewhat better interpersonal skills and are more connected to their social environment (Gabbard, 1995; Barlow & Durand, 1995). Ongoing research into these two disorders seems to support a genetic relationship (Dahl, 1993; Torgersen et al., 1993). Several theorists (Akhtar, 1987; Barlow & Durand, 1995) suggest there is oportunity for the person to be influenced by their environment.

From an early age, these individuals are unable to have long-lasting interpersonal relationships. This severely isolates them and reduces their capacity for maintaining connections with others (O'Brien et al., 1993). They often feel anxious with strangers and cannot banter or make small talk. They exhibit distortions in their thinking, eccentric perceptions, and "magical thinking." This makes the person appear unusual or odd to others. Often, these individuals manifest unusual perceptual experiences, such as feeling as if another person is in the room although they are alone. Their behavior is influenced by associated odd beliefs or by magical thinking inconsistent with cultural norms, including superstitions and belief in telepathy. Frequently, they believe they have special powers of thought and insight (Kaplan & Sadock, 1996).

Prevailing Pattern

Schizotypal personality disorder occurs in approximately 3 percent of the general population (Kaplan & Sadock, 1996). It is important for the practitioner to thoroughly explore the family history for evidence of schizophrenia, as there is a greater incidence found among first-degree biological relatives of people with schizophrenia (Kaplan et al., 1994; Stoudemire, 1994; Moore & Jefferson, 1996).

Differential Assessment

Oddities in behavior, thinking, perception, and communication (in addition to a strong family history of schizophrenia) distinguish those individuals with schizotypal personality disorders. In addition, these individuals exhibit two sets of qualities. First, they experience intense discomfort in interpersonal relationships and an impaired ability to form close relationships; and second, they often manifest cognitive or perceptual distortions, and eccentric behavior. In our earlier case illustration, Tyrone White was distant from others, but he is pictured more as a "loner." Unlike those individuals with schizophrenia (refer to Chapter 3), Tyrone has not lost total contact with reality. Ben Rogers, someone with a paranoid personality disorder, is characterized as hostile and suspicious, whereas Tyrone's affect is typified as anxious. As noted earlier, the schizotypal personality disorder can be distinguished from schizophrenia by the absence of psychosis. If psychotic symptoms are present, they are brief and fragmentary (Kaplan et al., 1994).

The following case describes a gentleman with schizotypal personality disorder.

The Case of Juan Enrique Martinez

His mother referred Juan Enrique Martinez, a 35-year-old single (never married) Mexican-American man, to our community mental health center's activities program. Mrs. Martinez seemed somewhat older than her stated age of 58 and looked really tired. She sounded worried as she told the social worker that her son "needs help making friends." The social worker asked for more details, and Mrs. Martinez added Juan has had a lifelong pattern of social isolation. She could not remember a time when her son had some "real" friends. He usually spends hours "doing nothing."

Mrs. Martinez said it all started when Juan lost interest "in just about everything" when he was about 13 years old. During that time, she took him to her parish priest, who said, "Juan will grow out of it; it's just a stage he's going through." She added, "Well, he never grew out of it, and he hasn't been able to keep a bunch of jobs including his last one as a postal worker." Apparently Juan did not show up for work on multiple occasions and could not deal with close contact working with the public. She stated, "I'm worried that Juan will lose his room in the boarding house because he now has no way to pay the rent, and he was picked up by the Metro Dade police. They charged him with disorderly conduct and said he was drinking. I know my son and he is not a drinker."

Mrs. Martinez added that Juan's appearance is becoming "more strange. He's been getting a lot of tattoos and now talks about wanting to get some body piercing done." She frowned, looked momentarily distracted, and then asked for the social worker's opinion about the health risks associated with body piercing. Mrs. Martinez admitted that her main concern bringing her to the mental health center was because Juan "is acting really weird." By that she means he believes he can sense "forces" around him; he is certain these forces are somehow against him, and he is highly suspicious about other people. These suspicious thoughts and paranoia worked against Juan in his dealings with the public in his last job; he also does not get along with those he knows well.

Mrs. Martinez sighed heavily and went on to say that it is harder and harder for her to communicate with her son. She added, "I worry that he will turn out to be just like my brother, Lorenzo, who was sent away to a mental hospital when he was 17. Everybody thought he was crazy. He used to hear voices and see things that no one else did. I remember during one visit that the doctor wanted me to convince Lorenzo to take his medicine. I asked, 'What for?' and the doctor looked at me kinda surprised and told me, 'I thought you knew!' Lorenzo is schizophrenic. I don't want that to happen to my little Juan."

During our first interview, Juan was distant and conveyed a high level of distrust. He described in intricate detail his somewhat uneventful everyday life. He told me that he really did not like people and did not want to join any group here at the center where he had to "talk to people." Juan then stood up, and with an almost forced air of bravado, walked out of the office saying, "If my mother wants to talk, she can join your group."

Assessment Summary

Juan's interpersonal pattern of relating shows that he is unable to form relationships or respond to others in a meaningful way. His sense of "forces" around him, suspiciousness, and paranoia contribute to keeping him socially isolated. The practitioner's conversation with Juan is difficult because of his odd communication style; for instance, he goes into intricate detail about his day, which, in reality, was uneventful. While his communication (and his appearance) can be characterized as "odd" and his perception of his social environment is subtly distorted, Juan does not show evidence of hallucinations or delusions characteristic of those with schizophrenia. Mrs. Martinez's concerns were clearly evident to the social worker, and seem to have increased over time; however, Juan is indifferent to his mother's worries.

Despite a close community, Juan is withdrawn from his social environment, and his recent job loss has further increased his isolation. In this case illustration, his

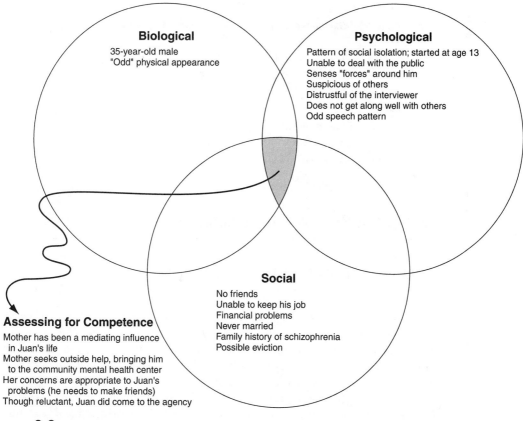

FIGURE 9-3

SCHIZOTYPAL PERSONALITY DISORDER

The interactions of the biological, psychological, and social factors in Juan Enrique Martinez's life.

isolation can be traced back to early adolescence. This is a time when peer influence is important, and yet it was during this period that Juan began to lose interest "in just about everything." His mother characterizes him as a socially isolated young man, and this pattern is evident throughout his life. Participation in the community mental health center's activities group might decrease Juan's social isolation, but his abrupt departure from the interview suggests this may be a frightening prospect for him. Mrs. Martinez points out that Juan tends to wander around "doing nothing." Juan's behaviors and appearance, while peculiar, are not provocative.

The involvement of "significant others" is important. As in Juan's situation, this is the vehicle within which he was brought to the mental health center. An examination of the biological, psychological, and social influences in his life (refer to Figure 9-3) shows that his mother has been a mediating influence in Juan's social environment. For example, she is the person in his social environment who brings him to the center for help with socialization, or to make friends. Though reluctant, Juan did come into the agency, and perhaps with time he would feel more comfortable participating in activities there.

According to the DSM multi-axial classification, Juan Enrique Martinez's diagnosis would be:

Axis I	303.00 Rule Out Alcohol Intoxication
Axis II	301.22 Schizotypal Personality Disorder
Axis III	None
Axis IV	Housing problems
	Financial problems
	Unemployment
Axis V	GAF = 60 (at intake)

CLUSTER B PERSONALITY DISORDERS

NARCISSISTIC PERSONALITY DISORDER

A heightened sense of self-importance and unrealistic notions of inflated self-worth characterize the individual with *narcissistic personality disorder*. This often disguises an underlying fragile sense of self-worth. As the name infers, individuals with this personality disorder tend to be self-absorbed, have a heightened sense of self-importance, and exhibit marked grandiosity. They see themselves as unique and special, deserving extraordinary treatment. Their sense of entitlement is striking. Others in their social environment might describe them as arrogant and boastful.

The major characteristics include:

- *Feelings of grandiosity*—These individuals not only feel superior to others, but they also believe they are unique and special. They are convinced they are entitled to "special handling" just because of who they are. Although they may envy others, their belief is that others envy them more. Their accomplishments, beauty, and talents are often self-exaggerated. They easily criticize others, but have a very difficult time receiving criticism.

- *Constant desire or need for admiration*—The person invariably seeks out adulation, admiration, and compliments from others. They are overly sensitive to what others think about them.

- *Lack of empathy for others*—The individual has good social skills, especially when it comes to beginning relationships with others. They can be very charming in securing others' admiration. Because they are so focused on themselves, they often are incapable of empathizing with others; relationships tend to wear very thin over time. As ultra-sensitive as they are about their own feelings, they have poor insight regarding the emotional needs of others, often feigning empathy when none exists.

- *"Fantasy world" preoccupation*—These persons have an active fantasy life, and maintain that they experience the best of everything, even when this is not true; for example, they might own a car just short of making it to the junk yard and their explanation is that their car is really a classic.

- *Possess overly high expectations*—If the person does not attain the unrealistic goals they have set for themselves, they will react with a strong sense of failure that brings about feelings of shame and worthlessness.

Most of us know people who think very highly of themselves, perhaps even a little beyond their actual abilities. However, individuals with narcissistic personality disorder possess this tendency to extremes. They exhibit an exaggerated sense of self-importance and a tremendous preoccupation for receiving attention from others (Cooper & Ronningstam, 1992). They have a lifelong pattern of needing admiration, and believe they are unique and special. The person considers their accomplishments to be greater than they are in reality. Essential features include "a pervasive pattern of grandiosity (in fantasy or behavior), a need for admiration, and a lack of empathy" (APA, 1994, p. 661). They tend to have a very rich fantasy "inner life" (Wilson et al., 1996), while masterminding their next venture bringing them fame and fortune. Interpersonal exploitation is very common (Akhtar, 1989). Although not considered to be a part of the DSM criteria, Cooper and Ronningstam (1992) suggest that underneath this individual's grandiosity and excessive need for admiration is a very vulnerable person with a fragile sense of self-esteem.

Prevailing Pattern

This personality disorder tends to be somewhat uncommon, and it occurs in less than 1 percent of the general population. Because of the individual's flair for being the center of attention, the practitioner will easily remember them. Information about this disorder's etiology is somewhat limited (Morrison, 1995; Moore & Jefferson, 1996), but it appears more in males than in females (Kaplan et al., 1994). The disorder has a tendency to be chronic and is difficult to treat because the individual must consistently struggle with looking at the impact of their behavior or its interplay with their life experiences. The person is prone to bouts of depression, handles the aging process poorly, and is more vulnerable to midlife crises than others.

The following case discussion illustrates the major features of someone with a narcissistic personality disorder.

The Case of Lawrence Shull

"Hello, is this Dr. Susan Gray?" a voice asked on the telephone.

"Why, yes," I replied. "Can I help you?"

"Well, you don't know me, but my name is Lawrence Shull and I've just moved to the South Florida area from New York."

"And so how did you hear about me Mr. Shull?" I asked.

Mr. Shull replied, "Well, first I called the Dade County Mental Health Association, then I checked with the National Association of Social Workers, then I carefully researched *Who's Who of Social Work Digest*, and finally I asked several local leaders about who was 'the best social worker' in town. That's how I got your name."

He added, "I heard you're the top person to see, and I'd like to make an appointment."

I replied, "Of course, I'll be happy to make an appointment with you. How is Thursday, the 4th, at 3:00 P.M.?"

"Perfect," Mr. Shull replied.

Our session took place three days later. Mr. Shull presented himself as a very refined looking gentleman. He was extremely well groomed, and what I would consider a "natty dresser." Although it was a typically warm tropical day, he wore a brown suit, matching tie, and expensive looking dress shoes. He confessed to me that he was 55 years old but added, with a wink, "I had a little surgical help from the 'top doc' in Manhattan. Everybody thinks I look ten years younger." He is six feet tall, 200 pounds, and looks as if he works out and takes extremely good care of himself. His nails were buffed and manicured and he had not a hair out of place. Though new to the South Florida area, he sported a bronze, suntanned appearance looking as if he spent a lot of time at the beach.

I asked Mr. Shull, "What brings you here?" He responded saying, "Please call me Lawrence, and by the way, may I call you Susan?" (I nodded yes.) "Well Susan, dear, it's quite a long and involved story, but the bottom line is I'm quite miffed at having to relocate because of my job. You see, I'm an underwriter for a very well known national tire chain. The problems all started when one of the managers there got jealous of my productivity level. You see, I sold lots of tires, shock absorbers, and brakes ... actually I sold more than all the other service writers put together." He was silent for a moment, and I prompted him to continue.

"The store manager is such a jerk! No, he's more than a jerk! He's a nitwit. He doesn't know how to run a business. I've been on the job for three months and I already know more than he does. I can't believe he disapproved of my selling style. Me! I was the best they ever had. He told me that I was unfair to the rest of the guys because I made deals for prices the store wouldn't support and customers had problems with my enthusiasm for selling." Mr. Shull continued, "Can you believe that! I was too enthusiastic?" (shaking his head slowly from side to side). "They are just envious of my success." Lawrence continued, "So it was suggested I relocate to South Florida. I took a big salary hit, and got a job demotion. Get this, I'm now an [chuckling] assistant service writer." He added, "You know Susan, they'll be sorry when I end up being the CEO and owning the damn company. They can't stop me!"

Upon further discussion, Mr. Shull stated that he abruptly broke up with his girl-friend of six months. "She was very dependent on me and I don't need that extra bag-gage to carry around. I need someone who is my intellectual equal, someone who complements me." Lawrence stated that he's "still looking for the right woman. The ones I've met just don't meet my needs." He continues, "You know Susan, I just real-ized all I've been talking about is me, me, me, and me. Why don't you tell me what you think about me and my problems? Do you think you can see me five times a week?"

When our session was over, we scheduled another appointment for the fol-lowing week.

Assessment Summary

Antisocial, histrionic, and borderline personality disorders often coexist with the narcissistic personality disorder, thus complicating the process of assessment. Lawrence Shull possesses less anxiety and his life is less chaotic than persons with borderline personality characteristics. Those with antisocial personality are fre-quently seen as arrogant and almost always evidence persistent exploitation of oth-ers; however, the intent of exploitation is for financial power or material gain (Kernberg, 1989; Meloy, 1992). In addition, they tend to relate a long history of impulsive behavior, associated alcohol and other substance abuse (Meloy, 1995; Cacciola et al., 1995), and frequent problems with law enforcement. For Lawrence, financial gain is not considered a key issue. Instead, he is forced to relocate and take a cut in pay while maintaining the idea of being the company's next CEO. His sense of personal glory and entitlement is the central focus of his life. Persons who have a histrionic personality disorder are also seen as self-absorbed and anxious to be the center of attention (Horowitz, 1995), but they are usually more willing to connect with others. This contrasts with Lawrence, who abruptly ended a six-month rela-tionship with his girlfriend (Moore & Jefferson, 1996). To further complicate assess-ment, persons with histrionic personality disorders show qualities of exhibitionism and interpersonal manipulativeness very similar to those associated with narcissis-tic personalities (Horowitz, 1995).

Those with an obsessive-compulsive personality disorder also complicate the assessment process. Here, too, the practitioner sees evidence of an air of superior-ity and marked condescension toward others. However, this smugness or sense of superiority hides a very vulnerable, fragile person. Individuals with a narcissistic personality disorder do not use smugness but rather gravitate toward malicious (pas-sive-aggressive) counterattacks in response to any criticism (real or perceived) that is directed toward them. Lawrence Shull, for instance, undercuts the prices of his coworkers at the tire company in order to succeed and then he perceives his boss as envious of his success.

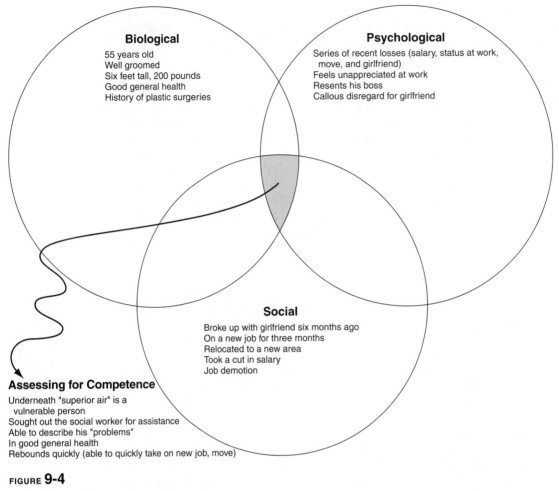

Biological

55 years old
Well groomed
Six feet tall, 200 pounds
Good general health
History of plastic surgeries

Psychological

Series of recent losses (salary, status at work,
   move, and girlfriend)
Feels unappreciated at work
Resents his boss
Callous disregard for girlfriend

Social

Broke up with girlfriend six months ago
On a new job for three months
Relocated to a new area
Took a cut in salary
Job demotion

Assessing for Competence

Underneath "superior air" is a
   vulnerable person
Sought out the social worker for assistance
Able to describe his "problems"
In good general health
Rebounds quickly (able to quickly take on new job, move)

FIGURE **9-4**

NARCISSISTIC PERSONALITY DISORDER

The interactions of the biological, psychological, and social factors in Lawrence Shull's life.

Understanding the various aspects of Lawrence's functioning helps to provide a more complete clinical picture and one that identifies his competencies that may be built upon. Within this framework, the difficulties that Lawrence brings to the interview are considered to be related to how he approaches problem solving. He is articulate in describing his "problems" and sought out the social worker on his own. Additionally, he is quite resilient in being able to "bounce back" regarding his job demotion.

Mr. Shull's diagnosis reads as follows:

> Axis I   V71.09 (No diagnosis)
>
> Axis II   301.81 Narcissistic Personality Disorder
>
> Axis III   None   *(continued)*

Axis IV   Employment problems
Axis V   GAF = 80 (at intake)

Histrionic Personality Disorder

An individual with histrionic personality disorder is not to be confused with those persons whose behavior can be characterized as being "hysterical"; the person with a histrionic personality has far greater problems relating to others. The individual with *histrionic personality disorder* is often described as colorful, dramatic, extroverted, excitable, and emotional. Underneath this flamboyant presentation is a deep-seated inability to maintain strong, reciprocal, and long-lasting friendships. These individuals attempt to acquire attention in inexplicable and unusual ways. A basic characteristic is a pattern of extreme attention seeking and highly expressive emotions. They tend to incessantly involve others in their life drama while keeping themselves the center of attention (Moore & Jefferson, 1996). Others frequently describe them as superficial, disingenuous, and unconvincing. While all of these characteristics are not found in all persons with histrionic personality disorder, they do serve as a means for assembling an initial basis for making an assessment.

The major characteristics include:

- *Excessive emotionality*—These individuals often have rapid shifts of emotion that may seem artificial. They can also be quite manipulative, using strong emotional outbursts to get their own way.

- *Attention seeking behavior*—They intensely crave attention from others, and feel uncomfortable when not the center of attention. These persons dress in extravagant, lavish, and provocative styles and use makeup, hairstyles, or clothes to gain further attention.

- *Easily influenced and susceptible*—Wilson et al. (1996) suggest these individuals are very impressionistic, generally become enthusiastic about the latest fad, and base their convictions predicated on very little evidence.

- *Self-centered/self-absorbed*—They tend to be unusually vain and self-absorbed. Relationships with others are apt to be superficial, with speech and emotional expression lacking genuine feeling or concern.

- *Concerns with "presentation"*—The individual's "personality" may change depending on circumstances as they attempt to engage whoever is present.

These individuals have a long-standing pattern of excessive emotionality and attention seeking, which seeps into most areas of their lives. They are often described as being provocative and sexually seductive. They are always overly concerned with their physical attractiveness. Often the need for approval can be so excessive that they will call attention to themselves through their speech, dress, behavior, and extreme emotions (Morrison, 1995). Women tend to dress and act seductively, whereas men tend to act "tough" or "macho." Relationships are inclined to be stormy and short-lived, as the person becomes easily bored with others; conversely, others may become fed up with their behaviors and leave. These individuals rarely maintain stable, enduring, and meaningful relationships. They are often described as shallow, lacking in substance, and without the ability to have reciprocal meaningful relationships with others.

Prevailing Pattern

This is a lifelong pattern of behavior, although symptoms generally tend to be modulated by the aging process. It remains unclear whether these persons just tend to burn out (Moore & Jefferson, 1996) due to the amount of energy it takes to maintain their character throughout the years. "Although this disorder tends to run in families, the basis for this aggregation is not known" (Moore & Jefferson, 1996, p. 277). These persons may get into trouble with the law, abuse substances, and act promiscuously (Kaplan et al., 1994).

Differential Assessment

Making the distinction between histrionic and borderline personality disorders is admittedly difficult. While both may be assessed for the same individual, the two disorders should be noted separately (Kaplan et al., 1994; McGlashan, 1993). Histrionic traits do occur in a number of other personality disorders; however, in each case there are certain specific differential points that help clarify making a correct assessment (First et al., 1995). They are:

- Individuals with a narcissistic personality may be quite self-aggrandizing, constantly searching for praise, and needing to be the center of attention but they usually lack the intense emotion seen in histrionic individuals.
- Individuals with borderline personality may be characterized as flamboyant and self-destructive; however, they have an enduring sense of emptiness and loneliness in contrast to histrionic individuals, who are seen as shallow and lacking substance.
- Those with antisocial personality disorder tend to be highly impulsive; however, they do not become dependent or deeply attached to others, as does the histrionic person.

The following case illustration provides an example of someone with a histrionic personality disorder.

The Case of Ms. Tamika Brown

During the course of a routine physical examination, Tamika Brown, a 43-year-old African-American single parent, suddenly started crying and blurted out to her doctor that she was thinking about committing suicide. She said she had been "playing with a razor and making marks on my arms." Tamika stated that she used to do this when she was a teenager to gain her mother's attention. The physician immediately made an emergency referral to a nearby county rehab center.

The social worker noted Ms. Brown's appearance as soon as she walked in. She was quite tall, almost six feet, and had what could be considered a naturally graceful style, but the first thing was Ms. Brown's unusual hair. It was braided but had what looked like "spikes" accentuating her forehead and was partially shaved in the back. Her clothes could be characterized as "dramatic"; everything was the color black, accented with animal prints, and extremely tight fitting. She wore about a dozen gold bracelets on each arm and a large, heavy gold chain around her neck. The first three or four buttons of her shirt were left unbuttoned revealing her bra (also black) and showing extensive cleavage. Her overall appearance could best be described as "distracting." When the social worker asked why she had been referred for an evaluation, Ms. Brown replied (laughingly), "I know something about psychotherapy and hoped to find a special therapist who understands me and will really help me. I promise to be your most interesting patient. You know, [chuckling] been there, done that?"

During the interview, Tamika described a "tortured childhood" that included an abusive alcoholic father, an absent mother, and being picked on by other children for being a "fat butt." When she became an adolescent she lost weight and began a "dedicated workout" regimen. Boys began to be attracted to her, but she completely ignored them. Instead, Tamika continued to exercise and study hard in school so she could "get out" of the neighborhood and as far away as possible from her family. In her early 20s, she had breast implants, lip augmentation, and surgical tightening of the buttock muscles to further accentuate her figure.

Tamika confided that she wants to be a model. Though currently working, she was somewhat vague and mysterious about her job. She showed this interviewer her professional photo portfolio including several seductive poses in bikini bathing suits, lingerie, and semi–nude shots. She belongs to a gym where "some very famous movie and television stars work out with me" and stated that it is "just a matter of time until I get discovered." She told the interviewer that "I have a much better body than some of those 'cows' and can't believe they still haven't asked me to work out with them. Well, it's really because they are jealous and can't compete with me." Tamika makes Herculean efforts to be seen around the "hot spots" in town. She dines in only the trendiest South Beach restaurants, making a dramatic entrance in a super-deluxe stretch limousine. She loves to wear the most revealing clothes she can find and says, "If 'ya got, flaunt it!" The South Beach location is important to her, because this is an area known for attracting celebrities. Tamika went on to say that she routinely sends photographs of herself chronicling the nights spent doing the town "big time" to local newspapers.

When asked about supports and relationships in her life, Tamika recounted multiple relationships that were short-lived and unsatisfying to her. She concluded, "I don't have a boyfriend right now. Geoffrey Halesander, the last one, was so shallow, and besides he didn't meet any of my needs. I like to be taken out and pampered, but all he wanted to do was sit around the house and watch television. How boring!" While the dialogue ends here, the worker's primary objective will be to assess the potential of Ms. Brown's suicidal ideation.

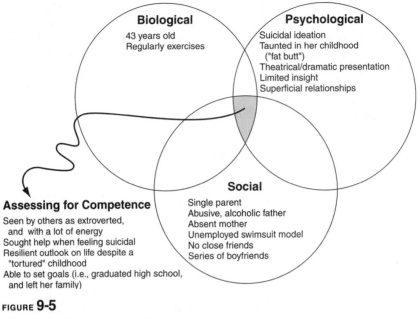

Biological
43 years old
Regularly exercises

Psychological
Suicidal ideation
Taunted in her childhood
 ("fat butt")
Theatrical/dramatic presentation
Limited insight
Superficial relationships

Assessing for Competence
Seen by others as extroverted,
 and with a lot of energy
Sought help when feeling suicidal
Resilient outlook on life despite a
 "tortured" childhood
Able to set goals (i.e., graduated high school,
 and left her family)

Social
Single parent
Abusive, alcoholic father
Absent mother
Unemployed swimsuit model
No close friends
Series of boyfriends

FIGURE **9-5**

HISTRIONIC PERSONALITY DISORDER

The interactions of the biological, psychological, and social factors in Tamika Brown's life.

Assessment Summary

What distinguishes people with histrionic personality disorder is their attention-seeking behaviors. Tamika reflects this characteristic way of relating to her social environment by being overly dramatic in her emotional displays, her attempts to be the center of attention, and her inability to be ignored. She is what could be considered self-centered, and appears unable to develop any degree of intimacy. Tamika has no insight about what went wrong with Geoffrey Halesander, her former boyfriend. In actuality, her ability to connect in a meaningful way had always been short-lived. As a consequence of her very strong need to be the center of attention, Tamika has few enduring friendships.

Tamika initially presented herself to the practitioner as an engaging, yet highly emotional woman. Upon closer examination, it became apparent that there was a shallowness of emotions and an inability to sustain meaningful relationships. When the practitioner began the interview, Tamika connected readily and seemed eager to please with her responses. However, Tamika was not in touch with her real feelings and was very vague about the details of her suicide attempt.

Using the competency-based model enables the practitioner to work collaboratively with Tamika in order to mobilize her strengths and coping abilities, locate resources, and begin to explore opportunities within her environment that may help pave the way for this client to achieve success. Despite a "tortured" childhood with an abusive, alcoholic father, she maintains a resilient outlook on life and has set some realistic future goals for herself. Tamika reports that she does not abuse or use drugs or alcohol.

According to the DSM multi-axial classification system, Tamika's diagnosis is as follows:

Axis I	V71.09 (No diagnosis)
Axis II	301.50 Histrionic Personality Disorder
Axis III	None
Axis IV	None
Axis V	GAF = 50 (at initial appointment)

ANTISOCIAL PERSONALITY DISORDER

The person with *antisocial personality disorder* is characterized by continual aso-cial or criminal acts, but this is not synonymous with criminality. These behaviors are initially described in childhood and intensify during adolescence. There tends to be a long and involved history of lying, theft, substance abuse, illegal activities, rejection of social norms, and lack of remorse for any hurtful actions directed toward others. "In the distant past, this disorder was known as 'moral insanity' a name that hints at the fundamental aspect of this disorder" (Moore & Jefferson, 1996, p. 269).

Because antisocial personality disorder results in a variety of problems with law enforcement, the legal system, and within families, it has been the subject of more clinical interest and research than any other personality disorder (Wilson et al., 1996). The essential features include a pervasive pattern of disregard for and violation of the rights of others occurring since age 15, with evidence of conduct disorder before age 15 (APA, 1994, 2000). As youngsters, they often acquire a reputation in the neighborhood for being a bully toward younger children and exhibiting cruelty toward animals. Sexual activity usually begins early, and some-times their "partner" is not a willing participant (Eppright et al., 1991). Overall, these youngsters appear out of control, and most efforts to discipline them have little or no lasting effect. Nothing seems to have an impact or the ability to touch them. They remain unmoved by any kindness shown, steal and destroy property for the pleasure of it (Adler et al., 1994), and habitually lie even when telling the truth is just as convenient. Although many of these individuals have a childhood marked by incorrigibility, school problems, or running away from home, "fewer than half the children with such a background eventually develop the full adult syndrome" (Morrison, 1995, p. 475). Therefore it is important to reserve this assessment for individuals who are over the age of 18 who have a history of symp-toms of conduct disorder before the age of 15 (Vankammen et al., 1991; Meloy, 1995; APA, 1994, 2000).

Major characteristics include:

- *Lack of remorse or empathy*—The person has no feelings or remorse for those they harm (Hare, 1991). They rationalize reasons for hurting or taking advan-tage of people (for example, "they should have known better than to trust me") and often blame their victim for making them act in a harmful manner because they consider themselves smart enough to "get away with it."

- *Defiance*—They do not feel they should obey societal norms or laws, but rather make their own rules.

- *Self-absorbed*—They are most often concerned with their own needs, wants, and desires, and do not care who gets in the way of getting what they want (Sperry, 1995).

- *Irresponsible*—They have problems fulfilling commitments, such as family, employment, or financial obligations. Their marriages tend to be troubled, violent, and short-lived. Being faithful in a relationship whether there is a marriage or not is a matter of convenience, and children are often viewed as being a burden.

- *Deceitful*—Being truthful is considered a matter of convenience; if a lie proves more useful, then that is what will be used. They use different aliases, changing names, occupations, and locations especially if they are running from the law. They are excellent at running confidence schemes for their own profit, pleasure, or power (Sutker et al., 1993).

- *Irritable and aggressive*—Reckless, violent, and cruel behavior is common (Stone, 1994). They are irritable with those in authority but seem comfortable when using aggression against others. Frequently they are involved in physical assault and confrontations; for example, there is a high incidence of reported domestic violence and child abuse (Robins et al., 1991), showing little or no concern for the safety of themselves or others.

A veneer of charm and a smooth and ingratiating seductiveness may mask their interest in exclusively meeting their own needs (Stoudemire, 1994). They often present themselves as fascinating, disarming, beguiling, and the ultimate con artist. They are also described as undependable, impetuous, and dishonest. They do things others find offensive, for example, stealing from family members or friends. Dr. Robert Hare (1993) so eloquently describes these individuals in his book *Without conscience: The disturbing world of the psychopaths among us*:

> Social predators who charm, manipulate, and ruthlessly plow their way through life, leaving a broad trail of broken hearts, shattered expectations, and empty wallets. Completely lacking in conscience and in feelings for others, they selfishly take what they want and do as they please, violating social norms and expectations without the slightest sense of guilt or regret. (p. xi)

They are often described as having a long history of being a rebellious problem child, and during their adolescent years continue a pattern of activities harmful to, and violating the rights of, others (Austrian, 1995; Kaplan & Sadock, 1996; APA, 1994, 2000). Many come to the practitioner's attention through a mandate of the court system. They generally recount extensive histories filled with arrests for fraud, theft, embezzlement, alcohol (DUIs) and drug use, and physical violence, and disregard for alimony and/or child support payments (Cacciola et al., 1995; Monahan & Steadman, 1994). Although most tend to have poor employment records, many do display a high degree of success in the business or corporate world. It is a mistake to assume that they reside in a poor neighborhood, ride a motorcycle, and wear torn T-shirts.

Prevailing Pattern

According to Kaplan et al. (1994), the prognosis for antisocial personality disorder is variable at best. They are at increased risk for substance abuse, alcoholism, vagrancy, suicide, criminal activity, repeated incarceration, and dying a violent death (Scully, 1996; Shader, 1994). Their antisocial disposition, tendencies, and attitudes tend to be chronic and lifelong; however, this pattern can shift over time. As individuals age (30+), the majority of them may "burn out," and gradually the frequency of their antisocial acts decrease (Kaplan et al., 1994; Moore & Jefferson, 1996). Often their antisocial behaviors are replaced with somatic behaviors, for example, hypochondriasis (Moore & Jefferson, 1996). "This is a serious disorder, with no known effective treatment. It is therefore a diagnosis of last resort" (Morrison, 1995, p. 475). Adds Stoudemire (1994), "In the psychiatric setting, antisocial personality disorder is viewed as one of the most difficult personalities to treat" (p. 187).

The following case discussion represents someone with behaviors considered "typical" of the antisocial personality disorder.

The Case of Luke Rossey

"I want to divorce my brother Luke," said Sara Rossey, weeping. "Isn't there anything I can do? Legal aid? The court system?" When this worker prompted her to continue, Sara related, "Luke is 23 years old and works as a cable installer, at least this week that is. He's had at least 20 different jobs, but he can't keep any of them. It's not that he's stupid or anything. In fact, when he was in school they tested his I.Q. and it was somewhere up in the 160s! Anyway, what he did last week was the last straw for me and my family, no matter how smart he is," she recounted.

"What happened?" asked the practitioner.

Sara continued, "He was caught threatening an elderly woman at knifepoint at a neighborhood ATM!"

"Tell me a bit more about Luke," I encouraged.

"Well, he was small as a kid, and all the other kids used to pick on him until one day they found out he killed two of their dogs and drowned a kitten. After that he got a reputation of being a 'bad boy.' He was left alone after that. Well, now that I think about it, I guess that's when he first started to be mean … I mean really mean. He would pick out some little kid and beat him up real bad. Luke was suspended lots of times from school. He also would steal from classmates, threaten teachers, and damage school property. Oh, and he was truant a lot of times, too. I mean weeks at at time he didn't go to school!"

She continued, "My poor mother really had a hard time with him. In her heart, I really think she had a hard time believing Luke could be so mean. Our dad died of alcohol and drug use when Luke was six years old. Mom raised the two of us by herself. She just couldn't control him. He joined a gang when he was almost 13 and was sent to juvenile hall for assault and battery of a police officer who was just doing his job breaking up a fight Luke was in the middle of. I think it was some kind of gang initiation rite. Luke got some shrink who told the judge that Luke was a victim of conduct disorder or something like that. They just slapped his wrists, and sent him to some country club youth ranch where he got time off for good behavior. I don't know what they meant by good behavior. As soon as he got out, he went right back to his old ways of boozing it up nonstop and using every drug he could get his hands on. I learned a whole new language. Have you ever heard the word 'shrooms' before?"

Sara continued, "When Luke turned 16, he was sent to the state youth program for nine months, because as soon as he got out of the 'country club' he was right back out on the streets causing even more trouble. He was busted selling drugs to an undercover cop. After he was released, Luke was sent to some kind of drug 'rehab' program. Some rehabilitation! That's where I think he learned more bad things he could do to people. He would relapse and then was just sent away again. My mom didn't want him to live at home anymore. She felt like a prisoner in her own home. Mom had to put a lock on every door, because if she didn't Luke would steal everything that wasn't nailed down. When Luke was a kid he hocked mom's heirloom wedding ring for ten bucks, and our dad's pocket watch for a bottle of booze. He doesn't care about anyone but himself. That's why I want to divorce him."

I replied, "It sounds as if things have been pretty rough for you and your family."

"You don't know the half of it," she sighed. "When Luke was 19, he joined the Army, and three months later he was court-martialed and thrown out on his ear. He beat up a captain who caught him selling drugs in the barracks. Luke came home after that. He wasn't home more than two weeks when his old girlfriend sued him for support of her baby. She named him as the father, but Luke wouldn't go for genetic testing, and denied the baby was his. I think he used to beat her up, too. Luke told me, 'Alyssa is a stupid bitch who wants me to support someone else's brat.' Can you believe that?"

Sara was asked if she ever saw evidence of psychotic behavior. She said, "No, he's only a mean son-of-a-...."

Assessment Summary

The roots of Luke's problems are recognized in his early childhood behavior that includes hurting animals, truancy from school, and stealing things from his parents while feeling no remorse. Luke's sister presented a history of his rebellious, problematic childhood and adolescence. The most common problems associated with antisocial personality disorder are substance abuse and dependence (First et al., 1995), acute anxiety states, delusional disorders, and/or factitious disorders (Morrison, 1995; Sperry, 1995). In Luke's situation, there is evidence of problems with substance abuse. The antisocial personality disorder should not be diagnosed if these behaviors occur exclusively during the active phase of schizophrenia or a manic episode (First et al., 1995).

"A criminal record, no matter how long, does not of itself qualify a person for a diagnosis of antisocial personality disorder" (Moore & Jefferson, 1996, p. 271). There

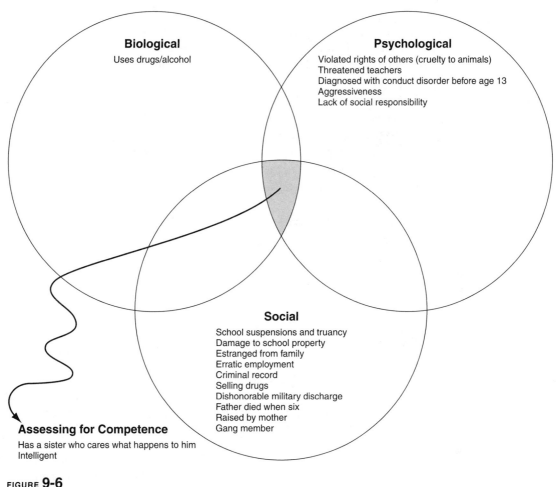

Biological
Uses drugs/alcohol

Psychological
Violated rights of others (cruelty to animals)
Threatened teachers
Diagnosed with conduct disorder before age 13
Aggressiveness
Lack of social responsibility

Social
School suspensions and truancy
Damage to school property
Estranged from family
Erratic employment
Criminal record
Selling drugs
Dishonorable military discharge
Father died when six
Raised by mother
Gang member

Assessing for Competence
Has a sister who cares what happens to him
Intelligent

FIGURE **9-6**

ANTISOCIAL PERSONALITY DISORDER

The interactions of the biological, psychological, and social factors in Luke Rossey's life.

is a difference between persons diagnosed with adult antisocial behavior and those with antisocial personality disorder; that is, the former manifest activities of a career criminal and these activities *fail to* pervade all aspects of their lives. Those with antisocial personality disorder manifest a sense of pervasive egocentricity (Moore & Jefferson, 1996), selfishness, reckless exploitation, lack of remorse, and failure to conform to social norms. Luke might come for counseling at the demand of others, such as an employer, the court system, or a spouse; it is very unlikely that he will seek out intervention on his own behalf or follow through with appropriate treatment.

Clearly, it would be easy to dislike Luke. He would be a very difficult client to work with, his behaviors are quite complex, and he is likely not to have a great deal of insight into his problems. Additionally, Luke is not motivated to come in and he does not have a problem with his behavior. As far as he is concerned, everyone else is the problem. However, the competency-based assessment has a preference for observation and systematic exploration rather than unsupported feelings. This requires the practitioner to be objective, and ultimately conclusions about how behavior is influenced can be reached more objectively.

Luke's diagnosis is:

Axis I	305.00 Alcohol Abuse
	304.30 Cannabis Dependence
	304.20 Cocaine Dependence
Axis II	301.7 Antisocial Personality Disorder
Axis III	None
Axis IV	Criminal record
	Estranged from family
	Unemployed
Axis V	GAF = deferred

BORDERLINE PERSONALITY DISORDER

An unstable mood, extremely poor relationships with others, and low self-image alternating between extremes of idealization and devaluation commonly referred to as "splitting" characterize the person with a borderline personality disorder. "In psychiatric hospital settings, the term 'borderline' was originally used to describe a kind of in-between state, a condition sharing features—borders—with both neurosis and psychosis" (Layton, 1995, p. 36). The term *borderline personality disorder* was not widely researched until it appeared in the DSM-III in 1980, and since then it has been too frequently used (Gunderson et al., 1991), inaccurately, to describe any observed form of personality disorder. "Prior to its addition to the DSM-III borderline individuals often were diagnosed in the DSM-II category of schizophrenia, latent type" (Sperry, 1995, p. 53). It was also subjected to a wide range of definitions and continues to be one of the most controversial personality disorder diagnoses (Gunderson & Links, 1995).

Although the disorder has been well described in the professional literature (Barlow & Durand, 1995; Dahl, 1993; First et al., 1995; Kaplan & Sadock, 1996; Stoudemire, 1994; Moore & Jefferson, 1996; APA, 1994, 2000), there is no consensus concerning its etiology or even the meaning of its notable features. There is a confusing hodgepodge of hypotheses suggesting the borderline is trying to conceal their *rage* directed toward the mother figure; is manifesting *depression* over loss of their mother; or spending their life energy ambivalently pursuing, seeking, and rejecting relationships resembling the original mother-child bond. Others suggest that this disorder results from a lack of "fit" between the mother and their infant (Layton, 1995). There is agreement that this disorder is characterized by a history of ambivalence, very unstable and intense relationships and moods, erratic and often self-destructive behaviors, feelings of boredom, poor self-esteem, poor impulse control, and a fear of abandonment (Stevenson & Meares, 1992; Moore & Jefferson, 1996; Sperry, 1995, Wilson et al., 1996; APA, 1994, 2000). Individuals may also have short-lived psychotic episodes (noted as micropsychotic episodes) when under severe stress, rather than a psychotic break. These symptoms are almost always transient and fleeting (Kaplan et al., 1994).

The major characteristics include:

- *Poor interpersonal relationships*—The person's primary fear is of being abandoned and left alone (real or imagined). They make heroic efforts searching for companionship yet at the same time struggle against being engulfed in a relationship.
- *Unstable self-image*—The person's life has been marked by uncertainty in major life issues, for example, occupation, education, values, and relationships with others.
- *Unstable emotions*—The individual's emotional state frequently fluctuates between extremes, dramatically going from euphoric mood to intense anger and rage in a matter of moments.
- *Marked impulsivity*—Reckless and self-destructive behaviors are important to note.

Prevailing Pattern

Assessing for a borderline personality disorder can usually be made by early adulthood when the individual has exhibited a pervasive pattern of unstable interpersonal relationships; frantic efforts to avoid real or imagined abandonment; alternating between extremes of idealization and devaluation; identity disturbance; recurrent suicidal behavior, gestures, or threats; chronic feelings of emptiness; inappropriate and intense anger or difficulty coping; and impulsivity in at least two areas, for example, spending money, sexual encounters, and substance abuse (APA, 1994, 2000; Sabo et al., 1995). The behaviors that make up this disorder are fairly stable and do not change very much over time. Although this is considered a chronic disorder, most individuals experience a lessening of symptoms as they reach their middle years (Moore & Jefferson, 1996; Rosowsky & Gurrian, 1992). Approximately 1 to 2 percent of the general population may qualify for the designation of borderline personality disorder (Kaplan et al., 1994; Moore & Jefferson, 1996; Morrison, 1995). It is applied to a far greater proportion of clients who seek out mental health care (Stone, 1994). Layton (1995) states:

> In the minds of many therapists, the borderline diagnosis has come to be a code word for trouble. The diagnosis signals a kind of impossible case—long, grueling work with the client often challenging the therapists equanimity over and over, withdrawing in a sulk or attacking in a rage, creating melodramatic scenes, threatening suicide, demanding more and more of the therapist's love and time, while the shaken therapist feels used, abused and manipulated, thinking he or she is often making no difference at all. (p. 36)

The borderline personality is characterized by gross impairment in behavior, cognitive and emotional styles, and interpersonal relationships:

- *Behavior*—These individuals perform physically self-damaging acts, such as suicidal gestures, self-mutilation, or inciting fights.
- *Cognitive style*—They experience their world and relate to others in terms of "black and white." The individual is often described as inflexible and impulsive (Sperry, 1995). Their inflexibility and impulsivity are characteristic of "splitting" or the inability to integrate contradictory qualities. The person tends to view others as "all good" or "all bad." The defense mechanism of projective identification is also associated with these individuals. By externalizing inner, unacceptable aspects of themselves, they may engage in relationships with others where the latter conforms to these perceptions. In this way, the person with a borderline personality disorder relates to others based on these externalized perceptions rather than endure what would otherwise be very painful self-castigation.
- *Emotional style*—The person's mood is characterized by *marked* shifts ranging from normal (euthymic), dysphoric, anger or intense rage. At the other extreme are feelings of emptiness, boredom, or experiencing a deep void.
- *Interpersonal*—They develop relationships rather quickly and intensely, while their social adaptiveness remains superficial (Sperry, 1995). The person is extraordinarily intolerant of being left alone and goes to great lengths seeking out the company of others, for example, making late night telephone calls to people they barely know or having indiscriminate multiple sexual affairs.

Differential Assessment

Clinical attention should be drawn to the possible coexistence of a mood, substance abuse, or eating disorder (Skodal & Oldham, 1991). Borderline personality disorder may be the "most over diagnosed condition in DSM" (Morrison, 1995, p. 479). The individual with histrionic personality disorder also shows extreme emotions but does not exhibit chronic feelings of emptiness or loneliness, self-destructive behaviors, or intensively impaired relationships. Differentiation between schizophrenia and the borderline personality disorder includes differences between prolonged psychotic episodes, and the presence of a major thought disorder. A relatively stable self-image and relative lack of self-destructiveness, impulsivity, and abandonment concerns distinguish paranoid and narcissistic personality disorders. The antisocial personality disorder is characterized by manipulative behavior motivated by the desire for power, control, or material gain versus a desire for nurturance. The person with a dependent personality disorder has abandonment concerns; however, individuals appease and submit in interpersonal relationships, unlike in the borderline personality disorder.

The following case discussion portrays a young woman with behaviors commonly seen in persons diagnosed with borderline personality disorder.

The Case of Suzie Hutchfield

This session takes place in a community mental health center. Suzie Hutchfield called and asked for an appointment for "someone to help me." An appointment was made for later that week. The following is an excerpt of the session.

"You know it's really hard to make something of yourself when your own father tells you that your never gonna make much of yourself," Suzie Hutchfield said. "Do you know what he told to me when I was 14 years old? I had just run away from home, 'cause he always smacked me around. When the police brought me home, my dad told me that I'd better learn to be good making money on my back because that's all I'll ever be good for."

She continued, "He was such a dumb shit. You know men have always been jerks, starting with him. He was no Prince Charming. He used to beat me and my younger brother up real good, and then he'd go drink his booze in front of the television set. Oh, and he had a girlfriend too, but I bet my mother didn't care."

Suzie is currently employed as a waitress in a delicatessen. However, she admits to having a series of jobs that "don't last too long." She goes on to add, "I've been married three times, and once I married the same man twice. Did I confuse you? Did you understand what I said?" I nodded my head in agreement. "Anyway, I can't seem to get it right even though I'm 42 years old. You know, I'm a single mom of two girls, and even at home I can't get things right. My oldest daughter, Candy, she's 16 and a real piece of work. She should be making A's, but skips school a lot. One of these fine days some 'goody two shoe' social worker is gonna haul me to jail because that kid's always truant." Suzie continued, "Now my little girl, Heather, she's the best. She's 11 years old and a better kid you never saw." She added, "Don't that beat all. I got one good kid and one bad one."

"What did you ask? Oh yeah, I remember now. My boyfriend, Bob, just moved in, but I'm not so happy about this arrangement. I think he's been cheating on me, but he tells me he's not. Twice last week I followed him after he left for his motorcycle repair shop. Anyway, he drove right over to his ex-girlfriend's house, and stayed there for two hours! When he came home, I confronted him, and he told me some cock and bull story that she needed some 'house maintenance' done. Some maintenance! I've been through this with him before, many, many times. I throw him out, and then he swears this is the last time, but it never is, and I still take him back." She said, "You know there's nothing more I hate than being alone, and if it means taking that bum back, well at least I know what I have, ya know? It's not that I need him. I've had lots of men in my life. I always have a man waiting in the wings. You never know what can happen. I really just don't want to ever be alone."

Suzie continued, "Can you keep a secret? [I nodded in the affirmative.] I met this orderly last week when I was in the hospital, you know for the 'cuts' and the cocaine? [It should be pointed out that she has been hospitalized several times for suicide attempts by cutting her wrists.] Anyway, I think he loves me, but he's not exactly a rocket scientist if you know what I mean. We found a broom closet and made out a coupla times. We even made a date for when I get out of here.

"You know, sometimes I feel so empty I'll do something really exciting for fun. My old social worker tried to tell me that I do these crazy things for attention. She's so stupid! Now on the other hand, you seem to be real smart and like you can help me. What do you think?

I once spent $2,000 at Payless Shoes. They're still waiting for me to pay." Suzie went on to say that she bought all different sizes in men's, children's, and women's shoes. The store manager told her that they had a no return policy and stamped her receipt to that effect. Despite this, Suzie still tried to return the shoes because she was worried that her credit card was charged over the limit. As a result of this incident, her credit card was canceled. Suzie also admits to long-term problems using alcohol and drugs, "but I'm not a drug addict or nothing like that. I just wanna smoke a little weed, drink a little wine, have a good time, and I don't hurt anybody."

Assessment Summary

Suzie's interpersonal relationships are characterized by a history of being very unstable, chaotic, and intense. She tends to be affected by self-destructive behavior, poor self-image, and a fear of being abandoned by others. Confronted by a boyfriend who is cheating on her, she makes a desperate attempt to maintain this flawed relationship by meeting someone else when she was hospitalized for a suicide attempt. Suzie presents mood reactivity related to her poor impulse control, as shown by buying $2,000 worth of shoes, multiple suicide attempts, and alcohol and drug use. Figure 9-7 summarizes the major biological, psychological, and social factors particular to Suzie's life. Of note, the multi-axial designation considers Suzie's many attempts at suicide and indicates her symptoms as "severe."

Historically, persons with borderline personality disorder have been stereotyped as being very difficult, demanding, impatient, and prone to acting out. Notes Layton (1995), often practitioners avoid working with someone like Suzie and tend to characterize the person by their diagnosis rather than those factors that make them unique as individuals. The competency-based assessment is concerned with individual differences and is sensitive to the factors that influence Suzie in her social environment. For instance, Suzie does convey to the practitioner some sense of wanting to make changes in her life.

Based on Suzie's past history, her current diagnosis is as follows:

Axis I	305.00 Alcohol Abuse	
	304.30 Cannabis Dependence	
Axis II	301.83 Borderline Personality Disorder, Severe	
Axis III	968.5 Cocaine Overdose	
	Old lacerations to both wrists	
Axis IV	History of childhood neglect	
	Occupational problems	
Axis V	GAF = 45 (at intake)	

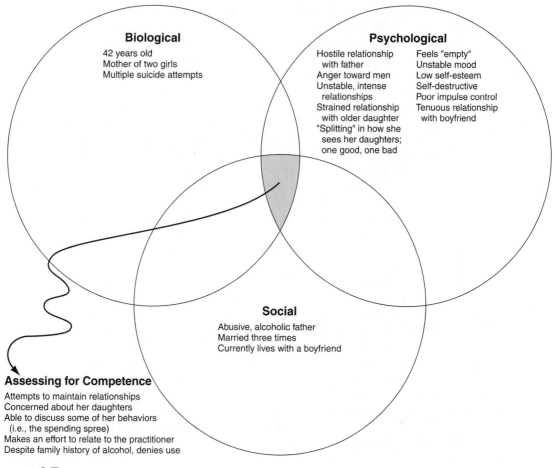

Biological

42 years old
Mother of two girls
Multiple suicide attempts

Psychological

Hostile relationship
  with father
Anger toward men
Unstable, intense
  relationships
Strained relationship
  with older daughter
"Splitting" in how she
  sees her daughters;
  one good, one bad

Feels "empty"
Unstable mood
Low self-esteem
Self-destructive
Poor impulse control
Tenuous relationship
  with boyfriend

Social

Abusive, alcoholic father
Married three times
Currently lives with a boyfriend

Assessing for Competence

Attempts to maintain relationships
Concerned about her daughters
Able to discuss some of her behaviors
  (i.e., the spending spree)
Makes an effort to relate to the practitioner
Despite family history of alcohol, denies use

FIGURE **9-7**

BORDERLINE PERSONALITY DISORDER

The interactions of the biological, psychological, and social factors in Suzie Hutchfield's life.

CLUSTER C PERSONALITY DISORDERS

AVOIDANT PERSONALITY DISORDER

The category of *avoidant personality disorder* was newly introduced in the DSM-III (APA, 1980), and it has a shorter history in the psychiatric literature than most of the other personality disorders (Sutherland & Frances, 1995). Its appearance was marked by considerable controversy, as some clinicians argued that there was too little distinction among the avoidant, the schizoid, and the dependent personality disorders

(Gunderson, 1983). The DSM-III advanced criteria emphasizing features considered typical of the avoidant personality disorder, that is, pervasive and generalized timidity, inhibition, and avoidance. DSM-III-R (APA, 1987) reflected some variation in perspective and attempted to demarcate this disorder more clearly from its differentially "close neighbors." Trait criteria such as "desire for acceptance" and "low self-esteem," initially considered central to the formulation, were removed, and new guideline parameters were added, for example, "fear of being embarrassed by blushing" and "fear of saying something inappropriate." These additions were considered fundamental to the core of the avoidant personality disorder construct (Sutherland & Francis, 1995). The current DSM criterion has been modified to differentiate between the avoidant and dependent personality disorders.

The prevalence of the avoidant personality disorder ranges between 1 and 10 percent of the general population (Sperry, 1995; Kaplan et al., 1994; Nietzel et al., 1998). No information is available about familial patterns or the proportion of men to women with the disorder. The empirical literature on avoidant personality disorder is sparse, with only a few references available of an empirical nature (Sutherland & Frances, 1995).

This disorder is often confused with individuals who can be described as "being shy." As the name suggests, people with avoidant personality disorder are highly sensitive to the opinion of others and therefore avoid most social relationships (Barlow & Durand, 1995). Because of their heightened sensitivity toward criticism and censure by others, they have a propensity to be self-effacing and anxious to please. These qualities often lead to marked social detachment. Additional features include feelings of low self-esteem; being standoffish or introverted; fear of closeness to and rejection by others; social awkwardness; and a chronic fear of being embarrassed. These characteristics persist throughout adulthood, affecting nearly all aspects of daily life. Individuals have a chronic, lifelong pattern of social withdrawal grounded in the anticipation of being rejected. They would like to have a relationship with others; however, the person is extremely sensitive to any form of criticism, making it nearly impossible for them to develop any relationships unless there is a strong guarantee of uncritical acceptance.

The main characteristics of avoidant personality disorder are constant feelings of inadequacy and ineptitude, especially in social situations:

- *Avoidance of social situations*—Individuals may ardently avoid social situations yet at the same time they desire social relationships.

- *Disengagement from social situations*—They are almost always detached from others, afraid of being embarrassed, criticized, or ridiculed (so that they withdraw from social situations whenever possible). This disengagement sets up a vicious cycle where the individual appears aloof and distant to others who mirror similar restraint toward them (Meleshko & Alden, 1993).

- *Desires relationships with others*—Although the person is inhibited and overly cautious, they long for affection and social acceptance, and are quite distressed by its absence.

- *Feelings of inadequacy*—They view themselves as socially undesirable. Although they want to be involved with others, low self-esteem and fear of rejection keep them from becoming involved.

• *Oversensitive to negative criticism*—They worry about embarrassing themselves and, as a consequence, do not try anything new or different.

Prevailing Pattern

These individuals are inhibited and overly cautious. They fear that new situations will "throw them a curve for which they are not prepared" (Nietzel et al., 1998, p. 422). Many are able to function as long as they stay protected in a "closed" or safe environment. Some individuals do marry and have families; being surrounded by familiar relationships and life circumstances that do not demand spontaneity is helpful. In the workplace, these individuals will often accept subordinate jobs, thus removing them from the realm of having increased responsibilities. These individuals are hypervigilant about being rejected, and they seek constant reassurance that others will like them. They tend to avoid occupations requiring social interactions, and generally do not attain very much personal advancement; they are instead seen as demure and eager to please (Kaplan et al., 1994; Stravynski, et al., 1994). If forced into a social encounter, they are usually very timid, inhibited, and afraid at every step of making a mistake that will bring the rejection they are sure is forthcoming.

Differential Assessment

Compared with those persons with schizoid personality disorder, who want to be left completely alone, the individual with avoidant personality disorder longs for social interaction and affection. They are not considered as querulous, irritable, irascible, or unpredictable, as are those with borderline or histrionic personality disorders. The differential picture is difficult to tease out between the avoidant and dependent personality disorders. However, the individual with the dependent personality has a greater fear of being abandoned or not loved than does the person with the avoidant personality disorder. For the practitioner, the clinical picture may be virtually indistinguishable. The individual with social phobia has problems around specific social situations, such as a speaking engagement, versus the personal relationship difficulties the avoidant individual experiences; however, the two often coexist (Zarate & Agras, 1994).

The following discussion portrays a young woman diagnosed with avoidant personality disorder.

The Case of Mabel Humphries

Mabel, a 33-year-old single woman, was referred to the Employee Assistance Program by her supervisor. The major complaint appeared to center around Mabel's unwillingness to change her working hours from nights to days; currently, she works the 11 P.M. to 7 A.M. shift in the hospital morgue.

The worker's first impression of Mabel was that she liked being "alone." She expressed herself in the following way: "Listen, it don't take much to keep me satisfied. As long as everybody stays outta my way, we'll get along just fine. I don't know what my supervisor told you, or what her problem is, but I don't want to work days. I like the peace and quiet of working the graveyard shift. That way I do my job and nobody's in my face. I guess I'm set in my ways. You see what I'm saying? I don't tell nobody my business and keep to myself. I always have, always will."

I asked, "Mabel, do you try to avoid the type of work that requires a lot of contact with people?" She answered, "Well, it's true I don't care to be around a lot of people, but mostly it's because they might not like me, you know." The worker followed this with a series of relationship-oriented questions:

- Have you ever turned down a promotion because you were worried other people would be critical of you?
- Do you worry about being rejected?
- Do you find yourself having trouble carrying on a conversation with someone you just met?
- Do you often feel inadequate in work or social situations?
- Do you usually feel like you are not as interesting or as much fun as other people are?

Mabel answered the above questions affirmatively and went on to add, "I was raised by a deadbeat alcoholic mother who never cared for anyone, including me. My mother always had trouble with people, especially men. I heard somewhere she had something called 'borderline personality disorder.' I'm not sure what that means, but it really made her one tough bitch. Anyway, she used to beat me and tell me I was no good. By the time I was 20, I believed I was no good. I mean a mother wouldn't lie, would she?" For a moment Mabel's eyes looked tearful, and I asked if she would like to have a drink of water. "No, don't waste anything on me, I'm fine," she replied.

When asked if she had any friends, Mabel replied, "No, I'm worried they'd see me as a loser. It's not like I haven't tried. I feel so stupid that I'm afraid they'll see me that way, too. After all, I don't have much to offer other people. I'm pretty much of a loner, and I don't like to go out and stuff like that. I guess that's one of the reasons why I don't make any friends. Sometimes I think they won't like me, so why bother? I pretty much keep to myself, and besides, what would I talk about? I don't do anything except wheel dead people into the autopsy room or the morgue holding room." Smiling, Mabel said, "Hey, I do have lots of friends, but they're all dead. Anyhow, I sure hope you can get my supervisor off my back and let me get back to work."

Assessment Summary

Mabel desires social interaction with others and is distressed by its absence. While she describes herself as a loner, Mabel is also struggling around the lack of interpersonal relationships. Persons with avoidant and schizoid personality disorders spend most of their time alone and isolated. The discrete differences are that Mabel is unhappy with her social interactions, whereas Tyrone White, described earlier in this chapter to illustrate schizoid personality disorder, prefers having no social contacts with others. Perhaps a more difficult differential assessment exists between persons considered avoidant and those noted as dependent. The next case, Walter Pearson, highlights some of the more salient features of the dependent personality

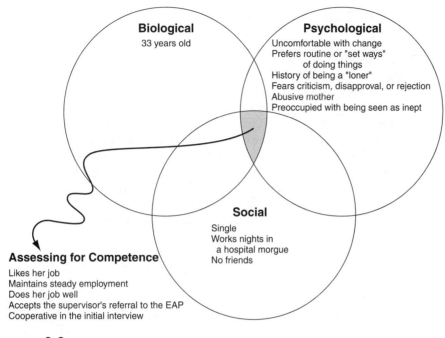

Biological
33 years old

Psychological
Uncomfortable with change
Prefers routine or "set ways"
of doing things
History of being a "loner"
Fears criticism, disapproval, or rejection
Abusive mother
Preoccupied with being seen as inept

Social
Single
Works nights in
a hospital morgue
No friends

Assessing for Competence
Likes her job
Maintains steady employment
Does her job well
Accepts the supervisor's referral to the EAP
Cooperative in the initial interview

FIGURE **9-8**

AVOIDANT PERSONALITY DISORDER

The interactions of the biological, psychological, and social factors in Mabel Humphries' life.

disorder. On the one hand, Mabel approaches interpersonal relationships with reluctance motivated by her fear of saying something foolish and looking inept. On the other hand, Walter Pearson's social isolation revolves around a clinging, submissive relationship with his mother.

The competency-based assessment serves as a guide in considering what information to obtain. A thorough understanding of Mabel's problems often demystifies using a "diagnostic label" and provides clinical insight into what seems to be a complicated symptom picture. The practitioner must be knowledgeable about many factors related to these presenting issues. While on the surface, it looks like Mabel has problems getting along with her boss, a thorough assessment reveals her underlying fears. At the same time, the practitioner appreciates the strengths in Mabel's personality and life situation. For instance, while fearful of criticism, she is willing to discuss with the practitioner "what's wrong."

Mabel Humphries' full diagnosis reads as follows:

Axis I	V71.09 (No diagnosis)
Axis II	301.82 Avoidant Personality Disorder (Principal Diagnosis)
Axis III	None
Axis IV	None
Axis V	GAF = 75 (at intake)

DEPENDENT PERSONALITY DISORDER

In 1952, the DSM-I included dependent personality disorder as a subtype of the passive-aggressive personality disorder. The category of dependent personality disorder received a great deal of criticism for presenting an overly narrow definition and for perpetuating possible gender bias toward women (Frances et al., 1995).

Dependent personality disorder describes a pervasive pattern of extreme inability to act independently of others. Some examples include allowing others to take responsibility for one's life and to make decisions for them; feeling helpless when alone; subjugating their needs to those of others; enduring mistreatment in order to maintain a relationship; and the inability to function when self-assertiveness is required. The person's dependency needs are so great they will often tolerate almost any kind of behavior on the part of others who seem to meet their needs. During the assessment, it is clinically relevant to ask whether there is a past or present history of abuse or battering.

Individuals with a dependent personality disorder go to great lengths to avoid undertaking or assuming positions of responsibility or leadership. Instead, they prefer to perform tasks under someone else's direction. It is important to discern that these individuals have more of a problem than just being indecisive. The disorder is more than being unsure about whether to order a tuna salad or a sandwich for lunch. What is so striking is the individual's inability to expedite decision making without exorbitant amounts of advice and reassurance. They want others to make decisions for them in all areas of their lives, including, for example, their occupation, where to live, how to dress, or even how to act. They cling tenaciously to others and make excessive sacrifices to win the slightest sign of appreciation (Hardy et al., 1995; Nietzel et al., 1998). At first blush, this dependency might seem like a compliment to someone; however, the excessive demands for reassurance eventually becomes so bothersome and irritating that most people are driven away. The tendency to be dependent on people is pervasive. This dependency also extends to the mental health system, the agency, and the practitioner.

To summarize, the central characteristics include:

- *Difficulty making any decisions*—The individual relies on excessive advice and reassurance from others, and avoids, at all costs, having to depend on themselves.

- *Excessive need for reassurance*—They are filled with feelings of self-doubt, passivity, pessimism, and helplessness and are uncomfortable when alone. The person often remains in relationships even when detrimental to their well-being.

- *Fear of rejection and abandonment*—The person is very reluctant to disagree with others out of fear of losing support and approval; it is not uncommon for this individual to live with someone who is controlling, domineering, overprotective, and infantilizing (Francis et al., 1995).

Prevailing Pattern

Dependent behavior begins by early adulthood and is present in a variety of contexts; for example, there is difficulty expressing disagreement, going to excessive lengths obtaining nurturance and support from others, being uncomfortable and helpless when alone, inability to make everyday decisions, and having difficulty initiating projects (Scully, 1996). The dependent personality disorder is more common in women than in men (Nietzel et al., 1998). However, little is known about the overall course of this disorder (Kaplan et al., 1994). What we do know is that individuals tend to exhibit impaired occupational functioning, and show little or no ability to act independently and without close supervision. Social relationships are apt to be limited to those they "depend" on, and subsequently the individual may endure mental or physical abuse as long as they remain unassertive and passive.

Differential Assessment

The differential assessment is a complicated process, because features of dependence are found in the other personality disorders as well as in other conditions, such as somatization disorder and agoraphobia. Dependence is a factor in histrionic and borderline personality disorders; however, the individual with the dependent personality disorder usually has a long-standing relationship with one main person on whom they are dependent versus a series of persons (Kaplan et al., 1994). This distinction is illustrated in the following case example.

The Case of Walter Pearson

Walter was referred to the employee assistance program (EAP) for an evaluation. His senior bank manager complained, "Walter requires too much direction, guidance, and time-seeking reassurance from others. This clearly interferes with his job responsibilities."

Walter Pearson is a 38-year-old African-American single male. He is an only child and was raised by a single-parent mother. "My momma has always spoiled me rotten," he relates. Mrs. Pearson, his mother, came to the interview at Walter's request. Mrs. Pearson jokingly told the interviewer, "As a baby, Walter had problems when I had to drop him off at the day-care center. 'Oooo wee,' did that feller cry. He also had problems when he started elementary school, and I guess he just wanted his momma!"

Walter broke in commenting, "Momma, do you remember when they sent me home from sleep-away camp? I cried so much, and I was so lonely that they put me on the first train home." Walter related that as a youngster most of the kids in the neighborhood made fun of him and called him a "momma's boy," but he didn't care.

He finished high school and was accepted to a small liberal arts college, where he earned his degree. Immediately after graduation, he came home because, "Momma needed me to help her with the business." At this point, he was looking eagerly toward his mother. The social worker had the impression, at this point, that his mother's approval was quite important to him. Almost imperceptibly, his mother smiled and nodded approvingly in Walter's direction. Walter currently lives at home with his mother. Although he used to rent an apartment nearby, he commented, "I didn't like the location and it wasn't safe, so I moved home after about three months."

Walter has done some dating, but hasn't found anyone "special," or "anyone that momma liked." He said, "Momma is very picky, and won't like anyone I date. I used to see a really nice girl, named Debbie McPhrew, but momma kept complaining about how talkative Debbie was." He continues, "I know I'm an adult, but momma does have my best interests at heart. Anyhow, my judgment hasn't always been the greatest. I've made lots of mistakes in my life." Walter's mother sat quietly by his side with a reserved but noticeable smile on her face. Periodically she would nod in agreement as if to reinforce Walter's comments about how much he needed her. He went on to say, "When Momma helps me make decisions, well, things I do seem better."

Walter has worked as a bank teller for the past five years. "My momma knew the manager who helped me get the job." Walter recently turned down a promotion, because "Momma thought it would be too much responsibility for me." He continued, "I was worried that I couldn't do a good job and that I'd make lots of mistakes. It's better that I stay in my present position."

Assessment Summary

Walter's story is an example of someone with a dependent personality disorder wherein we see a middle-aged man who continues to be bound in one way or another to someone else; in this situation, it is his mother. The vignette suggests that Walter lacks the initiative to make decisions or assert himself. Walter's dependency needs are so great that he accepts most suggestions his mother offers even if they are not in his best interests. He accepts this advice without question in order to avoid being rejected or criticized. In fact, he is willing to admit that his judgment is not "the greatest" except for when his mother intercedes on his behalf.

On closer examination, Walter's mother seems to want to keep him close to home and discourages any attempts he may have had in developing other relationships, such as with a girlfriend. On some level, Walter fears being separated from his mother and left to shift for himself. He maintains a submissive, clinging role in order not to be abandoned and looks to his mother for approval. His dependence on others is so great that his supervisor has referred him to the EAP office for help. Interestingly, Walter's mother accompanies him to the appointment.

An important social work value relates to appreciating human worth and respecting human dignity. The profession is committed to helping those who are oppressed and disempowered. In Walter's situation, his so-called "oppression" is not related to various forms of discrimination but arises from his dependence on his mother for her approval and advice. A competency-based assessment examines Walter's present functioning in relationship to past events, while considering biopsychosocial factors as well as environmental systems. This distinction adds clarity to the way that Walter relates to his world. Focusing on his strengths rather than deficits, the practitioner builds on his eagerness to please others, and, at the same time, fosters a relationship built on mutual respect and collaboration around problem solving.

Walter's diagnosis at this point would be as follows:

Axis I	V71.09 (No diagnosis)	
Axis II	301.6 Dependent Personality Disorder	
Axis III	None	
Axis IV	None	
Axis V	GAF = 70 (current)	

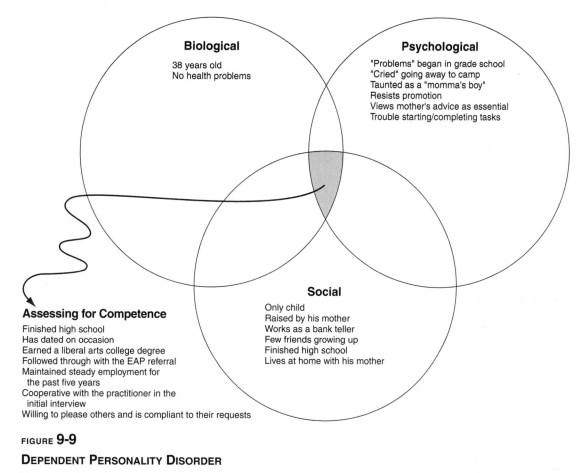

Biological

38 years old
No health problems

Psychological

"Problems" began in grade school
"Cried" going away to camp
Taunted as a "momma's boy"
Resists promotion
Views mother's advice as essential
Trouble starting/completing tasks

Social

Only child
Raised by his mother
Works as a bank teller
Few friends growing up
Finished high school
Lives at home with his mother

Assessing for Competence

Finished high school
Has dated on occasion
Earned a liberal arts college degree
Followed through with the EAP referral
Maintained steady employment for
  the past five years
Cooperative with the practitioner in the
  initial interview
Willing to please others and is compliant to their requests

FIGURE **9-9**

DEPENDENT PERSONALITY DISORDER

The interactions of the biological, psychological, and social factors in Walter Pearson's life.

OBSESSIVE-COMPULSIVE PERSONALITY DISORDER

Persons with *obsessive-compulsive personality disorder* do not have obsessions or compulsions as seen in OCD; perhaps the best word to describe their personality is "perfectionist." These individuals adhere to a high degree of rigidity, orderliness, and inflexibility, and they are emotionally constricted. They often have difficulties making decisions, and appear excessively moralistic. They are often characterized as headstrong. This disorder is often confused with obsessive-compulsive disorder (OCD), which is distinguished by thinking obsessions and performing compulsions. With this latter disorder, the practitioner encounters individuals who spend a great deal of time performing ritual behaviors such as checking, counting, or washing.

Some major characteristics of obsessive-compulsive personality disorder include:

- *Perfectionism*—These individuals have inflexible ethical standards that they believe everyone should follow. They do not delegate work to others because they fear things will not be done to their exacting standards. To all outward appearances, they seemingly stride through life with meticulous, regimental thoroughness.

- *Preoccupation with orderliness*—The individual is known to hoard and accumulate seemingly worthless possessions. They are often described as "pack rats" and stingy.
- *Difficulty with interpersonal control*—They over analyze things in an attempt to distance and detach themselves, as if this emotional spontaneity is too threatening to tolerate.

Prevailing Pattern

These individuals are more apt to seek intervention on their own than are people with other personality disorders. While they often have stable relationships and marriages (especially if the spouse is passive), they usually have few close friends and their lives tend to be constricted and joyless. Routines are rigidly adhered to and their occupational life is usually formal.

The individual tends to become "lost" in details and completely immobilized by indecision. Projects are ultimately left uncompleted. They feel more comfortable exercising control over others and greatly resist attempts at being controlled. These individuals appear to be supersaturated with upholding the highest level of scruples and are inflexible regarding moral and ethical matters. Consequently they are often described as cold, insensitive, single-minded, stubbornly rigid, frugal, parsimonious, and miserly to the point of being unwilling to part with any material possessions (Jefferson & Moore, 1996). Although this disorder tends to be chronic, there is some suggestion that symptomatology may abate as the individual enters middle and later years (Stoudemire, 1994).

Differential Assessment

Other disorders that should be ruled out include major depressive disorder, dysthymic disorder, and obsessive-compulsive disorder (OCD). Individuals with obsessive-compulsive disorder have true obsessions and compulsions that are not found in persons with obsessive-compulsive personality disorder. However, that is not to say that the person might not eventually develop OCD. Individuals with a narcissistic personality disorder, while concerned with perfection and correctness, focus on seeking adulation versus maintaining these behaviors out of fear and guilt. The following discussion illustrates a person with features of the obsessive-compulsive personality disorder.

The Case of Geoffrey Hales

Geoffrey Hales is a 45-year-old man who is married, and the father of two children: a boy who is 11, and a girl who is 9. He is employed as an electrical engineer for a nationally known company. Geoffrey, at his wife Irene's insistence, came in because of marital problems. The following is a synopsis of their initial interview.

Addressing the social worker, Mrs. Hales begins, "Marilyn, my husband is driving me crazy! No, I take that back, he's driven me crazy already! You gotta help him." When asked to elaborate on the problems that brought them to my office, Mrs. Hales continued, "Where do I start? He's never home, he's always working, we haven't been on a vacation in the 15 years we've been married. He's overworked and he never seems to sleep. He always brings work home with him and stays up until 3:00 A.M. most mornings working on the computer." She took a breath and continued, "Everything has to be just letter perfect, but it rarely is because he's constantly changing his work and nothing ever gets done. He can't even keep a secretary for more than three months because they can't stand his perfectionism. He doesn't have time for the kids or for me. We never go out because he's too involved with his work. I mean how many times can he rewrite a report? His current secretary calls him 'Mr. Four-R's.' It stands for rules, rigidity, regulation, and regimen. Boy! She sure pegged Geoffrey!"

Mr. Hales responded, "Irene, you know other people just don't do things the way I want them done." I asked if other difficulties were affecting their relationship. Mrs. Hales responded, "The house looks like we're ready to move out. He's got boxes scattered all around the place, and no one is allowed to touch anything. He says he is saving important information that he's going to use, but he never does. I jokingly call him a 'pack rat,' but it's not funny anymore. He can't throw anything away. We've got newspapers sitting in a corner of the living room dating back ten years! What's he going to do with all that junk?" Mr. Hales shrugged his shoulders and answered, "I guess I am a collector, and I think of it as waste not, want not." He continued, "Actually, I think its Irene who has the problem, not me, so why don't we talk about how disorganized she is around the house. She doesn't even know how to balance a checkbook."

Geoffrey went on to say that he runs his life by carefully making lists, meticulous planning, and, "I know that other people think that I'm a perfectionist but that's the only way you get things done in this world." Mrs. Hales retorted, "You might see yourself that way, but everyone else sees you as indecisive, preoccupied with details, and a procrastinator who never gets the job done." Mrs. Hales went on to say, "One of the reasons I insisted you come for help is that I've put up with your behavior for 15 years, and now it's time to stop. I'm tired of your 'it's my way or the highway' attitude." Mr. Hales replied tentatively, "I guess I am inflexible sometimes, and I know I turn people off, but it's only because I want things done right. I'm intolerant of people who bend the rules and try to cut corners." Irene turned to me and asked, "Do you think there is any hope for our marriage?"

Assessment Summary

Figure 9-10 provides an overview summarizing the major biological, psychological, and social features of Geoffrey Hales's life. Although his wife is quite unhappy and dissatisfied with his behaviors, Geoffrey is unaware of her discontent and continues to defend the importance of his need for orderliness and perfectionism. He is always working, and when he finishes a project he then feels the need to rework the details. As a matter of fact, getting the job done "correctly" seems to irritate co-workers, as illustrated by the secretary's comments about his work habits. Aside from an already troubled marriage, he seems to have no friends or interests outside of his job. In addition, Geoffrey Hales' preoccupation at getting things done properly comes at the expense of a family vacation.

Although Geoffrey's nonverbal behavior was not reflected in the vignette, it should be pointed out that his demeanor became quite preoccupied when he described the minutiae of his daily routine to the social worker. In the relationship with the practitioner, the person tends to replicate the preoccupations that dominate their life. It is important to recognize this parallel process, as it can provide clinical insight into the characteristic patterns that these individuals follow in relating to their social world. It is not unusual for Geoffrey Hales' wife to seek out coun-

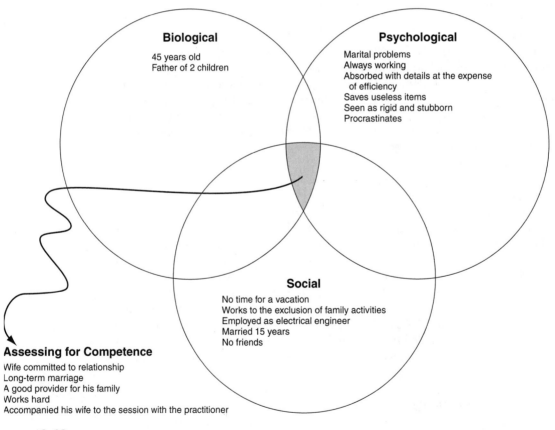

Biological
45 years old
Father of 2 children

Psychological
Marital problems
Always working
Absorbed with details at the expense
  of efficiency
Saves useless items
Seen as rigid and stubborn
Procrastinates

Social
No time for a vacation
Works to the exclusion of family activities
Employed as electrical engineer
Married 15 years
No friends

Assessing for Competence
Wife committed to relationship
Long-term marriage
A good provider for his family
Works hard
Accompanied his wife to the session with the practitioner

FIGURE **9-10**

OBSESSIVE-COMPULSIVE PERSONALITY DISORDER

The interactions of the biological, psychological, and social factors in Geoffrey Hales' life.

seling, since persons with personality disorders are often unaware of the impact their behavior has on others.

Clients do not exist in a vacuum. There is more to Geoffrey than his life story and a description of symptoms. The competency-based assessment helps to individualize Geoffrey while exploring the full range of factors affecting his life. He is very committed to his family and being a good provider. Since personality disorder features are ego-syntonic, Geoffrey was genuinely unaware of the distress his behavior created for his family.

Geoffrey Hales' diagnosis is:

Axis I	V71.09 (No diagnosis)
Axis II	301.4 Obsessive-Compulsive Personality Disorder, Moderate
Axis III	None
Axis IV	None
Axis V	GAF = 75 (current)

Summary

In sum, individuals with a personality disorder relate to others and to their social environment in rigid and inflexible ways. As they attempt to cope with stress or respond to problems in living in their usual way, matters only become worse. Unfortunately, the individual is largely unaware of the difficulties these behavioral patterns may pose and fails to recognize the connection to their personality. As a result, they generally do not seek out counseling on their own. If they come to the practitioner's attention, it is through a referral or coercion by others in their social environment to seek help.

The ego-syntonic nature of their behavior makes change difficult, and they are largely unmotivated to give up this characteristic disposition. The individual's behavior frequently elicits the kind of response from others that reinforces maladaptive traits. It is helpful for the practitioner to be aware of those distinctive ways that individuals with a personality disorder relate, since this process will more than likely emerge in the counseling relationship. Each case illustrated in this chapter shows that individuals with a personality disorder are very different from one another, and similarly, their strengths vary. Figure 9-11 provides an overview summarizing the major features of personality disorders.

Practitioner Reflections

The following activities are designed to encourage further reflections about the diagnostic categories of personality disorders. We recognize that it is a challenge for the practitioner to assess for personality characteristics and to distinguish among those features that may be helpful or those that may get in the way of coping and adapting to life's problems.

FIGURE 9-11

MAJOR CHARACTERISTICS OF EACH PERSONALITY DISORDER ORGANIZED BY "CLUSTER"

Activities

- Persons with a personality disorder generally do not come to the practitioner on their own. Problem-solving behaviors, though troublesome to others, are ego-syntonic, and the person's motivation for change is often limited. Looking back on the cases discussed in this chapter, imagine for a moment that this person is coming to your agency or office for the first time.

  How would you start the initial interview?

  What strengths can you identify?

  What might potentially get in the way of developing a therapeutic relationship with this client (and their family)?

  What is going on in this client's life that may be helpful in forming a therapeutic relationship?

- Imagine that you have been assigned to work with Mr. Shull after his social worker, Dr. Gray, left the agency. This is your first interview with him, and he says abruptly, "You know, Dr. Gray was the greatest and she knew everything about me. I just don't think you and I will be able to get along as well. My situation is so unique." And your response would be …

  Think about how you would respond to Mr. Shull. What features noted in his case vignette would influence your response?

REFERENCES

Akhtar, S. (1987). Schizoid personality disorder: A synthesis of development, dynamic and descriptive features. *American Journal of Psychotherapy*, 61: 499–518.

Akhtar, S. (1989). Narcissistic personality disorder: Descriptive features and differential assessment. *Psychiatric Clinician North America*, 12: 505–530.

American Psychiatric Association [APA]. (1952). *Diagnostic and statistical manual of mental disorders* (1st ed.). Washington, DC: APA.

American Psychiatric Association [APA]. (1968). *Diagnostic and statistical manual of mental disorders* (2nd ed.). Washington, DC: APA.

American Psychiatric Association [APA]. (1980). *Diagnostic and statistical manual of mental disorders* (3rd ed.). Washington, DC: APA.

American Psychiatric Association [APA]. (1987). *Diagnostic and statistical manual of mental disorders* (3rd rev. ed.). Washington, DC: APA.

American Psychiatric Association [APA]. (1994). *Diagnostic and statistical manual of mental disorders* (4th ed.). Washington, DC: APA.

American Psychiatric Association [APA]. (2000). *Diagnostic and statistical manual of mental disorders* (4th ed.-TR). Washington, DC: APA.

Barlow, D. H., & Durand, V. M. (1995). *Abnormal psychology*. Pacific Grove, CA: Brooks/Cole.

Cacciola, J. S., Alterman, A. I., Rutherford, M. J., & Snider, E. C. (1995). Treatment response of antisocial substance abuse, *Journal of Nervous and Mental Diseases*, 183(3): 166–171.

Cooper, A. M., & Ronningstam, E. (1992). Narcissistic personality disorder. In A. Tasman & M. B. Riba (Eds.), *Review of psychiatry* (Vol. 11). Washington, DC: American Psychiatric Press.

Dahl, A. A. (1993). The personality disorder: A critical review of family, twin and adoption studies, *Journal of Personality Disorders*, spring supplement, 86–99.

Eppright, J. D., Kashani, J. H., Robinson, B. D., & Reid, M. (1991). Comorbidity of conduct disorder and personality disorders in an incarcerated juvenile population. *American Journal of Psychiatry*, 150: 1233–1236.

First, M. B., Frances, A., & Pincus, H. A. (1995). *DSM-IV handbook of differential diagnosis*. Washington, DC: American Psychiatric Press.

Frances, A., First, M. B., & Pincus, H. A. (1995). *DSM-IV guidebook*. Washington, DC: American Psychiatric Press.

Gabbard, G. O. (1995). *Treatments of psychiatric disorders.* Washington, DC: American Psychiatric Press.

Goldstein, E. G. (1984). *Ego psychology and social work practice*. New York: Free Press.

Goldstein, E. G. (2000). *Ego psychology and social work practice.* New York: The Free Press.

Gunderson, J. G. (1983). DSM-III diagnosis of personality disorders. In J. Forsch (Ed.), *Current perspectives on personality disorders*. Washington, DC: American Psychiatric Press.

Gunderson, J. G., & Links, P. (1995). Borderline personality disorder. In G. O. Gabbard (Ed.), *Treatment of psychiatric disorders*. Washington, DC: American Psychiatric Press.

Gunderson, J. G., Zanarini, M. C., & Kisiel, C. L. (1991). Borderline personality disorder: A review of data on DSM-III descriptions. *Journal of Personality Disorders*, 5: 340–352.

Hardy, G. E., Barkham, M., & Shapiro, D. A. (1995). Impact on cluster C personality disorders on outcomes of contrasting brief psychotherapies for depression. *Journal of Consulting Clinical Psychology*, 63(6): 997–1004.

Hare, R. D. (1991). *The Hare psychopathy checklist—revised manual*. Toronto: Multi Health Systems.

Hare, R. D. (1993). *Without conscience: The disturbing world of the psychopaths among us*. New York: Pocket Books.

Horowitz, M. J. (1995). Histrionic personality disorders. In G. O. Gabbard (Ed.), *Treatment in psychiatric disorders* (2nd ed.). Washington, DC: American Psychiatric Press.

Kaplan, H. J., & Sadock, B. J. (1996). *The concise textbook of clinical psychiatry*. Baltimore, MD: Williams & Wilkins.

Kaplan, H. J., Sadock, B. J., & Grebb, J. A. (1994). *Synopsis of psychiatry*. Baltimore, MD: Williams & Wilkins.

Kernberg, O. (1989). The narcissistic personality disorder and the differential diagnosis of antisocial behavior. *Psychiatric Clinical North America,* 12: 553–570.

Layton, M. (1995). Emerging from the shadows, *Family Therapy Networker*, May/June 35–41.

McGlashan, T. (1993). Implications of outcome research for treatment of borderline personality. In J. Paris (Ed.), *Borderline personality disorder*. Washington, DC: American Psychiatric Press.

Meleshko, K. G. A., & Alden, L. E. (1993). Anxiety and self-disclosure: Toward a motivational model. *Journal of Personality and Social Psychology*, 64, 1000-1009

Meloy, J. R. (1992). *Violent attachment*. New York: Jason Aronson.

Meloy, J. R. (1995). Antisocial personality. In G. O. Gabbard (Ed.), *Treatment in psychiatric disorders* (2nd ed.). Washington, DC: American Psychiatric Press.

Monahan, J., & Steadman, H. (1994). *Violence and mental disorders: Developments in risk assessments.* Chicago: University of Chicago.

Moore, D. P., & Jefferson, J. W. (1996). *Handbook of medical psychiatry*. St. Louis: Mosby-Year Book.

Morrison, J. (1995). *The DSM-IV made easy*. New York: Guilford Press.

Nietzel, M. T., Speltz, M. L., McCauley, E. A., & Bernstein, D. A. (1998). *Abnormal psychology*. Boston: Allyn & Bacon.

O'Brien, M. M., Trestman, R. L., & Siever, L. J. (1993). Cluster A personality disorder. In D. L. Dunner (Ed.), *Current psychiatric therapies*. Philadelphia: W. B. Saunders.

Rapoport, J. L., & Ismond, D. R. (1996). *DSM-IV training guide for diagnosis of childhood disorders*. New York: Brunner/Mazel.

Robins, L. N., Tipp, J., & Przybeck, T. (1991). Antisocial personality. In L. N. Robins & D. A. Regier (Eds.), *Psychiatric disorders in America*. New York: Free Press.

Rosowsky, E., & Gurrian, B. (1992). The impact of borderline personality disorder in late life on systems of care. *Hospital and Community Psychiatry*, 43(4): 386–389.

Sabo, A. N., Gunderson, J. G., & Najavits, L. M. (1995). Changes in self-destructiveness of borderline patients in psychotherapy. A prospective follow-up. *Journal of Nervous and Mental Diseases*, 183(6): 370–376.

Scully, J. H. (1996). *Psychiatry*. Philadelphia: Williams & Wilkins.

Shader, R. I. (1994). *Manual of psychiatric therapeutics*. Boston: Little, Brown, & Company.

Siever, L. J., Bernstein, D. P., & Silverman, J. M. (1991). Schizotypal personality disorder: A review of its current status, *Journal of Personality Disorders*, 5: 178–193.

Skodal, A. E., & Oldham, J. M. (1991). Assessment and diagnosis of borderline personality disorder. *Hospital Community Psychiatry*, 42: 1021–1028.

Sperry, L. (1995). *Handbook of diagnosis and treatment of the DSM-IV personality disorders*. New York: Brunner/Mazel.

Stevenson, J., & Meares, R. (1992). An outcome study of psychotherapy for patients with borderline personality disorder. *American Journal of Psychiatry*, 149(3): 358–362.

Stone, M. H. (1994a). Early traumatic factors in the lives of serial killers. *American Journal of Forensic Psychiatry*, 15(2): 1–21.

Stone, M. H. (1994b). Characterologic subtypes of the borderline personality disorder, with a note on prognostic factors. *Psychiatric Clinics of North America*, 17(4): 773–784.

Stoudemire, A. (1994). *Clinical psychiatry for medical students*. Philadelphia: J. B. Lippencott.

Stravynski, A., Belisle, M., & Marcouiller, M. (1994). The treatment of avoidant personality disorder by social skills training in the clinic or in real-life settings. *Canadian Journal of Psychiatry*, 39(8): 377–383.

Sutherland, S. M., & Frances, A. (1995). Avoidant Personality Disorders. In G. O. Gabbard *Treatments of Psychiatric Disorders*. Washington, DC: American Psychiatric Press.

Sutker, P., Bugg, F., & West, J. (1993). Antisocial personality disorder. In P. Sutker & H. Adams (Eds.), *Comprehensive handbook of psychopathology* (2nd ed.). New York: Plenum.

Teyber, E. (1996). *Interpersonal Process in Psychotherapy* (3rd ed). Pacific Grove, CA: Brooks/Cole.

Torgersen, S., Onstad, S., Skre, I., Edvardsen, J., & Kringlen, E. (1993). "True" schizotypal personality disorder: A study of co-twins and relatives of schizophrenic probands. *American Journal of Psychiatry*, 150: 1661–1667.

Vankammen, W. B., Loeber, R., & Stouthamer-Loeber, M. (1991). Substance use and its relationship to conduct problems and delinquency in young boys. *Journal of Youth and Adolescence*, 20: 399–413.

Widiger, T. A., & Costa, P. T. (1994). Personality and personality disorders. *Journal of Abnormal Psychology*, 103: 78–91.

Wilson, G. T., Nathan, P. E., O'Leary, K. D., & Clark, L. A. (1996). *Abnormal psychology: Integrating perspectives*. Needham Heights, MA: Allyn & Bacon.

Zarate, R., & Agras, W. S. (1994). Psychosocial treatment of phobia and panic disorders. *Psychiatry*, 57(2): 133–141.

The DSM-IV Classification

This appendix provides the reader with an overview of the entire DSM-IV classification system. Our text covers selected diagnostic criteria. This decision is based on our beliefs about those disorders social workers most often encounter in their clinical practice. However, the DSM-IV is a lot easier to understand when the practitioner can visualize the overall landscape of this classification system. In the interest of completeness, it is provided here for your convenience.

NOS = Not Otherwise Specified

An "x" appearing in a diagnostic code indicates that a specific code number is required.

An ellipsis (…) is used in the names of certain disorders to indicate that the name of a specific mental disorder or general medical condition should be inserted when recording the name (e.g., 293.0 Delirium Due to Hypothyroidism).

If criteria are currently met, one of the following severity specifiers may be noted after the diagnosis:

> Mild
> Moderate
> Severe

If criteria are no longer met, one the following specifiers may be noted:

> In Partial Remission
> In Full Remission
> Prior History

DISORDERS USUALLY FIRST DIAGNOSED IN INFANCY, CHILDHOOD, OR ADOLESCENCE

Mental Retardation

Note: These are coded on Axis II.

317   Mild Mental Retardation
318.0   Moderate Mental Retardation
318.1   Severe Mental Retardation
318.2   Profound Mental Retardation
319   Mental Retardation, Severity Unspecified

Learning Disorders

315.00 Reading Disorder
315.1   Mathematics Disorder
315.2   Disorder of Written Expression
315.9   Learning Disorder NOS

Motor Skills Disorder

315.4   Developmental Coordination Disorder

Communication Disorders

315.31 Expressive Language Disorder
315.31 Mixed Receptive-Expressive Language
        Disorder
315.39 Phonological Disorder
307.0   Stuttering
307.9   Communication Disorder NOS

Pervasive Developmental Disorders

299.00 Autistic Disorder
299.80 Rett's Disorder
299.10 Childhood Disintegrative Disorder
299.80 Asperger's Disorder
299.80 Pervasive Developmental Disorder NOS

Attention-Deficit and Disruptive Behavior Disorders

314.xx Attention-Deficit/Hyperactivity Disorder
    .01   Combined Type
    .00   Predominantly Inattentive Type
    .01   Predominantly Hyperactive-Impulsive
            Type Disorder NOS
314.9   Attention-Deficit/Hyperactivity Disorder NOS
312.8   Conduct Disorder
        Specify type: Childhood-Onset Type/Adolescent-
        Onset Type
313.81 Oppositional Defiant Disorder
312.9   Disruptive Behavior Disorder NOS

Feeding and Eating Disorders of Infancy or Early Childhood

307.52 Pica
307.53 Rumination Disorder
307.59 Feeding Disorder of Infancy or Early
        Childhood

TIC Disorders

307.23 Tourette's Disorder
307.22 Chronic Motor or Vocal Tic Disorders
307.21 Transient Tic Disorder
        Specify if: Single Episode Recurrent
307.20 Tic Disorder NOS

Elimination Disorders

——.–   Encopresis
787.6   With Constipation and Overflow Incontinence
307.7   Without Constipation and Overflow
        Incontinence
307.6   Enuresis (Not Due to a General Medical
        Condition)

Specify type: Nocturnal Only/Diurnal Only/Nocturnal
and Diurnal

Other Disorders of Infancy, Childhood, or Adolescence

309.21 Separation Anxiety Disorder
        Specify if: Early Onset
313.23 Selective Mutism
313.89 Reactive Attachment Disorder of Infancy or
        Early Childhood
        Specify if: Inhibited Type/Disinhibited Type
307.3   Stereotypic Movement Disorder
        Specify if: With Self-Injurious Behavior
313.9   Disorder of Infancy, Childhood, or
        Adolescence NOS

DELIRIUM, DEMENTIA, AND AMNESTIC AND OTHER COGNITIVE DISORDERS

Delirium

293.0   Delirium Due to…*[Indicate the General
        Medical Condition]*
——.–   Substance Intoxication Delirium *(refer to
        Substance-Related Disorders for substance-
        specific codes)*
——.–   Substance Withdrawal Delirium *(refer to
        Substance-Related Disorders for substance-
        specific codes)*
——.–   Delirium Due to Multiple Etiologies *(code
        each of the specific etiologies)*
780.09 Delirium NOS

Dementia

290.xx Dementia of the Alzheimer's Type, With
        Early Onset *(also code 331.0 Alzheimer's
        disease on Axis III)*
    .10   Uncomplicated
    .11   With Delirium
    .12   With Delusions
    .13   With Depressed Mood
            Specify if: With Behavioral Disturbance
290.xx Dementia of the Alzheimer's type, With
        Late Onset *(also code 331.0 Alzheimer's dis-
        ease an Axis III)*
    .0   Uncomplicated
    .3   With Delirium
    .20   With Delusions
    .21   With Depressed Mood
            Specify if: With Behavioral Disturbance

290.xx Vascular Dementia
.40   Uncomplicated
.41   With Delirium
.42   With Delusions
.43   With Depressed Mood
        Specify if: With Behavioral Disturbance
294.9   Dementia Due to HIV Disease *(also code 043.1 HIV infection affecting central nervous system on Axis III)*
294.1   Dementia Due to Head Trauma *(also code 854.00 head injury in Axis III)*
294.1   Dementia Due to Parkinson's Disease *(also code 332.0 Parkinson's disease on Axis III)*
294.1   Dementia Due to Huntington's Disease *(also code 333.4 Huntington's disease on Axis III)*
290.10 Dementia Due to Creutzfeldt-Jakob Disease *(also code 046.1 Creutzfeldt-Jakob disease on Axis III)*
294.1   Dementia Due to…*[Indicate the General Medical Condition not listed above] (also code the general medical condition on Axis III)*
——.–   Substance-Induced Persisting Dementia *(refer to Substance-Related Disorders for substance-specific codes)*
——.–   Dementia Due to Multiple etiologies *(code each of the specific etiologies)*
294.8   Dementia NOS

Amnestic Disorders

294.0   Amnestic Disorder Due to…*[Indicate the General Medical Condition]*
        Specify if: Transient/Chronic
——.–   Substance-Induced Persisting Amnestic Disorder *(refer to Substance-Related Disorders for substance-specific codes)*
294.8   Amnestic Disorder NOS

Other Cognitive Disorders

294.9   Cognitive Disorder NOS

MENTAL DISORDERS DUE TO A GENERAL MEDICAL CONDITION NOT ELSEWHERE CLASSIFIED

293.89 Catatonic disorder Due to…*[Indicate the General Medical Condition]*
310.1   Personality Change Due to…*[Indicate the General Medical Condition]*

        Specify type: Labile Type/Disinhibited Type/Aggressive Type/Apathetic Type/Paranoid Type/Other Type/Combined Type/Unspecified Type
293.9   Mental Disorder NOS Due to…*[Indicate the General Medical Condition]*

SUBSTANCE-RELATED DISORDERS

[a]The following specifiers may be applied to Substance Dependence:

        With Physiological Dependence/Without Physiological Dependence
        Early Full Remission/Early Partial Remission
        Sustained Full Remission/Sustained Partial Remission
        On Agonist Therapy/In a Controlled Environment

The following specifiers apply to Substance-Induced Disorders as noted:

        [I]With Onset During Intoxication/[W]with Onset During Withdrawal

Alcohol-Related Disorders

Alcohol Use Disorders
303.90 Alcohol Dependence[a]
305.00 Alcohol Abuse

Alcohol-Induced Disorders
303.00 Alcohol Intoxication
291.8   Alcohol Withdrawal
        Specify if: With Perceptual Disturbances
291.0   Alcohol Intoxication Delirium
291.0   Alcohol Withdrawal Delirium
291.2   Alcohol-Induced Persisting Dementia
291.1   Alcohol-Induced Persisting Amnestic Disorder
291.x   Alcohol-Induced Psychotic Disorder
.5   With Delusions[I,W]
.3   With Hallucinations[I,W]
291.8   Alcohol-Induced Mood Disorder[I,W]
291.8   Alcohol-Induced Anxiety Disorder[I,W]
291.8   Alcohol-Induced Sexual Dysfunction[I]
291.8   Alcohol-Induced Sleep Disorder[I,W]
291.9   Alcohol-Related Disorder NOS

Amphetamine (or Amphetamine–Like)–Related Disorders

Amphetamine Use Disorders
304.40 Amphetamine Dependence[a]
305.70 Amphetamine Abuse

Amphetamine-Induced Disorders

292.89   Amphetamine Intoxication
          Specify if: With Perceptual Disturbances
292.0   Amphetamine Withdrawal
292.81   Amphetamine Intoxication Delirium
292.xx   Amphetamine-Induced Psychotic Disorders
    .11   With Delusions[I]
    .12   With Hallucinations[I]
292.84   Amphetamine-Induced Mood Disorder[I,W]
292.89   Amphetamine-Induced Anxiety Disorder[I]
292.89   Amphetamine-Induced Sexual Dysfunction[I]
292.89   Amphetamine-Induced Sleep Disorder[I,W]
292.9   Amphetamine-Related Disorder NOS

Caffeine-Related Disorders

Caffeine-Induced Disorders

305.90   Caffeine Intoxication
292.89   Caffeine-Induced Anxiety Disorder[I]
292.89   Caffeine-Induced Sleep Disorder[I]
292.9   Caffeine-Related Disorder NOS

Cannabis-Related Disorders

Cannabis Use Disorders

304.30   Cannabis Dependence[a]
305.20   Cannabis Abuse

Cannabis-Induced Disorders

292.89   Cannabis Intoxication
          Specify if: With Perceptual Disturbances
292.81   Cannabis Intoxication Delirium
292.xx   Cannabis-Induced Psychotic Disorder
    .11   With Delusions[I]
    .12   With Hallucinations[I]
292.89   Cannabis-Induced Anxiety Disorder[I]
292.9   Cannabis-Related Disorder NOS

Cocaine-Related Disorders

Cocaine Use Disorders

304.20   Cocaine Dependence[a]
305.60   Cocaine Abuse

Cocaine-Induced Disorders

292.89   Cocaine Intoxication
          Specify if: With Perceptual Disturbances
292.0   Cocaine Withdrawal
292.81   Cocaine Intoxication Delirium
292.xx   Cocaine-Induced Psychotic Disorder
    .11   With Delusions[I]
    .12   With Hallucinations[I]
292.84   Cocaine-Induced Mood Disorder[I,W]

292.89   Cocaine-Induced Anxiety Disorder[I,W]
292.89   Cocaine-Induced Sexual Dysfunction[I]
292.89   Cocaine-Induced Sleep Disorder[I,W]
292.9   Cocaine-Related Disorder NOS

Hallucinogen-Related Disorders

Hallucinogen Use Disorders

304.50   Hallucinogen Dependence[a]
304.50   Hallucinogen Abuse

Hallucinogen-Induced Disorders

292.89   Hallucinogen Intoxication
292.89   Hallucinogen Persisting Perception
          Disorder (Flashbacks)
292.81   Hallucinogen Intoxication Delirium
292.xx   Hallucinogen-Induced Psychotic Disorder
    .11   With Delusions[I]
    .12   With Hallucinations[I]
292.84   Hallucinogen-Induced Mood Disorder[I]
292.89   Hallucinogen-Induced Anxiety Disorder[I]
292.9   Hallucinogen-Related Disorder NOS

INHALANT-RELATED DISORDERS

Inhalant Use Disorders

304.60   Inhalant Dependence[a]
305.90   Inhalant Abuse

Inhalant-Induced Disorders

292.89   Inhalant Intoxication
292.81   Inhalant Intoxication Delirium
292.82   Inhalant-Induced Persisting Dementia
292.xx   Inhalant-Induced Psychotic Disorder
    .11   With Delusions[I]
    .12   With Hallucinations[I]
292.84   Inhalant-Induced Mood Disorder[I]
292.89   Inhalant-Induced Anxiety Disorder[I]
292.9   Inhalant-Related Disorder NOS

Nicotine-Related Disorders

Nicotine Use Disorder

305.10   Nicotine Dependence[a]

Nicotine-Induced Disorder

292.0   Nicotine Withdrawal
292.9   Nicotine-Related Disorder NOS

Opioid-Related Disorders

Opioid Use Disorders

304.00   Opioid Dependence[a]

305.50 Opioid Abuse

Opioid-Induced Disorders

292.89 Opioid Intoxication
        Specify if: With Perceptual Disturbances
292.0 Opioid Withdrawal
292.81 Opioid Intoxication Delirium
292.xx Opioid-Induced Psychotic Disorder
  .11   With Delusions[I]
  .12   With Hallucinations[I]
292.84 Opioid-Induced Mood Disorder[I]
292.89 Opioid-Induced Sexual Dysfunction[I]
292.89 Opioid-Induced Sleep Disorder[I,W]
292.9 Opioid-Related Disorder NOS

Phencyclidine
(or Phencyclidine-Like)–Related Disorders

Phencyclidine Use Disorders

304.90 Phencyclidine Dependence[a]
305.90 Phencyclidine Abuse

Phencyclidine-Induced Disorders

292.89 Phencyclidine Intoxication
        Specify if: With Perceptual Disturbances
292.81 Phencyclidine Intoxication Delirium
292.xx Phencyclidine-Induced Psychotic Disorder
  .11   With Delusions[I]
  .12   With Hallucinations[I]
292.84 Phencyclidine-Induced Mood Disorder[I]
292.89 Phencyclidine-Induced Anxiety Disorder[I]
292.9 Phencyclidine-Related Disorder NOS

Sedative- Hypnotic-,
or Anxiolytic-Related Disorders

304.10 Sedative, Hypnotic, or Anxiolytic Intoxication Dependence[a]
305.40 Sedative, Hypnotic, or Anxiolytic Abuse

Sedative, Hypnotic, or Anxiolytic Use Disorders

292.89 Sedative, Hypnotic, or Anxiolytic Intoxication
292.0 Sedative, Hypnotic, or Anxiolytic Withdrawal
        Specify if: With Perceptual Disturbances
292.81 Sedative, Hypnotic, or Anxiolytic Intoxication Delirium
292.81 Sedative, Hypnotic, or Anxiolytic Withdrawal Delirium
292.82 Sedative-, Hypnotic-, or Anxiolytic-Induced Persisting Dementia
292.83 Sedative-, Hypnotic-, or Anxiolytic-Induced Persisting Amnestic Disorder

292.xx Sedative-, Hypnotic-, or Anxiolytic-Induced Psychotic Disorder
  .11   With Delusions[I,W]
  .12   With Hallucinations[I,W]
292.84 Sedative-, Hypnotic-, or Anxiolytic-Induced Mood Disorder[I,W]
292.89 Sedative-, Hypnotic-, or Anxiolytic-Induced Anxiety Disorder[W]
292.89 Sedative-, Hypnotic-, or Anxiolytic-Induced Sexual Dysfunction[I]
292.89 Sedative-, Hypnotic-, or Anxiolytic-Induced Sleep Disorder[I,W]
292.9 Sedative-, Hypnotic-, or Anxiolytic-Related Disorder NOS

Polysubstance-Related Disorder

304.80 Polysubstance Dependence[a]

Other (or Unknown)
Substance-Related Disorders

Other (or Unknown) Substance Use Disorders

304.90 Other (or Unknown) Substance Dependence[a]
305.90 Other (or Unknown) Substance Abuse

Other (or Unknown) Substance-Induced Disorders

292.89 Other (or Unknown) Substance Intoxication
        Specify if: With Perceptual Disturbances
292.0 Other (or Unknown) Substance Withdrawal
        Specify if: With Perceptual Disturbances
292.81 Other (or Unknown) Substance-Induced Delirium
292.82 Other (or Unknown) Substance-Induced Persisting Dementia
292.83 Other (or Unknown) Substance-Induced Persisting Amnestic Disorder
292.xx Other (or Unknown) Substance-Induced Psychotic Disorder
  .11   With Delusions[I,W]
  .12   With Hallucinations[I,W]
292.84 Other (or Unknown) Substance-Induced Mood Disorder[I,W]
292.89 Other (or Unknown) Substance-Induced Anxiety Disorder[I,W]
292.89 Other (or Unknown) Substance-Induced Sexual Dysfunction[I]
292.89 Other (or Unknown) Substance-Induced Sleep Disorder[I,W]
292.9 Other (or Unknown) Substance-Related Disorder NOS

Schizophrenia and Other Psychotic Disorders

295.xx   Schizophrenia

The following Classification of Longitudinal Course applies to all subtypes of Schizophrenia:

> Episodic With Interepisode Residual Symptoms (*Specify if:* With Prominent Negative Symptoms)/Episodic With No Interepisode Residual Symptoms
> Continuous (*Specify if:* With Prominent Negative Symptoms)
> Single Episode in Partial Remission (*Specify if:* With Prominent Negative Symptoms)/Single Episode in Full Remission
> Other or Unspecified Pattern

.30   Paranoid Type
.10   Disorganized Type
.20   Catatonic Type
.90   Undifferentiated Type
.60   Residual Type

295.40   Schizophreniform Disorder
> *Specify if:* Without Good Prognostic Features/With Good Prognostic Features

295.70   Schizoaffective Disorder
> *Specify type:* Bipolar Type/Depressive Type

297.1   Delusional Disorder
> *Specify type:* Erotomanic Type/Grandiose Type/Jealous Type/Persecutory Type/Somatic Type/Mixed Type/Unspecified Type

298.8   Brief Psychotic Disorder
> *Specify if:* With Marked Stressor(s)/Without Marked Stressor(s)/With Postpartum Onset

297.3   Shared Psychotic Disorder

293.xx   Psychotic Disorder Due to…*[Indicate the General Medical Condition]*
.81   With Delusions
.82   With Hallucinations

Substance-Induced Psychotic Disorder (refer to Substance-Related Disorders for substance-specific codes)
> *Specify if:* With Onset During Intoxication/With Onset During Withdrawal

289.9   Psychotic Disorder NOS

Mood Disorders

Code current state of Major Depressive Disorder or Bipolar I Disorder in fifth digit:

> 1 = Mild
> 2 = Moderate
> 3 = Severe Without Psychotic Features
> 4 = Severe With Psychotic Features
>> *Specify:* Mood-Congruent Psychotic Features/Mood-Incongruent Psychotic Features
> 5 = In Partial Remission
> 6 = In Full Remission
> 0 = Unspecified

The following specifiers apply (for current or most recent episode) to Mood Disorders as noted:

> [a]Severity/Psychotic/Remission
> Specifiers/[b]Chronic/[c]WithCatatonic Features/[d]With Melancholic Features/[e]With Atypical Features/[f]With Postpartum Onset

The following specifiers apply to Mood Disorders as noted:

> [g]With or Without Full Interepisode Recovery/[h]With Seasonal Pattern/[I]With Rapid Cycling

Depressive Disorders

296.xx   Major Depressive Disorder,
.2x   Single Episode[a,b,c,d,e,f]
.3x   Recurrent[a,b,c,d,e,f,g,h]
300.4   Dysthymic Disorder
> *Specify if:* Early Onset/Late Onset
> *Specify if:* With Atypical Features
311   Depressive Disorder NOS

Bipolar Disorders

296.xx   Bipolar I Disorder,
.0x   Single Manic Episode[a,c,f]
> *Specify if:* Mixed
.40   Most Recent Episode Hypomanic[g,h,i]
.4x   Most Recent Episode Manic[a,c,f,g,h,i]
.6x   Most Recent Episode Mixed[a,c,f,g,h,i]
.5x   Most Recent Episode Depressed[a,b,c,d,e,f,g,h,i]
.7   Most Recent Episode Unspecified[g,h,i]

296.89 Bipolar II Disorder[a,b,c,d,e,f,g,h,i]
Specify (current or most recent episode):
Hypomanic/Depressed

293.83 Mood Disorder Due to...*[Indicate the General Medical Condition]*
Specify type: With Depressive Features/With Major Depressive-Like Episode/With Manic Features/With Mixed Features

——.– Substance-Induced Mood Disorder *(refer to Substance-Related Disorders for substance-specific codes)*
Specify type: With Depressive Features/With Manic Features/With Mixed Features
Specify if: With Onset During Intoxication/With Onset During Withdrawal

296.90 Mood Disorder NOS

ANXIETY DISORDERS

300.01 Panic Disorder Without Agoraphobia

300.21 Panic Disorder With Agoraphobia

300.22 Agoraphobia Without History of Panic Disorder

300.29 Specific Phobia
Specify type: Animal Type/Natural Environment Type/Blood-Injection-Injury Type/Situational Type/Other Type

300.23 Social Phobia
Specify if: Generalized

300.3 Obsessive-Compulsive Disorder
Specify if: With Poor Insight

309.81 Posttraumatic Stress Disorder
Specify if: Acute/Chronic
Specify if: With Delayed Onset

308.3 Acute Stress Disorder

300.02 Generalized Anxiety Disorder

293.89 Anxiety Disorder Due to...*[Indicate the General Medical Condition]*
Specify if: With Generalized Anxiety/With Panic Attacks/With Obsessive-Compulsive Symptoms

——.– Substance-Induced Anxiety Disorder *(refer to Substance-Related Disorders for substance-specific codes)*
Specify if: With Generalized Anxiety/With Panic Attacks/With Obsessive-Compulsive Symptoms/With Phobic Symptoms
Specify if: With Onset During Intoxication/With Onset During Withdrawal

300.00 Anxiety Disorder NOS

SOMATOFORM DISORDERS

300.81 Somatization Disorder

300.81 Undifferentiated Somatoform Disorder

300.11 Conversion Disorder
Specify type: With Motor Symptom or Deficit/With Sensory Symptom or Deficit/With Seizures or Convulsions/With Mixed Presentation

307.xx Pain Disorder
.80 Associated With Psychological Factors
.89 Associated With Both Psychological Factors and a General Medical Condition
Specify if: Acute/Chronic

300.7 Hypochrondriasis
Specify if: With Poor Insight

300.7 Body Dysmorphic Disorder

300.81 Somatoform Disorder NOS

FACTITIOUS DISORDERS

300.xx. Factitious Disorder
.16 With Predominantly Psychological Signs and Symptoms
.19 With Predominantly Physical Signs and Symptoms
.19 With Combined Psychological and Physical Signs and Symptoms

300.19 Factitious Disorder NOS

DISSOCIATIVE DISORDERS

300.12 Dissociative Amnesia

300.13 Dissociative Fugue

300.14 Dissociative Identity Disorder

300.6 Depersonalization Disorder

300.15 Dissociative Disorder NOS

SEXUAL AND GENDER IDENTITY DISORDERS

Sexual Dysfunctions

The following specifiers apply to all primary Sexual Dysfunctions:

Lifelong Type/Acquired Type/Generalized Type/Situational Type Due to

Psychological Factors/Due to Combined Factors

Sexual Desire Disorders
302.71 Hypoactive Sexual Desire Disorder
302.79 Sexual Aversion Disorder

Sexual Arousal Disorders
302.72 Female Sexual Arousal Disorder
302.72 Male Erectile Disorder

Orgasmic Disorders
302.73 Female Orgasmic Disorder
302.74 Male Orgasmic Disorder
302.75 Premature Ejaculation

Sexual Pain Disorders
302.76 Dyspareunia (Not Due to a General Medical Condition)
306.51 Vaginismus (Not Due to a General Medical Condition)

Sexual Dysfunction Due to a General Medical Condition
625.8   Female Hypoactive Sexual Desire Due to… *[Indicate the General Medical Condition]*
608.89 Male Hypoactive Sexual Desire Disorder Due to…*[Indicate the General Medical Condition]*
607.84 Male Erectile Dysfunction Disorder Due to…*[Indicate the General Medical Condition]*
625.0   Female Dyspareunia Due to…*[Indicate the General Medical Condition]*
608.89 Male Dyspareunia Due to…*[Indicate the General Medical Condition]*
625.8   Other Female Sexual Dysfunction Due to… *[Indicate the General Medical Condition]*
608.89 Other Male Sexual Dysfunction Due to… *[Indicate the General Medical Condition]*
——.–   Substance-Induced Sexual Dysfunction *(refer to Substance-Related Disorders for substance-specific codes)*
Specify if: With Impaired Desire/With Impaired Arousal/With Impaired Orgasm/With Sexual Pain
Specify if: With Onset During Intoxication
302.70 Sexual Dysfunction NOS

Paraphilias
302.4   Exhibitionism
302.81 Fetishism
302.89 Frotteurism

302.2   Pedophilia
Specify if: Sexually Attracted to Males/Sexually Attracted to Females/Sexually Attracted to Both
Specify if: Limited to Incest
Specify type: Exclusive Type/Nonexclusive Type
302.83 Sexual Masochism
302.84 Sexual Sadism
302.3   Transvestic Fetishism
Specify if: With Gender Dysphoria
302.82 Voyeurism
302.9   Paraphilia NOS

Gender Identity Disorders
302.xx. Gender Identity Disorder
  .6   in Children
  .85   in Adolescents or Adults
Specify if: Sexually Attracted to Males/Sexually Attracted to Females/Sexually Attracted to Both/Sexually Attracted to Neither
302.6   Gender Identity Disorder NOS
302.9   Sexual Disorder NOS

EATING DISORDERS

307.1   Anorexia Nervosa
Specify if: Restricting Type; Binge-Eating/Purging Type
307.51 Bulimia Nervosa
Specify type: Purging Type/Nonpurging Type
307.50 Eating Disorder NOS

SLEEP DISORDERS

Primary Sleep Disorders

Dyssomnias
307.42 Primary Insomnia
307.44 Primary Hypersomnia
Specify if: Recurrent
347   Narcolepsy
780.59 Breathing-Related Sleep Disorder
307.45 Circadian Rhythm Sleep Disorder
Specify type: Delayed Sleep Phase Type/Jet Lag Type/Shift Work Type/Unspecified Type
307.47 Dyssomnia NOS

Parasomnias
307.47 Nightmare Disorder
307.46 Sleep Terror Disorder
307.46 Sleepwalking Disorder
307.47 Parasomnia NOS

Sleep Disorders Related to Another Mental Disorder

307.42   Insomnia Related to...*[Indicate the Axis I or Axis II Disorder]*
307.44   Hypersomnia Related to...*[Indicate the Axis I or Axis II Disorder]*

Other Sleep Disorders

780.xx   Sleep Disorder Due to...*[Indicate the General Medical Condition]*
  .52   Insomnia Type
  .54   Hypersomnia Type
  .59   Parasomnia Type
  .59   Mixed Type
——.–   Substance-Induced Sleep Disorder *(refer to Substance-Related Disorders for substance-specific codes)*
        Specify type: Insomnia Type/Hypersomnia Type/Parasomnia Type/Mixed Type
        Specify if: With Onset During Intoxication/With Onset During Withdrawal

IMPULSE-CONTROL DISORDERS NOT ELSEWHERE CLASSIFIED

312.34   Intermittent Explosive Disorder
312.32   Kleptomania
312.33   Pyromania
312.31   Pathological Gambling
312.39   Trichotillomania
312.30   Impulse-Control Disorder NOS

ADJUSTMENT DISORDERS

309.xx   Adjustment Disorder
  .0   With Depressed Mood
  .24   With Anxiety
  .28   With Mixed Anxiety and Depressed Mood
  .3   With Disturbance of Conduct
  .4   With Mixed Disturbance of Emotions and Conduct
  .9   Unspecified
        Specify if: Acute/Chronic

PERSONALITY DISORDERS

Note: These are coded on Axis II
301.0   Paranoid Personality Disorder
301.20   Schizoid Personality Disorder
301.22   Schizotypal Personality Disorder
301.7   Antisocial Personality Disorder
301.83   Borderline Personality Disorder
301.50   Histrionic Personality Disorder
301.81   Narcissistic Personality Disorder
301.82   Avoidant Personality Disorder
301.6   Dependent Personality Disorder
301.4   Obsessive-Compulsive Personality Disorder
301.9   Personality Disorder NOS

OTHER CONDITIONS THAT MAY BE A FOCUS OF CLINICAL ATTENTION

Psychological Factors Affecting Medical Condition

316   ...*[Specified Psychological Factor/Affecting...[Indicate the General Medical Condition] Choose name based on nature of factors:*
        Mental Disorder Affecting Medical Condition
        Psychological Symptoms Affecting Medical Condition
        Personality Traits or Coping Style Affecting Medical Condition
        Maladaptive Health Behaviors Affecting Medical Condition
        Stress-Related Physiological Response Affecting Medical Condition
        Other or Unspecified Psychological Factors Affecting Medical Condition

Medication-Induced Movement Disorders

332.1   Neuroleptic-Induced Parkinsonism
333.92   Neuroleptic Malignant Syndrome
333.7   Neuroleptic-Induced Acute Dystonia
333.99   Neuroleptic-Induced Acute Akathisia
333.82   Neuroleptic-Induced Tardive Dyskinesia
333.1   Medication-Induced Postural Tremor
333.90   Medication-Induced Movement Disorder NOS

Other Medication-Induced Disorders

995.2   Adverse Effects of Medication NOS

Relational Problems

V61.9   Relational Problem Related to a Mental
         Disorder or General Medical Condition
V61.20   Parent-Child Relational Problem
V61.1   Partner Relational Problem
V61.8   Sibling Relational Problem
V62.81   Relational Problem NOS

Problems Related to Abuse or Neglect

V61.21   Physical Abuse of Child (code 995.5 if focus
         of attention is on victim)
V61.21   Sexual Abuse of Child (code 995.5 if focus of
         attention is on victim)
V61.21   Neglect of Child (code 995.5 if focus of
         attention is on victim)
V61.1   Physical Abuse of Adult (code 995.81 if focus
         of attention is on victim)
V61.1   Sexual Abuse of Adult (code 995.81 if focus
         of attention is on victim)

Additional Conditions That May Be a Focus of Clinical Attention

V15.81   Noncompliance With Treatment
V65.2   Malingering
V71.01   Adult Antisocial Behavior
V71.02   Child or Adolescent Antisocial Behavior

V62.89   Borderline Intellectual Functioning
         Note: This is coded on Axis II
780.9   Age–Related Cognitive Decline
V62.82   Bereavement
V62.3   Academic Problem
V62.2   Occupational Problem
313.82   Identity Problem
V62.89   Religious or Spiritual Problem
V62.4   Acculturation Problem
V62.89   Phase of Life Problem

ADDITIONAL CODES

300.9   Unspecified Mental Disorder (nonpsychotic)
V71.09   No Diagnosis on Axis I
799.9   Diagnosis or Condition Deferred on Axis I
V71.09   No Diagnosis on Axis II
799.9   Diagnosis Deferred on Axis II

MULTIAXIAL SYSTEM

Axis I   Clinical Disorders or Other Conditions That
          May Be a Focus of Clinical Attention
Axis II   Personality Disorders
          Mental Retardation
Axis III General Medical Conditions
Axis IV   Psychosocial and Environmental Problems
Axis V   Global Assessment of Functioning

APPENDIX

Assessing for Competency in Psychopathology

B

The following questions are designed to test your competency in psychopathology. Some items require you to apply what you know to a case study involving a hypothetical client. Other questions ask you to remember information about the various diagnostic categories. The section heading indicates the chapter where the answer can be found. You may want to answer these questions before reading the book in order to test your understanding of psychopathology. Alternatively, you may decide to attempt to answer these questions after reading the book and then review those chapters where you had the most incorrect answers.

CHAPTER TWO—COGNITIVE DISORDERS: DELIRIUM AND DEMENTIA

1. Dr. Johnson, a physician, referred his 73-year-old patient, Abner Smith, to you for a consultation. Mr. Smith has been having difficulty remembering and concentrating for the last three years. He came to the interview with his son, Jake. Abner Smith admitted to feeling depressed and anxious. His wife of 48 years died several years ago, and since that time he has lived alone in their house. Jake Smith added that his father seems to have changed over time; that is, his father leaves food cooking on the stove unattended; was found wandering around the neighborhood as if he was lost; and forgets the names of family members. These symptoms support the diagnosis of:

   a) Dementia
   b) Delirium
   c) Paranoid personality disorder
   d) Schizophrenia, paranoid type

2. Kenny Grayson accepted a new job in another town several hundred miles away, and he is worried about leaving his 72-year-old father behind. Kenny's father lives alone, is very confused, and is bowel and bladder incontinent. In addition, the senior Grayson suffered a mild stroke several years ago, which left a number of areas in his brain damaged. He is now showing signs of neurological impairment. What would be the most likely DSM-IV diagnosis for Kenny's father?

   a) Dementia due to a general medical condition
   b) Dementia of the Alzheimer's type
   c) Dissociative fugue
   d) Vascular dementia

3. The clinical picture of dementia, Alzheimer's type, includes all of the following symptoms, *except:*

   a) Sudden onset
   b) Individual gets lost in familiar places
   c) Night restlessness and difficulty falling asleep
   d) Short-term memory loss

4. The majority of people who experience an episode of delirium:

   a) Tend to progress rapidly to dementia without recovery
   b) Usually recover within several days or weeks after the causative factor is eliminated
   c) Do not recover unless treated with a carbamazepine protocol
   d) Should have psychosocial rehabilitation to support social and functioning skills that the individual may have lost in the earlier phase of the episode

5. Edna Trybus states that her mother, Hilda Walker, 75 years old, has become increasingly irritable and reclusive over the last four or five years. Mrs. Walker accuses her children of plotting to steal her house and her life savings. Mrs. Walker has been unable to care for herself; for example, she cannot cook her own meals, dress herself, or clean her home. Mrs. Walker is often confused in that she cannot remember her home address, her phone number, or her children's names. What DSM-IV diagnosis best describes Mrs. Walker's signs and symptoms?

   a) Agoraphobia, without panic disorder
   b) Delirium
   c) Pick's disease
   d) Dementia, Alzheimer's type

CHAPTER THREE—SCHIZOPHRENIA AND OTHER PSYCHOTIC DISORDERS

6. Mrs. Stacy Hill contacted the XYZ Mental Health Center because she is concerned about her 24-year-old daughter, Violet, who is displaying several psychotic symptoms at home including persecutory delusions, auditory hallucinations, incoherence, and loosening of associations. According to Mrs. Hill, her daughter was "just fine" until three months ago when this "strange behavior suddenly developed." There is some family history of schizophrenia. What would your diagnosis be?

   a) Schizophrenia, paranoid type
   b) Schizophreniform disorder
   c) Schizoid personality disorder
   d) Brief psychotic disorder

7. Sarah, age 23, gave birth to her first child three days ago. Her initial complaints consisted of insomnia, restlessness, and emotional lability that progressed to confusion, irritability, delusions, and thoughts of wanting to harm her baby. What is the most correct diagnosis?

   a) Brief psychotic disorder, postpartum onset
   b) Autoscopic psychosis
   c) Cotard's syndrome
   d) Induced delusional disorder

8. A delusional system shared by two or more persons was previously known as induced paranoid disorder and folie à deux. Persecutory delusions are most common, and the key presentation is the sharing and blind acceptance of these delusions between two (or more) people. What is the name of this disorder according to the DSM-IV?

   a) Pseudomentia
   b) Shared psychotic disorder
   c) Capgras disorder, not otherwise specified
   d) Schizophreniform disorder

9. Mario Walters believes that he has developed a major plan that would end all hunger, homelessness, and crime in the world. In addition, he believes the president of the United States, the Queen of England, and various important heads of state support his plan. This is an example of:

   a) Delusions of persecution
   b) Tangential thought
   c) Delusions of grandeur
   d) Neologism

10. Luther Ortega once met the criteria for schizophrenia. However, he no longer has the pronounced symptoms of disorganized speech or behavior, delusions, or hallucinations. Luther does occasionally exhibit odd beliefs and peculiarities of behavior. What would be the correct diagnosis?

    a) Schizophrenia, disorganized type
    b) Schizoaffective disorder, not otherwise specified
    c) Schizophrenia, residual type
    d) Schizophreniform disorder

11. This disorder is a delayed effect of taking long-term antipsychotic medication. The signs and symptoms of this disorder consist of abnormal, involuntary, irregular movements of the muscles in the head, limbs, and the trunk of the body. The most common symptoms include the twisting, chewing, and protruding thrusting movements of the tongue. This disorder is known as:

    a) Huntington's disease
    b) Gorsion dystonia
    c) Sydenham's chorea
    d) Tardive dyskensia

12. Echopraxia is:

    a) The pathological imitation of another person's movements
    b) Difficulty finding the correct name for an object (or objects)
    c) A condition in which the individual's speech is halting, laborious, and inaccurate
    d) Pathological persistence of an irresistible feeling that cannot be eliminated

13. The pathological repeating (over and over) of the same word or phrase just spoken by another person is called:

    a) Verbigeration
    b) Anologism
    c) Echolalia
    d) Hebephrenia

CHAPTER FOUR—MOOD DISORDERS

14. John Sanford constantly worries about his health, finances, job security, and the stability of his marriage. He worries about absolutely everything. Often, his worries keep him awake at night, causing him to be so fatigued at work that he cannot perform his duties adequately. His wife, Sharron, is becoming frustrated with him since he is so preoccupied with his worries that he is unable to do his chores around the house or help care for his children. What is John's most likely diagnosis?

    a) Panic disorder
    b) Simple phobia
    c) Generalized anxiety disorder
    d) Obsessive-compulsive disorder

15. Which of the following list of symptoms is the first sign of the beginning of a manic episode?

    a) Racing thoughts
    b) Hallucinations
    c) Hypergraphia
    d) A change in sleeping patterns

16. Which of the following symptoms is not apparent in a manic episode?

    a) The person is more talkative than usual or evidences pressured speech
    b) Distractibility—attention too easily drawn to irrelevant stimuli
    c) Excessive sleeping
    d) Excessive involvement in pleasurable activities

17. One subtype of Bipolar mood disorder is characterized by four or more episodes a year with mania and depression following each other. Which type is this?

    a) Seasonal affective disorder
    b) Double depression
    c) Rapid cycling
    d) Cyclothymia

18. _____ was formerly known as depressive neurosis and was considered less severe than major depressive disorder. This disorder is more common and chronic in women than in men. Its onset is insidious and occurs more often in persons with a history of long-term stress or sudden loss. This disorder often coexists with other psychiatric disorders, for example, substance abuse, personality disorders, and obsessive-compulsive disorder (OCD). Symptoms should include at least two of the following: poor appetite, overeating, sleep problems, fatigue, and/or low self-esteem. What is this disorder?

    a) Panic disorder
    b) Dysthymic disorder
    c) Schizoaffective disorder
    d) Posttraumatic stress disorder

19. Which of the following would not be present during a major depressive episode?

    a) Changes in sleep and/or appetite habits
    b) Anxiety
    c) Anhedonia
    d) Grandiosity

20. Maria Gonzalez, agitated and screaming, was brought to the emergency room of a local hospital by her family. The previous week, she heard that her former husband had been married in the Dominican Republic. Since then she has become increasingly agitated, developed insomnia, and is unable to eat.

    By the time she was seen in the emergency room and later admitted to the psychiatric unit, Ms. Gonzalez was alternately mute and mumbling unintelligibly in Spanish and English. She was given a small dose of an antipsychotic medication with no response. The social worker reported that Ms. Gonzalez had outbursts of bizarre behavior, had ideas of reference, complained of headaches, and felt "out of control." In addition, she cried, pulled her hair, rocked back and forth, and could not be consoled.

    Once assured by her family that she and her children would be well cared for, the psychotic-like symptoms resolved. She was discharged after three days in the hospital. Ms. Gonzalez's diagnosis would be:

    a) Ataque de nervios, a culture-bound syndrome
    b) Hysterical conversion disorder
    c) Panic disorder without agoraphobia
    d) Bipolar II disorder

21. Euphoria, boundless optimism, inflated self-esteem, and grandiosity are characteristic symptoms of:

    a) Bipolar disorder, manic type
    b) Schizophrenia, catatonic type
    c) Delusional disorder
    d) No mental disorder is present

CHAPTER FIVE—ANXIETY DISORDERS

22. Ilene has a tremendous fear of public speaking and she makes every effort to avoid formal speeches in front of others. This symptom may indicate:

    a) Specific phobia
    b) Nonspecific phobia
    c) Phenophobia
    d) Social phobia

23. Agoraphobia is defined as the fear and avoidance of:

    a) Anxiety-provoking events and situations
    b) Situations and places from which escape might be difficult or embarrassing
    c) Interactions with anxiety-provoking individuals
    d) Performing in public

24. Three basic types of panic attacks have been identified in the DSM-IV. These include all of the following *except:*

    a) Situationally bound
    b) Free floating
    c) Unexpected
    d) Situationally predisposed

25. A panic attack may be characterized by all of the following *except:*

    a) An abrupt experience of intense fear or discomfort
    b) Heart palpitations
    c) Sweating
    d) Elevated mood

26. Posttraumatic stress disorder may arise after any of the following events *except:*

    a) A traumatic wartime experience
    b) An earthquake, flood, or hurricane
    c) An allergic medication reaction
    d) Sudden death of a loved one

27. Dylan is extremely afraid of snakes. He makes every effort to never be in the presence of them or even to look at pictures of snakes. His phobia would be considered:

    a) Social phobia
    b) A complex phobia
    c) Agoraphobia
    d) A specific phobia

CHAPTER SIX—SOMATOFORM, FACTITIOUS, AND MALINGERING DISORDERS

28. The following symptoms are all necessary for a DSM-IV diagnosis of hypochrondriasis *except:*

    a) The individual is preoccupied with the fear of acquiring a serious/life-threatening disease
    b) The individual has a preoccupation with suing his or her doctor for not finding a serious/life-threatening disease
    c) The individual has a misperception of their bodily symptoms
    d) The individual experiences significant distress in their everyday functioning

29. Kenny Marks, a third-year medical student, returned to the student health services for the fifth time with complaints of diarrhea. After a thorough medical workup that included a barium enema and various other procedures, Kenny was told that there was no organic disease present. Despite this reassurance from several doctors, Kenny continued to test his stool for blood, and to believe that the doctors missed making the correct diagnosis. Kenny is exhibiting:

    a) Malingering disorder
    b) Hypochondriasis
    c) Body dysmorphic disorder
    d) Conversion disorder

30. Malingering disorder differs from factitious disorder in the following way:

    a) "Clanging" is more prominent in the factitious disorder than in malingering
    b) In malingering, there is an identifiable external gain
    c) There is evidence of displacement of anxiety left over from the oral stage
    d) Malingering is similar to factitious disorder but with fewer symptoms

31. Josette Saint-Jean, aged 27, recently experienced an episode of blindness that was short-lived. However, upon physical examination in a local emergency room, her eyes were found to exhibit normal dilation when exposed to light. Josette related that her current blindness occurred almost spontaneously when she witnessed an armed robbery at the local convenience store. She was fine until the police asked her to come down to the station and go through mug shots. What is your diagnosis?

   a) Dissociative disorder, not otherwise specified
   b) Depersonalization disorder
   c) Dissociative fugue
   d) Conversion disorder

32. _____ is characterized by the voluntary production of signs, symptoms, or disease for no other apparent goal than to achieve the role of being "sick." What is this disorder called?

   a) Conversion disorder
   b) Malingering disorder
   c) Factitious disorder
   d) Munchausen syndrome by proxy

33. Which of the following disorders was originally known as Briquet's syndrome?

   a) Dissociative identity disorder
   b) Somatization disorder
   c) Body dysmorphic disorder
   d) Hypochondriasis

34. Hope Udall is a shy, anxious-looking 29-year-old homemaker who is of normal appearance. Hope was hospitalized after an overdose of Valium washed down with some vodka. While in the hospital, she insisted on meeting the social worker in a darkened room. Hope was wearing a scarf pulled down over her face that partially covered her hair, eyes, and nose. The social worker asked, "What happened to bring you here?" Hope replied, "I have no friends and my husband just left me. It's just so hard to talk about. I don't know if I can, it's too embarrassing." After some discussion she revealed that she took an overdose and was in the hospital because of "her nose." She related to the social worker that her nose has "huge pock marks and ugly bumps." She believes she looks "grotesque and deformed." The social worker did not note any such appearance and, in fact, saw a lovely, normal-appearing young woman. According to the DSM-IV criteria, what would Hope's diagnosis be?

   a) Narcissistic personality disorder
   b) Body dysmorphic disorder
   c) Histrionic personality disorder
   d) Generalized anxiety disorder

35. The essential feature of this disorder is an individual's intentional production of an illness; that is, grossly exaggerating physical and/or psychological symptoms motivated by external incentives such as obtaining financial compensation through litigation or disability or avoiding military duty. This criterion meets which diagnosis?

   a) Malingering disorder
   b) Neuropsychiatric organizational disorder
   c) Hysterical conversion disorder
   d) Somatothymia disorder

CHAPTER SEVEN—DISSOCIATIVE DISORDERS

36. Nathan Roberts is being evaluated for a multitude of complaints that include "my perception of my environment often feels distorted or strange. For example, sometimes I feel I am suddenly engulfed by an overwhelming sense of being detached from my own body. During some of these episodes I am unable to understand people when they talk to me. The best that I can describe these symptoms is that I feel robot–like or like I'm really outside of my body." Mr. Roberts said that he has been experiencing these episodes since he was a teenager and that they were often accompanied by feelings of anxiety, panic, or depression. What is your beginning assessment?

    a) Dissociative fugue
    b) Depersonalization disorder
    c) Dissociative amnesia
    d) Dissociative identity disorder

37. Ling Wong is a 34-year-old woman who recently has survived the sinking of a ferryboat on the Mississippi River. She claims she has no memory for the events surrounding this disaster. Ling cannot explain how she got ashore. Her physical examination was unremarkable, and her cognitive ability is intact. She was distraught about the unknown fate of her husband, who was also aboard the ferry. She can remember everything but the event. Which of the following is Ling's diagnosis?

    a) Amnesia due to transient cerebral anoxia
    b) Dissociative amnesia
    c) Dissociative fugue
    d) Derealization disorder

38. Which of the following factors contributes to the difficulty in assessing dissociative identity disorder?

    a) These individuals are difficult to hypnotize because it is impossible to gain access to each of the separate "alters"
    b) Some of the presenting symptoms may appear to be symptoms of schizophrenia
    c) Few individuals report gaps in memory
    d) The different personalities are usually in conflict with each other

39. Which of the following is true of dissociative identity disorder?

    a) The separate identities are always fully developed
    b) There are rarely more than two separate identities
    c) It was previously known as multiple personality disorder (MPD)
    d) Each of the identities are completely aware of each other

40. When taking a client's history, an apparent cause of almost all cases of dissociative identity disorder is:

    a) An overactive imagination
    b) Lack of social support
    c) Severe physical and/or sexual abuse during childhood
    d) Familial predisposition

CHAPTER EIGHT—EATING DISORDERS

41. Which of the following is a feature found in both bulimia nervosa and anorexia nervosa?

    a) Excessive concern with body weight
    b) Excessive fear of being fat
    c) Bingeing
    d) Weight loss

42. Which of the following is considered the most severe medical complication associated with bulimia?

    a) Dental erosion
    b) Irregular heartbeat
    c) Electrolyte imbalance
    d) Hypertension

43. Each of the following is considered by the DSM-IV as an eating disorder except:

    a) Binge eating disorder (BED)
    b) Obesity
    c) Anorexia nervosa
    d) Bulimia nervosa

44. Twarla Jones is just under 5 feet tall and weighs 80 pounds. She has always been involved in cheerleading, the swimming team, and gymnastics in high school. When she turned 16 several months ago she became extremely fearful about gaining weight. Twarla initially began to limit her food and caloric intake. In addition, she began exercising excessively in order to prevent herself from gaining weight. Twarla calls herself "a blimp." However, her parents, teachers, and friends all reassure her that she is quite thin. Twarla's diagnosis is probably:

    a) Bulimia nervosa, purging type
    b) Anorexia nervosa, restricting type
    c) Eating disorder, NOS
    d) Bulimia nervosa, nonpurging type

45. _____ refers to self-induced vomiting or laxative misuse to influence body weight.

    a) Purging
    b) Excessive exercise
    c) Restricting
    d) Binge eating

46. Each of the following medical complications, except _____, is associated with anorexia nervosa.

    a) Dry yellowish skin
    b) High blood pressure
    c) Bradycardia (slow heartbeat)
    d) Electrolyte imbalance

Chapter Nine—The Personality Disorders

47. Perry Max lives his life every day following a very strict schedule. Perry must have everything perfect, in its place, and organized. He is devoted to his job as a plant manager and excessively follows rules and regulations without deviation. Perry has not taken a vacation in ten years. Although he loves his job, Perry has tremendous difficulty completing projects and getting his reports done in a timely fashion. Which personality disorder is this?

    a) Paranoid
    b) Obsessive-compulsive
    c) Dependent
    d) Avoidant

48. Jamie is a 19-year-old young man who was mandated to therapy by the court and assigned to you for an intake appointment. Reviewing the background materials, you notice that the client had been showing evidence of significant signs of conduct disturbance since the age of 14. He has a history of lying, stealing, selling drugs, and physically attacked his mother on several occasions. He shows no remorse and is indifferent to others' suffering. In session, the client seems surly and irritable. He blames others for his problems with the law. The best diagnosis for this client is:

    a) Cluster A personality disorder
    b) Antisocial personality disorder
    c) Oppositional defiant disorder
    d) Borderline personality disorder

49. Nancy has recently been assigned to you since her prior worker left the agency. You note from the psychosocial history in her file that she has a tendency to sexualize all relationships and displayed irrational emotional outbreaks to her prior worker. She likes to be the center of attention. Nancy also shows a tendency toward suggestibility, dramatization, and chaotic behavior. Her diagnosis would be:

    a) Schizoid personality disorder
    b) Histrionic personality disorder
    c) Borderline personality disorder
    d) Narcissistic personality disorder

50. According to his family, Barry, 28 years of age, has always been considered shy. He did not do well in grade school and dropped out before graduating high school. He is described as being isolated and having no friends. Barry has never dated and admits to having no interest in sexual activity. Despite adequate intelligence, Barry has never been able to keep a job. He prefers to live at home with his father and play computer games all day. He is so unmotivated and so isolated that he has never bothered to obtain a driver's license. Beyond Barry's reclusive nature and emotional aloofness, he has no desire to change and has refused going for counseling. What is Barry's diagnosis?

    a) Avoidant personality disorder
    b) Borderline personality disorder
    c) Schizoid personality disorder
    d) Dependent personality disorder

51. According to the DSM-IV, the ten personality disorders are divided into _____ clusters that are based on certain descriptive characteristics.

    a) 1
    b) 2
    c) 3
    d) 4

52. Cluster _____ personality disorders are characterized by odd and eccentric behaviors.

    a) A
    b) B
    c) C
    d) D

53. A pervasive distrust and suspiciousness of others characterize _____ personality disorder, such that the motives of others are interpreted as malevolent, and hidden meanings are read into benign remarks.

    a) Paranoid
    b) Schizoid
    c) Dependent
    d) Histrionic

54. Which of the following personality disorders is most closely related to schizophrenia?

    a) Borderline
    b) Antisocial
    c) Schizotypal
    d) Schizoid

55. This personality disorder is characterized by excessive expression of emotion and attention seeking.

    a) Obsessive-compulsive
    b) Histrionic
    c) Narcissistic
    d) Schizotypal

56. Which of the following personality disorders is best characterized by feelings of inadequacy, extreme sensitivity to negative remarks, and social inhibition?

    a) Avoidant
    b) Schizoid
    c) Dependent
    d) Borderline

57. Cluster C personality disorders are characterized by _____ behaviors.

    a) Aggressive and hostile
    b) Dramatic, emotional, and erratic
    c) Odd and eccentric
    d) Anxious and fearful

58. Persons with this personality disorder are described as having a preoccupation with orderliness, perfectionism, and mental and interpersonal control at the cost of being flexible and efficient.

    a) Narcissistic
    b) Histrionic
    c) Obsessive-compulsive
    d) Dependent

59. Cheyenne is described as having a tremendous amount of instability in interpersonal relationships, a poor self-image, marked impulsivity, and self-destructive behaviors. Her personality disorder would most likely be which of the following?

    a) Narcissistic
    b) Borderline
    c) Antisocial
    d) Paranoid

60. Cluster B personality disorders include all of the following except _____.

    a) Antisocial
    b) Borderline
    c) Histrionic
    d) Paranoid

ANSWER KEY

1. (a) Dementia
2. (d) Vascular dementia
3. (a) Sudden onset
4. (b) Usually recover within several days or weeks after the causative factor is eliminated
5. (d) Dementia, Alzheimer's type
6. (b) Schizophreniform disorder
7. (a) Brief psychotic disorder, postpartum onset
8. (b) Shared psychotic disorder
9. (c) Delusions of grandeur
10. (c) Schizophrenia, residual type
11. (d) Tardive dyskensia
12. (a) The pathological imitation of another person's movements
13. (c) Echolalia
14. (c) Generalized anxiety disorder
15. (a) Racing thoughts
16. (c) Excessive sleeping
17. (c) Rapid cycling
18. (b) Dysthymic disorder
19. (d) Grandiosity
20. (a) Ataque de nervios, a culture-bound syndrome
21. (a) Bipolar disorder, manic type
22. (d) Social phobia
23. (b) Situations and places from which escape might be difficult or embarrassing

24. (b) Free floating
25. (d) Elevated mood
26. (c) An allergic medication reaction
27. (d) A specific phobia
28. (a) The individual is preoccupied with the fear of acquiring a serious/life-threatening disease
29. (b) Hypochondriasis
30. (b) In malingering, there is an identifiable external gain.
31. (d) Conversion disorder
32. (c) Factitious disorder
33. (b) Somatization disorder
34. (b) Body dysmorphic disorder
35. (a) Malingering disorder
36. (b) Depersonalization disorder
37. (b) Dissociative amnesia
38. (b) Some of the presenting symptoms may appear to be symptoms of schizophrenia
39. (c) It was previously known as multiple personality disorder (MPD)
40. (c) Severe physical and/or sexual abuse during childhood
41. (a) Excessive concern with body weight
42. (c) Electrolyte imbalance
43. (b) Obesity
44. (b) Anorexia nervosa, restricting type
45. (a) Purging
46. (b) High blood pressure
47. (b) Obsessive-compulsive
48. (b) Antisocial personality disorder
49. (b) Histrionic personality disorder
50. (c) Schizoid personality disorder
51. (c) 3
52. (a) A
53. (a) Paranoid
54. (c) Schizotypal
55. (b) Histrionic
56. (a) Avoidant
57. (d) Anxious and fearful
58. (c) Obsessive-compulsive
59. (b) Borderline
60. (d) Paranoid

Glossary

Introduction to Glossary

The reader will no doubt recognize many familiar terms throughout this book. However, sometimes the same word will have different or specialized meanings when used in mental health practice. We have a highlighted those we felt needed further clarification. You will find them defined here.

Active or acute phase—in schizophrenia, the phase of the disease course in which psychotic symptoms are present; the active phase of schizophrenia is preceded by the prodromal phase and followed by the residual phase

Adjustment disorder—a maladaptive response of no more than six months duration to a specific psychosocial stressor, such as divorce or loss of a job; the response occurs within three months of the onset of the stressor event and impairs life functioning

Affect—observable manifestation of a person's mood or emotion; one of the "four A's" used to identify the splitting of external reality in schizophrenia, such as when affect is expressed by diminished emotions

Affectivity—the range, intensity, and appropriateness of a person's emotional responses

Agoraphobia—the person experiences anxiety about being in situations or places from which escape might be difficult, for example, in a crowded elevator

Agnosia—loss of recognition of familiar objects

Akinesia—complete or partial loss of muscle movement

Alexithymia—inability to identify and articulate feelings or needs, or to experience and express emotion except through physical symptoms; a common feature found in post-traumatic stress disorder and somatoform disorders

Alogia—a speech disturbance in which a person talks very little and responds to questions in brief, mostly concrete answers; this negative sign of schizophrenia is sometimes referred to as impoverishment of speech

Alters—additional identities that a person assumes within a dissociative state; alters are distinct personalities with cohesive characters, unique memories, attitudes, habits, facial expressions, and personal histories that are clearly different and apart from the "host" individual

Alzheimer's-type dementia—a chronic progressive disorder that begins with mild memory loss, progressing to deterioration of intellectual functioning, personality changes, and speech and language problems; this type accounts for more than 50 percent of all dementias

Ambivalence—positive and negative values that often exist simultaneously; can refer to uncertainty about taking a particular direction or frequent vacillation between two different perspectives or courses of action; one of the "four A's" used to identify the splitting of the external reality of schizophrenia

Amenorrhea—the absence of menstrual cycles, one of the signs used to assess anorexia nervosa

Amnesia—is the loss of memory of a person's identity or the loss of periods of time

Amnestic disorders—disorders characterized by prominent memory disturbances in levels of alertness or other cognitive complications that are found in delirium or dementia; associated features include disorientation, confabulation, emotional blandness, and apathy; three types of amnestic disorders include due to a general medical condition, substance-induced persistent amnestic disorder, and amnestic disorders due to multiple etiologies

Amyotrophic lateral sclerosis [ALS]—a rare illness that involves progressive muscle atrophy that develops slowly over a period of months or years

Anorexia nervosa—a major eating disorder in which affected individuals severely limit food intake, resulting in substantial weight loss and dangerously low body weight; there are two subtypes of anorexia nervosa, the *restricting type* in which there is an absence of binge eating and purging, and the *binge eating/purging type* in which binge eating is followed by self-induced vomiting and/or misuse of laxatives, enemas, or diuretics

Anosmia—absent sense of smell

Antisocial personality disorder—a Cluster B personality disorder; a pervasive pattern characterized by a long and involved history of lying, theft, substance use, illegal activities, rejection of social norms, and lack of remorse for any hurtful actions directed toward others; this disorder notes a disregard for the rights of others, which may begin as early as age ten

Anxiety—a mood state wherein the person apprehensively anticipates future danger or misfortune

Aphasia—impairment in the ability to formulate or comprehend language in any of its forms (reading, writing, or speaking) due to brain disease or injury

Aphonia—inability to create sounds or speak

Apraxia—impaired movement

"Arrangers"—persons with obsessive-compulsive disorder who are ruled by magical thinking and superstitions that fuel their strict need for orderliness and symmetry; "arrangers" compulsively and repetitively arrange particular items in a specific order

Associations—illogical thought processes; disturbance in thought processes (one of the "four A's") is used to identify the splitting of external reality found in schizophrenia

Ataque de nervios—is a culture-bound syndrome or a culturally accepted dissociative experience featuring uncontrollable crying, shouting, screaming, and seizure-like behaviors with the failure to remember the episode afterward; it lasts for a brief period of time and is perceived to be adaptive

Ataxia—impairment in control of voluntary muscle coordination

Auditory hallucinations—hearing voices that do not exist within the environmental context; the most common psychotic feature of schizophrenia, "voices" typically talk about, and to the affected individual

Autism—impairment in social interactions, communication, and restricted patterns evidenced by behavior, interest, or activity; used to identify the splitting of external reality in schizophrenia

Avoidant personality disorder—a Cluster C personality disorder; a pervasive pattern of social inhibition, hypersensitivity to criticism, and feelings of personal inadequacy; though individuals with this disorder desire relationships with others and are distressed by the lack of them, avoidance of social interactions and situations pervade their lives

Avolition—a negative symptom of schizophrenia that is characterized by lack of interest in and inability to initiate or sustain goal-directed activity

"Bashful bladder"—sometimes found in social phobia in which the affected person fears being unable to urinate when others are around such as in a public restroom

Binge—ingesting a much larger amount of food than most people would eat under similar circumstances

Binge eating—an eating episode where the individual eats "out of control" and is unable to resist the temptation to consume certain foods

Binge eating disorder [BED]—disorder characterized by recurrent binge eating, but without the inappropriate weight control behaviors that are a part of the bulimic picture

Biological predisposition—biological factors that can be passed on from one generation to the next that tend to increase the likelihood of developing a certain disorder

Biomedical model—a model or paradigm that delineates and describes diagnostic criteria to explain human behavior

Biopsychosocial framework—a perspective for examining an individual that validates the potential importance of biogenetic, psychological, social, and environmental factors in understanding human behavior from a medical perspective

Bipolar disorder—major mood disorder with a distinct period during which the predominant mood is either elevated, expansive, or irritable with several associated symptoms such as hyperactivity, pressured speech, racing thoughts, inflated self-esteem, decreased need for sleep, distractibility, and excessive involvement in potentially dangerous self-destructive activity

Bipolar I disorder—refers to severe manic symptoms accompanied by one or more periods of major depression

Bipolar II disorder—refers to the same patterns of symptoms found in bipolar I, but the major distinction revolves around the degree of disability; bipolar II is less severe, does not lead to psychotic behavior, and typically does not requires hospitalization

Body dysmorphic disorder [BDD]—disorder characterized by the affected individual's preoccupation about some imagined defect in their body, causing extreme self-consciousness and embarrassment, avoidance of activities, and body camouflaging

Body image distortion [BID]—a distortion in the way individuals view their body within the context of either eating or weight disorders

Borderline personality disorder—a Cluster B personality disorder; characterized by marked impulsivity, poor and unstable interpersonal relationships, and disturbances in affect and self-image

Brief psychotic disorder—psychotic disorder that includes one or more positive symptom(s) of schizophrenia (such as hallucinations, delusions, disorganized speech, or behavior) lasting more than one day but less than one month; this disorder often occurs following a severe life stressor

Bizarre behavior—patterns of conduct or demeanor far removed from normal and expected experiences

Bradycardia—slow heartbeat

Bulimia nervosa—a major eating disorder in which the affected person's "diet" leads to out of control episodes of binge eating followed by purging behaviors; there are two subtypes of bulimia nervosa: purging type and nonpurging type

Cardiac arrhythmia—irregular heartbeat

Cataplexy—stupor or motor immobility

Catatonic posturing—semistiff poses or postures made by persons with catatonic-type schizophrenia; this posturing can be remain fixed for hours or days

Catatonic-type schizophrenia—a type of schizophrenia characterized by unusual posturing, mutism or incoherent chatter, facial grimacing or making faces

Censure—within paranoid personality disorder, the tendency of affected individuals to blame others and believe others are generally ill intentioned or hostile toward them; hypervigilance against what is perceived as hurtful intentions of others

Centrality—within paranoid personality disorder, the belief of affected individuals that they are somehow the center of people's interest or attention

"Checkers"—persons with obsessive-personality disorder who are ruled by magical thinking and superstitions that fuel their strict need for orderliness and symmetry; "checkers" repetitively check and recheck particular items or situations in their environment, such as checking to make sure the door is locked or the iron is turned off

Clanging—a characteristic of disorganized speech in which the affected person primarily uses rhymes or puns to communicate with others

Clouding of consciousness—the inability to focus, sustain, or shift attention, in which affected individuals appear confused, bewildered, or alarmed

Cluster A—a grouping of personality disorders in which individuals are seen as "odd and eccentric" and includes paranoid, schizoid, and schizotypal personality disorders

Cluster B—a grouping of personality disorders in which individuals appear highly emotional, dramatic, or erratic and includes antisocial, histrionic, borderline, and narcissistic personality disorders

Cluster C—a grouping of personality disorders in which individuals are seen as fearful and anxious and includes avoidant, dependent, and obsessive-compulsive personality disorders

Cognition—ways of perceiving and interpreting one's self, other people, and events

Comorbid—describes the simultaneous existence of two or more diseases or syndromes within a single affected person

Competency-based assessment model—framework for better understanding human behavior, moving from individual intrapersonal factors to considering social, cultural, and environmental influences; the model seeks to understand human behavior from a multi-dimensional and dynamic ecological systems perspective

Competency-based practice—a framework for practice that underscores a focus on client strengths, resilience, and coping; additionally, the practitioner considers social environmental supports

Compulsions—repetitive behaviors such as hand washing, checking, or counting; compulsions act to prevent or reduce anxiety or distress, not to provide the affected person with pleasure; compulsions are performed to extinguish obsessional thoughts

Confabulation—unconsciously making up false answers when memory is impaired; most often seen in cognitive disorders

Continuous amnesia—a less common type of dissociative amnesia; affected persons experience an inability to remember all events from a given time up to and including the present time

Conversion disorder—a type of somatoform disorder in which the affected individual experiences a loss or change in physical functioning that suggests the presence of a physical disorder but cannot be explained by any physiologic mechanism

"Counters"—persons with obsessive-compulsive disorder who are generally ruled by magical thinking and superstitions that fuel their strict need for orderliness and symmetry; "counters" repetitively and compulsively count items a precise number of times

Creutzfeldt-Jakob disease—a fatal central nervous system disease known to cause degenerative, progressive brain deterioration, often confused with dementia; it is precipitated by an organism known as a prion (an infectious particle)

Cyclothymia—a minor mood disorder characterized by chronic or cyclic mood disturbance that lasts at least two years and has many of the same features found in a major depressive episode; numerous "up and down" fluctuating periods of hypomanic and depressive features are noted

Defense mechanisms—mental strategies that operate unconsciously to maintain balance between internal drives and the external world; according to psychoanalytic theory, defense mechanisms are used by the ego to reduce anxiety and mediate conflicting demands among the id, ego, and superego

Delirium—a syndrome characterized by temporary but prominent disturbances in alertness, confusion, and disorientation

Delusion—a psychotic symptom involving false or fixed belief based on incorrect deductions or misrepresentations of the person's reality that are not normative within the person's cultural or religious group despite incontrovertible, obvious proof or evidence to the contrary

Delusional disorder—a disorder involving fixed, false beliefs, contrary to reality (delusion); this disorder has no other features seen in schizophrenia, (such as prominent hallucinations, affective flattening, and additional symptoms of a thought disorder)

Delusions of grandeur—irrational belief that one is special, famous, or important

Delusions of persecution—irrational belief that others intend harm to the individual

Delusions of reference—irrational belief that the affected person is the object of discussion among others or that messages broadcast through the media are specially intended for him or her

Dementia—advancing, progressive, and degenerative condition, marked by a gradual deterioration of a broad range of cognitive abilities, characterized by prominent memory disturbances, often central nervous system damage, over a protracted period of time

Dependent personality disorder—a Cluster C personality disorder; characterized by pervasive pattern of extreme inability to act independently of others; submissive, clinging behaviors; maintenance of relationships despite mistreatment or fear of abandonment; and inability to assert oneself when needed

Depersonalization—feeling detached from one self or as an outside observer of one's own behavior; most prevalent in people with dissociative disorders

Depersonalization disorder—a dissociative disorder in which the affected person remains in touch with reality, but experiences the self as strange or unreal; recurrently they feel detached from their own body and surroundings, feeling as if someone else is in control and sometimes as if another person were observing them

Derailment—a characteristic of disorganized speech in which the affected person randomly leaps from topic to topic

Derealization—loss of one's sense of reality in the external world; affected persons may experience familiar objects or persons as strange and odd

Differential assessment—a consideration of a comprehensive range of diagnostic possibilities in the practitioner's evaluation and assessment process

Disorganized behavior—involves physical actions that do not appear to be goal directed, for example, maintaining unusual body positions, pacing excitedly, or taking off one's clothes in public

Disorganized speech—a style of speaking seen in individuals with schizophrenia that includes mimicking, disconnected or incoherent speech patterns, and/or the invention of new words

Disorganized type of schizophrenia—features include disrupted speech and behavior, fragmented delusions and hallucinations, and flat or silly affect

Dissociation—an alteration of consciousness characterized by estrangement from the self or the environment; can be a mechanism of defense to ward off the emotional impact of traumatic or abusive events and memories

Dissociative amnesia disorder—formerly known as psychogenic amnesia; a reversible amnesia, not attributed to ordinary forgetfulness, associated with some form of emotional, traumatic, or psychological stress wherein affected persons retain their generalized fund of life knowledge, but cannot remember important personal information such as their own name, age, or marital status

Dissociative disorder—a group of disorders precipitated by psychological conflicts featuring a disruption in the client's intrapersonal domain, specifically the mental functions of consciousness, identity, perception of the environment, and memory

Dissociative fugue disorder—formerly known as psychogenic fugue; affected persons experience confusion about their identity in which important personal details cannot be recalled; characteristically involves sudden travel away from home and work, or to another geographical location

Dissociative identity disorder [DID]—previously referred to as multiple personality disorder, this is considered the most serious of the dissociative disorders and features the presence of two or more discrete personality identities

Distorted body image [DBI]—an irrational perception that one's body shape and size is defective

Dizygotic twins—as in fraternal twins; twins developed by two separately fertilized ova and therefore no more closely genetically related than ordinary siblings

Dopamine—a catecholamine neurotransmitter that helps to regulate cognition, sensory processes, and mood

Double depression—coexistence of dysthymic disorder and major depressive disorder

DSM-IV—the fourth edition of the *Diagnostic and statistical manual*, published by the American Psychiatric Association, considered the standard tool for assessing psychopathology; the DSM-IV categorically classifies mental disorders by types and criteria

Dyskinesia—refers to an ability to perform voluntary movements

Dysmenorrhea—pain associated with menstruation

Dysphagia—an individual experiences difficulty swallowing

Dysphoric mood—refers also to the term dysphoria and is a general disatisfaction with life or feelings of unhappiness

Dysthymia—a minor mood disorder that is characterized by a relatively low-grade, but chronic depression often lasting for years; dysthymia differs from major depression in that symptoms are milder but more chronic

Early onset—refers to the presentation of a disorder or syndrome beginning prior to the expected age of onset

Echolalia—pathological repetition or mimicry of spoken words of others

Echopraxia—pathological repetition or mimicry of physical gestures and movements of others by a person with catatonic-type schizophrenia

Ecological perspective—a framework emphasizing dynamic interaction between persons and their environment; "goodness of fit" between individuals and their surroundings is achieved through mutual interaction, negotiation, and compromise

Egocentricity—having no regard for the thoughts, attitudes, or feelings of others; the irrational belief that the affected individual is the center or focus of interest and importance above all else and all others

Electrolyte abnormalities—low potassium levels that can disrupt signals to the heart, causing irregular conduction, as well as causing kidney failure

Environmental illness—a relatively new phenomenon, also known as total environmental allergy syndrome; a polysymptomatic disorder some consider to be associated with immune system dysfunction and allergy-like sensitivity to many compounds found in chemicals, foods, clothing, perfumes, and substances found in the air

Erythrophobia—persistent, irrational, and pathological dread of blushing in public

Euthymic—a description of mood that is characterized as normal, without depression or expansiveness

Excoriation—denuding of the skin often seen in those engaging in compulsive hand washing

Executive functioning—judgment, impulse control, and the ability to analyze, understand, and adapt to new situations

Factitious disorder—maintenance of the sick role for secondary gain in which the individual derives satisfaction from being considered ill

Flat affect—the observable absence of (or minimal presence of) facial expression as if the person is unaffected by the contextual environment that surrounds them

Folie à deux—also known as shared psychotic disorder, communicated insanity, infectious insanity, or double insanity; main features include a slow development of delusions resulting from being in a relationship with two closely associated persons

Full-blown episode—an episode in the disease process whereby the full spectrum of symptom criteria is experienced by the affected person

Generalized amnesia—a less common form of dissociative amnesia, this disorder encompasses a loss of memory that includes all the experiences during the person's entire life from infancy to present time

Generalized anxiety disorder [GAD]—formerly known as free floating anxiety; a disorder that features pervasive and nonspecific anxiety (anxiety not attached to any particular situation) and interferes in all aspects of life functioning

Globus hystericus—when swallowing, sensation of having a lump in one's throat

Grazing—binge eating in which affected individuals consume large amounts of food almost continuously throughout the day

Hallucinations—experiences of sensory events without environmental stimulation; tactile, olfactory, visual, and/or auditory hallucinations may be experienced during a psychotic episode

Hemiplegia—paralysis on one side of the body can be a presenting condition in conversion disorder

Hepatic encephalopathy—an altered mental state secondary to liver failure

Histrionic personality disorder—a Cluster B personality disorder; a pervasive pattern characterized by excessive emotionality, extreme attention-seeking behaviors, self-centeredness, self-absorption, and susceptibility; affected persons demonstrate an inability to maintain strong, reciprocal, and long-lasting friendships and are often described as colorful, dramatic, extroverted, excitable, and emotional

"Hoarders"—a person with obsessive-compulsive disorder who cannot throw anything away because of an irrational belief that if they do, something terrible will happen to them or to those they care about; "hoarders" feel compelled to save items like newspapers or string

Huntington's chorea—autosomal-dominant disorder the onset of which features personality changes, with affected persons demonstrating an inability to adapt to their environment; depression and psychosis may be experienced by affected persons

Hypersomnia—disturbance in regular sleep pattern in which the affected individual sleeps too much

Hypervigilance—obsessively concerned, defended, or watchful; within paranoid personality disorder, for example, the affected individual may be hypervigilant about perceived insults or harmful personal exploitation

Hypnotizability—refers to the ease in which someone can be hypnotized; links are noted between hypnotic suggestibility and increased risk of using hypnotic-like dissociation in anxiety-provoking situations

Hypochondriasis—a disorder of cognition and misperception of bodily symptoms, of at least six months duration, in which affected individuals are preoccupied with fears of having a serious or life-threatening illness without medical substantiation

Hypomanic episode—symptoms of at least four days duration that are less extreme and less disruptive than that of a full-blown manic episode

Hypotension—low blood pressure

Iatrogenic—adverse mental or physical condition caused by side effects from surgical or medical treatment

Ideas of reference—delusion in which the affected individual believes that the actions and speech of others somehow relates or refers back to them

Identity alteration—within dissociative states, condition in which an affected person's behaviors suggest that they have assumed new identities

Identity confusion—within dissociative states, condition in which an affected person is unsure of their own identity and who they are

Illness—refers to those experiences associated with disease that ultimately affect the person's state of being and social functioning

Illusions—perceptual disturbances in which things appear differently than they actually are in reality

Insomnia—difficulty maintaining or initiating sleep; there is a disturbance in regular sleep pattern in which sleep is interrupted; insomnia is the most common sleep complaint

Interpersonal functioning—characteristic ways of establishing and maintaining relationships with significant others; ways in which one communicates and interacts with others

Ipecac—also known as syrup of ipecac; solution used to induce vomiting

Korsakoff psychosis—amnesic disorder caused by damage to the thalamus resulting from chronic and heavy alcohol use

La belle indifference—an unrealistic degree of indifference or apathy in the face of one's own symptoms; seen in the conversion reaction

Lanugo—baby-fine hair found on the trunk, face, and extremities; commonly known as "peach fuzz"; often an indication of an eating disorder

Late onset—refers to the presentation of a disorder or syndrome beginning after the expected age of onset

Life stressors—within the ecological perspective, life stressors are difficult social or developmental transitions, traumatic life events, or other issues disturbing the existing "fit" between the individual and his/her environment

Localized amnesia—a type of dissociative amnesia also known as "circumscribed" amnesia; affected persons are unable to recall events that occurred during a particular time or following a profoundly disturbing event

Loosening of associations—incoherent speech in which connections among ideas are absent or obscure; commonly associated with schizophrenia

Magical thinking—irrational belief that one has powers defying laws of nature and physics that can cause or prevent events; while magical thinking is seen as pathological in adults, it is viewed as a normal part of the developmental process in children

Major depressive episode—also known as major depression; depressed mood with related functional changes in behavioral, physical, and cognitive areas of at least two weeks duration

Malingering—consciously maintaining the sick role for some material or financial gain; symptoms are intentionally produced by the individual to avoid some task, for advantage in legal actions, or to obtain disability

Mania—associated with the bipolar mood disorder, it is a period of abnormally excessive elevation or euphoric mood

Manic depression—currently known as bipolar disorder; extreme euphoric or heightened mood and depressive episodes at the same time, or during manic episodes alone

Manic episode—extreme mood elevation or irritability with related functional changes in behavioral, physical, and cognitive areas of at least one week duration

Medical model—framework that views the individual's problems as being "inside" of the person, resulting from a variety of causative factors that include genetic predisposition, internal conflicts, early traumatic experiences, and/or metabolic factors

Mental status exam—a practitioner's preliminary evaluation of a client's overall mental status including orientation to person, place, time, insight and judgment, mental and emotional state

Mixed manic episode—the person experiences both elation and depression or anxiety at the same time

Monozygotic twins—twins developed from singularly fertilized ova and who are thus genetically identical

Mood—pervasive and sustained emotion that affects every aspect of a person's life

Mood congruent—emotions that are seen to be normative to, or in sync with, the situation faced by the affected person

Mood disorders—also known as affective disorders; a group of emotional disturbances characterized by serious and persistent difficulty maintaining an even, productive emotional state

Morbid obesity—abnormal amount of fat on the body; the term is not usually used unless the individual is 30 percent over average weight for their age, height, and sex

Motor enervation—the nerve supply of a body part, or the stimulation of a body part through the action of nerves

Munchausen by proxy—a variant of factitious disorder; characterized by a caregiver deliberately falsifying another's medical history and subjecting the latter to unnecessary medical procedures and hospitalizations out of the unconscious psychological need to maintain the sick role, even though the sick role is experienced indirectly

Narcissistic personality disorder—a cluster B personality disorder; a pervasive pattern characterized by heightened sense of self-importance and unrealistic notions of inflated self-worth that often underlies a fragile sense of self-worth; marked grandiosity wherein affected individuals see themselves as superior to others, unique, and special; marked lack of empathy and need for admiration are also features of this disorder

Negative symptoms—also known as second-rank symptoms in schizophrenia, refers to characteristics that are notably absent but are normally present in people's experience (e.g., appropriate self care, full range of affect)

Negativism—disturbance of volition found in schizophrenia, characterized by a stubborn refusal to follow any course of action suggested or expected by others

Neologism—nonsensical words and phrases according to some form of special symbolism, created and uttered by a person with a thought disturbance

Neurasthenia—unexplained fatigue and lassitude

Neuropathic—describing or referring to any disease of the nervous system

Neurotransmitters—chemical substances, such as epinephrine or dopamine, that transmit nerve impulses across synapses to act on the target cell, either inhibiting or exciting it

Obsessions—recurrent thoughts (such as becoming contaminated by shaking hands), impulses (such as having to align things in a particular order), or fears that automatically occur, despite resistance from the affected person

Obsessive compulsive disorder [OCD]—a disorder characterized by recurrent obsessions and compulsions that are severe enough to be time consuming, causing the person marked distress or significant impairment; the most common obsessions are repeated thoughts, for example, being contaminated by germs. The most common compulsions are hand washing, checking, or counting.

Obsessive-compulsive personality disorder—a Cluster C personality disorder; characterized by pervasive pattern of adherence with orderliness, rigidity, and inflexibility accompanied by emotional restriction; affected persons are often described as perfectionists and have difficulty with interpersonal control

Onset—refers to the beginning phase of a disease or syndrome

Pain disorder—pain, as the primary clinical focus of attention, thought to be significantly maintained by psychological factors; preoccupation with pain that cannot be accounted for by any known medical or neurological condition; has also been previously known as somatoform pain disorder, psychogenic pain disorder, idiopathic pain disorder, and atypical pain disorder

Panic attack—sudden intense fear for which there is no logical explanation, in which the affected person experiences physiological symptoms (e.g., racing heart, increased rate of breathing, profuse sweating) accompanied by thoughts of dying or losing control

Panic disorder—recurrent, intense, and unpredictable episodes of extreme anxiety for which there are no rational explanations

Paranoia—condition characterized by groundless mistrustfulness and suspiciousness of others with a tendency to view others as malevolent

Paranoid personality disorder—a cluster A personality disorder; an enduring and pervasive pattern of groundless suspiciousness and inherent distrust of others; affected persons are often characterized as hostile, irritable, and angry

Paranoid type of shizophrenia—is a type of schizophrenia in which symptoms involve hallucinations with persecutory or grandiose content, and delusions of persecution, while the person's speech, motor, and emotional behavior remain relatively unimpaired

Paraethesia—refers to a sensation of numbness, prickling, or tingling experiences on the skin

Parkinson's disease—a slowly progressive neurological disorder that features tremors, postural instability, and impairment in fine motor movements

Pathophysiology—the study of how normal physiologic processes are altered by disease

Persecutory delusions—a feature in paranoid-type schizophrenia; fixed beliefs that remain unchanged, despite overwhelming evidence to the contrary, that others intend harm to the affected person

Perseveration—a characteristic of disorganized speech in which the affected person repeats the same word, phrases, or sentences over and over

Personality—a set of characteristics defining behaviors, thoughts, and emotions that become ingrained and usually dictate the person's worldview, lifestyle, and life choices; emotional and behavioral traits that characterize day-to-day living under normal conditions

Personality disorder—pervasive and enduring character traits that are extremely inflexible and maladaptive, and that cause significant functional impairment or subjective distress; characterized by an individual's impaired interaction within their social environment and with others

Person:environment fit—a concept found in the ecological model; the actual fit between an individual's or group's needs and their surroundings

Phobia—a common disorder in which a particular stimulant, object, or situation (e.g., heights, snakes, spiders) prompts overwhelming terror, obscuring all other experiences; a phobic episode may feature profuse sweating, racing heart, dizziness, and trembling; specific phobias may include fear of animals (animal type), fear of bodies of water (natural environment type), fear of medical procedures (blood-injection/injury type), or fear of being trapped in an elevator (situational type)

Pick's disease—a degenerative disease of the brain similar to Alzheimer's disease; differences include marked changes in personality early in the disease course with less impairment in memory than in Alzheimer's disease

Poor impulse control—behaviors in which the end result or consequences of actions are poorly anticipated; inability to appropriately delay action that may result in a poor outcome for the individual

Positive symptoms—also known as first–rank symptoms in schizophrenia; refers to characteristics that are notably present but normally absent in people's experience such as delusions and hallucinations

Postpartum blues—commonly known as "baby blues"; a temporary and nonpathological state of emotional disturbance that features sadness and general dysphoria experienced by a woman following the birth of her baby

Postpartum depression—a serious psychiatric condition requiring clinical intervention that occurs within four weeks of childbirth and is characterized by severe depression, apathy, or thoughts of harm toward the newborn and/or self, and delusions

Posttraumatic stress disorder [PTSD]—a specific set of symptoms developing after an individual experiences an extreme traumatic stressor event; PTSD symptoms may include intrusive recollection and reexperiencing of the trauma, avoidance of triggers that remind the person of the trauma, numbing of general responsiveness, hyperarousal or hypervigilance, and impairment in life functioning

Pressured speech—speech with a rapid, unremitting, urgent quality

Prodromal phase—a symptom indicative of an approaching disease characterized by the interval between the earliest symptoms and the appearance of the actual disease

Pseudocyesis—a false belief of being pregnant

Pseudoneurological symptoms—signs resembling sensory and motor symptoms without clinical or medical foundation

Psychodynamic model—framework that focuses on symptoms, behaviors, and underlying processes to explain human behavior

Psychomotor agitation—notable increase in physical restlessness as a result of inner tension; activity is usually meaningless and repetitive such as hand wringing, fidgeting, and foot tapping

Psychomotor retardation—commonly seen in major depression, observable decrease or slowing down of motor activity

Psychosis—the loss of reality testing and the impairment of mental functioning manifested by delusions, hallucinations, confusion, impaired memory, and the inability to function within the interpersonal domain

Psychotropic medications—medications used to alter the mental state in the treatment of mental illnesses, such as Resperdal for the treatment of psychosis

Purging—any activity aimed at ameliorating the perceived negative effects of an eating binge on body shape and weight, such as self-induced vomiting

Rapid cycling—within bipolar disorders, the occurrence of four or more separate bipolar episodes (in any combination) within a one-year period

Residual phase—or residual type, sometimes considered the "filler" category in the disease formulation of schizophrenia; this phase is characterized by improvement in the disease process such that schizophrenic features can no longer be ascertained; the residual phase follows the active phase in the disease process

Residual type of schizophrenia—a category reserved for persons who have had at least one episode of schizophrenia and who no longer display schizophrenic features; however, there is still some remaining evidence of bizarre thoughts and/or social withdrawal

Rumination—preoccupation with distressful thoughts or worries

Russell's signs—dorsal lesions that are by-products of repeated and constant friction of fingers being scraped back and forth across incisor teeth to cause vomiting

Schizoaffective disorder—this psychotic disorder features symptoms of both schizophrenia and a major mood disorder

Schizoid personality disorder—a Cluster A personality disorder; characterized by a pervasive pattern of social withdrawal and/or odd or strange mannerisms; includes magical thinking, ideas of reference, illusions, and derealization

Schizophrenia—a severe psychotic disorder characterized by hallucinations, delusions, disordered thought processes, and bizarre behaviors; schizophrenia is characterized by the presence of psychotic, disorganized, and negative factors

Schizophreniform disorder—psychotic disorder with symptoms similar to, but less severe than, those found in schizophrenia; this disorder must last less than six months (in contrast to symptoms in schizophrenia, which last more than six months) and must have prodromal, active, and residual phases

Schizotypal personality disorder—a Cluster A personality disorder; characterized by a pervasive pattern of behavioral eccentricities, extreme discomfort with and reduced capacity for interpersonal relationships, and cognitive and perceptional distortions

Seasonal affective pattern—within bipolar disorders, episodes that occur during a particular time of the year, for example, late fall or early winter

Secondary gain—accumulated discernable advantages gained from symptoms and behaviors as a result of being in the sick role

Selective amnesia—a type of amnesia found in dissociative disorders; affected persons have patchy recollections of an event while other portions of time are forgotten

Self-induced purging—self-forced vomiting characteristically found in some eating disorders, for example, the misuse of emetics (ipecac)

Serotonin—a neurotransmitter that plays a part in neurological processes such as memory and sleep, and that plays a role in some mood disorders

Sign—affective, behavioral, and emotional manifestations of conditions that are objectively observed by the clinician for diagnostic use

Social phobia—also known as performance anxiety; enduring and irrational fear that affected persons will somehow embarrass themselves or do poorly in performance-based or social situations; avoidance of these activities significantly and adversely impacts on individuals

Somatic complaints—preoccupation with illness or with bodily and physical symptoms

Somatoform disorder—represents a polysymptomatic presentation that begins early in life and is characterized by multiple bodily or somatic complaints

Somatoform disorders—cluster of "illnesses" that include physical symptoms that cannot be fully accounted for by a general medical condition

Somatoform disorder not otherwise specified [NOS]—residual category, assessed for individuals who have some symptoms suggestive of a somatoform disorder but who do not meet the specific diagnostic criteria for any of the other specific somataform disorders, including the undifferentiated type

Somatosensory amplification—the tendency for affected individuals to experience their own bodily sensations as being unusually intense, aversive, and distressing

Splitting—defense mechanism used in borderline personality disorder whereby the individual alternates between extremes of idealization and devaluation

Stereotypy—purposeless repetitive movements often seemingly driven and nonfunctional, such as folding a piece of paper along the same crease until it disintegrates

Stocking-glove anethesia—found in conversion disorder marked by symptoms of the loss of sensation in the hand or foot and the location of the loss of sensation is sharply demarcated

Stress—response to life stressors; characterized by anxiety, guilt, anger, fear, depression, helplessness, or despair

Suicidal ideation—thoughts of killing oneself

Sui generis—unique or singular aspect of a disorder

Sundowning—refers to the exacerbation of symptoms experienced by persons with delirium during the early evening hours

"Switching"—within dissociative disorder, a dissociation of the affected person into a fantasy world in order to escape or blunt some abuse or memory of abuse; in dissociative identity disorder [DID], "switching" specifically refers to the changing or movement back and forth between one personality-entity and another

Symptom—subjective, behavioral, and emotional manifestations of conditions experienced by the affected person and reported to the clinician for diagnostic use

Syncope—fainting

Syndrome—signs and symptoms that occur together that suggest direction for potential diagnostic and treatment formulations

Systemized amnesia—a less common type of dissociative amnesia in which a person loses memory pertaining only to certain categories of information, such as relating to their family or to work

Systems theory—theoretical framework; it does not attempt to explain human behavior, but asserts that human behavior can be viewed through three distinct frames of reference or "systems"

Tactile hallucinations—the feeling of bodily sensations or objects that are not present in the environment

Tardive dyskinesia—particular side effects from extended periods of taking high doses of antipsychotic medications, characterized by involuntary movements such as lip smacking, chin wagging, tongue thrusting, hand tremors, and unsteady gait; Cogentin may be prescribed to relieve these side effects

Thought broadcasting—irrational belief that the affected person's thoughts can be heard by other people without the use of written or verbal communication

Thought insertion—irrational belief that the thoughts of another person have been purposively placed inside the mind of the affected person

Tic—sudden, recurrent, and involuntary movements or vocalizations of the face, neck, head, or body

Toniclonic pseudoseizures—muscular spasms

Tourette's disorder—a tic disorder in which multiple involuntary movements or vocalizations occur; onset is prior to 21 years of age

Transient hypochondriac states (nonpsychotic)—condition characterized by the same criteria as hypochondriasis, except that symptoms last less than six months

Undifferentiated somatoform disorder—disorder in which individuals have one or more physical complaints that cannot be explained by any known general medical condition or pathophysiologic mechanism, or that grossly exceed the expected complaints of a medical condition; and the complaints of the person are below the threshold for meeting the diagnostic criteria for a specific somatoform disorder

Undifferentiated-type schizophrenia—disorder characterized by the exhibition of major features of schizophrenia without meeting full assessment distinctions for paranoid, disorganized, or catatonic type

Uremic encephalopathy—an altered mental status secondary to kidney failure

Vascular dementia—also known as multi-infarct dementia; this type of dementia is caused by at least one stroke

Vegetative features—bodily symptoms often seen in mood disorders, such as disturbances in sleep patterns (insomnia), poor appetite, and low energy

"Washers"—a person with obsessive-compulsive disorder who fears contamination, usually dirt or germs, and "cleans" in lieu of something bad happening to them or their family

Waxy flexibility—the semistiff quality of poses or postures made by a person with catatonic-type schizophrenia

Wernicke encephalopathy—deficiency in the vitamin thiamine arising from its poor metabolization in heavy alcohol drinkers; results in confusion, loss of muscle coordination, and unintelligible speech

Wilson's disease—an autosomal-recessive disorder that results in liver dysfunction and has symptoms of depression, irritability, psychosis, and dementia

Name Index

Subject Index

Note: Page numbers followed by *f* or *t* indicate figures and tables, respectively.

TO THE OWNER OF THIS BOOK:

I hope that you have found *Psychopathology: A Competency-Based Assessment Model for Social Workers* useful. So that this book can be improved in a future edition, would you take the time to complete this sheet and return it? Thank you.

School and address: _____

_____

Department: _____

Instructor's name: _____

1. What I like most about this book is: _____

_____

_____

2. What I like least about this book is: _____

_____

_____

3. My general reaction to this book is: _____

_____

_____

4. The name of the course in which I used this book is: _____

_____

5. Were all of the chapters of the book assigned for you to read? _____If not, which ones weren't?

6. In the space below, or on a separate sheet of paper, please write specific suggestions for improving this book and anything else you care to share about your experience in using this book.

_____

_____

_____

OPTIONAL:

Your name: _____ Date: _____

May we quote you, either in promotion for *Psychopathology: A Competency-Based Assessment Model for Social Workers,* or in future publishing ventures?

    Yes: _____ No: _____

    Sincerely yours,

    Marilyn R. Zide

    Susan W. Gray

FOLD HERE

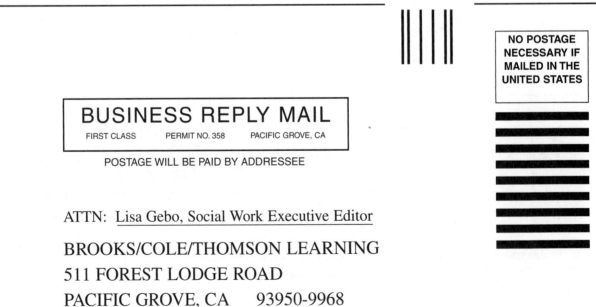

BUSINESS REPLY MAIL

FIRST CLASS   PERMIT NO. 358   PACIFIC GROVE, CA

POSTAGE WILL BE PAID BY ADDRESSEE

ATTN: Lisa Gebo, Social Work Executive Editor

BROOKS/COLE/THOMSON LEARNING
511 FOREST LODGE ROAD
PACIFIC GROVE, CA   93950-9968

NO POSTAGE
NECESSARY IF
MAILED IN THE
UNITED STATES

FOLD HERE